ALSO BY THE AUTHORS

EVERY SPY A PRINCE: THE COMPLETE HISTORY
OF ISRAEL'S INTELLIGENCE COMMUNITY

BEHIND THE UPRISING:
ISRAELIS, JORDANIANS, AND PALESTINIANS

THE IMPERFECT SPIES

FRIENDS IN DEED

Yossi Melman
Dan Raviv

Friends in Deed

Inside the U.S.-Israel Alliance

HYPERION

NEW YORK

LIBRARY OF CONGRESS CATALOGING-IN-PUBLICATION DATA

Melman, Yossi.
    Friends in deed : inside the U.S.-Israel alliance / Yossi Melman,
Dan Raviv. — 1st ed.
    p.   cm.
    Includes bibliographical references.
    ISBN 0-7868-6006-5
    1. United States—Foreign relations—Israel.   2. Israel—Foreign
relations—United States.   3. Zionism—United States.   4. United
States—Foreign relations—20th century.   I. Raviv, Daniel.
II. Title.
E183.8.I7M45 1994
327.7305694—dc20   93-42416
                              CIP

FIRST EDITION

10 9 8 7 6 5 4 3 2 1

Book design by Barbara M. Bachman

Endpaper maps drawn by Lisa Amoroso

TO BILLIE, YOTAM, AND DARIA

TO DORI, JONATHAN, AND EMMA

Mark Twain, after visiting the Holy Land, said it "always

brought to my mind a vague suggestion of a country as large

as the United States. I suppose it was because I could not

conceive of a small country having so long a history."

—THE INNOCENTS ABROAD, 1867

CONTENTS

CONTENTS

x

ACKNOWLEDGMENTS

There are many people in the various streams of the U.S.-Israel alliance who have our gratitude for helping to bring this project to life. We interviewed hundreds of government officials, military personnel, business executives, community leaders, lobbyists, and other activists all over the United States and Israel, and they were generous with their reminiscences, insights, and views.

Most of our sources are named in this book, although others who were sifted out in the editing process might note that true heroes do not always get their names in print. Some interviewees, especially in sensitive fields such as military and intelligence, prefer to remain anonymous.

We are especially grateful to our researchers—Zamir Dekel, Dania Drori, Smadar Golan, Ian McCary, and Nancy Zuckerbrod—and to the staffs of the Truman, Eisenhower, Kennedy,

ACKNOWLEDGMENTS

Johnson, Ford, Carter, and Bush presidential libraries and the *Ha'aretz* newspaper archive.

Our agent, Russell Galen, and the Hyperion team, including Brian DeFiore and Catherine Rezza, deserve special thanks for encouragement and support, as do the people of CBS News. And the love and patience shown by our families during the three years of producing this book defy description.

INTRODUCTION

As is said of ancient Rome, the alliance between the United States and Israel was not built in a day.

Indeed, there was no guarantee that this unique partnership would ever be built at all. It pairs two countries that are separated not only by five thousand miles of land and sea but by other obvious disparities. One nation is a giant superpower in the Western Hemisphere and the other, a tiny country in the Middle East. One has a quarter-billion people, while the other just celebrated reaching the 5 million mark. One extends from ocean to ocean, but the other could be contained in the State of New Jersey. The United States is rich in resources, while Israel has managed to make do with little. They have vastly different historical memories, which have led them down contrasting courses of experience and behavior.

Presented with these building blocks, it would have seemed difficult to imagine combining them into a partnership. Yet the relationship between the United States and Israel has come to be one of the strongest, if strangest, in history. It cannot be explained by one single event, personality, or motive. Rather it is the product of unexpected occurrences and dramatic coincidences forming a foundation on which dreamers, leaders, and ordinary people have added their intentional deeds.

Books on U.S.-Israel relations have fallen into three broad categories: historical accounts that chart the chronological progress, mainly dwelling on diplomatic developments; texts that narrowly focus on a single aspect of the relationship, such as the Jewish factor or strategic cooperation; and descriptions riddled with bias that search for evil motives and conspiracies.

Ours is an effort to explain the multilayered, patchwork-quilt nature of the U.S.-Israel relationship in a balanced and clear-sighted fashion. We try to tell the story in its chronological progression, particularly in Chapters 2 through 13. In the more recent period, powerful themes became apparent, so that Chapters 14 through 22 take a thematic approach to history. To avoid interrupting the narrative, we occasionally place relevant material, including letters from presidents, in the notes.

The major events, including the early days of American interest in the Middle East, are included as guideposts and turning points. So are the key components of the alliance: the common Judeo-Christian heritage, Christian fascination with the Holy Land, guilt and sympathy over the Nazi Holocaust, strategic motives, and democratic values—in addition to domestic politics, for while only two or three of every one hundred Americans are Jewish, their influence is greater than their numbers would suggest.

But even these explanations are insufficient. The alliance is more than the sum total of events and components. There are traits to be identified and patterns to be deciphered, connections to be exposed and new stories to be told.

All these, however, cannot be isolated from the people involved. Some famous but others unrecognized, they have contributed their efforts and ideas to constructing the alliance—at times according to a blueprint, at others improvised through personal initiative.

This is not a Hollywood romance or a fairy tale. The relationship has had its moments of happiness, but it contains anger and sadness as well. Sentiments have often clashed with hard interests. The basic trust has been colored by a measure of misunderstanding and suspicion, and as in some families there also have been scandals.

One important aspect of the friendship cannot be ignored: The United States has many allies, and Israel has only one. Israel is quite important to a few Americans, but of only occasional interest to most. To all Israelis, on the other hand, the United States is extremely important.

The alliance that has resulted from these unique circumstances is a broad relationship, extending from international politics to military affairs, from intelligence cooperation to financial ties, from show-business celebrities to notorious gangsters, from enthusiastic lobbyists to influential media people, and from Zionist Jews to fundamentalist Christians.

It is not our intention to compile a catalogue or an encyclopedia of all the deeds and all the doers. So much has occurred between the two nations that to include every fact would obscure the true picture. Instead the alliance can be examined by highlighting the major events that built it, dipping into the memories of the builders, and adding analysis that binds them together.

Some events have been omitted or presented in brief, and some of the people involved will not find themselves between the covers of this book. There was, regrettably, insufficient space for all the events and all the dramatic players. The word "drama" derives from the same Greek root as "to do," and the tale of how the United States and Israel became friends is truly deeds turned into a striking drama. This is the inside story of that drama.

FRIENDS IN DEED

CHAPTER ONE

HANDSHAKES

The momentous yet momentary physical contact at the White House between Yitzhak Rabin, retired general and now prime minister of Israel, and his nation's archenemy, Yasser Arafat, was immediately recognized as the handshake of the decade. In a less obvious fashion, the abandonment of Israel's war against the Palestine Liberation Organization in September 1993 also encapsulated the Jewish state's relations with its friend and sponsor, the United States.

After all, the U.S. president, Bill Clinton, stood behind the handshakers with his own arms outstretched, framing his guests—with the flair of a slick impresario, but also the pride of a father at a ceremony that felt like a cross between a Jewish bar mitzvah, an Arab wedding, and an American barbecue.

To the three thousand guests on Clinton's South Lawn and the tens of millions of television viewers around the world who watched in disbelief, it was clear that while Arafat happily extended his hand to his foe there was more than a second's hesitation on Rabin's part. With a weak smile of distaste, he did, however, accept the obvious cues of the president's body language—the spreading of the arms meant to introduce the two warring leaders to each other in a civilized fashion.

Clinton did not touch Rabin, to prod him toward the historic handshake. The fact is that, whether on September 13, 1993, or throughout the relationship spanning nearly half a century, the United States usually can impose its will on Israel without twisting any arms. If persuasion and heavy hints are ignored or misinterpreted, coercion may be threatened. But just as the United States has learned that its best interests are served by letting Israel pursue its own agenda and freely express its wishes, both sides have learned that if America's vital interests are imperiled, the Israelis will do best by stepping aside and letting the United States exercise its prerogatives as a superpower.

Two of Clinton's predecessors were also at the ceremony. There was Jimmy Carter, smiling like the godfather of a baby called Peace; but his deeds were a decade and a half old. More than the other former presidents, it was George Bush who might have the right to claim most of the credit. "Let history be the judge without my trying to shape history," he comments modestly.

But it was the Bush administration, through its deeds, that sculpted the landscape to make new horizons visible. "I felt a quiet satisfaction from the fact that without Desert Storm, the handshake would not be taking place."

Indeed, it was while on assignment from Bush during the Gulf War against Iraq that another handshake—less publicized and far more casual—became part of the same process of learning lessons. It occurred nearly three years before the Rabin-Clinton-Arafat encounter, and it involved only Americans—although on Israeli soil. Yet as a small piece of the complex and interwoven relations between the two countries, it helped propel the Middle East toward its rendezvous with peace.

The handshake between two Americans, at a road junction near Tel Aviv, ordinarily would seem no big deal to Israelis long accustomed to opening their land to U.S. influence. But this encounter came at an extraordinary time. It was January 21, 1991, and the Americans had come to save Israel—from its enemies; but also, they believed, from itself.

A lieutenant colonel in the camouflage uniform of the United States Army introduced himself as Harry Krimkowitz. His gas mask, suddenly a mandatory wardrobe accessory for everyone in Israel, hung from his belt.

The civilian he met was one of his masters from the Pentagon: Paul Wolfowitz, undersecretary of defense for policy. The two men, surrounded by U.S. and Israeli officials and military personnel, exchanged a few pleasantries, but the substance of their conversation was unmemorable. It was the symbolism of why they had come to this muddy field, just south of Israel's largest city, that counted.

Surrounded by winter rain puddles, standing near brown and green nets meant to hide this emplacement from enemy planes, the two Americans represented two aspects of a unique policy at a unique time in America's ambiguous alliance with Israel— an unprecedented friendship between a superpower and a far-off, tiny state. The fact that both Krimkowitz and Wolfowitz were Jewish and had relatives in Israel added an extra dimension, at least in the eyes of many Israelis.

Lieutenant Colonel Krimkowitz, commander of two batteries of Patriot missiles, had been flown to Israel from his base in Germany two days earlier, under urgent orders issued by President George Bush. The military objective: to use the missiles, designed for shooting down airplanes, to intercept Soviet-made Scud missiles fired at the Jewish state by Iraq. Perhaps the Patriots could foil Saddam Hussein's strategy of complicating the

Gulf War by attacking Israel—even worse, by using the poison gas warheads he had amassed.

Krimkowitz's mission also had a psychological objective: to make the Israeli people feel that someone was doing something, so that their government would agree to absorb the missile strikes and do nothing. One of Bush's key war aims was that Israel, the Middle East's foremost military power, take no action.

Saddam's military and industrial complexes were already being pounded by thousands of sorties a day by U.S. and allied bombers, and the American president did not want the added complication of Israel's air force entering the fray—a development that could shatter the support he had won from Arab leaders to join the United States in a war against one of their own.

For most Israelis, the presence on their soil of Krimkowitz, four Patriot batteries, and the attendant crews of over seven hundred U.S. Army men and women was the most profound evidence of America's commitment to ensure the survival of Israel. What greater expression could there be of shared strategic interests, military cooperation, the common values of two democracies, the attachment of the Christian majority to the Holy Land, and the American public's determination that the Jewish nation should never again face the threat of lethal gas, as in the Nazi Holocaust?

It seemed only natural that Bush was promising Prime Minister Yitzhak Shamir and his cabinet the moon, just so long as they did not exercise their right of self-defense.

But like the moon, this fabled partnership had its dark side. In the dramatic days of Bush's Operation Desert Storm, he sent some soldiers and envoys to Israel; not because he trusted Shamir and his ministers, but largely because he did not.

Shamir and Bush had had a bumpy relationship since the president's term began two years earlier, and now he was asking a huge favor: Please do nothing. Naturally, he sent two officials who were well liked in Israel—Wolfowitz, of medium build, and the portly Deputy Secretary of State Lawrence Eagleburger—to ask in person.

Their mission was no less important than the defensive task of Krimkowitz and his missile crews: to ensure that Israel would not damage Bush's strategic goals in the Gulf War. Eagleburger and Wolfowitz, senior and experienced Washington hands, were dispatched by the administration like two bodyguards sent by a Mafia boss to "protect a friend" while also keeping an eye on him so he doesn't do anything the boss wouldn't like.

If the Jewish lieutenant colonel symbolized cooperation, trust, and the clear U.S. concern for the fate of Israel, Wolfowitz and Eagleburger blended those sentiments with the undercurrents of suspicion and fear in the relations between Washington and Jerusalem. That is not how they put it publicly—as Eagleburger spoke of America's "affection" for Israel—and even privately they sympathized with the country's plight as a victim. But still, their job was to make the victim act helpless, all in the service of helping Bush create what he would later proclaim a "new world order."

These were difficult days for the government in Jerusalem. Israelis were puzzled as to why their fabled army, the Israel Defense Forces, sat bound and gagged. Yet even as dozens of Iraqi missiles struck their country, the Israelis did not shoot back. They put their faith in the United States—in its bombers and in its political promises. Shamir and his cabinet soon had great misgivings.

As the smoke of war cleared in March 1991, U.S.-Israel relations had done an about-face. Before the war they had seemed to be at their finest hour; now they returned to a sour and ugly time. Mistrust seemed to overwhelm shared interests, and Bush and Shamir clashed over some of their most cherished concerns. Operation Desert Storm and its aftermath proved to be a crossroads for the two countries. The ecstatic highs and the extreme lows, during such a short period, reflected most of the fundamentals of an intense roller-coaster ride that had begun four decades earlier on tracks laid long before.

CHAPTER TWO

FROM THE HOLY LAND TO THE HOLOCAUST

The very first contacts between the United States and the Land of Israel contained the early elements of the alliance and its unique patterns still found today. Religion, of course, has always stood at the center of the connection—with the Judeo-Christian heritage providing spiritual strength to the bond. Conscience, guilt, and the allure of the Promised Land for both Jews and Christians all played a role and still do. In addition, well-placed Jews in American society have helped turn their countrymen's attention toward Zion.

The early nineteenth century witnessed a wave of Protestant revivalism throughout the United States and especially in New England. It was this religious sentiment that moved American missionaries, during this period, to travel to foreign lands and spread the Word. Among their destinations was Palestine, as the Holy Land was known then. These Americans joined hundreds of Europeans who had arrived before them: fellow mis-

sionaries, merchants, adventurers and diplomats, spies, archae-
ologists, and charlatans of all sorts.

The European powers' main concerns, in Turkish-ruled
Palestine, were to keep watch over Christian holy places and to
continue to run the churches, monasteries, and missions that
had been there for hundreds of years. European churches experienced a burst of evangelicalism, which powerfully stressed the
immediacy of the relationship linking God, the people, and the
Bible. This spread, with a wave of European immigrants, to
the United States. Evangelicalism of various shades focused
interest on the land where the Bible stories had unfolded.

An important facet that tightened the missionaries' attachment to the Holy Land was the "millenarian" strand of evangelicalism—a belief in the millennium, Christ's thousand-year
reign on earth associated with his Second Coming.

Many of today's U.S. fundamentalists still adhere to mille-
narianism, and the Jews play an important part in the scenario
of the Last Judgment and Redemption. In the New Testament's
Book of Revelations, the return of the Jews to their ancient
homeland was set as a necessary precondition for the Second
Coming of Christ. That, in its simplest terms, is why evangelicals support Jewish sovereignty in the Holy Land.

To the American missionaries, the Bible was a living reality,
and pilgrimage to Palestine represented the opportunity to experience it literally. For Christians, almost every place where
Jesus and his disciples set foot is hallowed ground. Jerusalem is
especially charged with religious sentiment.

Following an example set by European countries, President
Andrew Jackson signed an agreement in 1830 with the Turkish
authorities granting special privileges to American citizens in
Palestine. The United States was allowed to appoint consuls
in Constantinople, the capital of the Ottoman Empire, and in
Palestine. At first these consuls happened to be European Jews

who resided there, but in time special representatives were sent from the United States.

There was even an expedition by the U.S. Navy in early 1848, when three ships—transported by land from the Mediterranean port of Haifa to the Jordan River—sailed into the Dead Sea, where Lieutenant W. F. Lynch found "the waters a nauseous compound of bitters and salts." The navy men visited the small Jewish community and the Christian holy sites in Jerusalem, moving Lynch to predict that the fall of the Ottoman Empire would "ensure the restoration of the Jews to Palestine." The first part of his prophecy came true in seventy years; an entire century would pass before the fulfillment of the remainder.

In the meantime, the consular agreement with Turkey made it easier for Christian adventurers to set out for the Holy Land. American missionaries arrived with little more than the banner of religiosity and civil virtue. Unlike the Europeans who had property and vested interests, the Americans wanted to do more than set up churches and preach among the natives— mainly Muslim Arabs—so as to convert them to Christianity. The contingent from the United States put more emphasis on providing the local population with education and medical care.

By the 1860s the first American community in Palestine was established. This so-called colony crystallized around the controversial figure of George Washington Joshua Adams, an actor and Mormon Millenarian. He was an eternal adventurer who had already established his own church in Maine. Adams, who would prove to be an alcoholic and a crook, had set himself one great aim in life: He would return the Children of Israel to the Promised Land, so as to realize the visions of the Old Testament prophets and pave the way for the coming of Christ.

To prepare the biblical land for the Jews, he organized 150 supporters, raised money, and set sail for Palestine. After a voyage of forty-two days, they landed on the Mediterranean coast at Jaffa in August 1866. Well organized, they brought horses and carriages with them, and their music teacher even brought a piano. With the support of the American consul, Adams purchased land to the north of the ancient port and constructed his settlement.

The settlers had planned to support themselves by farming, but the harvests were disappointing. Life became harsh and enthusiasm waned, as Bedouin Arabs attacked them, raped some of the women, and stole their property. Poisoned water and outbreaks of disease killed thirteen members of the group. Then Adams's alcoholism was exposed, as well as his involvement in land speculation.

The group collapsed under the pressure. Some of its wooden houses remain today in the slums of modern-day south Tel Aviv, where an effort is being made to rehabilitate them as an artists' colony.

In 1867, a little over a year after their arrival and the opening of their settlement, most members of Adams's congregation were on their way back to the United States—some on a ship that, by coincidence, also carried Samuel Clemens. The author, famous under his pen name Mark Twain, had been assigned to tour Palestine by several newspapers that were inspired by the new religious revivalism.

In reporting his impressions, Twain did not spare the Holy Land his scorn. Of its landscape, he wrote that there were "no flowers, nor birds nor trees." Its inhabitants, he found, were "simple, superstitious, disease-tortured creatures" and "ill-clad and ill-conditioned savages."

His word portraits were of Arabs "quarrelling like dogs and cats" and Bedouins "whose sole happiness it is, in this life, to cut and stab and mangle and murder unoffending Christians." He was hardly more complimentary to the small Jewish community in Palestine, so that even now there are some patriotic

Israelis who will not forgive the American writer's insulting attitude to what he saw.

Such harsh descriptions did not scare off the pious travelers who continued to flock to Palestine—to visit, travel, or even settle there. In September 1881 a group of Presbyterians led by Horatio Spafford, a lawyer and real estate agent from Chicago, reached Jerusalem. Ten years earlier Spafford had lost all his property in the Great Fire in Chicago. As if this was not enough, two of his children then drowned. Following these calamities, the family was expelled from its local church and decided to establish its own congregation.

Spafford then had a vision that led the entire congregation to move to the Holy Land. The group, called the Newcomers, acquired a building in Jerusalem. Their Arab neighbors referred to the place as the "American Colony," and it functioned as a missionary settlement offering religious studies to local Arabs. The community fell apart within a decade, but the building remained in the care of the Spafford family for many years to come. Today it is one of the most prestigious hotels in the city, popular among foreign diplomats and journalists. Many of the meetings between Palestinians and American officials who come to Jerusalem to discuss peace prospects take place in the American Colony Hotel.

Though during the twentieth century the religious pull of Palestine lessened, the attachment of Christians to the Holy Land has always played an important role in their support of Jewish causes. As Zionism became the political movement of the Jews, American Christians gave moral and political support. And after Israel was established in 1948, this support was one of the foundations for the special relationship between the new state and the United States.

Even before statehood, American Jews who sought to take part in their country's diplomatic outreach toward the Holy Land were able to do so. Time and again a Jew was appointed as

U.S. ambassador to Turkey—in the years when the Ottoman Turks ruled Palestine. The first in this line was Solomon Strauss, given the job in the 1880s on account of his friendship with President Grover Cleveland. As soon as he had assumed his position, the new ambassador began supporting the Zionist movement, which had only recently been established in eastern and central Europe.

The Zionist mission was to return the Jewish people to its homeland, known in Hebrew as *Eretz Israel* (the Land of Israel), and to gain statehood. But Jewish immigrants were denied entry to Palestine by the Turkish authorities, and if they somehow did get in, they found themselves threatened with deportation. Ambassador Strauss used his influence to prevent these expulsions, setting himself up as a quasi-Zionist lobbyist in the court of the Ottoman sultan.

When Strauss returned to the United States, he was replaced by another Jewish ambassador. Still later the most remarkable of all was Henry Morgenthau, Sr. Serving through the difficult years of World War I, he proved himself the guardian angel of Palestine's persecuted Jewish community. "He saved it from starvation and probably extinction, thus preserving it for the ultimate statehood," says his granddaughter, historian Barbara W. Tuchman, who adds the irony that Morgenthau was opposed to the Zionist movement in the United States. He believed that life for American Jews was best in America.

Still, recognizing the humanitarian needs in Turkish-ruled Palestine, in November 1914 he cabled leaders of the American Jewish Committee in New York—mostly German-born Jews who were anti-Zionist—as follows: "Palestinian Jews facing terrible crisis. Belligerent countries stopping their assistance. Serious destruction threatens thriving colonies. Fifty thousand dollars needed by responsible committee . . . to establish loan institute and support families whose breadwinners have entered army conditions. Certainly justify American help. Will you undertake matter?" It was signed, "Morgenthau."

The sum was raised in two days, cabled to a bank in Constantinople, changed to gold, and carried in a suitcase to Jerusalem by Morgenthau's son-in-law. Later food, money, and medicine were transported from the United States by thirteen warships: a precursor to Jewish lobbying, Jewish fund raising, and military airlifts. This was the first time that American Jews organized themselves to assist their brethren in the Land of Israel. "By these measures," says Tuchman, "the nucleus of the future state of Israel survived."

In 1915, after Turkey joined the war on Germany's side, Morgenthau sent the American warship *Tennessee* to the port of Jaffa to pick up Jewish refugees—suspected by the Turks to be British sympathizers—and to bring them to safety in Egypt. The *Tennessee* made a few sailings back and forth on the same route, bringing out six thousand Jews altogether.

When Eliezer Ben-Yehuda, the scholar who was the driving force behind the revival of Hebrew as a spoken language, needed financial support, the same German-born Jewish leaders in the United States who had heeded Morgenthau's call provided money and a house for the Ben-Yehuda family.

It was World War I that greatly accelerated the change in the U.S. attitude to the Middle East. America became interested in the world, and President Woodrow Wilson's ideas—including the right of self-determination—inspired the peoples of the Middle East, the Zionists as much as Arab nationalists.

Between the two world wars, however, the United States withdrew into an isolationist shell and left the Middle East political playground to France and Great Britain. At first, most American Jews showed little interest in Zionism—or even disdain for it. They had their minds primarily on finding a niche in America's way of life or channeling their socialist beliefs from eastern Europe into fortifying the U.S. labor movement.

But an active minority did support Jewish nationalism. Zionism's supporters were keenly aware of the ideological, political, and religious schisms that still exist today. They formed their own local groups in America's big cities and were inspired by occasional visits by Palestinian Jews, including the future prime ministers David Ben-Gurion and Golda Meir. A growing number of socialist labor activists joined the Zionist movement, and union leaders would become a bedrock of support for Israel.

But before that occurred came the greatest calamity ever to befall the Jewish people, and neither the Zionists nor the non-Zionists could stop it. The U.S. government was among the many that displayed indifference to Adolf Hitler's Final Solution.

From the moment in 1933 when Hitler and his Nazi party rose to power in Germany, their hatred for Jews was crystal clear. Jews were stripped of their civil rights and then their property. Some were lucky to be expelled; others were jailed. There were limited diplomatic protests from Washington, London, and Paris, but very little was done to assist the Jews. Most Western countries denied them entry visas.

An especially painful case was that of the American ocean-liner, the *St. Louis*, filled with Jewish refugees on the eve of war in 1939. The ship pulled into various ports in western Europe and the Western Hemisphere—including American harbors—but in every case was turned away. The U.S. and European press covered the story, but with governments unwilling to set a precedent for mass immigration, the vessel had to return to Germany, where the Jews were doomed.

Even Palestine had been closed to them, because of the British governors who had taken over from Turkey after World War I. Britain had permitted the Zionists to start building a "Jewish national home," as spelled out in the Balfour Declaration of 1917; and between the wars more than 300,000 Jews had come in from Europe, the majority from Poland. But in 1936 the Arab inhabitants of Palestine rebelled against the British and demanded an end to Jewish immigration. Concerned that the Arab revolt might spread into oil-rich neighboring countries, thus harming their economic interests, the British gave in and imposed limitations on Jewish immigration.

The new fixed quotas blocked the way to the Land of Israel just when Jews needed it most. The Zionist movement and the Jewish community in Palestine, led by Ben-Gurion, did what they could to smuggle in European refugees. But only a few thousand safely reached the shores of their Promised Land.

When Hitler saw that no country in the world was prepared to take in Europe's Jews, he started to murder them en masse. The most audacious killing machine in history became an industry, turning German precision and efficiency to the task of rounding up and transporting victims. Nearly 6 million Jewish people were killed in a program aimed at wiping out an entire race and religion.

It is undeniable that information about Nazi atrocities reached the outside world during their fairly early stages. The Final Solution plan had been adopted in January 1942 during a secret meeting of Nazi leaders at Wannsee, near Berlin, and soon afterward the use of firing squads to kill Jews gave way to the high-productivity gas chambers of the death camps: Auschwitz, Treblinka, Sobibor, Belzec, Chelmno, and others. The gray smoke that issued from the crematoria's chimneys showed that the factories of death worked around the clock.

It took only a few weeks, in the summer of 1942, for fragmentary information on the unfathomable killing industry to start reaching the West. Horrifying accounts of Auschwitz were smuggled out by Polish resistance fighters and by the diplomats of neutral countries, such as Portugal, Sweden, and Brazil. Even more credible and documented information was transferred by German industrialist Edward Schulta, whose conscience about the evil deeds of his compatriots would not allow him to remain silent. He gave the information to Jewish representatives in neutral Switzerland. From there British and American diplomats relayed the news to London and Washington, and by the end of 1942 it had definitely reached Prime Minister Winston Churchill and President Franklin Roosevelt. Perhaps unwilling to believe the reports, the Western leaders suppressed them.

Indeed, the stories from central and eastern Europe were nothing short of unbelievable. Even the leaders of the prestate Jewish community in Tel Aviv were unable to comprehend that their coreligionists—their families—in Europe were being slaughtered. Documents that recently came to light show that in Ben-Gurion's Jewish Agency, the fate of European Jewry elicited little talk and no action. The Hebrew press dismissed the first, smuggled reports as "unfounded rumors" spread by "sensation mongers."

The tragic fact is, however, that even if they had taken the issue more seriously, the Zionist leadership could have done very little. It was a nationalist, political movement, with neither a true army nor the apparatus of a state. There was little money, and the Jewish community in Palestine was ruled by foreign occupiers who seemed indifferent to the fate of the Jews. The British were not doing anything, even though they and the Americans were the only ones who could.

But even when the United States knew beyond doubt about Germany's systematic murder of the Jewish people, America did nothing to provide shelter. In the sad history of World War II, this is perhaps the most tragic chapter. America still refused to grant entry visas to Jewish refugees, and the British choked another escape route by keeping the strict limits on Jewish immigration to Palestine.

Roosevelt and Churchill calculated that if they spent too much effort, bombs, and money on saving the Jews, this would detract from their main objective: rooting out the Nazi enemy. According to the logic of Washington and London, the persecution and murder of Jews would stop only when the Nazi monster was stopped.

But why was there no effort, at least, to slow the terrifying pace of the mass killing? During 1943 and '44 pleas from Jewish leaders in the United States and Great Britain grew ever more vociferous to the effect that the death camps in Poland, or at least the railway tracks leading to them, should be bombed. The same urgent request was smuggled out of the concentration camps themselves. If the system of transporting Jews to the death camps on crowded and inhuman train boxcars had been stopped, fewer Jews would have reached the camps and fewer would have perished in the gas chambers.

Military commanders retorted that they had only limited resources and would have to choose priorities. An absurd climax came in August 1944, when Allied warplanes flew out to attack oil refineries and chemical plants that happened to be close to the Auschwitz concentration camp. Some bombs accidentally fell on an inmates' barrack and a house used by German guards. For a few days the doomed prisoners were elated. Even though some of their friends had died in the bombardment, they felt that their liberation must be imminent.

But as the days passed, everything returned to the normalcy of their hell. The Germans went on operating the gas chambers. The Jews went on being murdered. And the Allies went on bombarding German military, strategic, and industrial targets.

Some small rays of light punctured the gloom of the Holocaust's bleak reality. These were mainly the work of individual Americans, diplomats, government officials, and servicemen who were moved by the news and the descriptions of Jewish suffering. They decided on their own, in spite of Roosevelt's inaction and sometimes against the president's expressed opinion, to bring help to European Jews.

One of them was Israel Gaynor Jacobson, whose life story is typical of an American Jew of his generation. He was born in

May 1912 in Buffalo, to a family of Jewish immigrants. His father, Morris, had been imprisoned in Russia on account of socialist activities and was sent to Siberia for a life sentence of forced labor. He bribed his way out of prison and made his way to a ship bound for the "Golden Land," as the entire United States was then known among European Jews. There he joined relatives who had already found refuge in America. Like many of his fellow Jewish immigrants, Morris Jacobson became a laborer and stuck to his socialist ideals, which he now combined with support for Jewish causes.

When his son was born he gave him two names: Israel and Gan-Or (Gaynor), Hebrew for "garden of light." The boy was raised to be proud of his roots, in the face of anti-Semitic attacks by local members of the Ku Klux Klan. The combination, in the interwar years, of radical Jewish socialism with exposure to anti-Semitism was typical of the Jewish-American experience of the time.

Gaynor Jacobson was sent to Sunday school every week to receive some *Yiddishkeit*—education in Jewish heritage and tradition. Judaism and Zionism remained important components in his life. Even his studies at Columbia University in New York did not manage to subdue this. His enrollment in 1928 to this prestigious school was "a near miracle," Jacobson recalls, "considering Columbia was not in the habit of admitting too many Jews." The Great Depression interrupted his studies, because his family could not afford both the tuition and their mortgage, but Jacobson did earn a master's degree in social work from the University of Buffalo. He then directed his professional work toward issues concerning Jewish welfare in the United States and abroad.

Jacobson still remembers vividly what a great impact the deportation of the *St. Louis* refugees had on him and his generation. From that moment in 1939, he pledged he would help his

fellow Jews. During the war he worked with the small number
of European refugees who had managed to escape and settle in
the United States. He was then hired by the American Jewish
Joint Distribution Committee, widely known as the Joint. This
organization had been founded in 1914, after America's ambassador, Morgenthau, appealed in his cablegram from Turkey to
his Jewish friends to help the Jews of Palestine.

The Joint had been active between the wars in distributing
relief to Jews in distress all around the world. Now, in World
War II, the Joint had set itself the task of rescuing Jews from
occupied Europe.

Jacobson's first foreign assignment led to an important development in the future alliance between America, its Jews, and
Israel. The Joint sent him to Italy late in the war, and there he
forged working relations with underground agents of the Jewish community in Palestine. These agents would become,
within a few years, the master spies of the newborn intelligence
community of Israel.

In Italy and elsewhere in Europe, they were working for the
same purpose: to save Jews, to help Holocaust survivors recover
from their war traumas, and to smuggle them to Palestine.
These were the first seeds of clandestine cooperation between
American Jews and envoys from the land of Israel. These seeds
would, with time, yield impressive fruits—especially in bringing the new nation hundreds of thousands of new citizens. The
Joint and other organizations, and Jacobson in various capaci-
ties, would continue to cooperate with Israeli intelligence to
rescue and smuggle Jews from Yemen, Morocco, Iraq, and
other places where they were in danger.

"For us, the generation who witnessed the Holocaust," says
Jacobson, "the words 'never again' have a clear and special significance." And this was true not only for Jews.

Jacobson believes that encountering the emaciated survivors

of the death camps left indelible marks on any American involved in World War II: servicemen, diplomats, other government officials, Jews and non-Jews alike.

In the 1940s, he recalls, "The various agencies and bodies of the federal government still refused to participate in our humanitarian efforts, but there were always individuals who were ready to offer help or who turned a blind eye. Human compassion could not remain untouched by the sight of the Jewish tragedy."

This was, in fact, the beginning of the road toward the vote at the United Nations General Assembly in November 1947 that approved the UN partition plan for Palestine. This, in turn, paved the way for the first independent Jewish state after more than two thousand years. And on this there was a rare consensus between the two superpowers that emerged from the war, the United States and the Soviet Union.

The Holocaust was, and still is to an important degree, a major factor in relations between Israel and the United States. The now-confirmed facts—seen on newsreels—of gas chambers, trains, and human suffering on an unprecedented scale left the public at large with a deep feeling of guilt for having stood by passively, without trying even the minimum to prevent the catastrophe. The leadership of the Western world, especially in America, could not escape the guilt.

A shamefaced, remorseful postwar West now supported the Jewish demand for an independent state in Palestine. American soldiers in Europe had seen for themselves what the Jews had suffered. Upon returning home and taking jobs in key positions—including the White House, the State Department, the Central Intelligence Agency, and the Pentagon—they did not forget the Holocaust. They could not forget. This fact profoundly influenced their positive attitude toward Jews and Israel.

After declaring its independence in May 1948, and even

while fighting and winning a war for survival, the new Jewish state knew full well how to exploit these sentiments and to take advantage of them. In the American Jews and the officials of postwar administrations, Israel saw the levers for advancing its own interests.

CHAPTER THREE

PULLING LEVERS

The most useful lever in bringing America's Middle East policy around to a pro-Israel course was found in the person of another Jacobson. However, aside from their shared surname, Eddie Jacobson of Kansas City had little in common with Gaynor Jacobson, the Jew from Buffalo who helped Jewish refugees from Europe's Holocaust.

The two men symbolize the two aspects of the leverage system developed by Israel and its friends in the United States. One is the practical side, which takes action to reach objectives needed by the Israeli government. The other aspect is personal, working to obtain American support for Israel's political needs.

This is where Eddie Jacobson's story fits in: the story of a man whose most important asset was his friendship with President Harry S Truman; and whose most important achievement was persuading Truman to recognize the newborn State of Israel, the very first American step into the alliance.

Sergeant Jacobson met Lieutenant Truman during World War I at an army camp in Oklahoma, where they were both waiting for action in France. They ran the regimental canteen together and became lifelong friends. After the war they opened a haberdasher's shop in Kansas City.

Truman's partner was born on New York's Lower East Side in 1891, to poor Jewish parents from Lithuania. He experienced the petty anti-Semitism that was endemic to society at the time, but Jacobson would not be deterred when it really counted for Israel.

The moments of truth came in early 1948. American Zionists and officials of the Jewish Agency, in effect Israel's prestate government, could tell that trouble was brewing for them in Washington almost immediately after the previous November's UN vote for partition of Palestine. The United States had voted "yes," but while Ben-Gurion prepared to declare statehood upon the departure of the British, there were definite rumblings of a change of heart in the Truman administration.

The State Department, led by General George C. Marshall, was concerned that identifying with a Jewish state would harm America's standing in the Middle East, especially when U.S. companies were seeking favorable terms for drilling in the Arab oil world.

The Department of Defense, under James V. Forrestal, also expressed the view that Israel would be an obstacle to advancing American strategic and military interests. And the Pentagon would continue to be hostile ground for Israel for over a decade to come. Forrestal's experts said the Jews would be hopelessly outnumbered by the Arabs, and the United States—if it made any commitment to a weak Jewish state—would have to send troops to its rescue. But Forrestal's unstable personality limited his influence; in 1949 he would commit suicide.

General Marshall's voice, however, could not be ignored. He was a war hero—commanding more respect than the president, who, after all, had only the questionable mandate of inheriting the White House upon Roosevelt's death.

Marshall's State Department was leading a turn away from partition, despite the U.S. vote in favor. American diplomats proposed instead that a UN trusteeship keep Jews and Arabs under a single administration until they could sort out their differences. Prominent among them was Dean Rusk, a middle-level official singled out by a journalist covering the UN as having "tried the last-minute maneuver that almost untracked the Palestine partition decision in 1947 and dissembled about it." A future secretary of state, he would be remembered negatively by Israeli officials and by American supporters of the Jewish state, who together would get into the habit of dividing the world into two camps: "for us" and "against us."

Ben-Gurion insisted that nothing would stop him from pronouncing statehood. His envoys in the United States wanted to know whether the shift to trusteeship was imagined or real, a State Department chimera or a White House fact. But Truman would not tell them. The president was suddenly refusing to see any Jewish or Zionist lobbyist.

The Zionists knew that Truman was sympathetic. On several occasions he had stated his commitment to the concept of a Jewish homeland as promised by Britain's Balfour Declaration of 1917. An avid Bible reader, Truman occasionally recited Deuteronomy 1:8, "Go in and take possession of the land which the Lord hath sworn unto your fathers, to Abraham, to Isaac, and to Jacob."

Cynics noticed that Truman sounded most enthusiastic about Jewish concerns when appearing at Democratic party rallies in states with relatively large Jewish populations, notably in New York, where around 14 percent of voters were Jews. But it was known that he had backed his words with deeds. At the end of World War II Truman had persuaded the British government to permit 100,000 Jewish Holocaust survivors who were still in Displaced Persons camps in Europe to settle in Palestine.

American Jewish leaders had not counted on Truman's support, however. They had heard of the president's Jewish partner, and they learned that Eddie Jacobson was a member of the social service organization B'nai B'rith. In mid-1947 a senior B'nai B'rith officer telephoned Jacobson, asking him to speak to Truman about the 100,000 refugees. "Harry Truman will do what's right if he knows all the facts," Jacobson replied. "If I can help supply them, I will. But I'm no Zionist, so first I need the facts from you."

Jacobson went to the White House to lobby Truman on the Displaced Persons issue. And in November, just days before the UN vote on partition, Jacobson was there again—writing in his personal diary, after the vote: "Mission accomplished."

But still, despite the sentiments of the U.S. president, there were lingering doubts over whether Truman favored full, independent statehood for the Jews.

The most troubling months were in early 1948, when pro-Zionist Americans realized that the president had been freezing them out since the start of the year. At one cabinet meeting Truman was so annoyed by Jewish pressure that he snapped, "Jesus Christ couldn't please them when he was on earth, so how could anyone expect that I would have my luck?" He had had it with lobbyists. He found Rabbi Abba Hillel Silver, the foremost leader of America's Zionist Jews, particularly abrasive; after all, Rabbi Silver was an active Republican.

Truman later wrote of "Jewish pressure" for "the extreme Zionist cause," adding: "I do not think that I ever had so much pressure and propaganda at the White House as I had in this instance." He turned down all requests for appointments on the subject of Palestine.

So what was to be done now? How could Israel's founders and supporters win the backing of their most prized ally? These were the questions pondered by Aubrey Abba Eban, the eloquent Cambridge graduate who at age thirty-two was senior diplomatic representative in Washington for the state-to-be. How would he find a path to the president's heart so as to ensure America's continued support for the partition plan? The challenge, in essence, was how to get into the White House without using the Jewish leaders who had so antagonized the president.

Eban hit upon the idea of arranging a meeting, at this critical juncture, between Truman and Chaim Weizmann, president of the World Zionist Organization and elder statesman of the Jewish Agency for Palestine. The two had already met in November 1947, just before the UN vote, and Weizmann had enthralled Truman with a lecture on how Jews could make the Negev Desert bloom, persuading the president to keep the Negev in the territory of the future state. Naturally, Eban hoped that Weizmann could be the secret, successful weapon again. But Truman, sick of being lobbied, would not see even Weizmann.

Eban and his friends in the American Jewish community decided to reactivate the Eddie Jacobson lever, to tip the White House toward the conviction that creating a viable Jewish state was necessary and unstoppable. Contacted again through B'nai B'rith, Jacobson immediately penned a letter to Truman, imploring him to meet with Weizmann. Truman wrote back that there was no point in having a meeting on a problem that was "not solvable."

Jacobson then flew to Washington from Missouri and walked into the White House without an appointment. Admitted, as usual, to the Oval Office, he was surprised to find Truman refusing to talk about Palestine and railing against "disrespectful" Jews. Jacobson later wrote that his "dear friend, the President of the United States, was at that moment as close to being an anti-Semite as a man could possibly be."

The visitor gathered up the courage to argue back. Pointing

to a miniature statue of President Andrew Jackson, Truman's hero, Jacobson said: "Well, Harry, I too have a hero, a man I never met but who is, I think, the greatest Jew who ever lived." The analogy between Chaim Weizmann and Jackson was spurious—but it worked.

Jacobson said Weizmann "is a very sick man, almost broken in health, but he traveled thousands of miles just to see you and plead the cause of my people. Now you refuse to see him because you were insulted by some of our American Jewish leaders." Jacobson had tears in his eyes as he turned to his friend. "It doesn't sound like you, Harry, because I thought you could take this stuff they've been handing out."

Truman gave in, saying "You win, you bald-headed s.o.b." And on March 18 he met with Weizmann, although the Zionist leader was ushered quietly into the White House so as not to be spotted by reporters. Once again, theirs was a meeting of the minds and spirits. The American president pledged that he was still committed to the original UN partition plan that guaranteed Jewish statehood.

The Zionist levers had worked. Eddie Jacobson went back to selling hats and ties in Missouri, and Weizmann returned to his hotel suite in New York to await the invitation to be Israel's first president. Not informed about the secret Truman-Weizmann meeting, however, the State Department declared the next day that the United States would recommend abandoning the partition plan. Shocked to read that in a newspaper, the president jotted down a note: "I'm now in the position of a liar and a double crosser," adding that there were people in the State Department "who have always wanted to cut my throat."

In the ensuing confusion came a protest by Eleanor Roosevelt, the widow of the late president, who was now serving as a U.S. delegate to the United Nations. She submitted her resignation. Her sons, Franklin Jr. and Elliott, were active in Democratic Party politics and started floating the idea of drafting

General Dwight D. Eisenhower as the presidential candidate for the Democrats in 1948.

Truman did not publicly contradict the State Department announcement, but he did summon Eddie Jacobson and reassured him that he still stood behind his promise to Weizmann and favored a Jewish state.

Nevertheless, there was one more great hurdle in Washington: in the Oval Office, beyond the reach of Jewish lobbyists, on May 12, 1948. Two days before the expected end of the British mandate and the declaration of a Jewish state, Truman wanted to have it out—once and for all—with the anti-Zionist establishment in his own government. The president refereed a fiery debate between two camps: one led by his advisors Clark Clifford and David Niles, and the other by Secretary of State Marshall.

According to Clifford, Truman had instructed him to prepare a case for Jewish statehood "just as though you were to make an argument before the Supreme Court." In the Oval Office debate, Clifford argued that the United States should announce that it looked "with favor on the creation of a Jewish state," even before Ben-Gurion's declaration of independence.

Marshall countered that such a declaration would only trigger a war, so the United States must delay recognition to allow more time for diplomacy. His camp also questioned whether the Jewish state would ever be a friend to America, displaying a file full of intelligence reports that suggested the boatloads of Jews arriving in Palestine were riddled with Communist spies.

Clifford, confident that he was voicing the president's own feelings, responded: "It is important for the long-range security of our country, and indeed the world, that a nation committed to the democratic system be established there, one on which we can rely. The new Jewish state can be such a place. We should strengthen it in its infancy by prompt recognition."

Marshall, in disgust, questioned why Clifford—a domestic policy advisor—should even be taking part in the debate. The secretary of state implied that Clifford was advising Truman to think only of Jewish votes and campaign contributions, with the presidential election less than half a year away. Marshall shocked everyone in the room by saying that if he lost the argument, he would probably vote against Truman.

Technically, Marshall won. The United States would not announce recognition of the Jewish state before the new nation was declared. But the secretary of state could see where Truman stood. U.S. recognition was inevitable, once Ben-Gurion did make his declaration. Marshall considered it unwise, he blamed it on politics, and he never exchanged another word with Clifford.

Clifford would deny for decades that he was lobbying for Zionism so as to win Jewish votes. But America's Jews would be grateful to Truman. Many of them shared Niles's feeling, as an advisor to both presidents, that had Roosevelt lived things would probably have been different; and there might not be a Jewish state.

Wealthy members of the community would swell Democratic party campaign coffers, and in the normal give-and-take of U.S. politics, this would give them increasing access to the halls of power in Washington. The close, though not exclusive, identification of Jews as Democrats would persist through the electoral triumphs of John F. Kennedy and Lyndon B. Johnson in the 1960s.

But at the time of Israel's birth, a substantial portion of American Jewry felt uncomfortable about a state overseas that might make claims on their allegiance. That very week the American Council for Judaism issued a statement denying any support for Ben-Gurion: "We reaffirm our belief that in the modern world, a people cannot be both a universal religion and a nation. Our nationalism is American, our religion is Judaism, our loyalty is indivisible, and our homeland is only in the United States of America."

While some Jews saw Israel and the United States as an either-or situation, it was ironic to see non-Jews who enthusiastically embraced both. Whether moved by biblical inspiration or Holocaust guilt, Israel's first champions on Capitol Hill were often from states with hardly any Jewish voters. New Mexico senator Dennis Chavez told a huge rally in Madison Square Garden: "The Hebrews have forged a nation for themselves! This is a fact, whether the British like it or not; whether the oil companies like it or not; and whether the anti-Semites like it or not. Perhaps one of these days the Middle East division of the State Department may become aware of it."

On May 14 Ben-Gurion read Israel's declaration of independence to an emotional crowd in a Tel Aviv museum. He was not absolutely certain of official American support. But it was "now or never," according to Moshe (Shertok) Sharett, soon to be Israel's foreign minister, whose attitude could reverberate through history as the basic policy of his nation: "We won't commit suicide to gain a friendship."

Just as Ben-Gurion announced the restoration of Jewish sovereignty in the ancient land of his people, the Jewish Agency office in Washington was sending the White House a formal request for recognition. Only when the new prime minister revealed what the new country's name would be was the word "Israel" hurriedly handwritten into the request.

Eight hours later, when Israel's independence took effect at midnight in the Middle East, the United States became the first nation to recognize the Jewish state. The announcement by the White House came at 6:11 P.M.—11 minutes after midnight on Israel's historic day of birth, May 15: "The United States recognizes the provisional government as the de facto authority of the new State of Israel."

It had become a recognition race, with Washington determined to beat Moscow: the first volley in the battle to ensure that Israel never fell into the Soviet Union's sphere of influence. The State Department was unhappy about Truman's decision but found some solace in outracing the Soviets.

Truman quickly chose his nation's first envoy to Israel, intentionally ignoring the ranks of the State Department and choosing a Gentile Zionist: James G. McDonald, a Protestant of Scottish and German descent who had represented the United States at conferences on refugees. He would be caught in the middle of many arguments, but he almost always defended Israel's viewpoint and was first in a long line of ambassadors to Israel who fell in love with the country.

He was not officially an ambassador, but rather the "Special Representative of the United States to the Provisional Government of Israel," for Truman's recognition of the state was de facto rather than de jure. Yet McDonald and his family were warmly received in Tel Aviv ninety days after the establishment of the state—only the second foreign diplomat stationed in Israel, for in this race the Soviets had beaten the Americans.

The neighboring Arab countries had responded within hours to Israel's declaration of independence by invading from all sides, so McDonald was in a country at war, occasionally hearing gunfire or seeing tracer bullets in the distance. When the on-again, off-again truces were in force, he transmitted Washington's warnings to Israel not to violate them. But the cease-fire lines were often untenable, and a typical Ben-Gurion reply became another Israeli litany to be repeated for decades: warning Truman and the State Department "that they would be gravely mistaken if they assumed that the threat or even the use of United Nations sanctions would force Israel to yield on issues considered vital to its independence and security."

McDonald did more than understand the flavor of the remarks. He swallowed them whole and digested them in a letter to Clifford: "An indefinite truce is, from Israel's point of view, equivalent to a death sentence to be executed at the convenience of the Arabs."

In another precursor to issues that would long haunt the U.S.-Israeli relationship, the Truman administration urged Ben-Gurion to be more flexible over territory. Washington did not insist that tiny Israel, defending itself from an onslaught, try to live in the narrow confines of the 1947 UN partition plan. But the United States foresaw only minor modifications and asked Israel, during the various truces, to withdraw from some of the captured land and permit the return of Palestinian Arab refugees.

Israel snapped back that by forcing such withdrawals, "the United States would gain no further friends in the Middle East and would lose one existing friend." McDonald recorded that he "felt this analysis had much logic." International political pressure would not force Israel to give up land for which it had sacrificed blood, following Arab aggression. At least not for another nine years.

The Americans were delighted when Israel held its first parliamentary elections on January 25, 1949, and were far from surprised when Ben-Gurion's labor party, Mapai, came in first among nearly a dozen parties that won seats in the K'nesset. Indeed, Washington was relieved that the Communists had only four seats out of 120 and that other left-wing parties were kept out of the cabinet, soothing U.S. fears that Israel might become a Soviet satellite.

While Israel flirted with the Soviet bloc for two more years, the results of the national vote clearly signaled that Israel was drifting toward the Western camp in the Cold War.

The elections cleared the way for Truman's more formal, de jure, recognition of Israel. But Jerusalem's reaction reflected the poverty of the fledgling state. Foreign Minister Sharett said the offer to upgrade the U.S. Mission in Tel Aviv to full "embassy" status was flattering, but Israel was not sure that it could afford a comparable embassy in Washington.

McDonald wrote Sharett a "personal and confidential" note to advise him that it was worth it. "Israel, in the nature of things, is and must remain a symbol of a dream fulfilled and of a larger promise held out," the ambassador wrote. "Whatever adds dignity and prestige strengthens the State, not only among Jews here and everywhere but also among its neighbors."

Whereas McDonald could write directly to the White House when a crisis needed to be averted, he also knew what his nominal masters at the State Department demanded. At a gathering of U.S. diplomats from the entire Middle East, he gained plaudits for his own written summary of the points he should pound home to Israel:

1. To see the problem of . . . Jerusalem in perspective, to recognize the overriding interests of the international community . . .

2. To show realistic moderation in the current and prospective bilateral peace negotiations . . .

3. To soften—on grounds of enlightened self-interest, if not common humanity—its rigid attitude on [Arab] refugees.

4. To consider the view of those American experts who contend that unrestricted "ingathering of the [Jewish] exiles" will mean economic disaster for Israel.

5. To understand that the U.S. Government's benevolent attitude might be jeopardized if Israel should not take these suggestions into account.

Throughout the long history of the alliance, Israel would always stubbornly reject the first and fourth points, would insist it was being flexible and humane on the second and third points, and would try not to panic about the fifth point.

But how could a poor, newborn country avoid panic when the giant patron was occasionally perceived to be rationing its goodwill? The new Israelis, however, quickly found that there were many avenues to explore in America, the land of opportunity—official and unofficial, open and covert, in Washington and elsewhere between the two shining seas. One of these was to be found over the Copacabana nightclub, just off Fifth Avenue.

Inside Hotel Fourteen—at 14 East 60th Street—was the headquarters for Israeli activity in the United States. The hotel owners, ardent Zionists, had offered several suites for free. In the basement was the Copacabana. Upstairs were the young Jewish envoys, led by Teddy Kollek.

Kollek was born in 1911 in a small village near Budapest, Hungary. He was one of the lucky few Jews permitted by the British to move to Palestine, in 1935, before Hitler took over most of Europe. He became the founder of a kibbutz on the shores of the Sea of Galilee, not far from the place where, according to tradition, Christ walked on water.

Before long Zionist leaders including Ben-Gurion realized that Kollek was not cut out to be a farmer. They decided to exploit his charm and worldliness and made him their senior intelligence operative—both in the prestate underground and after statehood. His assignments took him to Cairo, Istanbul, London, and Italy during World War II. There he met American intelligence officers and Jewish activists—people who, like Gaynor Jacobson of the Joint, were trying to rescue Jewish refugees. These acquaintances would help Kollek when he began his New York assignment in October 1947.

Kollek, Ben-Gurion, and the other leaders of the ruling labor movement were building a new society in the land of Israel, based on justice, equality, austerity, and other traditional socialist values. Influenced by their own backgrounds in eastern Europe, they modeled key parts of their society on Soviet-style centralism, bureaucracy, and planned economy. Pro-Israeli votes at the UN and the supply of weapons by Communist Czechoslovakia helped Israelis overlook the evil sides of Joseph Stalin's dictatorship, even as they danced to Russian folk music.

In sharp contrast, the United States was looked upon with scorn—its politics, society, and culture seen as shallow, materialistic, and aimless. It was only to be expected that Teddy Kollek, who had grown up on socialist values, might feel lost in New York. Surprisingly, the very opposite turned out to be the case.

He enjoyed the relaxing and stimulating sides of New York. In the Copacabana, below his office, he recalls hearing Lena Horne and jazz musicians from Harlem. Whatever the cultural and political shock, he was coping and quite happily so.

"I actually started liking America," Kollek says as he thinks back to his first encounter with the world capital of capitalism. It did not take much time for Kollek to shed his socialist past. He became the strongest advocate of American interests in the Israeli leadership.

In the eighteen months of his sensitive New York assignment, Kollek and his people took liberties that often balanced on the thin dividing line between the legal and illegal. Israel had official diplomats in Washington and at the UN, but manpower was stretched so thin that everyone performed double duty. Kollek found himself fund raising through the established machinery of the United Jewish Appeal (UJA) but also was involved in recruiting influential Jews such as Eddie Jacobson as political levers. But Kollek's main mission was to search for the practical levers.

Israel's 1948–49 War of Independence against the Arabs required skilled military personnel and hardware. Kollek and his colleagues looked for American Jewish veterans with World

War II experience who might be persuaded to volunteer for the fledgling Israeli army.

Kollek's most famous catch was David "Mickey" Marcus. He was a West Point graduate and army colonel who ended up in the U.S. military government in Germany after the war. By the time he was ready to settle down with his wife in Brooklyn, where he intended to start a legal practice, Kollek entered the scene and managed to claim him for the Zionist-Israeli cause. Colonel Marcus went to Israel at the beginning of the War of Independence under the pseudonym of Mickey Stone.

He was given the rank of general and served as a special advisor to Prime Minister Ben-Gurion. His job was to help organize the Israeli army on sound, modern foundations. But he never got very far with the project. On a dark night in June 1948, Marcus left his headquarters for a walk. The Israeli sentry challenged him for a password and when Marcus could not remember the Hebrew word, the sentry assumed he had caught an Arab infiltrator and shot him dead.

He was by no means the only foreign volunteer. There were thousands of them, some Jewish, others not, from a multitude of countries. They made a significant contribution, numbering one out of ten in the inexperienced new army. Most came out of sympathy with Zionism, because of the Holocaust, and because they identified with the small country that was struggling for survival. Some, however, were adventurers and misfits.

About half of the volunteers came from America. And the long arm of Kollek's search reached as far as the Pacific Ocean. There, on Tinian Island, were squadrons of B-17 and B-29 bombers, better known as the Flying Fortresses. These huge and clumsy airplanes had been used in August 1945 to drop the atom bombs on Hiroshima and Nagasaki in Japan.

A pilot based on Tinian, Harry Eckerman, was surprised to be approached by a seaman suggesting he should volunteer for the

Israeli air force. Like other Jewish pilots who got similar requests, Eckerman recalls with astonishment, "How did they know we were Jews? And how were they able to find us in this forgotten place?" Eckerman himself declined the suggestion. "One war was enough for me." But even those pilots who did accept the offer never solved this mystery.

The secret was that this was an inside job. The Israelis had very good contacts, informers, and assistance in the Pentagon.

In his memoirs, Kollek confesses that "we engaged in secret intelligence gathering." And U.S. Army Intelligence suspected that a Pentagon official working on veterans' affairs was supplying Israel with names and personal details of ex-soldiers ripe for recruitment. Suspicion was cast on Lieutenant Colonel Elliot Niles, "formerly a high official of the B'nai B'rith," who happened to be the brother of President Truman's pro-Israeli aide David Niles.

Altogether, dozens of American pilots were recruited to serve in Israel's tiny air force—still exceeding the number of airplanes available. Kollek and his team had a much harder time getting the planes than the people.

The U.S. government had imposed an arms embargo on all sides in the Middle East conflict. The real victims of this decision were the Arabs, because the Jews in Palestine had a fairly smooth-running supply of weapons and equipment, thanks to the purchasing networks run by Kollek and others. They had even managed to lay their hands on some used planes, U.S. Army surplus, which they flew over with the volunteers and reassembled in Israel.

The key figure in the airplane procurement was Adolph (Al) Schwimmer, a former TWA flight engineer. Part Zionist and part adventurer, Schwimmer became the Jewish state's prime arms smuggler in America. He was subcontracted by Kollek to run a network of his own that operated in South America, Hawaii, and the Philippines. His team bought every piece of hardware it could lay its hands on: tanks from corrupt South American governments whose leaders and officials were bribed, ammunition from California, and other goods such as blankets, tents, and canteens from army surplus dealers throughout the United States.

Schwimmer, in turn, recruited Herman "Hank" Greenspun, future publisher of the *Las Vegas Sun* and soon to be dubbed the "Robin Hood of the gambling community." Born in 1909 and raised in New Haven, Connecticut, Greenspun was a New York lawyer during the Depression and an outstanding U.S. Army captain in World War II, serving under General George Patton in Europe. He received the Silver Star for bravery as well as honors from the French government.

After the war, Greenspun was one of the first to foresee the Sun Belt boom and moved to Las Vegas. He gained fame in 1954 by courageously opposing Joe McCarthy's witch hunt against "Communists." In one of his newspaper columns headlined "Where I Stand," Greenspun accused the senator from Wisconsin of being a Communist himself.

The publisher was even more active and heartfelt in his support of Israel. "I knew every wrinkle on the painted face of Theodore Herzl, the founder of the Zionist movement," Greenspun wrote in his autobiography, explaining how he became a Zionist "before I could even identify a picture of George Washington."

When he was approached by Schwimmer in December 1947, Greenspun did not hesitate for a moment before joining Teddy Kollek's smuggling network. "How could I forget the childhood beatings I took because I was a Jew?" Greenspun wrote later. "The Jews will always be hounded, driven, and burned unless there is a Jewish state to give them stature and refuge. My conscience answered."

In a response more melodramatic than even Hollywood would dare invent, Greenspun literally dropped what he was doing. He skipped the party he was planning for that night, celebrating the launch of his own radio station, and immediately flew to his new assignment in Hawaii. He did not even say good-bye to his young wife.

Greenspun was so eager to help Israel that he sometimes pestered Kollek's New York office with telephone calls. His travels took him also to Mexico, the Dominican Republic, Guatemala, and Panama, where he organized false documents, bank guarantees, and arms shipments to Israel.

Perhaps more controversial were his connections with Jewish gangsters. In Las Vegas, before he joined Kollek's network, Greenspun was for a few weeks the well-paid public relations man for Benjamin (Bugsy) Siegel's Flamingo Hotel, in which Meyer Lansky had invested some of his mob money. Greenspun insisted "it was a legitimate business," with the Andrews Sisters and Jimmy Durante entertaining the guests at the "grand opening" in 1946. "Besides," he wrote later, "I was curious to see the notorious Bugsy Siegel in action."

Following World War II and the Holocaust, Siegel, Lansky, and a third gangster, Mickey Cohen from Los Angeles, experienced a surge of Jewish patriotism and enthusiastically passed the word to Israel that they would like to help.

Reuven Dafni, an envoy of the Palestinian Jewish underground, had a meeting with Bugsy Siegel in a Los Angeles restaurant as early as 1946. "Do you really want to tell me that the Jews in Palestine have taken up arms, shoot, fight?" asked the gangster with some surprise.

"Yes," answered the Israeli envoy.

Bugsy looked him straight in the eyes. "When you say 'fight,' you mean 'kill'?" Again, Dafni answered in the affirmative. "Then I'm your man," responded Bugsy.

From then on, the Israeli delegate used to get occasional telephone messages bidding him to go to the same restaurant, where bags filled with five- and ten-dollar bills would be awaiting him. In the envoy's estimate, Siegel contributed, all in all, some $50,000—an enormous sum in those days.

After Siegel was murdered in June 1947, employee Greenspun kept for a while in touch with other men of his ilk and invested in another casino hotel, the Desert Inn, where his new partners were Moe Dalitz and his notorious gang of bootleggers from Cleveland. Soon, however, he denounced his partners and became a staunch opponent of Las Vegas mobsters.

"When my husband solicited contributions to the UJA, he didn't care where the money came from," his widow, Barbara Greenspun, recalls. "Heads of the Mafia organized charity dinners." He would get them to donate money, and he achieved the same success with the controversial leader of the Teamsters union, Jimmy Hoffa, even bringing him to Jerusalem in 1956 to dedicate a children's shelter that was financed by the union and was named for Hoffa.

"During the long, prejet flight a poker game started," Greenspun wrote. "It continued all the way across the Atlantic." Although Greenspun won $114 and Hoffa hardly gambled at all, some newspapers picked on the Teamsters leader by writing that he had lost $200,000 on the journey to Israel. A few months later, Hoffa was arrested and charged with fraud and associating with organized crime. Yet the *Las Vegas Sun* "tried to see and render Hoffa's side of the picture," according to Greenspun, whose loyalty to the union boss had been strengthened by their joint fealty toward Israel.

Kollek, too, had personal encounters with Jewish and Italian-American gangsters in New York—finding they were a gateway to the powerful labor unions that dominated America's seaports. These contacts helped lead to fruitful relations between Israel and the U.S. labor movement, which in due time became one of the main levers for American support of Israel.

In times of emergency, when Israel was at war but American ports were on strike, unions ordered their members to release shipments. More than once they turned a blind eye to Israeli agents smuggling military hardware.

Kollek admits in his memoirs, "We even established contact with the Mafia, and once with the famous organization Murder Inc. headed by Albert Anastasia . . . [who] was pointed out to me once." Whether by coincidence or not, Kollek also found himself within earshot of Anastasia's assassination in the Park Plaza Hotel during one of the frequent battles between organized crime families. "One morning I walked through the lobby to the barbershop and there was a great ruckus," he writes. "Shots were heard, people were scattering, and on the barbershop floor lay Anastasia who had just been shot."

The gangsters had suggested that if the Israelis would simply draw up a hit list, naming the enemies of the Jewish people, they would take care of the rest. Kollek politely declined the offer.

The connection between Kollek's network and organized crime, and its involvement with arms smuggling, aroused the suspicions of the Federal Bureau of Investigation. What really worried the law enforcement agencies were the developing relations between Israel and its American agents, on the one hand, and Czechoslovakia, on the other.

The Israeli network's offices in New York were put under FBI surveillance, its people were followed, and its telephones were tapped. Kollek, aware of this, tried to shake off his tail. He moved his offices from Hotel Fourteen to another building, and, as he says, "We had to be extremely careful." Despite all the precautions, the Israeli network was eventually rounded up.

Kollek was tipped off by well-informed U.S. government sources and managed to return to Israel in April 1949, but the other members of the network were less lucky. Ten Americans who had been working with Kollek were indicted and charged with conspiracy to violate U.S. law. Schwimmer also got away, via Canada and Czechoslovakia, to Israel. But after the War of

Independence was over, he went back to America and turned himself in. He was convicted in Los Angeles federal court in February 1950 and fined tens of thousands of dollars, not just for arms smuggling to Israel but also on account of his secret deals with Czechoslovakia.

Federal investigators had evidence that Schwimmer had delivered an American training aircraft and a radar system to that Communist country; and it was assumed that Soviet military analysts had received the equipment. Schwimmer's deliveries appeared to be part of the payment for Czechoslovakia—encouraged by Moscow—being Israel's main arms supplier.

Hank Greenspun was acquitted in his first trial. However, in his second trial he pleaded guilty to protect Kollek and other Israeli officials and was convicted by the Los Angeles court in July 1950 on charges of violating U.S. neutrality and of smuggling arms to Israel. His fine was $10,000 and the deprivation of his right to vote and his right to be elected to public office. Other defendants were sentenced to short jail terms. The Israeli government had arranged their legal defense and also raised money to pay the fines.

Many years later Kollek and some of his coconspirators portrayed their activities as a combination of ideology and adventure—juvenile thrills, which were justified as contributions to the Jewish state's struggle for life.

Lest their activities be seen as a failure, they did not cause lasting harm to relations between the United States and Israel. In fact, the fringe benefits were enormous. In addition to connections with gangsters and labor unions, Greenspun helped open the world of American show business to his Israeli friends. He introduced Teddy Kollek to Frank Sinatra, who became a great supporter of Israel and visited the country several times.

As early as 1948 Sinatra became involved in a clever escapade to help Israel. He spent many friendly hours with Kollek in the Copacabana, under the Zionist envoy's office, just when a boat full of ammunition and guns for Israel was delayed in New York Harbor. The captain refused to sail without being paid in advance. Under surveillance by FBI agents neither Kollek nor his lieutenants could bring him the money. So Kollek asked Sinatra, over a few drinks after his performance, to be a secret courier.

Without hesitating, Sinatra agreed. The next morning, while Kollek went out through Hotel Fourteen's main door with his tail in pursuit, Sinatra slipped through the back door with a suitcase full of cash. He headed to the harbor and handed the money to the impatient captain, who within weeks brought the newborn Israel what it needed.

Sinatra and many other Hollywood figures became open supporters of the Jewish state, often thanks to Kollek's knack for finding the emotional soft spots of big stars. Edward G. Robinson, famous for playing gangsters and whose Jewishness was not known to most movie audiences, played his role with gusto in a film used for UJA fund raising for Jews in Palestine—demonstrating how to lean on recalcitrant contributors.

Other actors and singers found it was fashionable to visit Israel, where the government and people warmly received them.

Similar star treatment has been given by Israel to American Jewry from all walks of life. It is a special bond, built and shored up by Kollek from his early years lobbying and smuggling in the United States, through his role as an accredited diplomat, and on to his long career as mayor of Jerusalem. He was among the first to recognize that the Jews of America—no matter how insecure they may feel as a minority in their country—feel ten feet tall when they think of Israel.

And when they visit, they are accorded such great respect that they might feel they have a second, welcoming home. Army generals and cabinet ministers receive them for private briefings. Jewish delegations from the smallest American towns get attention, a sense of importance, warmth, and a boost to the ego.

American Jews who give even more receive more. Al Schwimmer, for example, became an establishment figure in Israel and a confidant of Ben-Gurion, Kollek, and Shimon Peres. Schwimmer was the founder and chairman of Israel Aircraft Industries, the largest military contractor in the country. In the late 1970s he resigned, but in business on his own he returned to the world of intrigue. He would feature in the Irangate affair, which was to sour Israel's relations with the United States.

Hank Greenspun was also remembered by the State of Israel. Its diplomatic envoys, helped by influential American Jews, repeatedly appealed to Washington for the reinstatement of his civil rights. The Israeli-Jewish lobbying bore fruit when President Kennedy pardoned him in October 1961 and restored Greenspun's rights to vote and to be elected. Greenspun then exercised his newfound right, running for governor of Nevada as a Republican and losing. When he died in July 1989, his many Israeli admirers mourned the loss of a colorful, enthusiastic, and daring supporter. His family contributed over a million dollars to build a plaza, in his memory, at the entrance to Jerusalem's Botanical Garden.

Perhaps the greatest bonus of Kollek's network was the special link it developed with the American intelligence community. The FBI would continue to harbor suspicions about Israel for many years to come, with some federal investigators viewing American Jews as potential agents of Israel. But the Jewish state, meanwhile, succeeded in gaining the trust of an even more influential American institution, the Central Intelligence Agency.

The CIA was not just another lever to enhance Israeli interests in the United States. It became a central factor in the building of the alliance and a real partner.

CHAPTER FOUR

THE INTELLIGENCE LOBBY

The Israeli and U.S. intelligence communities found a reluctant matchmaker in Fred Gronich, an otherwise forgotten American soldier. He was born in New York in 1916, the son of Jewish immigrants from Austria. World War II brought him to North Africa and Europe, as a colonel serving under General Dwight D. Eisenhower in organizational planning and in processing battlefield intelligence.

He made a lot of friends who would make the U.S. military their career, including a senior army officer who was reassigned from the general staff to the Central Intelligence Agency at its formation in 1947.

Like many American Jews, Gronich was thrilled in November of that year when the United Nations partition vote endorsed plans for a Jewish state. Still, the thirty-one-year-old colonel had no plans to go there.

Mutual friends introduced him to Teddy Kollek, who tried to

persuade him to join the fight for Jewish independence, and to Colonel David Marcus, another U.S. Army veteran who had already heeded the call.

It was after Marcus was killed, in June 1948, that Gronich flew to Tel Aviv to contribute himself to the cause. It was certainly an act of philanthropy, because neither the state nor the Jewish Agency paid him salary or expenses. "Frankly, they didn't have any money," recalls Gronich, who is happy that he can never be labeled a mercenary. "All they did was buy me a life insurance policy."

Kollek had arranged the kind of reception that would make a man feel important, if not secure, because Gronich was immediately introduced to the top echelons of the Israeli army and later taken to meet Ben-Gurion. From that moment and for the year and a half to come, the American was firmly in the inner circle around Israel's first prime minister.

Gronich traveled out to the front lines: in the north, against the Syrians and Lebanese; along the east, against the Trans-Jordanians and Iraqis; and in the south, against the Egyptians. He recalls being occasionally surrounded by interpreters and guards, "because they were still under trauma after Mickey Marcus was killed. But most of the time my only shield was a bilingual woman army driver who was one of the most courageous and colorful soldiers I ever met."

His goals were similar to those of Marcus: to advise Ben-Gurion, who was his own defense minister, on a permanent structure for the new Israel Defense Forces. "I urged him and the general staff to push for the rapid establishment of officer and noncommissioned officer schools for infantry, artillery, armor, communications, and staff training," Gronich says, "because what they had was an improvisation that grew like Topsy to fit particular challenges as they arose."

The American advisor's military work also had the potential

of helping to create a country as free as the United States. "Ben-Gurion said this would be an army reflecting a democratic society," says Gronich, who at Ben-Gurion's request obtained a copy of *The Federalist Papers*, so the prime minister could read the debates and discussions of America's founding fathers. "He locked himself away with those papers and studied the U.S. Constitution they wrote."

At the end of 1948 Gronich flew to the United States to recruit more high-level volunteers and paid consultants with battle experience. Although Ben-Gurion had not yet decided Israel's orientation between East and West, he did believe that his nation would need support from the United States and especially from its Jews.

Gronich had heard of plenty of Jewish soldiers willing to volunteer, but the two senior U.S. officers he really wanted were—ironically—Gentiles. "Non-Jewish would be better," he says, "because in Israel, if you weren't a Jew, they would listen to you!"

Both officers were willing to go, inspired by sorrow over the Holocaust and by admiration for the Israeli army's early triumphs on the battlefield. One was a general who would have been a human bridge between the military establishments of the United States and Israel. But the Department of Defense would not let them go. "I found a lot of hostility in the Pentagon," says Gronich, who returned to Israel empty-handed.

He reassumed the false identity that Ben-Gurion had thrust upon him for security reasons. Everyone, from Israel's military commanders to his landlady on Tel Aviv's Yarkon Street, where his room overlooked the Mediterranean, knew the American only as "Fred Harris." The prime minister's daily diaries, although published, refer to "Fred" or "Harris" but without explaining who he was.

"While Ben-Gurion may have found it politically convenient to give me a nom de guerre," Gronich recalls, "I myself was not trying to hide from anyone. Actually, it became an amusing situation."

The advisor drove around the newborn state in a khaki uniform, without emblems of rank, and wearing the type of cap worn by Admiral William "Bull" Halsey as he defeated the Japanese fleet in the Pacific. With the prime minister's approval, the general staff authorized Gronich's access to all military bases and invited him to sit in on nearly every strategy session.

The trust lavished on a foreign soldier, who appeared to be counseling Ben-Gurion on American organizational practices, aroused harsh resentment among many Israeli officers. Most were the leftist children of socialist kibbutz farms, their political leanings accentuated by the fact that most of Israel's weapons were coming from the Communist world.

It was no surprise, then, that they labeled the American a spy. A leftist member of the K'nesset asked Ben-Gurion a parliamentary question: "Who is General Harris?" A Communist newspaper then violated wartime censorship by repeating the question on its front page, adding: "Why are you selling out the state to the Americans?" Israel's Communists then repeated the question on posters, which the police scurried around the country tearing down.

The political Left assumed that "Harris" was controlled by the U.S. Embassy in Tel Aviv, but in fact the military attachés there had no idea there was a senior American so close to Ben-Gurion. They asked the Israeli authorities to have General Harris, if he existed, contact the embassy.

Gronich's only contact with the first U.S. ambassador to Israel, James McDonald, was a mere mistake. He bumped into him at a cocktail party, introduced himself as Fred Gronich, and chatted about nothing that touched upon Ben-Gurion's overburdened military. The ambassador did not, however, make the connection between Gronich and Harris.

By late 1949, months after the war was over, Gronich realized that the Israelis were ready to be on their own, and his presence was causing some dissension in the army. So he went home.

"I left, after eighteen months, with a sense of mission accomplished—but not finished." The United States was not embracing Israel as a part of its worldwide strategy. Many American officials still saw Israel as more a threat to U.S. interests than an asset.

Gronich would still be called upon, from time to time, to help Israel—finding access to senior officials in Washington, where the Israelis were locked out. This was especially tough for the new state's first intelligence men in Washington. Operating under diplomatic cover from their embassy, they felt stranded in territory that could be described as hostile.

"The doors of the CIA, defense intelligence, and not to mention the FBI, remained closed to us," recalls Meir "Memi" de Shalit. He was the semiclandestine representative of Israeli intelligence in the U.S. capital from 1949 to 1954, serving in the foreign ministry's Political Department, which was the forerunner of the Mossad, Israel's overseas espionage arm.

De Shalit's formal boss at the embassy was Abba Eban, but Eban was also accredited as Israel's ambassador to the United Nations and thus spent most of his time in New York. The person truly in charge at the embassy was Teddy Kollek, who had returned to America in 1950.

The FBI was far from wild about the fact that the ringleader of the earlier Israeli conspiracy, responsible for smuggling arms and volunteers, was back in Washington as a senior diplomatic representative. Lacking the evidence to prosecute him, however—the other members of the network had shielded Kollek in their trials—the FBI's attempt to block his return failed.

Kollek and de Shalit invested a lot of effort into breaking out of what was called "Point Four." Based on the fourth section of Truman's inaugural address in 1949, the aid program of that name sought to help developing nations while promoting America's political influence in the Third World. Point Four, however, had hardly any money compared to the Marshall Plan—the multibillion-dollar brainchild of the secretary of state that financed the reconstruction of Europe and Japan.

So Israel was left in the corner, classified with the poor and developing nations offered tiny lollipops called technical assistance. In Israel's case, this amounted to only $3 million or $4 million per year—in no way sufficient to fulfill the rocketing economic needs of a country opening its doors to hundreds of thousands of immigrants from Yemen, Iraq, and eastern Europe. In the first three years of its existence, Israel doubled its population to 1.2 million.

Kollek, de Shalit, and Eban felt they had to break the shackles of Point Four, but Eban recalls having trouble getting the Americans to pay any attention. "They'd gone through this emotional climax of recognition and the establishment of the state. Then their view was 'Okay, that's finished, so now we can turn to something more important.' They had the Cold War becoming colder and colder; the Soviets gave the impression they would conquer Europe; and there was the McCarthyite madness in America."

When he arrived in Washington in 1950, Eban says he "found America's relationship with Israel was not institutionalized." Once or twice President Weizmann might be granted an audience at the White House, "because Truman likes him, but you can't establish a tradition based on gimmicks, and Weizmann's health was sinking."

Because the United States did have enough of an attention span to help hammer out armistice agreements, to stabilize the

Middle East, "our problems were much more economic than military," says Eban. "Our challenge was to get into the aid program of the United States."

The young Israeli ambassador launched a precedent that would grow into a tradition: lobbying Congress. "Truman had told us that he would recommend that Israel receive aid in proportion to its size," Eban recalls, "but in proportion to our size is quite useless to us! We would need at least ten times that much." Friends in the White House, such as David Niles, suggested to Eban that he start digging on Capitol Hill for support.

"I got thirty-five senators, from both parties, to initiate legislation to make Israel eligible for assistance," says Eban, adding that State Department officials sarcastically thanked him for even talking to them. "It was said without any indignation. American officials were beginning to understand, very early, that we behaved in a very different way."

No other nation was sending its ambassador, behind the executive branch's back, to ask Congress for money. The pitch was largely emotional, touching on the tragedy of the recent past, but the unsaid focus was practical and political. "I would speak about the Holocaust," Eban says, "but what mattered to Senator Douglas was to get elected in Illinois, and it mattered to Senator Taft to get elected in Ohio. Those were the issues!

"It was a bit awkward," Eban admits, "an ambassador going around lobbying," so a new brigade of lobbyists was brought in: Americans who actually voted in the elections, specifically the Jews who were important—far beyond their small numbers—as political activists and campaign contributors.

Eban and Kollek found a coordinator for the project: Isaiah L. Kenen, a Canadian-born Jewish journalist who had helped Israel as the first spokesman for its UN delegation. "I asked Si Kenen to come to Washington and spend three weeks," says Eban, "but thirty years later he was still there."

Kenen formalized the lobby into a small but effective organization that would eventually name itself the American Israel Public Affairs Committee—AIPAC.

Kollek also phoned up his old Hollywood connections. Among the many who heeded the call was Barney Balaban, president of Paramount Pictures, who loaned members of his company's public relations department to the Israeli cause.

The combination of PR and private lobbying, both of which emphasized the phenomenally high cost of Israel's challenges in defense and immigration, yielded impressive and quick results. A majority in the House and Senate agreed to allocate $65 million for aid to Israel, and the federal Export-Import Bank granted loans totaling another $70 million.

The figures may seem small by today's standards, but $135 million represented nearly three times the foreign currency that Israel had been able to earn from exports in 1950. American aid was not only symbolic, but a genuine measure of relief for the country's economic burden.

Eban and Kollek had started something that would form a pattern in U.S.-Israeli relations for decades to come. Other countries had tried to mobilize influential American citizens on their behalf, but never with the rapid and significant success scored by AIPAC. The systematic and organized lobbying would only grow in magnitude, as would its successes.

Kenen, the PR veteran, took care to register with Congress as a domestic lobbyist and not as an agent of a foreign country. The head of AIPAC always sought to make it clear that he did not take orders from Jerusalem, and that his wish for stronger U.S.-Israeli relations was an emphatically pro-American policy.

Eban found yet another means of protecting Israel's interests, by suggesting a more coordinated forum for consultation among the largest American Jewish institutions. He had heard U.S. officials complain that they were fielding the same questions from, and explaining their policies to, a dozen or more prominent Jews in separate, sometimes tiresome conversations.

Now, in the early 1950s, with Israel having consolidated its statehood, all the major American Jewish groups turned pro-Zionist. They welcomed Eban's idea of coordination, and from its beginnings in May 1951, the Conference of Presidents of Major American Jewish Organizations expanded into a recognized spokesman for American Jewry, with access to the highest levels of the U.S. government.

The Conference and AIPAC were both products of the lessons learned from the traumas of sweet-talking the Truman administration: not to bet all of your money on one horse, whether the steed is the president or his Jewish partner in a Missouri haberdashery. It is preferable, instead, to develop ways of maneuvering among the various centers of power in U.S. politics.

"Lobbyist" is an unpopular label in America's public lexicon. But the vocation is part of the political system, and Israel's friends in the United States take on the role with relish because they are certain that they have a good product to sell. Rather than stressing the carrots and sticks that are implicit in a system that encourages financial contributions to election campaigns, American Jews and Israeli diplomats speak of what the two nations share: democratic values and strategic interests.

While this may suggest Israeli interference in internal U.S. affairs, it was certainly not a one-sided act. American diplomats, from the very first year of the relationship, have stuck their noses, hands, and checkbooks into Israeli politics. It was not mere coincidence that when the United States granted its first loan to Israel, on the eve of the first parliamentary elections in 1949, Ambassador McDonald timed the announcement to weaken the political parties on Israel's radical left, while boosting Ben-Gurion's mainstream Mapai.

In Washington, success whetted Kollek's appetite for financial support from Israel's backers in America. He laid the groundwork for Israel Bonds, a permanent institution that would become the most successful seller of a foreign government's securities in U.S. history. For Israel, it was a cheap way of borrowing money while engaging the involvement and goodwill of supporters around the world.

"The economic odds were against us," Kollek writes in his memoirs. "Who would even consider buying bonds from such a small and poor country?" Moreover, American Jews who wanted to send money to Israel already had the United Jewish Appeal, and why should the UJA want competition? Still, the highly persuasive Kollek talked the Jewish organizations into giving his idea a chance. Kollek also secured the support of America's leading banks and financial institutions, many of them owned or administered by Jews, to underwrite the bonds.

Again, Jewish connections were put into action to obtain clearance from the Securities and Exchange Commission for the sale of interest-bearing Israeli notes. It was highly unusual for a foreign government to be granted permission to sell its own treasury bonds, in competition with the American government's issues. This resulted from the creativity of Israel's leadership and the goodwill of highly placed Americans.

Among the enthusiastic supporters was Henry Morgenthau, Jr., son of the ambassador to Turkey who had helped the Jews of Palestine during World War I. "He was galvanized," says Barbara Tuchman, the historian and his niece, "by the failure of his ceaseless effort as Secretary of the Treasury under Roosevelt, to make the president take some effective action to save Jews from Hitler's Final Solution."

With his experience of selling America's War Bonds to finance the crucial battle against Japan and Nazi Germany, Morgenthau agreed to become the chairman of the United Jewish Appeal and head of the Israel Bonds campaign, thus closing a historic circle.

The success of Israel Bonds set yet another precedent. Having consolidated its initial breakthroughs in the Truman administration, in Congress, in the labor movement, and in Hollywood, the Jewish state now had its foothold in the financial community. This connection would go on to function as a wonderful fund-raising tool. Whenever Israel needed a loan it had an address: the big U.S. banks and Wall Street.

Ben-Gurion underlined the importance of Israel Bonds by flying to the United States to launch their sale in May 1951. A full three years after the establishment of the state, this was the first visit to the United States by an Israeli prime minister.

Israel was in the news, and perhaps surprisingly it was seen not as a beggar nation but as an exciting project with a pioneer spirit reminiscent of America's westward expansion. The new country radiated freshness and youth, captivating the American imagination. Ben-Gurion flew from city to city to open the local Israel Bonds offices and was received with extraordinary enthusiasm. Madison Square Garden was packed with 20,000 cheering spectators, and another 20,000 New Yorkers crammed the sidewalks outside to listen to the prime minister's speech blare out over loudspeakers.

One of the first investors was the International Ladies' Garment Workers Union. Here again was the start of a tradition: the massive purchases of Israel Bonds by America's largest trade unions.

Ben-Gurion's historic visit also produced the opportunity for which Kollek and Israel's intelligence operatives had been waiting—the notion of bringing the two countries closer that Fred Gronich had visualized two years earlier as a volunteer with the Israeli army. Since returning to America, Gronich had occasionally helped Kollek with advice and with preliminary introductions to some of his U.S. Army friends.

By the middle of 1950 he had managed to set up a meeting at the Statler Hotel in Washington between Kollek and James Jesus Angleton, a senior operative at the CIA. It was a useful chat, and while it had no immediate follow-up it would lead to Angleton's becoming the biggest ally that Israel ever had in the U.S. intelligence community.

More than twenty years later an Israeli intelligence officer who met with him recalled: "Angleton would be our guardian angel. Whenever we needed him, he was there. Always helpful." Angleton, in turn, called Israel "the best friend the United States ever had."

The Israelis felt grateful. In the first years after their independence, they could see that the American military and intelligence had little taste for working with Israel. Dealing with the Jewish government, in a sea of oil-rich Arabs, was still considered not worth the risk. But as Ben-Gurion's May 1951 visit approached, the atmosphere changed. Israel's popularity was evident among the general public. Its diplomats had managed to get some influence on Capitol Hill, and Congress had already appropriated some foreign aid.

Probably most important was the change in the international situation. The competition and tension between the United States and the Soviet Union had greatly escalated, the Truman Doctrine had made "containment" of the Soviets the new national priority, and every corner of the globe would henceforth be seen through the Cold War prism.

America, fighting in Korea to confront the Soviet- and Chinese-backed North, tried to enlist the support of all UN members, and Israel was no exception. The United States asked Ben-Gurion to send a small, symbolic military unit to South Korea, and he and his aides were willing to do so. But a majority of cabinet ministers blocked the move, clinging to the ideology of nonalignment.

It soon became clear, however, that Moscow was not impressed. Soviet dictator Stalin required a kind of loyalty—total obedience—that the satellite states of eastern Europe were displaying. Ben-Gurion saw no reason to give up the freedom to act on the international stage, so Stalin abruptly dropped Israel. At the same time, Stalin launched a campaign of anti-Semitism throughout the Communist bloc. Many of the satellites halted Jewish emigration and published vicious attacks on Israel and Zionism in the state-owned media.

Ben-Gurion's visit to America was the watershed in Israel's passage from neutrality, tinged with pro-Soviet sentiments, to a pro-Western orientation in general—a pro-American one in particular. Israel started getting frequent visits from U.S. experts in many fields: water, agriculture, industry, and construction.

There was also the propaganda equivalent of junk mail. An American cultural organization—which was nothing but a CIA front—distributed books, magazines, records, and films in Israel, with the aim of counterbalancing Communist publications and broadcasts. Thus was "the American way of life" promoted and introduced to an Israeli public just starting to dream of U.S.-style affluence.

In 1951 Israel felt sufficiently confident to ask, for the first time, for U.S. arms. Though the request was turned down, it planted the seeds for a process that would finally and decisively draw Israel into the U.S. Cold War camp.

Another sapling was planted at CIA headquarters in May of that year, when Gronich played an indirect role in arranging a meeting between Ben-Gurion and the intelligence agency's director, General Walter Bedell Smith. "Israel was very isolated," recalls Gronich, who had served with Bedell Smith in World War II, both in North Africa and in London, "and I was asked if I could possibly help establish a contact."

He was a very close acquaintance of another general who was one of Bedell Smith's deputies at the CIA and a colonel in U.S. military intelligence. "Look, fellas," Gronich told them, "it's stupid to operate the way you do, depending on the British for basic information on an area which is critical to American strategic interests. It's about time you talk to the Israelis, a nation in the Middle East, and have your own evaluation and your own contacts."

They agreed, and Ben-Gurion's visit to Bedell Smith was set. At that point, Gronich says, he stepped aside, "for a very good reason: What I don't know, I can't talk about!"

The prime minister brought Kollek with him to the lunch, while Bedell Smith was joined by his deputy and eventual successor, Allen Dulles. Ben-Gurion and Bedell Smith had met once before, in 1946, when the general was Eisenhower's chief of staff and the Jewish Agency leader was in Germany to visit the Displaced Persons camps. Ben-Gurion remembered that the American had been very helpful, from a Zionist point of view, by giving permission for Hebrew classes to be taught in the camps.

From the tone of the conversation six years after the end of the war, it seemed that the fate of the Jews was still fresh in the general's mind. It was clear to the Israelis, from Ben-Gurion down, that the Holocaust factor was a strong card to play when seeking support in the United States.

The prime minister proposed that the two countries' intelligence communities cooperate, and Bedell Smith responded favorably.

Israel's semi-intelligence man in Washington, Memi de Shalit, recalls: "Teddy came up to me and said: 'I have an interesting job for you.' " Kollek told de Shalit about the new agreement for an ongoing liaison relationship between the CIA and the Mossad, the agency that Ben-Gurion had created only one month earlier. The prime minister, fearing leaks from his talkative ministers, was not even telling his own cabinet about the breakthrough.

De Shalit felt honored to be the first liaison officer. In addition, "This was a great relief for me. After having dealt for a year and a half with economic affairs, I could now do the real thing for which I had been trained: intelligence."

On the CIA's side, the chosen liaison officer was James J. Angleton. He and de Shalit met that very evening. "Up until that day," the Israeli stresses, "there had been no contacts between the CIA and the Mossad."

Angleton was a man of sharp contrasts. An intellectual who spent part of his childhood in Italy, he was recruited into the pre-CIA Office of Strategic Services (OSS) during World War II and got to know some of the Palestinian Jews' secret agents who were trying to save their brethren in Europe. The Holocaust factor had an impact on Angleton, according to his Israeli contacts.

But it was not on the strength of horrible memories, nostalgia, or personal passions that Angleton was given this job. The reasons were basically negative. The CIA's own Near East department was doubtful of Israel's strategic value. The agency's Arabists had fostered excellent contacts with military officers and politicians from Cairo to Baghdad, and the Americans felt capable of engineering coups d' état as they had done in Syria in 1949.

Bedell Smith and Dulles, however, were interested in having a wider variety of contacts and sources in the region. They insisted on pursuing their cooperation program with the Mossad but totally compartmentalized it beyond the reach of their Near East desk. The counterintelligence department, headed by Angleton, was put in charge in the hope that Israel could contribute information on Soviet activities.

He handled the "Israeli account" personally for twenty-three years, until a policy dispute prompted his ouster in 1974. Within the CIA, Israel was forbidden territory for anyone without permission from Angleton. Meanwhile, he continued in charge of foiling espionage plots by the Soviets and their allies, building his own reputation among intelligence agencies worldwide as a zealous opponent of communism.

The Americans suspected that among the many Jewish immigrants from the Eastern bloc, some Soviet agents must have been planted—some as longtime moles who might emerge from their burrows in the decades to come. Angleton's job was to dig up moles wherever they might be.

"Jim impressed me," de Shalit says of the mysterious spy-catcher. "He seemed detached and acted with great·caution and circumspection."

In contrast to Angleton's style, Kollek displayed enthusiasm in his eagerness to please the Americans. Though intelligence relations are usually characterized by their carefully rationed give-and-take, Ben-Gurion himself ordered his people to provide the United States with information unconditionally. This was done in the hope of gaining the suspicious Americans' trust.

Kollek and de Shalit began sending Angleton evidence that—just as the CIA would wish—Israeli counterintelligence agents were checking every incoming batch of immigrants, on the lookout for Communist spies. The Israelis explained, moreover, that it might actually be possible to profit from the eastern European immigrants, who were often in the educated elite of the countries they left. The newcomers could give the West up-to-date information about events and trends behind the Iron Curtain.

Kollek remembers that "our people talked with immigrants, translated what they told us into English and passed the material on to the Americans. The CIA was interested in any crumb of information from the East Bloc, from the price of bread and train timetables, to the description of the lines of people that were waiting to get into the food shops." He estimates that about a quarter of all the information on the Soviet Union and its allies obtained by the United States during the 1950s came via Israel.

While it was widely assumed that a written cooperation pact was signed by the CIA and the Mossad, the truth—says de Shalit—is that "there was no written agreement at all."

Most of the meetings with Angleton took place in the Israeli liaison's house on Massachusetts Avenue, and occasionally in restaurants. "He came, two or three times a week, to my house in the early evening," recalls de Shalit, "and often stayed until the early hours of the morning. It happened more than once that his wife, Cecilia, phoned at about 4 A.M. to find out whether the meeting was still going on."

Angleton and de Shalit's conversations were the beginning of a long friendship that ended only with the American's death in 1987. Both men were born on the same date, December 9. The American was four years older than the Israeli, and they used to send each other birthday cards.

Angleton made a point of visiting Israel at least once a year, adding a few more people on each trip to his growing list of friends—both within the intelligence community and outside it. Among the reciprocal guests was Reuven Shiloah, the first director of the Mossad who made several trips to Washington to add flesh to the bare bones of clandestine cooperation.

There were moments of tension, however. In 1952 and 1953 the FBI concluded that some of the Mossad and Military Intelligence personnel stationed in Washington by Israel were involved in espionage. Elyashiv Ben-Horin, who worked with de Shalit, tried to recruit Arab diplomats in the United States as informers and future spies in their own home countries. This was standard practice for Israeli intelligence operatives in Washington and other Western capitals where they might rub shoulders with Arabs, but it did not sit well with the Americans. The Jordanian military attaché double-crossed Ben-Horin: pretending to be recruited, but in fact tipping off the FBI. In a Washington restaurant, the Jordanian officer prodded his Israeli controller into an argument, and an FBI surveillance team intervened when Ben-Horin lost his temper and pulled a gun.

It was only thanks to his diplomatic immunity that the Israeli agent was not arrested. The State Department, to which the FBI referred the case, declared Ben-Horin persona non grata and he hastily left. Although he went on to a remarkable career in the Israeli foreign service, including a term as ambassador to Germany, he was blacklisted by the United States and was refused an entry visa for many years.

The FBI, which never put much trust in cooperation between the CIA and the Mossad, also received information that Israel's military attaché, Colonel Chaim Herzog, was involved in attempts to steal defense technology. The FBI insisted that Herzog, too, should be expelled. But the evidence against him was inconclusive, and since his term in Washington was about to end anyhow, the case was dropped.

Herzog returned to Israel, where he was promoted to the rank of general and named director of Military Intelligence—an odd choice if he had never been involved in the world's second oldest profession. Unlike Ben-Horin, Herzog never had a problem entering the United States; in fact, he made many visits as president of Israel in the decade that began in 1983.

Angleton was furious with Israel. "This is not the way friends behave," he reproached his Israeli contacts. "Friends do not engage in secret activities against each other."

The Israelis played the innocents. "Our activity on American soil," one explained to Angleton, "was not directed against the U.S. but against the Arabs."

Angleton and the CIA did not seem to buy the explanation, yet the Israelis also felt certain that the Americans were collecting intelligence data on Israel. The difference was that no proof could be found, because rather than use human agents the United States was mainly employing its technological edge.

Electronic surveillance of many kinds kept close watch on military and industrial activities in Israel, using high-tech equipment manned by the ultra-secret National Security Agency more than by the merely secretive CIA.

The NSA eavesdrops on telephone and radio conversations in almost every country on earth, and Israel had little doubt that its military codes had been broken by the Maryland-based agency.

The Israelis also believed that just as they were listening in on the telephone conversations of foreign diplomats in Tel Aviv, the FBI was intercepting the conversations of Israelis posted in New York and Washington. But, as they had no hard evidence to back up their assumption of being watched, all they could do was be more careful.

During the 1950s Israel never charged anyone with spying for America. This was disappointing to some Israelis, who had hoped to balance the Ben-Horin and Herzog cases. Instead, the Mossad liaison had to eat humble pie and promise never to do it again. The tension between the two sides began to subside by the end of 1953.

"Angleton started asking us for small favors," de Shalit recounts. "Once he asked if we could get him gold coins. For them, getting gold coins was not an easy affair. It was very easy for us. We got them from friends in Europe and passed them on to the Americans." The CIA used the coins to pay their agents behind the Iron Curtain.

On another occasion Israeli intelligence was asked to arrange work for the wife of a Soviet defector to the West. Angleton wanted to keep the defector happy and talkative, so he focused on the woman, who was a musician. He asked Israel to pull strings with a prominent Jewish violinist on the international concert circuit. The Israelis tried, but the violinist found her performance too discordant.

The CIA, for its part, began helping Israel by providing intelligence equipment: bugging devices, radio receivers, and broadcast gear to be installed on the border between Israel and Syria to transmit disinformation to the enemy. The CIA also invited Mossad and Military Intelligence personnel for training and courses. The Pentagon was not yet extending this type of hospitality, so it was the clandestine community that made the landmark offer—the first time the U.S. government gave Israel defense-related equipment.

The cooperation peaked in April 1956, when an Israeli agent in eastern Europe accidentally managed to get hold of a highly secretive speech by Nikita Khrushchev. The secretary-general of the Soviet Communist party had delivered the address two months earlier at a closed session of the 20th annual party congress. His speech—three years after Stalin's death—was the first official account of the wartime dictator's horrific crimes against his own people, doubtless providing clues on the damage done to Russia's economic and military strength.

Western intelligence agencies, and above all the CIA, were desperate to obtain the speech. They trawled through their contacts in Europe but repeatedly came up empty. It was the Israelis who succeeded. Allen Dulles, by that time, was director of the CIA, and Republican Dwight Eisenhower had replaced Democrat Truman as president in 1953.

Dulles would later describe acquiring the speech as the outstanding achievement of his career. But he never revealed that Israel had scored the triumph. The Israelis, in turn, never told the Americans how they got the document.

The turning point had been in December 1955 when Victor Grayevski, a Polish journalist, made his first visit to Israel. In fact, he was the first Pole given permission by his government to visit Israel as a tourist. Until then the only Poles who got to see the country were Jewish immigrants who took the one-way trip, government officials, or members of delegations who came to promote relations between the two countries.

The tourist visa and the passport granted to Grayevski enabled him to visit his sick father, who had become paralyzed since moving most of the family to Palestine in 1947. The month that Grayevski spent in Israel changed his worldview and transformed him into a Zionist.

He was a Communist party member and an editor at the official Polish Press Agency, in charge of news from the Soviet Union. Grayevski considered himself a loyal and dedicated Pole. But his stay in Israel convinced him that the only place for Jews to live was in their own country. He decided that after returning to Poland, he would put in an official request for permission to emigrate.

In the meantime, word was leaking out of Moscow that Khrushchev had delivered a startling speech about the Stalin years. Foreign delegates had not been permitted to attend that session, but seven copies—each fifty-eight pages in the original Russian, bound in red and marked "Top Secret"—were sent to the Communist bloc's heads of government.

The recipient comrade-leaders were urged to look after their copy as after their own child. They were allowed to read the document but were ordered not to reproduce it.

When Eduard Ohab, head of the Polish Communist party, read the speech, he was shocked. Khrushchev's sharp criticism of Stalin was, in the context of the period, close to heresy. Upset and excited, Ohab felt the need to share his feelings with his aides. He had a few copies made.

One of these got into Grayevski's hands, after the journalist charmed a secretary into lending him the text for just a few hours. Still acting out of newfound Zionist zeal, he decided to give the document to Israel as a gift. He could have sold the information to the Americans or to other Western diplomats whom he had met at cocktail parties, but his trip through Israel affected him so profoundly that he offered Israeli intelligence the intelligence coup of the decade for free.

Grayevski turned to a trusted friend, who was often in touch with Israeli diplomats in Warsaw. The friend photographed the fifty-eight pages, gave the film to the Israelis, and handed the document back to Grayevski for return to the party offices.

Within a few days the Khrushchev speech—in Russian and Israel's Hebrew translation—reached Prime Minister Ben-Gurion and Teddy Kollek. They held an emergency meeting, which concluded with the decision to transfer the information as a gift to the CIA. The document, exactly as photographed in Warsaw, was carried by a courier to Washington, where it was quickly taken to the director of the agency.

President Eisenhower's senior officials were astonished that Israel had achieved what the entire large and wealthy CIA had failed to do. Tiny Israel was finally joining the big leagues in the sport of intelligence.

Eisenhower, Dulles of the CIA, and his brother Secretary of State John Foster Dulles decided to leak the Khrushchev text to newspapers. The speech was then read over the U.S.-financed radio stations beaming programs to the Soviet Union and other Communist countries. American authorities even launched balloons carrying leaflets about the speech from Austria and West Germany into the neighboring Communist lands.

Victor Grayevsky—who later settled in Jerusalem—may not have intended to help U.S.-Israeli relations, but his decision to send the Khrushchev text to his newly discovered spiritual homeland illustrates the political power of coincidence.

Kollek and de Shalit, meanwhile, were urging Angleton to tell his boss, Dulles, and the president about CIA-Mossad cooperation and how well it was going. The Israelis wanted Eisenhower to appreciate them, but Angleton—as was his habit—seemed to be keeping it all under his hat. Khrushchev's speech was such a scoop that the top leaders were now told of the credit Israel deserved.

There would be many joint projects, in military and intelligence affairs, in the future. Israeli officials were thankful for the liaison between the clandestine communities, because the general tone of relations was deteriorating after the transition from Truman to Eisenhower.

Without the Khrushchev speech and the intelligence lobby, things would have been even worse.

CHAPTER FIVE

FITS AND STARTS

As Harry Truman's term neared its end in 1952, Israel and its friends in the United States knew that they were losing their hero in the White House. When it became clear that Dwight Eisenhower, a hero to all Americans, would be the next president, their task was to ensure that he would be just as friendly.

Pro-Israel lobbyists were looking to the future and knew that political change was as inevitable as the change of seasons, so they wanted to invest in both political parties. And the 1952 campaign represented their first coast-to-coast challenge.

They mounted their own campaign of personal visits to party leaders, focusing simultaneously on dozens of senators and congressmen who had displayed sympathy toward Israel. There was, for instance, Hubert H. Humphrey, the Minnesota Democrat who was "more of a Zionist than many Jews," according to a former aide, Washington lawyer Max M. Kampelman. He recalls that at the start of Humphrey's long career in the Senate in 1948, there was little political benefit to reap from support-ing the newborn state, yet "his enthusiasm was unbounded and he exulted in Israel's creation, feeling both a secular and a Christian religious fulfillment."

Si Kenen, the AIPAC founder, geared up his forces for the Republican national convention in Chicago, in July 1952, by contacting the senator who they felt was likely to be chosen as Eisenhower's running mate. They were correct, and Califor-nia's Richard M. Nixon promised to help insert a strongly pro-Israel plank into the party platform. Nixon cautioned them that John Foster Dulles would likely be the new secretary of state and might not be so sympathetic.

In a forerunner of successes that AIPAC would have every four years at the party conventions, the Republican platform did—in the end—declare its friendship and support for Israel as a sanctuary for the Jewish people that "appeals to our deepest humanitarian instincts."

Nixon then wrote a Kenen aide that he was delighted to have helped draft the positive plank. "I am proud that our country has been an effective champion," he added, "in the settlement of Jewish refugees in Israel and the development of that coun-try."

The Republicans had a great year, wresting control of the White House and both houses of Congress from the Democrats for the first time in twenty years, but due to the impotence of vice presidents in the American system, it would be more than two decades before Nixon could act on his political reflex to support Israel.

As for Eisenhower, American Jews had noticed that he rarely spoke about their favorite subjects: Israel and the Holocaust. They tried to engage him, hoping that his heart was in the right place, since he had—after all—had the searing experience of liberating survivors from Nazi concentration camps in Europe.

"We were talking with Eisenhower about Dachau," recalls

Max M. Fisher, one of the biggest Jewish contributors to Republican campaigns. "He was accused by some Jewish organizations of not giving the people there enough food. He told me, 'Max, you can't force-feed people who've been starving. You'll make them sick.'" Eisenhower did tell Jewish supporters that whenever an officer would make an anti-Semitic remark, he would send them to the Dachau or Auschwitz death camps, "and that would cure him."

But all signs were pointing to an "even-handed" policy on the Middle East, and that would not be good enough for Israel. Ambassador Abba Eban pictured his country as the defendant who, when assured by the judge that "this court will grant you justice," replies frankly: "That's exactly what frightens me. I'm looking for mercy."

Israel's friends began to fear they would get little mercy from Eisenhower, who showed little sympathy toward the young country's determination to shore up its defenses. Israeli diplomats would ask the United States for weapons, to correct an imbalance of forces. This would mean lifting the U.S., British, and French arms embargo imposed on the entire Middle East in 1950. Eisenhower infuriated the Israelis by saying there was no point in giving more arms than a tiny nation of 1.7 million people could absorb. Considering that Egypt alone had a population of 40 million, this U.S. attitude would leave Israel forever outgunned.

Eisenhower was not even certain that he—in Truman's position—would have supported Israel's birth; but now that it was an accomplished fact, he would have to live with it.

And on the campaign trail, the retired Supreme Allied Commander spoke of the need to improve relations with the Arab countries that had been angered by early U.S. recognition of Israel. Israel's supporters thought they could sniff the scent of oil interests when they heard Eisenhower say, "We must support the legitimate aspirations of the Arab world."

To learn more of what the conflict was all about, Dulles toured the Middle East in May 1953. It represented the first trip to Israel by a secretary of state. However, the Israelis were unimpressed. They noted that he brought the Egyptian president a silver revolver, but in Israel "offered no gift except an abundant quantity of advice." The fact-finding tour resolved nothing. The Israelis remained suspicious, and the Arabs, concerned.

One of the Arab world's many complaints about Israel centered on water rights. In an arid region where water is more important than oil to most people, arguments over rivers and streams nearly drowned U.S.-Israel relations in the first months of the Eisenhower administration.

The trouble began in the summer of 1953, when Israeli engineers started a big diversion project along the northern section of the Jordan River, aimed at irrigating the Negev Desert to the south. Jordan and Syria, sharing the same water, howled in protest that their share was being stolen. The United States understood Arab concerns and joined the United Nations in ordering Israel to stop the project. Ben-Gurion refused.

Around the same time, Israel complained bitterly that Palestinian refugees infiltrated from Egypt, Jordan, and Syria to steal livestock, to ruin crops, and—much worse—to attack isolated farms. Perceiving the incursions as a threat to its security, Israel retaliated, sometimes without correlation between the crime and the punishment. In the choreography of Arab-Israeli escalation, the early steps were being danced.

As would happen repeatedly in the long conflict, there was in 1953 one particular Israeli military offensive that became the lightning rod for misunderstandings with Washington. It was an October attack by a commando force led by a young colonel, Ariel Sharon, whose exploits in decades to come would trigger more controversy. His soldiers crossed into Jordan, and in the course of a search-and-destroy mission aimed at terrorists who had fled, they attacked the village of Qibiya and killed sixty-nine men, women, and children. Sharon would later explain that the deaths were an unintentional "tragedy" that occurred because of indications that the villagers had left and Qibiya "seemed completely deserted."

Ben-Gurion instructed Ambassador Eban to lie, to tell Washington and the UN that the raiders had not been Israeli soldiers but enraged farmers and settlers. No one believed that tale, and it only fueled the Eisenhower administration's anger.

The U.S. counsel in Jerusalem, S. Roger Tyler, interpreted that and other retaliation raids as an extremely dangerous "Israeli game," suggesting that the Jewish state wanted more territory—"that she wants peace but only on her own terms."

With typical paternalism toward Israel, Tyler's cable to the State Department said: "She must be patient and know that we will support her if she does, and that because we disapprove certain of her acts does not mean we are deserting her. But there is a limit."

The Qibiya raid, along with the water diversion, had crossed that line. And the White House coupled its condemnation with a suspension of all aid to Israel—the first time the United States tried pulling its own, powerful economic lever to affect the Jewish state's behavior. At stake was only $26 million, to be sure, but this also was a tug-of-war over who needed the money and who needed Israel.

At a time of economic hardship in his country, Ben-Gurion knew the answers. Eisenhower's aid freeze was a shock, and Israel could barely afford its historic ingathering of Jews from Iraq, north Africa, and eastern Europe. The government had already imposed rationing on food and other supplies. Officials feared the economy would simply collapse if the U.S. welfare checks—so hard won by a unique lobby—were to stop.

The Israelis promised to behave themselves, showing a sense of disgrace under pressure that would become a behavior pattern. Occasionally U.S.-Israel relations would resemble a dysfunctional family. Uncle Sam felt it had to deal with an *enfant terrible* that acted as it pleased without regard for the elder's feelings; Israel was convinced that it had to do whatever it deemed necessary for its security; but when Uncle Sam looked as if it would not tolerate another moment of defiance, the problem child would clean up its room and wash behind its ears—especially if Uncle Sam tightened the purse strings.

The Israelis halted their irrigation project and pledged to cooperate fully with Ambassador Eric Johnston—the first of many presidential envoys the United States would send to the Middle East—who had been charged by Eisenhower to mediate the water dispute.

It took Johnston two years and twice as many trips to the region, but he did work out a compromise for water-sharing in the Jordan Valley. Israel then scored points by being the only interlocutor to agree to the plan. Jordan and Syria refused to sign on, although in fact everyone played by the new rules and warfare over water was averted.

The Eisenhower administration's overriding goal was not just to prevent bloodshed but "to step in to counter the weight of the Soviet," as the president wrote in his memoirs. The resulting "New Look" policy claimed to be based on "friendly impartiality" to Israelis and Arabs, but the conflict between them was considered an obstacle to U.S. friendship with the Arab world in the fight against communism. Based on the mathematics of resources and territory, the Israelis had very little to offer, and thus concessions were demanded of them in order to please the Arabs. To the administration, Israeli flexibility was the key to a pro-Western Middle East.

And on the Arab side, Egypt was the key—the most important prize for the West. The United States did its best to get along with the ultra-nationalist president, Colonel Gamal Abdel Nasser, who had overthrown King Farouk in early 1952, and to try to woo Nasser into the Western camp. The CIA provided personal security to him, while Nasser continued for years to play East and West against each other.

A shock to Washington, and to Jerusalem, came when Nasser signed a massive arms deal with the Soviet bloc. Tension was already on the rise after an unusually large Israeli retaliation raid on the Gaza Strip killed nearly forty Egyptians and wounded more than a hundred on February 28, 1955. The raid, described by Egypt as the worst "butchery" since the 1949 armistice, is linked by Israeli historians to the fact that David Ben-Gurion had returned to the post of defense minister just a few days earlier—as an emphatic statement that he would not tolerate Arab terrorist activity. But the U.S. Embassy in Tel Aviv quickly reported to Washington that Prime Minister Moshe Sharett seemed to be "in full agreement" with Ben-Gurion, indicating impatience, toughness, and a belief by Israel that force was the only language the enemy would understand. Underlining a fairly constant political reality in Israel, the embassy report said military action was generally popular in the country and thus could be seen as a pre-election move.

Another piece of the background puzzle was Project Alpha, a joint U.S.-British initiative aimed at bringing peace to Israel and its neighbors. The ambitious product of a series of secret meetings in Washington and London, the plan was secretly sent to Sharett and the governments of Egypt, Syria, and Jordan.

It suggested that Israel and Jordan should exchange some land, to make their borders and highways more secure. Jordan would gain access to the Israeli port of Haifa. Israel would cede a small part of the Negev Desert to Egypt, to permit a land connection with Jordan. Israel would have to accept between 75,000 and 150,000 Palestinian Arab refugees and would have to pay compensation to others. The money would be loaned by Western governments and banks.

In exchange for all its concessions, Israel would be granted a guarantee by the United States and Great Britain that its new borders would be secure. The Arabs would have to agree to end their economic embargo of Israel. Egypt would permit Israeli ships to use the Suez Canal. Israel would be supplied with weapons and would join pro-Western alliances.

No one in the Middle East seemed enthusiastic about the plan, and U.S. officials suspected that the large Israeli raid on Egyptian forces in Gaza was meant to torpedo Project Alpha. It sank with barely a trace.

Another development in February 1955 made Egypt feel threatened: the formation of a plainly anti-Nasser alliance comprising Britain, Iran, Pakistan, Turkey, and Iraq. U.S. officials arranged financing for the new, mini-NATO, which became known as the Baghdad Pact.

Nasser, desperate for support in the only coin that matters in the Middle East—weapons—lost patience with the West and turned to the East. He shocked Washington and its allies on September 27, 1955, by announcing a huge purchase of armaments from Czechoslovakia. This was the first entry into this regional market by Communist arms suppliers. It would become a long-term investment, yielding political and strategic dividends for Moscow.

Israel, deeply concerned that Egypt had a new arms source, tried to reap some advantage from the situation, asking the West to respond to the Czech deal by arming the Jewish state. Prime Minister Sharett visited Washington in November 1955 for a short chat with Eisenhower and a longer one with Dulles. In addition to asking for weapons, Sharett opened the door to a renewal of U.S. peacemaking efforts. He said that in a process of "give and take" Israel would be prepared to discuss "exchanges of territory" with Egypt but without surrendering "vital points such as Eilat" or allowing Israel to be cut in two.

There were other levers to press for military and political

support. Motivated by Eban and other Israelis, leaders of the American Jewish community stepped up their lobbying efforts in Washington, claiming that Nasser was an open Communist agent and anti-American. Now united as the Conference of Presidents of Major Jewish Organizations, they convinced former President Truman, former first lady Eleanor Roosevelt, and labor union leaders to call publicly for U.S. arms deliveries to Israel. But the fact that these were all Democrats had only limited impact on a Republican administration.

As Eisenhower and Dulles saw it, moreover, arming the Israelis might not defuse tensions but only accelerate an arms race. It could tempt Israel to embark on adventures that would tip over the delicate apple cart that Washington was attempting to erect: a proposed system of alliances that would bring the Middle East and the Persian Gulf under a pro-Western tent.

Under Dulles's "domino theory," the fear was that when one country fell to Soviet domination, others would follow. The Western aim was to set up a bulwark so that none would fall.

Israel's participation, at least openly, was out of the question. Due to Arab hostility, there was no formal place for the Jewish state in Muslim-based pacts. But the secretary of state and his brother, CIA director Allen Dulles, found intelligence again to be a useful tool. They encouraged the Mossad to establish cooperative relationships with intelligence services and government ministries on the edges of the Middle East. Aside from serving American, anti-Communist interests, this "peripheral concept" became a Mossad favorite, allowing the espionage agency to maintain covert ties with Muslim nations such as Iran and Turkey.

And when Israel renewed its request for arms, the United States no longer rejected it outright. While still fearing that open sales to Israel would annoy the Arabs, American officials referred the Israelis to France and Canada, encouraging the

Comfortable with each other: President Johnson *(left),* holding a grandchild, and Eshkol *(second from left)* listened to country music at the LBJ Ranch in Texas on January 7, 1968. Israel's ambassador Ephraim Evron *(third from left)* smoked a cigar. *(Yoichi R. Okamoto, courtesy of LBJ Library Collection)*

On the first official visit of an Israeli prime minister to the United States, Levi Eshkol *(left)* and President Lyndon B. Johnson *(right)* reviewed the honor guard on the White House lawn on June 1, 1964. *(Cecil Stoughton, courtesy of LBJ Library Collection)*

John F. Kennedy *(right)* visited Israel in 1951 with his friend and fellow congressman Franklin D. Roosevelt, Jr. *(center),* two of the first U.S. legislators to take part in the tradition of touring the Jewish state. Here they listen to Prime Minister Ben-Gurion. *(courtesy of John F. Kennedy Library)*

Foreign Minister Golda Meir visited President Kennedy at his family's compound in Palm Beach, Florida, on December 27, 1962. JFK delighted Golda by dubbing Israel "a close and intimate ally." *(courtesy of John F. Kennedy Library)*

Keeping a secret: Victor Grayevski, who emerged from Communist-controlled Poland to find a renewed Jewish heritage in Israel, provided Israel and, in turn, the United States with one of the Cold War's greatest intelligence coups: the text of a secret speech by the Soviet leader Nikita Khrushchev in 1956. In Jerusalem, he stands among his gifts from foreign radio stations as director of Israel's broadcasts to Eastern Europe. *(Nitsan Shorer)*

The troubles are over: Prime Minister Ben-Gurion *(left)* visited the White House on March 10, 1960, and met with President Dwight D. Eisenhower *(center)* and C. Douglas Dillon *(right)*, deputy under secretary of state for economic affairs. The Suez/Sinai campaign of 1956 had given the United States a new appreciation for Israel's fighting abilities and independence. *(National Park Service, courtesy of Dwight D. Eisenhower Library)*

Labor's ties to Israel: Jimmy Hoffa *(circled in the front row),* then vice president of the Teamsters' Union and later its controversial president, was proud to attend the dedication of an orphanage named in his honor in Jerusalem in August 1956. The event underlined the strong links between Israel and the American labor movement, and Las Vegas publisher and former gunrunner Hank Greenspun *(circled in second row)* worked hard to fortify the connection. *(courtesy of Barbara Greenspun)*

Visiting the White House on May 8, 1951, Israel's first prime minister, David Ben-Gurion *(right)*, discussed the Middle East map with President Truman *(left)* as the Israeli ambassador, Abba Eban *(center)*, listened in. During that visit to the United States, Ben-Gurion launched the sale of Israel Bonds and initiated the intelligence connection between the CIA and the Mossad. *(National Park Service, Abbie Rowe, courtesy of Harry S Truman Presidential Library)*

Herman "Hank" Greenspun *(far right)*, then a U.S. Army captain, accompanied the supreme allied commander, General Dwight D. Eisenhower, inspecting a damaged tank after the D-Day invasion in France in 1944. After the war Greenspun smuggled guns to the prestate Jewish forces and introduced Israelis to key contacts in organized labor and organized crime. *(courtesy of Barbara Greenspun)*

Eddie Jacobson *(left)* chatted with his friend, President Harry S Truman, in 1945 in the haberdashery shop they used to run together in Kansas City. Jacobson was one of the "Jewish levers" applied by Israel and its supporters in the United States during the 1948 debate over recognizing the newborn state. *(courtesy of Harry S Truman Presidential Library and the Kansas City Star)*

Henry Morgenthau, Jr., the U.S. Treasury Secretary during World War II, later chaired the Israel Bonds project that helped build the Jewish state's economy. His was a family tradition, started by his father, who as U.S. consul in Turkey persuaded fellow American Jews to send aid to starving Jews in the Holy Land during World War I. *(courtesy of American Jewish Joint Distribution Committee)*

Henry Morgenthau, Sr.,'s initiative led to the founding of the American Jewish Joint Distribution Committee. Leaders of "the Joint" are seen in 1919, overseeing the first postwar shipment of kosher meat to starving Jews in Poland. Later the Joint helped Israeli intelligence bring Jews to Israel from many countries. *(courtesy of American Jewish Joint Distribution Committee)*

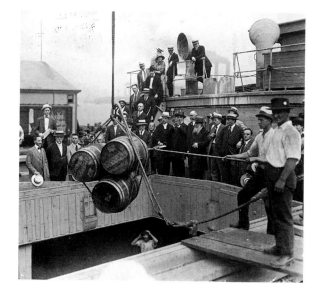

As LBJ's dog listens carefully on January 8, Eshkol *(left)* and Johnson discuss the Middle East, seven months after Israel's lightning victory in the Six-Day War. *(Yoichi R. Okamoto, courtesy of LBJ Library Collection)*

A shared joke: President Nixon and Prime Minister Golda Meir got along extraordinarily well. They are seen at the White House before revelations of military unpreparedness during the Yom Kippur War forced her out of office in April 1974 and before the Watergate scandal forced his resignation two months later. *(courtesy of Israel Government Press Office)*

President Richard M. Nixon *(right)* received a gift, a Jewish encyclopedia, from Israel's ambassador and future prime minister Yitzhak Rabin *(left)* on January 28, 1972, during one of their many White House meetings. Israel and the United States had cooperated in the Jordan crisis of September 1970, but later would go through the tense days of the Yom Kippur War of October 1973. *(The White House)*

Nixon, desperate to regain respect lost in Watergate, reviewed an honor guard of air force cadets in June 1974 as the first U.S. president to visit Israel. *(courtesy of Israel Government Press Office)*

One of the leading American Jewish philanthropists, Max M. Fisher *(right)*, was a successful fund-raiser for the Republican party and thus enjoyed access to Nixon and, here, to President Gerald R. Ford *(center)* and Secretary of State Henry Kissinger *(left)*. In the Oval Office in February 1975, they discussed Israel's bitter negotiations with Egypt. *(The White House)*

Secretary of State Kissinger *(left)* often chatted with Isaiah L. (Si) Kenen *(right)*, founder of America's pro-Israel lobby, AIPAC. Friends of Israel found that Kissinger, despite his Jewish heritage, was tough on Israel when mediating in the Middle East. But Kenen and his successors at AIPAC, especially in the 1980s, would increasingly find open doors and willing listeners in the U.S. government's highest echelons. *(courtesy of AIPAC)*

A rainy day for President Ford *(right)* and Israel's Prime Minister Yitzhak Rabin *(left)*, as they emerge from a White House meeting where they discussed the declared "reassessment" of U.S. policy toward Israel in 1975. *(courtesy of Israel Government Press Office)*

Israel's most ardent pro-American, Jerusalem's mayor Teddy Kollek *(left)*, in February 1972 showed the ancient walls of his city to Henry Ford II *(right)*, the automobile magnate whose support for Israel defied both his grandfather's famous anti-Semitism and the Arab economic boycott. *(courtesy of Max M. Fisher)*

A hero's home: The residence near Tel Aviv of Moshe Dayan *(center)*, the Israeli general most celebrated in America, with its splendid collection of Holy Land antiquities, was a favorite stop on a VIP tour of Israel. His visitors in February 1972 included Henry Ford *(left)* and Max Fisher *(right)*. *(courtesy of Max M. Fisher)*

President Jimmy Carter *(right)* would be surprised in May by Rabin's defeat in the Israeli election after Rabin's get-acquainted visit to the White House on March 5, 1977. Carter would have to reformulate U.S. policy. *(courtesy of Israel Government Press Office)*

Walks and talks in the Maryland hills: Prime Minister Menachem Begin *(left)* adhered to his formal attire while President Jimmy Carter *(center)* and Egypt's president Anwar Sadat *(right)* tried to relax during thirteen days of tense negotiations at Camp David in September 1978. *(courtesy of Jimmy Carter Library)*

The Holocaust factor: The President and Rosalynn Carter visited Yad Vashem, Israel's national memorial to the six million Jewish victims of the Holocaust, accompanied by Prime Minister Begin, officials of Yad Vashem, and a cantor. This was in March 1979, when Carter risked his prestige by traveling personally to hammer out the Israeli-Egyptian peace treaty. *(courtesy of Jimmy Carter Library)*

The triple handshake: Prime Minister Begin *(right)* and President Sadat *(left)* were linked by President Carter *(center)*, after the signing of Israel's first peace treaty with an Arab country, on the White House lawn on March 25, 1979. *(courtesy of Jimmy Carter Library)*

governments in Paris and Ottawa to supply planes and other military equipment.

Arms deliveries, despite the U.S. quest for stability, only added to instability and tensions in the Middle East. By the end of 1955, in every major capital, it was obvious to all but the blind and deaf that a clock had started counting down toward war—a second round between Israel and the Arabs.

It was to head off the inevitable that Eisenhower launched a diplomatic mission, code-named Project Gamma. Unlike Alpha, this time there would be a specific presidential envoy, and he was even more senior than water-mediator Eric Johnston: a former navy secretary and future treasury secretary, Robert Anderson. A Texas businessman, favored by many Republicans to be a presidential candidate four years hence, Anderson dipped his toe into the unfamiliar waters of shuttle diplomacy. His was a direct approach, urging Ben-Gurion and Nasser to meet face-to-face to settle their differences.

Anderson spent the first two and a half months of 1956 hopping between Jerusalem and Cairo in a small plane with intermediate stops in Athens and cover stories concocted by the CIA. Only a very few officials and intelligence operatives in Israel knew about Anderson, who was housed in an apartment opposite the prime minister's office to preserve secrecy. He was quietly blazing a trail for the secretive, grueling journeys of negotiation and mediation that would characterize many attempts by future secretaries of state and presidential envoys.

Still, the Anderson mission failed. Nasser did tell the envoy that he harbored no "hostile intention" toward Israel, but the Egyptian leader insisted on getting part of the Negev as a land corridor to Jordan—a suicidal bisection, in Israel's view. Nasser insisted that Israel take back Arab refugees, which the Israelis saw as a ploy to outnumber the Jewish people in their own country. He almost agreed to a summit meeting with Ben-Gurion, but expressed his fears of being assassinated like Jordan's King Abdullah in 1951 after his talks with Israelis.

Ben-Gurion insisted on direct negotiations with Egypt—a policy stand that would be a hallmark of Israeli diplomacy, a guidepost bent only rarely when there was much to be gained. In one of his reports to Washington, Anderson wrote that Ben-Gurion told him "he was willing to concede things that Nasser never dreamed of, but only if he could discuss matters with him personally."

Project Gamma died in March 1956. As described by Eisenhower in a diary entry, "Nasser proved to be a complete stumbling block." Lest that seem too pro-Israeli, the president criticized Ben-Gurion for refusing to cede territory while demanding weapons "as a means of ensnaring the U.S. as a protector."

Israel, in fact, was busily—but secretly—bringing itself under the protective umbrella of two other powers: France and Britain. A series of clandestine meetings among the countries, without Washington's knowledge, led to the outbreak of fighting on October 29, 1956. War had long been expected, but not in this form: the French and the British, in collusion with the Israelis, invading Egypt and seizing the Suez Canal because Nasser had just nationalized it.

Eisenhower was simply shocked, although he had received intelligence reports indicating an Israeli military buildup that might lead to action against Jordan or Egypt around the end of the year. A few months after Egypt was invaded, CIA director Allen Dulles felt he had to defend his agency's performance. "I have heard a number of comments recently from congressional sources to the effect that the United States intelligence community failed completely to produce any advance warning of the immense [size] of an Israeli attack against Egypt," he wrote to his brother, the secretary of state.

On October 25, the CIA director insisted, "the U.S. military attaché reported substantial evidence of Israeli mobilization to a level higher than any attained since the armistice of 1949." There were two cables from the attaché the next day, reporting "very large scale" movements of trucks and taxis heading toward southern Israel, the activation of army reservists including the Israeli drivers working for the U.S. Embassy, "and that all units, posts, camps, and stations of the Israeli Defense Forces were on standby alert."

The CIA concluded on October 27 that this activity "probably indicates preparation for a limited objective action against Egypt or Jordan." Immediately after the Israeli attack on October 29, the CIA added a warning that "the British and French are prepared to and probably will intervene with force in the Middle East as opportunity occurs in connection with the Israeli-Egyptian action."

The intelligence chief gently complained that the White House did not treat the reports as being that serious, in the belief that "the mobilization was not full and that Israel's preparations were to meet the possibility of border action."

President Eisenhower was certainly preoccupied by the final days of his reelection campaign, and he resented the distraction of a war in the Middle East. He lashed out at Ben-Gurion's "overestimate of my desire to avoid offending the many voters who might have either sentimental or blood relations with Israel. I emphatically corrected any misapprehension of this kind he might have."

Vice President Nixon expressed concern about Jewish support, saying the campaign might "lose some Israeli votes," but he also noted that "there weren't many" anyway.

As the Israeli-British-French conspiracy rolled on, Eisenhower wrote: "I gave strict orders to the State Department that they should inform Israel that we'd handle our affairs exactly as though we didn't have a Jew in America."

The president was determined to roll back aggression, even

when the aggressors were erstwhile friends of America. An angry dispute raged on for months between Washington, on one side, and London, Paris, and Jerusalem on the other.

Israelis were proud that their army was talented enough to seize the entire Sinai, right up to the Suez, in a matter of days. Ben-Gurion was carried away with the popular euphoria, announcing to his astonished parliament that a biblical Jewish kingdom would be reestablished in the Sinai. After all, Moses had led the Israelites out of slavery in Egypt and had received the Ten Commandments at Mount Sinai.

But officials who devoted their careers to building relations with the United States, including Teddy Kollek, had their doubts. He wrote that things would have been much better "if the Americans had been told even an hour beforehand and not felt slapped in the face by their friends and allies."

Implicitly acknowledging that some Israeli officials had begun to suspect that all his friendships in the United States were making him too ardent a pro-American, and almost an American agent, Kollek sardonically noted "the reasoning presented to Ben-Gurion about keeping the Suez plan from me was that I wouldn't keep it secret!" He threatened to resign, but did not.

For Britain and France, the war was a disastrous straw that broke their backs as great powers. Militarily, their paratroops had no trouble lining the canal. But politically, the British and French found themselves confronting not only a defiant Nasser but an angry United States.

The Soviet Union sent letters to Britain, France, and Israel, threatening military strikes against them. And the United States was not lifting a finger to deter the Soviets. America's inaction sent Ben-Gurion into a panic. "It was a nightmarish day," he wrote in his diary, having no choice but to take seriously the Soviet threat to hit Tel Aviv with missiles. Even when going to war without U.S. permission, the Israelis had assumed that Washington would stop Moscow from acting.

But instead it was almost as if Eisenhower were using the Soviet hammer to press harder on Israel, Britain, and France. In every forum, including the UN, America demanded that they accept an immediate cease-fire and a complete withdrawal of their forces.

To back up its demand, the United States cut off all financial and technical assistance to Israel, including deliveries of surplus food, gobbled up by needy immigrants still pouring into the Jewish state. For the second time in three years, America was trying to influence Israeli behavior by wielding the aid lever.

Administration officials began to whisper about economic sanctions, or perhaps even expelling Israel from the UN, if it did not pull its troops out of the Sinai.

Ben-Gurion accepted the cease-fire but still hoped to retain the captured peninsula. In an effort to repel the White House assault, he ordered Ambassador Eban to mobilize friends in the United States.

Eban embarked on an unprecedentedly organized effort to interfere in American policy making. Reaching out to both major parties, he secured a promise of help from Rabbi Abba Hillel Silver—a key Republican Jew with White House access—even though Silver considered the Sinai invasion "an error of judgment."

Eban and the Israeli cause received especially impressive support from the American labor movement, led by the AFL-CIO's Walter Reuther and George Meany, with their legal advisor Arthur Goldberg, a Jew who would distinguish himself further as a UN ambassador and Supreme Court justice.

"Many people in organized labor, and certainly many leaders, were Jews, and they responded to our requests on the basis of emotional identification with us," recalls Ephraim (Eppy) Evron, a special Israeli envoy to America's unions and later ambassador to the United States. "The leadership was strongly anti-Communist, so we also played that string."

The unions had some clout with Republicans on Capitol Hill. Labor lobbyists somewhat aggressively told Senator William Knowland, the Republican minority leader, that he would be "very sorry" if the United States went along with UN economic sanctions against Israel.

Support from the Democratic majority leader, Senator Lyndon B. Johnson, was more predictable. "I feel that I should tell you most frankly how disturbed I have been by recent stories in the press," he wrote to Secretary of State Dulles, referring to plans for sanctions. "It is my hope that you will instruct the American delegation to the United Nations to oppose with all its skill such a proposal if it is formally made."

The administration was concerned about Capitol Hill's almost stunning tilt toward the Israeli side of the Middle East dispute. "We have a very nasty situation on the Hill," Dulles complained. At a bipartisan meeting with legislators, an official summary said, "the president said he was aware of congressional opposition to sanctions against Israel."

Behind the scenes, a CIA memo advised that "economically, the imposition of sanctions would be especially serious because of Israel's continuing dependence on outside supplies and financing, not only for continuation of its immigration program and furtherance of economic development but also for maintenance of its present standard of living."

The memo, dated February 19, concluded "that a U.S.-supported program of economic sanctions, effectively applied, would eventually compel Israel to yield—probably within a period of three to twelve months." The CIA was wrong. Even without sanctions, it would take Israel only two weeks to bend to American and international pressure.

U.S. officials began to whisper about changing the tax laws to put pressure on Israel. Why, some asked, should contributions to a foreign country—however charitable their intent—be deductible from taxable income? Jerusalem was concerned, because private contributions by U.S. Jews then totaled some $150 million per year, a significant contribution to Israel's annual budget.

Secretary of State Dulles held pro-Israeli lobbyists at bay, complaining bitterly: "I am aware how almost impossible it is in this country to carry out a foreign policy not approved by the Jews. Marshall and Forrestal learned that. I am going to try and have one." Dulles said Jews control the media and that they put enormous pressure on congressmen. And the administration noted that 90 percent of the letters it received against imposing sanctions were from Jews.

In the standoff between giant and tiny nations, no wonder Israel blinked first. The United States kept up its pressure, and Ben-Gurion finally gave in, after negotiations dotted by mini-crises in Washington and at the UN in New York. The prime minister completed his descent from the "Jewish kingdom" around Mount Sinai by announcing on March 1, 1957, that his troops would pull out of the Sinai and Gaza.

There were negotiations, however, with Eban and Foreign Minister Golda Meir, who was visiting the United States and the United Nations. The result was an extremely important set of U.S. guarantees. Eban and Meir made sure that it was in writing from Dulles, and Israeli officials would find themselves waving this aide-mémoire, dated February 11, in America's face a decade later. The Eisenhower administration's assurances included Egypt's responsibility to prevent guerrilla attacks from its territory against Israel, and the formation of a UN peacekeeping force to ensure that no Egyptian troops were in the Sinai.

The aide-mémoire also specified the right of Israeli shipping to use the vital port of Eilat by passing through the Egyptian-controlled Strait of Tiran. "The United States believes," the formal memo said, "that the Gulf of Aqaba constitutes international waters and that no nation has the right forcibly to prevent free and innocent passage in the Gulf and through the Straits giving access thereto."

Realizing that Egypt might again be tempted to close the Strait of Tiran, the United States said it "is prepared to exercise the right of free and innocent passage." If the United States failed to make a convincing demonstration, Israel would be entitled to use force under the UN Charter's right of self-defense. Eban also obtained a U.S. promise to send its own ships through the strait, to demonstrate that the Gulf of Eilat was open to all.

Was this enough to justify having fought a war? At least the maritime routes to Africa and Asia were again assured, and at least the prime minister had a cable from Eisenhower to read and reread: "I believe that Israel will have no cause to regret having thus conformed to the strong sentiment of the world community."

The Israelis would eventually rue the day they gave up Sinai, but they found consolation in the almost instantaneous repair of their damaged relations with the United States. As early as April 1957, American ships started patroling the Red Sea and farther north toward Israel, sending the Arabs a signal that the Jewish state had a protector. A report to the Pentagon and State Department said: "The U.S. flag oil tanker *Kern Hills*, under charter to the Israeli government, entered the Gulf of Aqaba through the Straits of Tiran and discharged a cargo of oil at the port of Elath. The world at large might generally assume that the U.S. Navy was prepared to back up official United States Government statements, made at the time of Israeli withdrawal from the Gaza Strip and Sharm el-Sheikh, that we regarded the Gulf of Aqaba as international waters."

Ben-Gurion was determined never again to be totally isolated from foreign support. More specifically, Israel had learned that only at its peril could it go to war without first ensuring that it had a green light from the United States. And since then Israel has almost always tried to coordinate its major military campaigns with Washington.

The clash with America had been traumatic and sour, but as the Bible suggested, "From the bitter comes the sweet." The State of Israel, less than nine years old, had demonstrated its military prowess, and this gained Israel a great deal of credibility and respect—not least from the U.S. defense establishment.

Now, for the first time, the United States openly invited Israel to join its new strategic line-up: the Eisenhower Doctrine. Ben-Gurion accepted gladly. He had long harbored hopes of signing formal pacts between Israel and the Western world. While there still would be no formal defense accord or treaty, the Eisenhower Doctrine was as close as he would get.

The American president realized, even before the Suez crisis was over, that by focusing on individual trees—such as details of the Israeli withdrawal—he might be missing the wider regional forest and the Soviet bear lurking within. His new doctrine pledged American support, including troops, to any accepting nation threatened by aggression from Communist-backed neighbors.

As an indication of vastly improved relations, Abba Eban by mid-1957 became one of the very few ambassadors who met frequently with Secretary Dulles and his top advisors. As they discussed Middle East security issues, above all, three outstanding issues recurringly arose.

Israel asked for increased U.S. economic aid for the absorption of tens of thousands of new immigrants and for the construction of a national water system. In addition, Israel requested weapons from the United States.

More broadly, the Jewish state wanted security guarantees to deter Arab and Soviet aggression. "A specific U.S. warning to the Soviet Union," as Ambassador Eban's request was summarized in a State Department memo, "was particularly important to Israel, which was without formal contracts for mutual defense with other states."

But the American responses were only mildly positive, at best. On economic aid, Dulles indicated that a little bit more food aid and development loans would be made available. On weapons, he seemed unwilling to go any further than to suggest that "where there was a clear case of a U.S. replacement item needed by the Israelis, with no alternative source of supply available, it would seem reasonable to supply it."

Washington would not, however, provide any explicit guarantee of Israel's defense because "broadening our formal commitments in this respect raises complex constitutional issues," as an internal memo to Dulles put it. However, "both Nasser and the Soviets are aware of our deep interest in the independence of Middle East states."

American interests and the Eisenhower Doctrine were quickly tested, by Egypt's Nasser rather than by Moscow, and the United States was making preparations for the challenge. "If we choose to combat radical Arab nationalism and to hold Persian Gulf oil by force if necessary," a July 1958 memo from the National Security Council said, "a logical corollary would be to support Israel as the only strong pro-West power left in the Near East."

That same month, when Nasser-inspired Arab nationalists overthrew Iraq's government and tried to do the same in Jordan and Lebanon, there was no doubt that Israel was on the West's side. Ben-Gurion granted British paratroops permission to overfly Israel on their way to Jordan, while Eisenhower sent U.S. Marines to the shores of Tripoli, Lebanon.

In Washington, Eban was surprised that Dulles—no friend of Jewish lobbyists—suggested to him that they might help press Congress to support the president's dispatch of troops to the Middle East. It was ironic, but only the first of many occasions on which a U.S. administration would ask pro-Israel lob-byists—the only powerful group that cares about foreign aid and events abroad—to help with a non-Israel issue.

Eban recalls mourning the loss of a friend when Dulles died, because of "the intimacy that had arisen between the two governments during the short period when the United States went over to a policy of containing and even resisting Nasser's disruptive policies." News of the death reached Eban on a transatlantic oceanliner, after he resigned as ambassador in 1959.

Proudly ending twelve years at the UN and in Washington—the second half, truly a period of fits and starts—Eban had many mementoes, including a photograph from President Eisenhower on which he had inscribed: "Abba Eban, a distinguished representative of Isreal." Eban says he was "sustained by the conviction that future presidents would know how to spell our country's name."

Eisenhower himself was coming to recognize that Israel offered some strategic advantages, and the intelligence liaison relationship was reenergized. It was only a few months after the Suez war that the CIA asked the Mossad to supply samples of Soviet-made hardware that Israel had captured in the Sinai. Such treasures are not always shared free of charge, but for the sake of political healing Israel complied. The United States gained excellent insights into the latest products of Soviet military industry.

The cooperation between intelligence agencies had, in fact, continued on a fairly even keel throughout the upheavals of the 1950s. As then-Mossad chief Isser Harel recalls, "In contrast to the crisis and hostile atmosphere on the political and diplomatic level, on the interservice level the relationship continued being orderly, correct, and even friendly."

The Mossad was encouraged by the CIA to penetrate the awakening continent of Africa. While the United States might be rejected by newly independent black nations, suspicious of superpower imperialism, Israel was seen as an imaginative and progressive success with a lot to offer. Through the late 1950s and early 1960s, Israeli experts in agriculture, construction, and military training were welcome guests and contract employees in over thirty African countries. Israelis helped jittery leaders form their own bodyguard brigades. The CIA secretly underwrote some of these projects, occasionally with labor union funds from the AFL-CIO, in the belief that Israel's influence was pro-Western. Evron, the Israeli envoy to the American labor movement, says the U.S. government and unions far preferred Israeli experts in Kenya, Ghana, and Tanganyika to Communist advisors from the Soviet Union or China.

The intelligence channel also contributed to the U.S.-Israel alliance by clearing the way for arms deals. There is new evidence that the Eisenhower administration did sell equipment to Israel's military after the 1956 war—not, as previously claimed, sanctioning only the CIA's delivery of electronic bugging gear to Israeli intelligence.

The breakthrough came only in the final year of the administration, after President Eisenhower played host to Prime Minister Ben-Gurion on March 10, 1960. The meeting was almost imposed on the Americans. "An invitation to receive an honorary degree from Brandeis University could serve as a pretext for a trip at a time convenient to the president," the post-Eban Israeli ambassador Avraham Harman suggested to the post-Dulles secretary of state Christian Herter.

Finding Herter to be a solid bureaucrat but unenthusiastic about a Ben-Gurion visit, Harman added: "The prime minister had no interest in press conferences, public appearances, or congressional courtesies. He had had all of this during his visit in 1951 and did not want the experience repeated." The Israeli embassy even promised to work closely with the U.S. government "to avoid activities which may make the visit a matter of embarrassment."

In an already grand tradition of political calculation, it was the calendar that persuaded the administration to greet the Israeli leader: it was an election year and the Republican party could not afford to annoy Jewish voters. As something of a compromise, Ben-Gurion's visit to the White House was officially labeled "unofficial."

Before turning to business, according to the official State Department summary, the prime minister's small talk included the observation that he had been watching television the previous day and thought that Eisenhower "looked a little tired."

The president shrugged off the apparent rudeness, politely explaining that "it was a matter of lighting" and "any appearance on television always brought shades of opinion on how he looked, that some people in his own family would say he looked well, while others would say he looked not so well."

When Eisenhower remarked that "it had been many years since he had last seen the prime minister," Ben-Gurion tried to refresh the memory by saying, "It was fifteen years ago, just after the end of World War II." In case the hint about remembering the Holocaust was not fully clear, he gave the president a gift: "an album of photographs of DP's in Germany, many of whom, after having been liberated by the armies under General Eisenhower's command, came to Israel and are good and useful citizens."

As the conversation got down to brass tacks, it became clear that Ben-Gurion had one main subject: asking that Israel be allowed to purchase U.S. weapons, especially Hawk antiaircraft missiles. It was a matter of genuine security, he explained, when Egypt "could send fifty bombers over Tel Aviv one day and destroy Tel Aviv without too much trouble." If Nasser were to defeat Israel, "he would exterminate the Jews just as Hitler exterminated them in Germany."

Ben-Gurion did add, grimly: "Mr. President, the Jews will

fight to the last. I know this phrase is commonly used but I assure you, you may take it literally."

Eisenhower reassuringly replied that "American policy would not stand for the destruction of any nation." But the official summary added: "In the long run, he does not believe that security lies in arms."

While Israel's shopping list was considered by the U.S. bureaucracy, Ben-Gurion could not resist "noting how the Israelis had surprised even U.S. intelligence agencies when launching the Sinai campaign." So, as a State Department memo reported, "he stressed Israel could easily keep secret the fact that the U.S. was supply missile weapons." Some U.S. officials, however, felt this was a veiled threat that if the Israelis did not receive what they needed, they might find it necessary to repeat their military feat of 1956.

The Americans had their own proposal for a concession by Israel: an agreement to permit a small number of Palestinian refugees to return to their old homes in the new Jewish state while paying compensation to others. Ben-Gurion rejected the suggestion by saying, "as far as Israel is concerned, there is no possibility for repatriation. Even a small number would be like poison."

A newly declassified portion of Ben-Gurion's diaries, written at the start of 1960, says that in relations with the United States, "Everything is okay, and last year we received more grants than in any other year."

In April 1960, after the prime minister returned from his talks in Washington, his diary noted that Israel's military attaché Colonel Aharon Yariv, who would soon be chief of military intelligence, negotiated delivery of a "sophisticated radar including interception-control system," as described by Ben-Gurion. Israel also received an airborne system to detect submarines.

The prime minister wrote that the systems were worth $20

million, but the Department of Defense had given a $3 million discount and easy payment terms for the rest. "The Pentagon was very sympathetic to our needs and, unusually, responded quickly."

Doubtless aware that whatever inroads he had made with Eisenhower would expire with the end of his presidency in January 1961, Ben-Gurion kept asking Washington all through 1960 about the Hawk missiles.

The response was that U.S. forces did not immediately have enough to spare. This was a lie, as Secretary of State Herter admitted privately to his aides. According to their notes, he "found it difficult to understand why we are refusing to allow Israelis to buy Hawk missiles." Noting that "we had told the Israelis that Hawks were unavailable," Herter "was concerned by what appeared to be dishonesty on our part" because the missiles, by the end of 1961, "could be produced for the Israelis."

Other U.S. officials saw things differently. "Actually, we have done quite well by the Israelis," said one State Department memo. "We are (a) making an arms offer of a magnitude ten times that of any previous arms supply to Israel, (b) providing Israel with electronics equipment of an advanced type not available to many of our allies, (c) affording Israel an opportunity to develop scientific know-how many years in advance of its neighbors."

Only after Eisenhower handed the presidency to John F. Kennedy did Israel get its missiles—but in total secret.

It was left to the young Democrat, determined to introduce fresh ideas into foreign policy and far more beholden than the Republicans to Jewish voters, to raise U.S.-Israel relations to new heights.

CHAPTER SIX

NEW FRONTIERS

Although John F. Kennedy was violently taken from the American people before he could complete a single term in office, his thirty-four months of stewardship contributed greatly to turning U.S.-Israel relations into an alliance.

The politics underlying his own electoral success had a lot to do with it, because Jews in the Democratic party were among Kennedy's most fervent supporters. As early as 1951, the then-congressman had visited Israel, in part to expunge the Jewish community's impression of his father as a sympathizer with Nazi Germany before the United States entered World War II. In the 1960 campaign the dashing young senator told a Jewish audience: "Friendship for Israel is not a partisan matter; it is a national commitment."

But this was more than domestic politics influencing foreign policy. Kennedy and his national security team had figured out that rather than fear what a militant Israel might do—a concern felt by the last administration—it would be easier to live with an Israel that was getting the resources it needed to defend itself. Then Israel would not have to commit wild or unacceptable acts.

The necessary resources would include money, weapons, and political support for the bedrock fact that the Jewish people deserved their own state. It was important to have good relations with Arab countries, not least to ensure oil supplies to the West; but if the Arabs were still insisting that Israel had no legitimacy, then their argument was anachronistic and just plain wrong.

Kennedy's secretary of state, Dean Rusk, because of his past hostility to the creation of Israel, was not considered the young nation's friend. Yet he and the president were beginning to realize that Israel could be useful to the United States—something that Eisenhower, in his first term, and Truman both missed. There was the possibility of building up Israel as a base for U.S. influence and power projection in the Middle East.

But there were obstacles. Kennedy was moved by the plight of an estimated 600,000 Palestinian Arabs who lost their homes in Israel's 1948 War of Independence and since then were scattered around the neighboring countries—almost all in pitiful shantytowns. And from a political point of view, he considered them a thorn in the side of any effort to bring peace and stability to the Middle East.

The Kennedy administration proposed several solutions, all of them pressing Israel to take back at least 10 percent of the refugees. Secretary Rusk urged the president to try to achieve "progress on the refugee question and specifically the need for a significant gesture by Israel on the key element of repatriation."

Another obstacle was Israel's nuclear ambitions. In December 1960, in the twilight between the Eisenhower and Kennedy administrations, American U-2 spy planes flew over a largely

completed construction project in the Negev Desert that the Israelis were calling a "textile plant." The U-2 photographs of
the Dimona site helped U.S. analysts conclude that it was an
atomic plant. Because Washington started peppering Jerusalem
with questions, Ben-Gurion decided to make a public statement. The U.S. Embassy in Tel Aviv told Washington, in a secret telegram on December 3, that "Ben-Gurion was planning
to announce a new university located near Beersheba and
would also mention a new 10 to 20 megawatt nuclear reactor
designed by Israel with some French equipment."

Five days later an alarmed National Security Council convened in Washington to formulate a U.S. response. CIA director Allen Dulles, according to the minutes, "reported that Israel
was constructing, with French assistance, a nuclear complex in
the Negev. This complex probably included a reactor capable of
producing weapons-grade plutonium."

The CIA report added: "The French were apparently supplying equipment and training to the Israelis and were flying in
the necessary fuel elements. Apparently the Israelis intend to
announce shortly that a new university is being established
with a small reactor, exclusively of Israeli design and intended
solely for scientific research. CIA and Atomic Energy Commission experts believe, however, that the Israeli nuclear complex
cannot be solely for peaceful purposes."

Dulles, at this point, passed around the table photographs
taken by the U.S. Air Force and apparently by intelligence
agents in Israel. When asked whether the photos could be used
publicly, the CIA chief said he "would like to check with the
army, which had obtained the photographs." A deputy secretary of defense, James Douglas, was less cautious, saying, "I believed there was no risk in using the photographs since they
could have been taken from a road which runs near the facility."

Vice President Richard Nixon, a month after losing the presidential election, suggested that Israel's nuclear construction project "should be a major intelligence target since such facilities posed a danger, even in friendly countries."

Dulles responded that "the U.S. had known about the construction of a facility in Israel for some time, but had only recently identified it as a nuclear facility." He assured the vice president that "CIA operatives were constantly on the watch for nuclear facilities."

The discussion ended with a promise by Secretary of State Christian Herter "to talk to the Israeli ambassador soon," because of "the serious implications of this development." The Arab countries and the Soviet Union would "undoubtedly interpret the Israeli nuclear facility as intended for production of weapons," said Herter, adding that "the fact the facility cost between $40 and $80 million at a time when we were providing aid to Israel raises serious questions."

The next day Israeli ambassador Avraham Harman was duly summoned to the State Department, where Herter showed him "photographs of installation south of Beersheba," in the stilted language of a department telegram to the U.S. Embassy in Tel Aviv. The secretary of state "pointed out overall scope of installation, diameter containment building and capacity power lines far in excess research reactor requirements. U.S. scientists and industrial representatives have recently noted scale and high secrecy of Israeli atomic program, as well as French involvement in large scale nuclear reactor."

Herter complained that the "obvious inconsistency between [our] information and projected Israeli announcement gives us great concern. Knowledge of potential nuclear weapons capacity would have very disturbing impact on Middle East and affect U.S. interests."

American concerns were also made known to France, because

the foreign ministry in Paris promptly stated that French cooperation with Israel was aimed at "peaceful utilization" of atomic power.

On December 21, Ben-Gurion admitted in the K'nesset, Israel's parliament, that his nation had received a nuclear reactor from France. He declared that it was for peaceful purposes.

Because the public announcement was so brief, the Israeli government felt it had to provide a little more information to Washington. Ambassador Harman went to the State Department again, telling Secretary Herter: "The reactor is estimated to cost $5 million a year in addition to local currency costs for the conventional structures." More important, as the department paraphrased Harman, "The appraisal of United States experts regarding the facility was wrong. The size was not 100 to 300 megawatts, but rather 24 megawatts."

The ambassador seemed to have been well briefed by Israeli atomic experts, as he added: "The structure observed in the photographs was only a water tower, this was a water-cooled and not an air-cooled reactor."

But the secretary of state and other U.S. officials at the meeting were equally well informed, grilling the Israeli with questions, such as "whether the rating of the reactor was 24 megawatts thermal or 24 megawatts electrical?" They explained that "in the latter case the size would be in the range of the U.S. estimate." They wanted to know "whether the reactor would include any power-generating facilities to draw off useful electrical power" and, above all, what about "plutonium safeguards?" Emphasizing the "concern that might be aroused if plutonium were known to be floating around loose," the Americans raised the possibility of "inspection by visiting scientist?"

The ambassador, evidently embarrassed, time and again said that he "would have to inquire," repeating the official Ben-Gurion line that "the purposes are the development of scientific knowledge for eventual industrial, agricultural, medical, and other scientific purposes" as "part of the general program of development of the Negev." The Americans, dissatisfied, pressed for more details.

Only decades later did it become apparent that Dimona, built on-site by hundreds of French engineers, had been part of the price that France paid for Israel's participation in the Suez conspiracy of 1956.

The nuclear and refugee issues stood at the center of Ben-Gurion's talks with Kennedy in May 1961—a meeting at New York's Waldorf-Astoria hotel. Ben-Gurion was on a fund-raising tour, but just as ten years earlier with Truman and fourteen months earlier with Eisenhower, he used the opportunity to meet the president.

"I was amazed at such a young boy," Ben-Gurion—known in Israel as the "Old Man"—later reminisced. "He was already about forty, but he looked twenty-five. I couldn't imagine that such a young boy would be elected for the presidency. Really, I didn't take it seriously."

Kennedy, on the other hand, was told by his advisors to be careful in dealing with the veteran Israeli leader. "He lacks suavity and is usually gruff though not unkind in manner," said a sketch of the seventy-four-year-old Ben-Gurion prepared by the CIA and the National Security Council. "In negotiation he can be excitable, determined, and even contemptuous," and since he "has a tendency to speak at length before allowing interruption (last year he spoke over an hour before President Eisenhower could speak), you may wish to make our [points] at the start of your meeting."

America's side of the conversation, said written suggestions from Secretary of State Dean Rusk, should stress "the unique close ties which bind our two countries together, which should

be a source of assurance to Israel," but also "the need for progress on the refugee question and our firm opposition to Israel's
developing a nuclear military capability."

Kennedy brought up his refugee and nuclear concerns, and
Ben-Gurion—while making no commitments—was willing to
talk about both at length, giving Kennedy the feeling that Israel
would listen. In return Ben-Gurion raised the question of Israel's need for weapons, and he asked for the Hawk antiaircraft
missiles already discussed with Eisenhower.

Now it was Kennedy's turn to be noncommittal, promising
only to consider the request, although he knew "Israel is seriously vulnerable to surprise air attack." As the meeting was
nearing its end, he may have felt that Ben-Gurion was disappointed. As the Israeli later recalled, "he stood up and took me
to a corner away from the people and said: 'You know I was
elected by the Jews. I have to do something for them.'

"I was shocked! I'm a foreigner. I represent a small state. I
didn't come to him as a Jew, as a voter. And he told me, 'You
know, I was elected by the Jews of New York. I will do something for you.' Then he went back and continued our conversation."

Ben-Gurion felt that "Kennedy's wish to bring about peace
and to secure at least a status quo" was not new, but "the
change which I felt was a new and different type of American. It
was not only youth. Eisenhower did not take a real deep interest in political questions at all."

The Israeli leader remembered being surprised when he met
a U.S. military commander who knew everything about Eisenhower's private talk with Ben-Gurion because the president
had told him during a card game. "I cannot imagine President
Kennedy sitting all evening and playing cards," Ben-Gurion
laughed. "This was the difference."

Yet it would take over a year for the prime minister to draw
his own lucky card. The good news was delivered in August

1962 by his "Jewish liaison," Myer (Mike) Feldman, for Kennedy was the first president with the concern and political instinct to have a full-time aide to maintain contact with the Jewish community.

Feldman, on a visit to Israel, told Ben-Gurion and his aide Teddy Kollek that five batteries of Hawks would now be sold. Israel would pay $21 million—a large arms package at the time, but of moderate proportions when compared with the many weapons sales to Israel in the decades to come. Kennedy thus became the first American president openly to sell arms to Israel.

It was only two months later that Kennedy faced his greatest crisis: the nuclear confrontation with the Soviets over their missiles in Cuba. Despite distractions of the Cold War and Vietnam—and perhaps because of them—his administration began to recognize Israel's strategic potential.

The president discussed the wider issues, in December, when he invited Golda Meir to the Kennedy family compound in Palm Beach, Florida. He chose not to see the Israeli foreign minister in Washington, so as to give the talks less of an official character. The talks went well, from Meir's point of view, with Kennedy speaking of a "partnership" between the United States and Israel—the first time a president used such language.

Moreover, he said America's "special relationship" with the Jewish state was comparable to U.S. links with Britain, adding that even without a formal treaty Israel was considered a "close and intimate ally."

The president repeated his insistence, however, that Israel could not be America's "exclusive friend" in the region. "If we pulled out of the Arab Middle East and maintained our ties only with Israel," Kennedy said, "this would not be in Israel's interest."

What did interest the Israelis most were American arms. In

April 1963 Ben-Gurion cabled to Kennedy: "Hawk is appreciated, but Government of Israel regrets that in light of new offensive weapons being prepared by Israel's neighbors, Hawk alone is not a deterrent." Ben-Gurion was not satisfied. He wanted tanks and airplanes. And he was beginning to feel that Israel's primary supplier, France, might not remain forever a reliable source. Ben-Gurion was thinking of the United States as Israel's future arms benefactor.

Despite Kennedy's basically friendly attitude toward Israel, the nuclear issue continued to bother him. American intelligence was increasingly certain that the supposedly peaceful atomic plant at Dimona, whose existence was reluctantly admitted by Ben-Gurion, was designed to make atomic bombs.

Ironically, it was not the only atomic reactor in the country, because President Eisenhower had given Israel its first—albeit a small, research plant—as part of his Atoms for Peace program in 1955. Eisenhower, optimistic about technology and its uses, used the special aid program as a Cold War weapon. He believed that if America provided small nations with reactors, they would use them for benign research and would be grateful to the United States. What Eisenhower had in mind was one thing; what the recipients did was another. Israel placed its American gift at Nahal Soreq, fifteen miles south of Tel Aviv, and used it to upgrade its nuclear know-how.

In the final weeks of the Eisenhower administration, the State Department was concerned whether the public "would clearly distinguish between the small U.S.-assisted reactor and the new reactor." A report to the embassy in Tel Avid said Israel had still not satisfied Washington with answers to key questions: "Is a third reactor in either the construction or planning stage? What are the Government of Israel (GOI) plans for disposing of plutonium which will be bred in the new reactor? Can Israel state categorically that it has no plans for producing nuclear weapons? Will GOI agree to adequate safeguards with respect to plutonium produced? Will GOI permit qualified scientists to visit new reactor? And if so, what would be earliest date?"

The United States had required regular visits to Nahal Soreq by UN inspectors from the International Atomic Energy Agency (the IAEA), checking that nuclear materials were not recycled for military uses. But Israel could live with the inspections, because the much larger Dimona facility was firmly under its own lock and key.

Now Kennedy's administration was demanding that Dimona be opened to inspection. Presidential envoy Feldman recalled that when he promised the Hawks would be delivered, he also got the Israelis to promise that they would permit the United States to inspect the Dimona plant.

However, Israel's policy of total secrecy included deceiving the United States. Abba Eban recalls that when a team of American inspectors arrived at Dimona, "it cost us a hell of a lot of money to arrange it so their inspectors wouldn't find out what was going on." False walls were erected, doorways and elevators were hidden, and dummy installations were built to show to the Americans, who found no evidence of the weapons program secreted underground.

The president was not going to drop the issue. The CIA's Office of National Estimates provided arguments, in early 1963, that Israeli nuclear weapons would make the Middle East more polarized and thus more dangerous. Israel, the report said, would rely on its nuclear strength to take a harder line on many issues, while Arabs would increasingly resent the West and turn toward Moscow.

Without revealing his source, Kennedy echoed the same line when he met in April 1963 with Shimon Peres—Ben-Gurion's loyal aide in the defense ministry. Despite the usual protocol of dealing with officials at their own level, the president canceled a meeting with a congressman when he heard Peres was in town. The subject was atomic.

In his Oval Office, Kennedy turned to the Israeli and said: "You know that we follow with great interest any development of nuclear potential in the region. That would create a most dangerous situation. For that reason, we have been in close touch with your effort in the nuclear field. What can you tell me about that?"

Peres, taken aback, did not wish to reveal anything but also hoped to please the president. So he came up with a reply that would become Israel's official, ambiguous explanation. "We will not introduce nuclear weapons into the region," he told Kennedy. "We will not be the first to do so."

The United States was finally figuring out that Israel was not interested in atoms merely for peace, despite its refusal to reveal anything. Ben-Gurion had made the fateful decision to acquire nuclear capability, but it was thought best not to tell anyone: not the Israeli people, not friends in America, and not enemies in the Arab world. Unguarded rhetoric might trigger an arms race with unthinkably disastrous consequences.

The Middle East remained fairly quiet during Kennedy's term, and the seeds planted by Israel for better relations could not blossom because an assassin's bullets on November 22, 1963, in Dallas tragically brought unexpected change in the White House.

Israel's leadership also changed hands in 1963: a nonviolent change, yet also traumatic because Ben-Gurion—who had resigned from office for a while in the 1950s—was now genuinely retiring. One of the state's founding fathers was brought down by dissenting factions within his Labor movement.

The movement chose the finance minister, Levi Eshkol, to take over from Ben-Gurion. Relations with America, as always, loomed large over other policy points on the new government's agenda, but Eshkol seemed to have little in common with the new U.S. president, Lyndon B. Johnson. Eshkol could hardly be more east European, and there was no reason to hope he would get along especially well with President Johnson, whose roots were so plainly in America's Southwest.

There was, however, the significant advantage that Johnson, although having few Jewish constituents in his home state of Texas, was close to factions in the national Democratic party that had many Jews in them. They were liberals who strongly supported his plans for racial desegregation and other social reforms. Organized labor was comfortable with both L.B.J. and Israel, and the unions encouraged their connection. The AIPAC lobby's director, Si Kenen, had known Johnson well as Senate majority leader and described him as "front-rank, pro-Israeli."

The explanation can be found in Christian dogma. The president's grandfather, a devout fundamentalist, had taught young Lyndon the evangelical doctrines. Christ's Second Coming would follow the return of the Jews to their ancient homeland; Jerusalem must be their capital; and Johnson could achieve grace by helping the Jews.

This he did, as a young congressman during World War II, fighting insensitive American bureaucrats to bring hundreds of Jewish refugees from Nazi-occupied Europe to Texas. The survivors were in awe of him. One of his first acts as president, newly sworn-in, was to dedicate a synagogue in Austin. There, Lady Bird Johnson recalled, "Person after person plucked at my sleeve and said, 'I wouldn't be here today if it weren't for him. He helped get me out.'" Johnson's good deeds were appreciated by the Jewish community at large, which took it for granted that he was pro-Israeli.

The personal factor at the top was very helpful to U.S.-Israel relations. Johnson liked to take stock in person of the people with whom he was dealing, and he and Eshkol found a common language. While Ben-Gurion had met with Presidents Truman,

Eisenhower, and Kennedy, those had all been during unofficial "private visits." In June 1964 Eshkol became the first, truly invited Israeli prime minister to enjoy the official hospitality of the White House and the U.S. government. The talks focused primarily on Israel's military requests, as have most of the summits since.

Johnson and Eshkol were the first American president and Israeli prime minister to establish personal rapport. Not every such pairing has had that advantage; but when there, a good relationship between two leaders has helped protect and promote the alliance.

Israelis appreciated a gesture by Johnson in August 1966, when Zalman Shazar was welcomed in Washington on the first official state visit by an Israeli president. The post is merely ceremonial, yet the two heads of state did discuss Israel's request to purchase warplanes from the United States.

Over his entire five years in office, Johnson enjoyed the company of Eppy Evron, the former envoy to the labor unions and now the minister—or number-two official—in Israel's Washington embassy. How the soft-spoken diplomat and the compulsively loquacious president got along so well is simply a mystery of personal chemistry. There was cordiality, but little warmth, between the president and Ambassador Avraham Harman. So it was Harman's nominal deputy who became the strong man of the embassy. After all, anyone who has entrée to the White House is likely to be a more effective envoy.

Evron managed to establish the closest friendship a diplomat for a small country has ever forged with an American president. On a purely social visit—with his family—to the L.B.J. Ranch in Texas, Evron even had the dubious distinction of finding himself stuck in a ditch with Johnson. The president was driving Evron around in his Jeep, and while talking rather than paying attention Johnson slipped off the road into the gully.

The two men laughed about it, while the Secret Service rushed to get a tractor and fish them out.

"The atmosphere of the relations, from the start of the 1960s, was wonderful," recalls Kollek. A man much experienced at using personal contacts in the United States, he appreciates the change that was taking place under both Kennedy and Johnson. "A great openness was created in the relations between the two countries, through human and personal encounters."

On a larger scale, it was discernible in parts of the tiny, relatively poor Jewish state that a process of Americanization had begun. Israel's political and fashion trends have tended to run in tandem. As soon as the country became independent, it was the British style that still dominated systems of government, justice, and education. English was the only foreign language taught at school, and London was seen as the center of the world.

In the late 1950s, as it became obvious that France was Israel's chief arms supplier and diplomatic backer, Israelis fell in love with French music, food, and films. French was added to the school curriculum. But when the diplomatic honeymoon with Paris cooled, Israelis abruptly halted their francophile cultural affinity.

As political relations with the United States improved, Israelis became far more interested in America. At first, money and military assistance were more welcome than Hollywood movies, hamburgers, baseball, or the general trappings of consumerism. Members of Israel's elite still believed, even as they toned down their socialism in the 1960s, that everything European was superior. But Israelis were gradually embracing the allures of the world's most successful capitalist society.

Especially helpful in promoting the cultural convergence between the two societies was the Hollywood connection first made by Kollek through his gangster friends. Israelis became so adored that even Marilyn Monroe hastened to be in their company. As early as May 1956, an Israeli soccer team was invited to a packed Yankee Stadium in New York to celebrate the country's eighth birthday. Monroe's arrival was flamboyant, in an open car with John F. Kennedy—then a senator starting to run for president. Providing contrast in the car was Abba Eban, the very image of restrained diplomacy. Years later, Eban could not forget that Kennedy had remarked: "While both of us have great assets, hers are more visible."

Movie stars, television producers, writers, and journalists became frequent visitors to Israel, with enough mutual admiration for everyone to enjoy. American performers and celebrities fell in love with the young and vibrant country, its pioneering spirit, its ideals, and the determination of its people—combined with the easygoing atmosphere of an open society that artists always prefer.

Israel was happy to be portrayed as the most impressive country on earth. Actors—whether Jews, such as Kirk Douglas and Danny Kaye, or Gentiles such as Frank Sinatra and Sophia Loren—visited the Holy Land, shot movies, and had a great time. Kollek took care of their every need. The army took them on special tours and happily loaned military equipment and soldiers as "extras" when the movie cameras were rolling.

When they returned to Hollywood, the celebrities could usually be counted on to appear at fund-raising events for Israel or the many Jewish charities.

Strengthening the bond, they were tremendously popular in Israel. Just as actors and singers love to have an autographed photograph of themselves with the Israeli prime minister on their wall, successive prime ministers have felt the same way. Sinatra visited Ben-Gurion and was received lavishly, with no less pomp than visiting heads of state. Even after leaving office, Ben-Gurion was considered one of the world's great statesmen of the century. His peerless image lifted Israel's to mammoth proportions, a magnetic mother lode for celebrities.

Israel cooperated fully in the filming of *Cast a Giant Shadow*, knowing that Kirk Douglas's portrayal of Mickey Marcus—the American Jewish colonel who died an Israeli general—would create a legend. Sinatra costarred in the movie, which showed Israel as a cause worth dying for.

Kollek's memoirs describe driving from Jerusalem to Tel Aviv with the liquor for a party with his friends. "Kirk cooked an excellent meal, and Yul [Brynner] supplied the cigars. It was a jovial occasion, and we all got a little drunk."

But the biggest parties, as recalled by Kollek, surrounded the shooting in 1960 of *Exodus*, the huge movie based on the Leon Uris novel that had already tugged on the emotional heartstrings of readers in dozens of countries.

"It has been the fulfilling experience of my life as a writer," Uris recalls. "I was just plain pissed off about the Holocaust, and I wanted to hurl that in the face of the Christian world. And when I went to Israel, I saw I had a lightning story in my hands. So I wanted to use it to light a fire under the Jews, to tell them we were better than the other Jewish writers would have you believe with all their self-pitying writing that made 'Jewish mother' a dirty name."

The film version would reach hundreds of millions more with the basic message: Jews who survived the horrors of Nazism had now fought for survival in Israel and richly deserved their sovereign state.

Starring Paul Newman and, literally, a cast of thousands, the movie was fabulous public relations. The world saw the Newman character, Ari Ben-Canaan, as the embodiment of Israel: a tough fighter, farmer, and patriot, but also a sentimental lover.

Exodus and the other films and books of that period were a double-edged sword, however, because in building a myth, they raised expectations beyond all proportions. The image of

Israeli as superhero was mostly in the eye of the beholder, but it led to disappointment when the real-life stars of the Middle East drama failed to live up to their mythic reputations.

Paul Newman had loved Israel in the belief that the aspirations of American liberals were being fulfilled there, but was turned off when he read headlines suggesting Israel's fight against the Arabs was not as pure as its official line had professed. "Later, he wrote me a letter filled with disappointment," Kollek recalled. "He felt we have betrayed our own ideas."

Through most of the 1960s, however, Israel was the darling of American public opinion. This was the result not only of personal rapport among leaders or the box-office appeal of Tel Aviv's beaches. In the real politics of international affairs, the Middle East continued to make few waves in Washington. Johnson was devoting even more energy than Kennedy to a new battle against a Soviet surrogate: the rapidly escalating war against the Communists in Vietnam.

When little attention was paid to the Middle East and the tiny sparks of hope for a negotiated settlement there, the United States and Israel got along better. In the Johnson years, America was not trying to please or appease the Arabs to draw them into peace talks; nor was Israel being pressed to make concessions on the refugee issue that had vexed the Truman, Eisenhower, and Kennedy administrations.

The Cold War, meanwhile, became more acute, prompting nations throughout the world to identify with either one major bloc or the other. The most important Arab countries, notably Egypt, flocked to the Soviet-sponsored camp; so the United States felt it comfortable—indeed, almost imperative—to welcome Israel into the Western fold.

American aid to the Jewish state increased dramatically during the Johnson presidency. It totaled only $40 million in the 1964 fiscal year, the last budgeted by Kennedy. In fiscal 1965 the aid jumped 75 percent to $71 million, and it soared again to $130 million the following year.

Israel was then in a severe economic recession and sorely needed the money. So few jobs were being created that many Israelis—especially young, productive citizens—left the country. The search for employment often took them to the United States, marking the first massive movement of people from Israel to the United States, in the opposite direction from the fervent hopes of Zionist activists. By 1966 tens of thousands of Israelis had moved to America, and they and their children would at times serve as human bridges between the two nations.

The precise composition of U.S. aid was changing, too. Eisenhower and Kennedy had given only development loans and deliveries of surplus food. When Kennedy did sell the Hawk missiles, Israel had to come up with the cash to pay for them. Johnson, however, was the first president to permit the use of American aid money to pay for U.S. weapons purchased by Israel. American Jewish fund raising would not have been sufficient to pay for the security-related shopping spree approved by Johnson. In 1965, 20 percent of U.S. aid was military; while in 1966, the military proportion was over 70 percent.

Since one measure of friendship is the delivery of weapons—especially to a country in a constant state of war—it should be remembered that Truman, however friendly in tone, maintained an arms embargo; Eisenhower only rarely succumbed to pressure to help Israel keep an eye on Soviet spies and submarines; and Kennedy sold only defensive systems.

It was Johnson who broke new ground, lifting the military side of U.S.-Israeli friendship to new heights. He agreed in 1965 to sell offensive systems such as 250 M-48 tanks and then, even more important, attack aircraft.

Abba Eban, promoted to foreign minister in January 1966, set out on an around-the-world tour to promote Israel's diplomatic interests. His old stomping ground, Washington, was a key stop. Working with Evron, he brought personal persuasion to bear on President Johnson and Secretary of State Rusk, winning a contract to purchase forty-eight Skyhawk bombers.

This was, of course, not merely the result of Eban and Evron having winning personalities. The political background had included sometimes bitter discussions between U.S. and Israeli officials over Johnson's plans to deliver arms to conservative Arab nations such as Jordan. Prime Minister Eshkol resorted to what would become standard practice for Israel: calling on Jewish lobbyists in America to try and block the sales. If they could not succeed, then he insisted on receiving more arms than Jordan.

As part of the bargaining, Johnson's emissaries told Israel that it could expect higher levels of military aid if it would persuade the American Jewish lobby to stop protesting sales to moderate Arabs—to "put these matters into proper perspective," as the State Department put it, because "this was an essential part of our relationship" with the Arabs.

Calling the Skyhawk sale to Israel "a deliberate exception," the State Department also suggested to the president: "We have no intention of becoming Israel's principal supplier of arms."

The final decision, however, was Johnson's, and he seemed attracted by the notion that—by supplying modern bombers—he was supplanting France as Israel's favorite weapons wholesaler. This had always been Israel's goal, and now its defense dream was coming true.

The Johnson administration was divided, however, on the ramifications of the Skyhawk sale. One group feared that it would give the Israelis a delivery system for nuclear bombs. Officials of this school said the United States should at least demand that Israel sign the nuclear Non-Proliferation Treaty, which Israel refused and still declines to sign.

The other school embraced two classes of thought: One, including the CIA's master of the Israeli account, James Angleton, did not care about Dimona and the nuclear program, or even looked the other way.

The other class believed that the best way to slow the Israelis' nuclear ambitions was to keep them militarily happy. "If Israel is unable to obtain its valid conventional arms requirements," a State Department briefing paper said, "those in Israel who advocate acquisition of nuclear weapons will find a much more fertile environment for their views."

This appeared to reflect an agreement by Eshkol to trim spending on the Dimona atomic facility in exchange for the unprecedented increase in U.S. weapons sales. Eshkol, as a former finance minister, had feared anyway that the nuclear program could bankrupt his country.

No government documents are available to prove a specific agreement to scale down the nuclear program, but there is circumstantial evidence. On May 18, 1966, Eshkol amplified the policy formulation that Shimon Peres had said privately to President Kennedy three years earlier. Eshkol declared from the K'nesset rostrum that Israel "would not be the first to introduce atomic weapons in the region." This remains official policy, despite the worldwide assumption by the 1980s that the Dimona project had produced two hundred nuclear warheads.

On May 19 the Eshkol government announced that it was purchasing the Skyhawks, using military sales credits offered by the United States. The deal's value exceeded the cumulative total of all American arms previously supplied to Israel.

Johnson offered yet another sweetener—quite literally: assistance in developing a system to "use nuclear energy to turn salt water into fresh water." A joint U.S.-Israeli Seawater Desalination Project was established, with the goal of generating electricity in the same process. Engineers and technicians from two Israeli agencies, the Electricity Company and the

Atomic Energy Commission, flew to California and Pennsylvania for training in a technique originally developed in Oak Ridge, Tennessee. Senator Albert Gore, Sr., was a major proponent of the project on the American side, and his son—as senator and vice president—would continue the family line of support for Israel. Studies were conducted at a small model plant constructed in Ashdod, twenty-five miles south of Tel Aviv on the Mediterranean coast.

It is surprising that the United States, while applying pressure on Israel to give up its military options in the nuclear field, was supplying Israel with sophisticated nuclear technology. But it seemed obvious that Israeli scientists were hard at work in the nuclear field, so the best America could hope for was to divert that to energy and desalination projects—rather than producing nuclear bombs.

It took a few years for the United States to realize that its diversionary effort had failed. Israel's nuclear scientists may have slowed their work on weapons, but they did not stop. The small reactor at Nahal Soreq, provided by Eisenhower, and the new research facility at Ashdod had the effect of giving Israelis more hands-on experience in the nuclear field. The desalination project proved uneconomic and was shut down.

While the United States tried to contain the Israeli nuclear program, containing the Soviets was considered even more essential—especially when President Johnson was sinking deeper into the mud of Vietnam. Tiny Israel tried to demonstrate that it could help, that its contribution to the Western cause could be more important than Arab oil. Luckily for them, Israeli intelligence agents secured a bonanza for the West at a perfect time.

The Mossad lured an Iraqi air force pilot into defecting with his MiG-21, flying to an Israeli base in August 1966. The plot was complicated, and the bribery expensive. But the Israelis knew that the United States would be interested. The fighter plane contained the most modern Soviet aeronautics, of the type that U.S. pilots might confront over Vietnam, Europe, or wherever East-West conflict might develop.

Pentagon experts enjoyed examining it, and the Johnson administration was as elated as Eisenhower's had been a decade earlier when Israel provided the secret Khrushchev speech.

The intelligence channel between the United States and Israel would continue to be unknown to the public, but insiders recognized what an important role it played in a sharp crisis in the spring of 1967. U.S. attention was forced back onto the Middle East when Egypt's President Nasser broke the 1957 post-Suez agreements, marched his soldiers back into Sinai, and threatened Israel.

Because the United States had its foreign-policy mind almost solely on Vietnam, the crisis fell like a bombshell on Washington. There were many causes: Nasser's gamble that Egypt and its partners could defeat Israel; his delusion that the United States would let that happen; and the Soviet Union's desire to stir up trouble. The Soviets apparently calculated that Washington would be too busy with Vietnam to respond effectively; and however the crisis or war in the Middle East might turn out, it was likely to increase Moscow's influence.

Moscow sent Cairo false intelligence reports on an alleged military buildup in Israel, saying it posed a threat to Syria. Nasser concluded that the time had come to unite Egypt and Syria in a campaign against "Zionist aggressors." He ordered UN observers to leave the Sinai, sent his own army into the peninsula, and a few days later closed the Strait of Tiran to Israeli shipping—thus erasing all of Israel's gains from the 1956 Suez war.

At the starting point of the crisis, on May 15, 1967, the Eshkol government mobilized reserve soldiers—publicly charging that Nasser had committed an act of war by attempting to strangle Israel. Eshkol hesitated, however, to attack the Egyptian forces, because the traumatic 1956 Suez rift with the United States was still so fresh in Israeli minds, more than a decade later.

For the first time Israel had a first step to take before ordering its forces into battle: coordination with America. Eppy Evron, in the Washington embassy, was assigned the task of explaining his country's predicament to the Johnson administration; and Eban was sent there to help press the case on May 26.

They met the president and Secretary of State Rusk and demanded that they fulfill the U.S. commitments outlined in the aide-mémoire that John Foster Dulles had handed to Eban in February 1957. At first the Americans did not understand what the Israelis were talking about. Johnson and his top aides did not know about the letter, and when the Israelis displayed a copy of it, U.S. officials searched their files but could not find the original. The president sent an advisor to ask Eisenhower what he remembered about any promises.

"Administration officials promised that they would honor their commitment, but they never asked us what that commitment was," Evron recalls. "To us it was clear that the Americans were required to break the naval blockade on Eilat."

But Vietnam did have a restraining effect, because Johnson did not wish to risk congressional and public wrath by sending even more U.S. forces into harm's way in yet another part of the world.

At the height of dramatic, often blunt negotiations—with the Israeli envoys expressing concern for their nation's very existence—they suggested something new: a formal defense treaty with the United States. Israel's military chief of staff, General Yitzhak Rabin, sent the idea to Washington so that the United States would be forced into a decision: either concrete action, or leaving Israel free to act on its own.

President Johnson was not interested in codifying an official alliance, but he did order that Israel be helped with the cost of maintaining its reserve forces on alert. General mobilization was bringing the Israeli economy to a halt, and there was a fear of fiscal collapse within days. To Johnson, as long as the Israelis did not attack, the United States would pay the bills to keep their army as a deterrent.

The Americans were not quite binding Jerusalem's hands, as they would in 1991, but what were the Israelis to make of the sentence that Johnson carefully read to Eban from a card prepared by his aides: "Israel will not be alone unless it decides to go alone"?

The United States had still not learned that Israelis prefer to hear exactly what their interlocutor is thinking—rather than enigmatic sentences—but the message seemed to mean this: Wait for the Egyptians to attack, and if they do you'll beat Nasser, with our help if necessary.

When Eban returned to Jerusalem, reporting no breakthrough at his Washington talks, Eshkol and his cabinet were faced with a tough decision. "Now it was clear to us that the Americans would not do anything to break the blockade," Evron recalls: "Johnson tried to organize an international naval force, but it didn't work. He also sent letters and envoys to Cairo to persuade President Nasser to reduce the tension by returning to the status quo ante, but in vain. We knew that, in the end, we would have to shatter the blockade ourselves."

Still, despite domestic political pressures and his generals itching for a preemptive strike on Egypt, Eshkol was reluctant to attack so long as the United States stood in opposition.

But the Israeli prime minister was also unwilling to live much longer with Nasser's noose around his nation's neck. The Israelis decided to have one last go at persuading Johnson that they had no choice but to fight.

Eshkol searched for an alternative to the usual channels of ambassadors—even foreign ministers. In the prime minister's view, Eban had failed to bring a clear reading of the American president's attitude. Eshkol felt cornered by events: the Egyptians on the border; the Israeli public panicking; the economy collapsing; the newspapers infected with jingoism; and his army demanding action; yet not knowing what the United States would and would not support.

Israel now activated the two best assets it had managed to establish over the preceding two decades in the United States: influential Jews and the intelligence lobby.

The hectic deliberations in Jerusalem were contrasted by the tranquility of the United States during a long Memorial Day weekend. The president left Washington on May 27, to spend a four-day holiday at his Texas ranch, entertaining friends. To help him prepare for a Democratic party fund-raiser in New York the following week, his guests included party contributors and activists who happened to be Jewish. Even better for Israel's cause, none of Johnson's advisors on foreign policy was there.

An old friend of the president who also did not trust his advisors—especially Secretary of State Rusk—was Supreme Court justice Abe Fortas. Appointed by Johnson and fiercely loyal to him, on one hand, but also a supporter of Israel and Jewish causes, he stepped forward as an intermediary between Israeli diplomats in Washington and the president. Fortas gave Israel one more route for figuring out Johnson's attitude.

Whether through Fortas or the friends at the L.B.J. Ranch, the arguments by Israelis and American Jews did not have to be more sophisticated than reminding the president of the Holocaust, saying that Jews can never again allow themselves to be defeated, and portraying Nasser as a bully who only understands force.

Johnson had been pro-Israeli as a senator, and his true colors—somewhat grayed by three and a half years in the White House—now shone through. In the course of a long weekend, he changed his mind.

The first to feel the change was Meir Amit, the Mossad chief, sent to Washington on May 30 for one last test of American intentions. He traveled under a false name, hoping to hear the truth about what U.S. defense and intelligence chiefs could tolerate, if not support.

Amit had separate meetings with his CIA counterpart Richard Helms, with the agency's James Angleton, and with Defense Secretary Robert McNamara. Amit now reveals that during his talks with McNamara, the defense secretary was speaking with Johnson on the telephone. That encouraged Amit to believe that whatever McNamara said, he was voicing the president's wishes. And McNamara was not pressing Israel to restrain itself from military action. What a difference a week made, to the astute.

The Mossad chief was perceptive enough to pick up the nuances, perhaps more so than Eban, who as a professional diplomat always searched for the precise and correct words. Amit had long had a cooperative relationship with the CIA; its director, Helms, had been understanding of Israel's needs; and—as Amit recalls—"Just like Helms, so was McNamara now. He told the president that Israel could do the job itself."

Amit and Evron could tell that Johnson had ordered a change of signals. Evron recounts: "From a red light, opposing war, we understood that the light had changed to yellow," meaning Israel could proceed with caution. "The Americans didn't give us a green light to go to war, but they signaled to us that they would not repeat what the Eisenhower administration had done in 1957" in forcing the Israelis to give up their war gains.

"On June 3, at seven o'clock in the morning, I saw McNamara and gave him a list of military equipment—including tanks and planes—that we needed urgently. McNamara looked at the list and said, with a smile, 'Even if we decide to give you these, we won't get a chance to deliver because the war will already be over.' "

That day, Evron adds, "I received a letter from Rusk to Eshkol which said, 'We were happy to exchange views with General Amit.'

"To me," he concludes, "what McNamara said—plus the letter from Rusk—constituted the yellow light."

Amit rushed back to Israel and on June 4 delivered a report to the cabinet sharply different from Eban's the previous week. The United States, the Mossad chief said, would at least tolerate an Israeli attack.

Amit also reported on the intelligence assistance he received in Washington: Helms and the CIA had given him aerial photographs taken by U.S. reconnaissance planes, transcriptions of coded messages deciphered by the National Security Agency, and evaluations of the movements, traffic communications, and planning of the Arab armies.

Both aspects—the intelligence package and the yellow light starting to appear greenish—helped convince the cabinet to vote for a preemptive strike on Egypt, Jordan, and Syria, the campaign that in six days would give Israel new frontiers and new problems.

Johnson wrote in his memoirs, "I have never concealed my regret that Israel decided to move when it did." Whether that is precisely true, he certainly preferred that there be no Middle East war. But when Israel seemed to have no alternative but to fight, he undeniably wanted America's friends to defeat Moscow's clients.

The president had every reason to be confident, because he had read several U.S. intelligence reports that stated—point blank—that Israel was strong enough to defeat the combined Arab armies in ten days or less. One of the reports had come from the CIA station chief in Tel Aviv, an American spy the Israelis welcomed into their midst.

CHAPTER SEVEN

I SPY

Even when a war seems about to begin, a CIA operative can treat himself to a relaxing lunch, and the Agency's station chief in Tel Aviv was contentedly munching on his usual Danish lox on toast. As always, the smoked salmon was sliced one-sixteenth-inch thin, with a wedge of lemon and a little caviar at the side.

It was noon on Sunday, June 4, 1967, and even though John Hadden's job was to know everything, he could not know that the very next morning would mark the beginning of the war that in six days would transform the political, military, and demographic map of the Middle East.

He did know that war was certain. Sitting in the cool shade of the Samuel Hotel bar, sipping his daily martini, the lanky, fair-haired forty-year-old with the cover job at the U.S. Embassy had told his headquarters what to expect. Now it was up to the Israelis or the Arabs to choose the time.

If the Israelis struck first, as was likely, they would win in a few days. If the Arabs attacked, highly doubtful with Nasser choosing to squeeze Israel into bankruptcy, then it would take the Jewish state a week or more to win.

Hadden had even joked to Washington that if Egypt's air force tried to raid Tel Aviv, the island of Cyprus had better be careful because the Egyptians were equally likely to go two hundred miles off-course and bomb Larnaca.

With all the political intelligence to be gathered and written up—reporting, for instance, that the Israelis seemed honestly to expect six thousand casualties—Hadden had to keep lunch short. There was less than the usual kibitzing with the bartender, David Horn, a Polish Jew who always had great stories to tell about the early 1950s, when he worked at a hotel where American diplomats had the entire second floor, the Soviets had the third, and the bar was an amazing meeting place for the spooks of East and West.

As usual, the bartender was dressed in a neatly pressed light-blue shirt and tasteful tie. If Horn was not an informant for the Israelis, Hadden felt, they were missing the opportunity to use a great eavesdropper. If he was, then he would probably be reporting that the American had been too busy for a long, lingering lunch.

Hadden had to assume that everyone knew who he was. It was the only assumption to make in a small and talkative nation, even if he did not go around with a sign around his neck that said "CIA station chief."

Certainly the Israelis who really mattered knew who he was. This was not like being posted in Communist Prague or East Berlin, where you would remain undercover although it would still be prudent to assume people knew who you were. In Tel Aviv, Hadden's job was primarily to liaise with the top people in the Mossad: to maintain a constant dialogue and, when appropriate, to coordinate the formal exchange of data.

Hadden remembers a diplomatic dinner at a private Israeli home in 1963, his first year as head of the Tel Aviv station, when he was placed across from Colonel David Carmon, the number-two man in Israeli military intelligence. Hadden had just begun taking private lessons in Hebrew, and he overheard the hostess murmuring something to Carmon about hoping the American would drink too much and then talk too much.

Should the CIA man tell Israeli intelligence that he understands Hebrew? And how to embarrass them politely? Hadden turned to Carmon with a smile and said: *"Nichnas yayin, yotzeh sod!"* which is Hebrew for "Wine goes in, a secret comes out!" He enjoyed the wonderful look of horror on the colonel's face. The next day Carmon ordered everyone in the military intelligence agency—known in Hebrew as Aman, but the CIA insisted on referring to it by its American equivalent, G-2—not to speak Hebrew around Hadden. Intelligence officials with a sense of humor had jokingly Hebraized his name, John Hadden, into "Yochanan Ha-Dan."

During the spring 1967 crisis, he expected to be in Israel another year or so and was already thinking of the advice to give his successor. Learn Hebrew, for one thing. Your professional peers will be afraid of you, but ordinary Israelis will speak more freely. And that is what matters for intelligence men.

He would also warn the newcomer not to be like the other U.S. Embassy diplomats, who fell quickly into one of two camps: those who adored Israelis and their country, and those who couldn't stand them. "No matter what you really feel, you're going to get absolutely nowhere unless you're one of their friends," he recalls. "You are going to be worthless to the United States government if you don't reserve some part of your brain to be friendly and share their interests. When you're in Hamburg, you sail. When you're in Austria, you ski. When you're in Israel, you dig."

Hadden would, in fact, tell his successor to take up archaeology, to buy a shovel and a book by Josephus, the Jewish-born Roman historian. Hadden observed that Israelis are obsessed with their past, and the history of the country is buried in the soil. "Josephus is really interesting. Really. Here's this renegade Jew, this Jew who betrayed his race and his nation as almost no other Jew has ever done. He becomes a general in the opposing army. It would be just as though Arik Sharon went to Baghdad and became a general in the Iraqi army—whereupon the Iraqi army destroys the Third Temple and he starts writing books about the Jews."

Digging, in the literal sense of sifting dirt, had already led the CIA station chief to an extraordinary fortnight of private conversations with the great icon of modern Israel, David Ben-Gurion. This stroke of luck for American intelligence came in 1965, when Hadden's wife was working on a dig—with some other "embassy wives" who had taken up archaeology as a hobby—at an ancient Jewish site near the Dead Sea. It was a Friday night, and John Hadden drove the three hours from Tel Aviv to visit.

By coincidence or not, this was a perfect pretext for him to take the road most traveled by American spies in Israel—the route past Dimona. Israeli officials knew that U.S. diplomats, especially military attachés, were taking every opportunity to snap a few quick photographs of the nuclear reactor there, also occasionally taking a sample of the surrounding soil for radioactive analysis.

While sitting around the campfire Mrs. Hadden began to suffer severe stomach pain, and Hadden decided to rush her to Beersheba, still known as "Abraham's town" in honor of the Hebrew patriarch and now the largest city in the Negev Desert. He headed for the home of an Israeli newspaperman with whom he often had long chats. The man insisted that Mrs. Hadden go right to bed in his home, while he fetched a doctor—

fortunately trained in San Antonio with "American English better than mine," Hadden says.

In how many countries would a CIA man feel comfortable hospitalizing his wife in a remote desert town? But not only did Mrs. Hadden undergo surgery that removed part of her colon; there was the extra bonus of the lady sharing the semiprivate hospital room with her. It was none other than Paula Ben-Gurion, wife of Israel's retired first prime minister.

Ordinarily the Agency station chief would be too busy to drive to Beersheba every day, even to visit his wife; but he did, because David Ben-Gurion showed up every afternoon too. The spy and the legendary politician spent hours chatting over the fourteen days that their wives were roommates.

While Paula Ben-Gurion, who was a former nurse from Brooklyn, hastened her own recovery by "Jewish-mothering" Mrs. Hadden, the two men spoke about Zionism, about the fascinating characters who had founded the state, and about the United States with the kind of relaxed frankness that filled in some of the gaps in Hadden's education about Israel.

"Imagine two weeks with Churchill!" he enthuses. "And that's what it was like!"

While he could not promise his successor equally lucky and insightful coincidences, Hadden would tell the new man that this was a "dead-end job" for a career builder. The Tel Aviv station was "fascinating," but any American intelligence officer who worked there would be destroying his chances of ever being sent to an Arab country.

Despite the ups and downs of U.S.-Israel relations, there was surprisingly little to do—at least in the intelligence field, in Hadden's view, because "Washington was interested only in fighting the Russians." The few Soviet spies in Israel were "completely bottled up by Israeli counterintelligence."

So a newcomer should prepare to stay here a long time, Hadden would suggest, learn a lot, and have some fun. It takes years to build up all the contacts really to understand the country, he would say with a grin, and "it's going to take you more than two years for the Israelis to realize that you're not working for Saudi intelligence."

Getting Israelis to chat is pretty much the same as persuading any foreigner to talk, Hadden says. But Israeli intelligence is suspicious. "The Mossad and G-2 aren't going to treat you as an ally, even if you do get some Israelis to accept you as part of the family." This is not an allied country like Britain, he believed, nor is it an enemy zone like East Germany. This place is something else, unique unto itself.

Hadden, a man of contradictions, is clearly fond of Israel and its people and fascinated by their past. Yet as a professional, emotionless intelligence operative, he believes only in interests. Nearly everyone on both sides may say the United States and Israel are "friends," but Hadden believes it is nothing like true, old friends who "played together and went to school together."

Perhaps more harshly, Hadden notes that he had great respect for three statesmen—George Marshall, James Forrestal, and Dean Acheson—who were all convinced that America's greatest diplomatic mistake was recognizing the State of Israel. Harry Truman, however, had been influenced by "one of his old army buddies," Eddie Jacobson, "so he cried," as Hadden puts it. "Harry cried, everybody cried, and Israel was recognized."

But Truman still refused to send any weapons, so the Israelis had plotted and worked to change U.S. policy. Hadden had no criticism of that. "They were at war, so they can't be blamed for doing anything. You can only blame the other side for going along."

Hadden had long ago been critical of the Israelis for their machinations in October 1956. He believes that when Israel invaded Egypt and took America's "eye off the ball," it made the Soviets believe they could get away with invading Hungary. At the time he was a CIA operative, based in Germany since 1945, and aware of east European operations.

He had already gotten used to the idea of Jews who were rough and tough. When, like other American servicemen at the end of World War II, Hadden saw Holocaust survivors, he judged Jews to be the cleverest in the Displaced Persons camps at smuggling goods and smuggling themselves to Mediterranean ports to sail to Palestine.

Still, when the CIA transferred him to Israel in 1963, Hadden prided himself on arriving as a "totally blank sheet."

By 1967 one of the tricks he had learned in Israel was that he could predict, in his political and military observations to headquarters, a crisis or dramatic blow-up every year; and in one form or another, events would prove him correct. There would always be some guerrilla raid or Israeli retaliation to boost tension, and Washington would think him a genius.

The Economics Section in the embassy, on the other hand, should have learned the opposite: not to predict crises. Its reports in 1948 began by saying, as Hadden recalls them, "The state of the Israeli economy is such that it cannot survive. By any known measure, given the figures for imports, exports, and GNP, you see that they cannot survive. Financially, they are going to go under in the next twelve months."

The first year went by, and nothing happened. The Economics Section said, "They got through '48, but they won't get through '49." Forty-nine went by, and Israel survived. The same thing happened in 1950.

By 1954 or '55, the embassy's economists caught on and started predicting—every year—an economic "miracle" that Israel was going to survive, in spite of every indicator being against it. That miracle, of course, became an annual event.

Hadden had also learned from watching the wild, roller-

coaster rides during formal government-to-government meetings to exchange intelligence. These liaison meetings had
begun after Ben-Gurion's 1951 meeting with CIA chief Bedell
Smith, but to Hadden they never made for a relaxed workday.

With a "cooperative country," such as the West Germans
with whom he had dealt for over a decade, their negotiators
would come to the table bearing their secrets like cards held to
their chests. The two sides would take turns, each playing a card
by turning over some information, until finally the Americans
got most of what they wanted and the Germans got most of
what they wanted. If each side felt that it got more than the
other guy, then the intelligence-sharing session went well.

But sessions with the Israelis were "crazed," according to
Hadden. They would come in, "stiff-necked and clutching their
files." Instead of offering some data, "they would stage a para-
chute drop twenty miles behind our lines"—in the form of a
forty-five-minute diatribe on all the terrible challenges to Israel's security, listing all the intelligence and military material
they needed for their survival.

"Christ! There you were in your chair," Hadden recalls,
"and they were shouting way over behind you! Absolutely
outrageous! They were asking for the goddamned moon!"

The station chief felt he had learned how to deal with it. As
advisor to Angleton and other high-level negotiators, he would
tell them to listen respectfully, paying very close attention and
taking careful notes. Then the Americans would speak for
forty-five minutes without interruption. When the Israelis
tried to cut in, the trick was to say "Wait! You had your 45
minutes. . . ." It showed seriousness, he thought, because—in a
Russian style that Israel's leadership generally adopted—if you
don't speak for three-quarters of an hour, you clearly don't
have much to talk about.

The only proviso was that the U.S. monologue would *not*
deal with the points raised by the Israelis. The Americans,

whether from the CIA or other agencies, would ignore everything the Mossad or Israel had just said. And the Americans would do their best to be just as "outrageous"—making demands and landing twenty miles behind their lines. Then the two sides could approach back-to-back toward a point where they would reach an agreement, rather than front to front as with other exchanges with allies.

It was a unique style of interchange, and a lot of U.S. officials had trouble with it. Some were speechless with rage, but Hadden says he could barely contain his laughter. "Just hold on to your hat," he would advise his colleagues, "and take the ride!"

The station chief was not overly impressed by Israel's efforts to become more Americanized in the 1960s. He found that Israel often behaved like "a People's Republic encased in bureaucracy, centralized and authoritarian." Any Israeli who did not belong to the ruling Labor party had little say in local or national affairs.

This made Hadden somewhat skeptical about Israel's claim to be the only democracy in the Middle East. Also, the kibbutz members who were prominent in the nation's institutions were the kind of ideologues who had maps of the world on their wall that showed the socialist world in red—and included Israel.

But the American spy could not help but admire the Israeli intelligence community, which was small and efficient. Israel had the advantage of loyal citizens who had been born and raised in dozens of foreign countries, who had what Hadden calls "the fund of languages that is the sine qua non for any intelligence work." Mossad headquarters "always had someone in there who can listen to a tape from any part of the world and understand it," while the CIA might have to play a recording to an exotic outsider to get a translation—and then never know where the secret was going next.

His admiration for Israeli intelligence reached its peak in the crisis of 1967. He knew that the Israelis would win because of their superior knowledge of Arab society and military structures, but he also advised them not to rush into battle. Hadden told his Israeli counterparts: "The President of the United States is a very important friend to have. Give him a chance! Wait for three weeks! Have him in your pocket!"

Israeli intelligence, like the military, was running out of patience from the beginning of the crisis and did not see the benefit in looking good in Johnson's eyes. One Israeli official used a Hebrew-Russian word in responding to Hadden: "But that is just *kosmetika!*"

"Yes," Hadden lectured the Israelis, noticing the cultural divide on the importance of how a nation's actions appear on the global stage. "For you guys cosmetic appearances aren't important, but in our world, that's image and it's all-important."

Israel did not need U.S. help to win the war, anyway. "It was a piece of cake," Hadden says. "It was all over by 10:30 A.M. on the first day, when Israel destroyed Egypt's air force. That was the only card the Arabs held."

One of the few surprises, as the Israelis moved toward victory on three fronts in six days, was their attack on the *Liberty*, a U.S. Navy spy vessel off the coast of Egypt, on the fourth day of the war. Israeli warplanes and ships bombed, strafed, and torpedoed the electronic surveillance ship, killing thirty-four Americans and wounding many more.

"It became clear that it was a complete and total error," Hadden recalls. His contacts with senior Israelis showed that they were "terribly embarrassed that by moving too fast, the air force had gone and bombed the ship—as though racing its own navy—assuming it was an Egyptian ship without really looking."

If the Israelis had really wanted to eliminate an American spy ship, he says, it would have been easy for them to paint their planes and boats with Egyptian markings and blame Egypt. As for the lingering suspicions, mainly among U.S.

Navy personnel, that Israel's attack was deliberate so that America could not monitor a ground offensive onto Syria's Golan Heights, Hadden responds: "That's ridiculous. What's a U.S. ship near Egypt going to find out from there?"

Israel paid over $100 million in compensation to the dead sailors' families, and the top officials of both nations put the *Liberty* incident behind them. "This is small potatoes, no matter what exactly happened," Hadden said with his hard realism. "This isn't the real heart of our national interest, so let's move on."

CHAPTER EIGHT

APOCALYPSE NEVER

AIPAC, the pro-Israel lobby in Washington, had never had it so good. Just three weeks earlier, when the Middle East crisis began in May 1967, AIPAC had been broke. Its director Si Kenen had to pay for letters, telephone calls, and telegrams to government officials, politicians, and commentators out of his own pocket. But by the time that Israeli forces were in command of the entire Sinai, the West Bank of the Jordan, all of Jerusalem, and the Golan Heights, AIPAC's bank accounts were suddenly healthy and would never again be in the red. New supporters, moved by events, were for the first time convinced of the importance of lobbying for the Jewish state and were sending in fat checks.

More important, American Jewry opened its hearts and purses to Israel itself. In two weeks Jews in the United States made emergency contributions amounting to more than $100 million—almost double the amount typically raised in an entire year—by far the biggest fund-raising campaign for Israel.

There was an instant transformation from the paralyzing fear that the vulnerable Jewish state was being strangled to absolute euphoria at the totality of its military triumph.

America's relief that Israel was not destroyed—for that is how baldly the crisis was put in the prewar media—translated to joy from coast to coast. The Israeli victory also won the country a new generation of activists in the United States.

"It was the Six-Day War that made me a Zionist," recalls Seymour Reich, a New York lawyer who would become one of the leaders of the American Jewish community. Although he was very active in the social action organization B'nai B'rith, "I hadn't been formally affiliated with any Zionist movement. But Israel's survival seemed to be at stake in the days before the war, and afterward I saw a march through Times Square of people carrying an Israeli flag, and onlookers throwing coins and bills into the center of the flag."

Reich was touched and redirected his time and efforts to active lobbying for Israel. Yet the same scenes that electrified him and an entire generation of American Jews depressed Edward Said.

Said, a Palestinian professor in New York, will never forget the pro-Israeli streets of Manhattan in June of 1967. "One could sense the feeling of elation in the air."

It was not a feeling that Said shared. His people had just been defeated by Israel once again. Yet he could not deny that all around him, "People waved to each other and raised their fingers in the V sign for victory." He recalls "how one could overhear complete strangers proudly telling each other, 'Well well well, look at how we beat them!'

"What amazed me was the fact that the emotions were shared not only by Jews, which could have been understandable, but by non-Jews as well. For me as an Arab, it was a humiliating experience." Now a professor of literature at Columbia University, Said shifts uncomfortably in his chair as he pinpoints the Six-Day War as the lowest point for the Arabs and the clear zenith for Israelis and their Jewish supporters in the United States.

Even as the mood of Israelis and Jews soared rapidly from low to high, the Arabs suffered the opposite psychological slide. In the Middle East, Arab leaders had persuaded their publics that the war was an opportunity to avenge the defeats of 1948 and 1956 by destroying Israel. The masses were summoned to the streets of the major Arab capitals, where they chanted slogans such as "In blood and fire we will redeem you, O Palestine!"

Israeli movie theaters showed newsreels of the Arab rallies before the main feature attraction—and the audience knew this was not to be a fictional Shootout at the O.K. Corral with bogus bullet holes. The Arab crowds were crowing about liberating Palestine and driving the Jews into the Mediterranean. The fanatics in the films would close their hands around their throats—a gesture with symbolic meaning well understood by the Israeli public.

When their government and the United States seemed unable to provide any solution, the Israelis' sense of security and self-confidence became fragile. Despite having long managed to relegate Holocaust memories to the back of their minds, they were again thinking of Auschwitz. The Arabs were perceived as the new Nazis who were seeking to destroy the Jewish people, as if finishing off what the Germans had begun. Many Israelis saw themselves as the reincarnation of eastern Europe's ghetto dwellers, wiped off the face of the earth.

The sudden lack of Israeli confidence had spread to American Jews. At hundreds of emergency meetings to raise cash to help Israel, organizers preached the apocalyptic possibility that the Jewish state's very existence was in peril. The CIA's assessment that Israel would have an easy time defeating all of its Arab neighbors was, after all, a secret.

When the Israeli troops did win, therefore, American Jews felt they were witnessing a modern-day miracle. The warm glow of divine redemption illuminated Jewish communities, reflecting the beacon of triumph lit by Israel's army. Defense Minister Moshe Dayan's eyepatch became a symbol of courage and triumph.

Thanks to Dayan and the other war heroes, Jews all around the world felt a new pride. At the various celebrations of the six-day victory, they marveled at how Jews were not only doctors and accountants. They were now warriors, fierce and daring in the defense of their land.

For some in America, the line between fiction and fact began to blur. The *Exodus* factor had created the enjoyable image of brave and bold Israeli pioneers, and now genuine heroes had stepped out of the pages of books and off the movie screen.

For many American Jews, at all levels of society, the Israeli victory provided a window for understanding their roots. It was a kind of internal revival for the eminent writer Henry Roth. Born in 1905 among his fellow Jews in the Lower East Side of New York, the young Roth moved to heterogeneous Harlem. Had the family stayed in the Lower East Side, "I'm sure I would have been a lot happier," says Roth, in his late eighties. "I might have been a rabbi—who knows?"

Instead, the stimulation of a mixed community led him in 1934 to write *Call It Sleep*, a lively account of immigrant life in New York City at the turn of the century. He innovatively had his colorful characters speaking in a combination of street slang, high-brow English, and Yiddish prose, creating one of the best novels on early Jewish life in America.

But Roth then suffered writer's block for over sixty years, struggling to produce another novel. His creative energies were diverted by politics, as he became a Communist and did his best to forget Judaism. "I thought I was writing a proletarian novel," he recalls.

Still blocked in 1967 Roth realized that he could not escape his past. The outbreak of the Six-Day War and the mortal danger to Israel made it deeply uncomfortable for him to maintain his allegiance to the worldwide Communist movement—which echoed Moscow in unequivocal support for the Arab side. "I felt a great deal of dread," he said. "I felt as if I were personally under attack." From that point, Roth began "heading back to being a Jew."

"I found myself identifying intensely with the Israelis in their military feats, which repudiated all the anti-Jewish accusations we had been living with in the Diaspora," Roth added. "I had the need for us to be warriors.

"I adopted my ex post facto native land. Suddenly I had a place in the world and an origin. An intellectual excitement seized hold of me that forced me to set down what was going through my mind, to record my thoughts about Israel and my new reservations about the Soviet Union.

"Strangely enough this dead author may be going through a resurrection. I started writing again in the summer of 1967."

Like Roth, many Jews had long felt strange about the crossroads faced, decades earlier, by their grandparents or great-grandparents in eastern Europe. Until Israel's soldiers performed their historical rewrite on the battlefield, it had seemed that the families choosing America were enjoying health and wealth; those staying in Europe had mistakenly opted for death; while those who had gone to Palestine had chosen—at best—a difficult and dangerous life. Many Jews sensed that the Israeli Army had now redeemed the suffering of an entire people.

"I remember my father listening to the radio with great emotion during the June crisis," says Steven Hartov, then a fourteen-year-old in Connecticut and now an Israeli-American writer in New York. "Especially engraved in my mind is a broadcast from Jerusalem, describing how Israeli paratroops conquered the Old City and the Wailing Wall. That radio broadcast was a turning point in my life. From that moment, I paid attention to what was happening in the Middle East."

Hartov's was a fairly typical American, middle-class Jewish family. His mother was Austrian and got out of Nazi-ruled Vienna on the last train to Holland in 1938, when she was thirteen. From the Netherlands, her family sailed to America. "My mother was one of the few lucky ones who obtained a visa to enter the U.S. Most of her relatives died in the Nazi death camps."

His father was born in America to parents from Hungary who were Conservative Jews, but more religiously observant than most. "My grandparents went to synagogue every day, and my grandfather always wore a *yarmulke*. My parents were less religious. They didn't keep kosher and went to temple only on the holidays."

Young Hartov did go to a Jewish Sunday school, but there was little talk of Israel or Zionism. "What impressed me more were my mother's stories about the Holocaust."

Suddenly, with the Middle East crisis of 1967, the concept of Israel meshed with fears of a new Holocaust. "The nearly obsessive listening of my father to the radio during the Six-Day War, together with the same story in all the major magazines and newspapers, triggered me.

"As a kid, I was brought up with the notion that a Jew must be strong, but I hadn't found anyone like that in America. Reading about Israel and the war made me realize that I might find it there."

All through high school, Hartov recalls, he continued hearing the siren call of the Jewish state. "I had an uncle who visited Israel right after the war, and he came back with fascinating stories. I swallowed every word I heard or read about Israel. I bought every book. I searched out Israelis in America and got friendly with them. But it wasn't enough. I wanted to sense the real thing. I wanted to be there."

He made his move in the spring of 1973. "I was twenty and in the middle of college. One day I tell my parents, 'I'm going to Israel.' They were in shock and tried to stop me. In the end, they gave in. My father said, 'Okay, do what you want, but with your own money.'"

Hartov did not have the cash, so to fulfill his Zionist dream he became a merchant seaman and sailed to South America. From there it was on to Italy, and by then he had saved some money and told the captain that he wished to leave. Permission was denied, so Hartov jumped ship and flew to Tel Aviv.

Two weeks after he arrived on a kibbutz, the Yom Kippur war broke out, and the anxieties surrounding the conflict had the greatest emotional impact on Hartov, finally "pushing me over from casual tourist to future citizen."

He spent a year traveling all over Israel and then returned to Boston University. After graduation in 1976 he went back to Israel, and this time it was *aliyah*.

The word, in Hebrew, literally means "going up," but *aliyah* is known to Jews as the process of moving to Israel. Those who make the ascent are greeted with great assent. On the other hand, Israelis who leave their country permanently are said to have committed *yeridah*, a "descent" heavily laden with disgrace.

Having made *aliyah*, complete with the instant citizenship offered by Israeli law to any Jew, his identification with Israel was so complete that he altered his identity. After changing his name from Schonberger to the Hebraic "Hartov," he joined the Israeli army.

"I wanted to be a paratrooper, a fighter, to be a strong Jew," he says. "Leon Uris's *Exodus* was my substitute for the Bible, and I suspect that those fantasies sustained many of us through the harsh realities of the initial stages of *aliyah*."

But Hartov adds that fact could clearly be distinguished from fiction after only a few weeks of the hardships that were basic training for the paratroops. "I distinctly remember coming home on leave to Jerusalem one weekend after a grueling eighty-kilometer forced march. My friend mentioned that Leon Uris was in town, working on another book. My response was 'If I had the strength, I'd go over there and kill him!'"

Hartov's transformation from Connecticut schoolboy to Israeli soldier is emblematic of the change in an entire generation of American Jews. The Six-Day War was, for them, an earthquake that shook their sense of identity out into the open. Young Americans did not have firsthand knowledge of Nazi atrocities or the survivors' struggle to establish a Jewish state. Until 1967 being Jewish, affluent, and American did not seem to have a lot to do with Israel.

Now they had shared a shock. They were no longer simply the children or grandchildren of Jews who had made the fateful decision to seek new lives in America. The drama was no longer a relic of generations past, because in 1967 they saw their parents' old fears resurface, and they all were cheering a great victory. This was their first experience of collective identity.

It was easy to get swept up in the long history of the Jewish people. First, it was interesting. But it also felt right. Israel seemed clean and pure—a young nation fighting for its life against evil enemies and long odds.

For young Jews, most of them liberal in their political outlook, Israel's perceived purity was wonderful when compared with the bogus motives and brutal militarism of America's quagmire in Vietnam. Many of the student-age liberals rejected materialism, at least in their rhetoric, and Israel's idealism stood in praiseworthy contrast.

On a more practical level, the Jewish state offered refuge from the icy winds of the draft. Rather than be summoned to serve in the Vietnam War, Jews had an open invitation to pick oranges on a kibbutz or just to relax on the beaches of the Mediterranean and Red seas. Thousands of young Jews came to Israel—some, like Hartov, joining Israel's army no matter what they thought about Vietnam.

In addition, largely because of all the good press Israel was getting worldwide after the Six-Day War, tens of thousands of non-Jews came on long visits from dozens of countries. Sun, sea, sex, and often hashish combined to make Israel a magnet for the curious and the adventurous. A tiny country, formerly almost ignored by the peripatetic hip, was suddenly the place to be.

The popular love affair with Israel could hardly be ignored by the American administration. True, when the war broke out and there were public doubts that Israel would win, AIPAC's director found some legislators hard to pin down, and they did not even return his calls. But after victory was clear, "Representatives and senators who had been evasive," Si Kenen recalled, "were now staunchly pro-Israel."

Everyone loves to identify with an underdog hero, and the concept appeals even to rigid bureaucrats. But U.S. interests are not defined merely on sympathy and emotion, and the fact is that Israel's swift victory—even if fully expected by the CIA—changed political and strategic perceptions in Washington.

Key American interests in the Middle East were immutable: ensuring the flow of Arab oil to Western allies; blocking Soviet attempts to gain new allies that might offer warm-water ports to its fleet; and avoiding crises that might entangle U.S. troops in the region. But the pursuit of interests had to change with circumstances.

Pre-1967 policy declarations tended to focus on "security" and "stability," but Washington policy makers were not actually doing much about it in the Middle East. There was the occasional foray by a peace envoy, and there were some relatively small arms sales from time to time. But American leaders usually thought they could and should be even-handed, and this usually led them throwing up their hands in disgust at their inability to broker peace between Israel and the Arabs.

The 1967 war transformed the game rules. U.S. interests remained the same, but there was a significant change among Israel's supporters: Few, if any, would ever again fear the destruction of the state. The excellence of its armed forces and the buffer of added territory now suggested that the apocalypse would never occur. Israel was the smallest country in the region, but at age nineteen it had emerged as the strongest military power and had proved that its place in the Middle East was permanent.

The Johnson administration reacted by embarking on a new path: on one hand, more direct and active diplomatic involvement aimed at bringing peace; and, on the other hand, more military support for Israel.

The first indication that priorities had changed—and that the United States would not, as in 1957, force the Israelis to surrender the land they had captured—came on June 19, only one week after the end of the war. President Johnson delivered a speech in Washington enunciating basic principles for solving the Arab-Israeli conflict. He said that Israel must give up territory, "but there must also be recognized rights of national life, progress in solving the refugee problem, freedom of maritime passage, limitation of the arms race, and respect for political independence and territorial integrity."

The next, more significant indication came in the United Nations, where a Jewish U.S. ambassador, Arthur Goldberg, repulsed Arab and Soviet diplomatic assaults on Israel. Having helped forge the connection between American unions and the Jewish state as a senior lawyer for organized labor, Goldberg had risen to the bench of the Supreme Court. Johnson then persuaded him to resign as a justice, and Goldberg found that as ambassador to the UN he could integrate his love of the United States with his affection and concern for his fellow Jews.

Hoping to help grant Israel peace but always watching out for its safety, Goldberg was one of the architects of the famous Resolution 242 of the UN Security Council. Adopted in November 1967, it called for Israeli withdrawal from occupied land—without specifying if it meant all the territories—in return for peace agreements and Arab recognition of Israel's right to live within secure and recognized boundaries.

Resolution 242 still stands as the basic charter for Middle East peace efforts and the launching pad for cease-fires and accords that would temper the regional conflict.

While Israeli officials were initially dissatisfied with the UN resolution, they eventually concluded that they had scored an achievement by avoiding a call by the world organization for an immediate withdrawal.

When the Eshkol government passed messages, through U.S. diplomats, offering to return almost all the captured land in exchange for comprehensive peace agreements, the humiliated Arab leaders rejected all compromises. In Khartoum, Sudan, in August 1967, they declared their famous "three nos": no peace, no recognition, and no negotiation with Israel.

The Israelis also tried secret diplomacy, with Eban and other officials meeting several times with Jordan's King Hussein. Israel offered to give up most of the West Bank, but Hussein wanted every inch of land. The United States was kept informed, and President Johnson told Eban: "You can try your best, but my feeling is he won't settle for just 73 percent. But go ahead and try."

The refusal of the Arabs to compromise only fortified the U.S.-Israel alliance. Israel's government felt free to "create facts on the ground," in the euphemistic phrase of many Israeli officials, and after annexing Arab East Jerusalem, they began building Jewish settlements in the West Bank, Gaza Strip,

Golan Heights, and Sinai peninsula. The United States made its opposition clear from the start, but Washington's stand on settlements was like the old joke about the weather: There was plenty of talk, but no one did anything about it.

Finding no other hook on which to hang a political and military strategy in the Middle East, the Johnson administration threw in its strategic lot with Israel. In January 1968, when Eshkol flew to the United States for his second visit—considered a victory tour by the large delegation of officials and journalists accompanying him—the president extended a friendly invitation to the L.B.J. Ranch.

"The president wanted the meeting to take place in a relaxed atmosphere," Israeli diplomat Evron recalls, "so we showed up without ties and jackets." Johnson took his honored guest on a private tour of the cattle ranch, this time staying on the road, and Eshkol—who as finance minister had worked closely with Israeli farmers—was impressed by the spacious fields of truly Texan proportions.

What also impressed Eshkol was the president's large chair, complete with remote-control buttons. The Israeli leader took the liberty of sitting down and relaxing, but when it was pointed out that this was Johnson's place, Eshkol said: "So what? It's very comfortable."

Also underlining the casual atmosphere was Eshkol's method of eating oranges. He took a big bite, tearing off the peel with his teeth. Johnson seemed a little surprised, but then picked up another orange and did the same. The large entourage of Israelis and Americans laughed.

The rural summit was not, however, designed primarily for atmospherics and scenery. The two leaders got to the heart of the U.S.-Israel alliance: military and political cooperation. Rather than talk in generalities, the Israelis preferred to make a specific request: fifty F-4 Phantom jets, then considered the state of the art of fighter-bombers. These, combined with the

Skyhawks previously sold by the Johnson administration, would mean a qualitative leap forward for Israel's military. Almost fully weaned off of French supplies, Israel's air force would begin a close and valuable association with the U.S. Air Force.

The president expressed concern about the Middle East arms race, but fully blamed the massive Soviet resupply to Egypt and Syria. In the end-of-summit declaration, Johnson said he would "keep Israel's military defense capability under active and sympathetic examination." Privately he ordered that the fifty warplanes be built for Israel.

The Pentagon and the State Department opposed the sale, so Johnson hesitated—even after personal political stakes were eliminated by his surprise announcement in March 1968 that, with the divisive Vietnam War escalating, he would not be running for reelection that year.

Pro-Israel lobbyists persuaded both presidential candidates, their warm friend Vice President Humphrey and the cooler former Vice President Nixon, to speak out in favor of the Phantom sale. But the effort focused on the lobby's most effective channel: Congress.

Surprisingly, AIPAC's tactics were challenged by, of all people, the envoy of the country the lobby was trying to help. Yitzhak Rabin, the former army chief of staff, had just taken over as Israeli ambassador to Washington, and he decided that he knew better. First, the House approved an amendment that would require President Johnson to sell at least fifty Phantom jets to Israel. Rabin was very pleased.

But AIPAC director Kenen advised Rabin that the language would not hold up. The House amendment would have to be rewritten as a "sense of Congress" resolution—basically, a recommendation to the president—because no one could order the White House to do anything. Rabin "refused to believe us,"

Kenen recalled. It was "the first of my many differences with him."

Johnson, meanwhile, continued to have differences with his own bureaucrats over aid to Israel. Some of his senior advisors insisted that Jerusalem be forced to sign the nuclear Non-Proliferation Treaty. Other administration officials expressed concern that the Phantoms would enable Israel to use the nuclear bombs the state was assumed to have. The aircraft sale, they argued, would send a signal that America had no objection to Israel's nuclear program.

However, Johnson was inspired by his Christian roots and moved by Jewish lobbyists' reminders of the Holocaust. He stuck to what he considered his promise to Eshkol. In a preelection farewell chat with Foreign Minister Eban, the president asked him to tell the prime minister that "Lyndon B. Johnson has kept his word." In announcing the sale of the Phantoms, he referred to the congressional resolution—the rewritten product of AIPAC's quiet but energetic lobbying. It would become a pattern for presidents to pretend that Congress was forcing them to do what they intended to do anyway.

CHAPTER NINE

UNIMPEACHABLE TIES

As he completed his third week as president, Richard M. Nixon summoned Max Fisher—the nation's foremost Republican Jew, at least as measured by the amount of money he had managed to raise: nearly 10 percent of the $36.5 million Republican campaign war chest of 1968. "It was February 9, 1969, and he called me into the Oval Office," Fisher recalls. "I had told him before the election that I did not want a cabinet post, so now he told me, 'Max, I'm making you my advisor on the Middle East and Jewish affairs.' "

Fisher, who knew very well that William Rogers was secretary of state and Henry Kissinger was national security advisor, told the president that he could happily live without a title. "One thing about us Jews, we don't have any popes," he said to Nixon. "No top man. But I'll be happy to be one of your advisors."

His first official mission came less than three weeks later, as part of a four-man delegation representing the United States at the Jerusalem funeral of Prime Minister Levi Eshkol. Labor party leaders selected Golda Meir as his successor. In Israel and America, questions arose as to how the changes at the top—in both capitals—would affect relations.

Above all were the doubts about Nixon's track record and personality. On the campaign trail in 1968, Nixon became the first presidential candidate to stress that the Jewish state must have arms superiority. "Israel must possess sufficient military power to deter an attack," Nixon declared. "Sufficient power means the balance must be tipped in Israel's favor."

American Jews and Israelis were not, on the whole, persuaded by Nixon's campaign rhetoric. Both groups had created a rapport with Democratic administrations over the past eight years and now feared a return to the fits and starts of the 1950s. "We assumed," Abba Eban says, "that he would continue Dwight Eisenhower's reserved attitude to Israel."

Many Americans had heard rumors that Nixon was anti-Semitic, and indeed the White House tapes released as a result of Watergate would eventually confirm the rumors. "Nixon shared many of the prejudices of the uprooted California lower-middle class from which he had come," wrote Kissinger, who was surely in a position to know. "He believed that Jews formed a powerful cohesive group in American society, that they put the interests of Israel above everything else, that their control of the media made them dangerous adversaries."

On election day in November 1968, fewer than one out of five Jews voted for the Republican, while four out of five voted for Humphrey.

Kissinger, in his memoirs, portrays himself as Nixon's antithesis when it came to Jews. "My own starting point was at the opposite end of the emotional spectrum," he wrote. "Though not practicing my religion, I could never forget that thirteen members of my family had died in Nazi concentration camps. I had no stomach for encouraging another Holocaust by well-intentioned policies that might get out of control."

But Kissinger's attitudes were suspect, in the eyes of Israeli and American Jews. He tried to dispel the distrust by telling Jewish leaders that he went to his elderly parents' Passover Seder banquet and even asked the traditional Four Questions. "Of course I read Hebrew," Kissinger boasted. "With the vowels, I read pretty well."

Still, Israelis saw him as a "detached Jew," their standard phrase to describe someone who shows no enthusiasm about the Jewish state.

Both Kissinger and Nixon—despite their or anyone's claims about emotions—were motivated, above all, by the *realpolitik* of the Cold War and power politics. Of the president, Eban recalls: "Throughout his term of office, I rarely heard him say a sentimental word about our country and its cause, and his utterances about Jews in America were rarely free from irascibility. But whenever Israel's security was at issue or in hazard he would supply our needs.

"And the Nixon Doctrine added up to this: If you get people—such as Israelis—who are willing to defend themselves without American troops, that's a blessing so help them do it!"

Perhaps the only Israeli with an emotional hold on Nixon and Kissinger was the new prime minister, Golda Meir. She certainly had no linguistic obstacle, having been a teacher in Milwaukee in her youth. Born in the czarist Russian Empire, she had witnessed a pogrom against the Jews of her town. Her family brought her to America, where she became a socialist Zionist. After moving to prestate Israel, she often spoke about the need for Jewish security.

When she took office in 1969, many Israelis still felt like political orphans because of Ben-Gurion's death six years earlier. With Meir's installation, the orphaned Israelis could find comfort from their loss of a "big daddy" in the "strong mommy" who was now their leader. Israeli and American Jews seemed to melt in her presence, as she reminded them of the archetypical Jewish mother.

As the prime minister known universally as "Golda," she radiated simplicity, toughness, and determination. Nixon remembers her "extreme toughness and extreme warmth." Kissinger describes her as "shrewd, earthy, elemental."

Meir's personal chemistry with the two Americans, added to their *realpolitik*, had an immediate impact on the most sensitive and secretive issue between their countries: Israel's nuclear program. Nixon and Kissinger shared a contempt for the 1968 Non-Proliferation Treaty and issued a National Security Decision Memorandum, stating that "there should be no efforts by the United States government to pressure other nations" to sign the treaty.

As a further illustration of Kissinger's apparent support for Israel's nuclear monopoly in the Middle East, Eban recalls a meeting he had as early as 1963 with the then professor. "He asked me, 'Are you making atomic weapons?' And I said, 'No.' He said, 'I don't believe you, and if it's true that you're not, you'd be crazy.'"

During Golda Meir's first visit to the White House in September 1969, Nixon is said to have surprised her by asking "Tell me, do you have any toys?"

She did not understand, but he persisted. "Military toys? I'm talking nuclear."

Finally understanding that he was gently probing about Israel's secret arsenal, Meir replied, "No, Mr. President."

"Well, if you do, you'd better be careful." It was as much concern as Nixon ever expressed about a nuclear Israel.

In fact, Nixon and Kissinger were so little concerned that they stopped the inspections of the atomic plant at Dimona. This was a sharp deviation from previous U.S. administrations, especially Kennedy's, with its insistence that the nuclear program be stopped. The new White House team had apparently concluded that an unquestionably strong Israel would be good for American interests: pushing the Arab states to negotiate peace by dispelling their dreams that they could, with Soviet assistance, wipe out the Jewish state.

More light-heartedly, when a reporter asked Meir whether Israel would ever use nuclear bombs, she got a laugh by responding: "I thought we hadn't done so badly with conventional weapons!"

At that first summit and in other visits, the Israeli prime minister pressed for concrete evidence of improved relations: more fighter-bombers and low-interest loans. She herself called it her "shopping list."

She kept asking for more Phantom and Skyhawk jets, at one point writing to Nixon: "It is true that our pilots are very good, but they can be good only when they have planes." The president was reluctant, out of concern that Arab states would not reestablish diplomatic relations with the United States.

Israel's friends in Washington, including Max Fisher, sought out all the administration's pressure points. Fisher recalls that when he asked Kissinger to help get the warplanes, the national security advisor backed off, saying Nixon had told him to butt out of Arab-Israeli affairs—in part because of his religion.

The lobbyists were realizing that even when U.S. relations with Israel were clearly rising to a higher plane, there were endless complications. As in other periods, they learned how to play one faction of the administration off against the other. When Kissinger's national security avenue was closed and the State Department was dismissed as even-handed, friends of Israel turned to an unusual channel that should have had nothing to do with foreign affairs or arms sales: the attorney general.

John Mitchell, Nixon's political confidant who would later be at the center of the Watergate scandal, was approached by

Fisher and agreed to help. Attorney General Mitchell would argue this case, for Israel. "We had a situation where Henry Kissinger, who was Jewish, was on the National Security Council, and the secretary of state, Bill Rogers, was a little mixed up in his perception of the Middle East," Mitchell recalled. "And so, we handled things like the Phantoms outside of the State Department and the NSC." Israel got its planes.

Mixed up or not, Rogers was in charge of Middle East policy, and he surprised Israel in December 1969 by announcing a new peace initiative for the region. Golda Meir had thought, based on her meeting three months earlier with Nixon, that his policies were quite favorable. But now the "Rogers Plan" contained the kind of language Israel had not heard since the Six-Day War: a call for near-total withdrawal and peace agreements with the Arabs that did not quite constitute the full treaties demanded by Israel.

Meir's government complained through every possible forum. The prime minister herself took the trouble to write to Max Fisher, believing he could influence Nixon. "We are passing through difficult days," she wrote, and then sent "emissaries" carrying intelligence reports showing how the Rogers Plan would undermine Israel's security.

Fisher went into action, as if to prove that he was not merely the "court Jew" to Nixon, as some Democrat-leaning Jews were whispering in Meir's ear. His years of political generosity seemed to pay off, when Nixon authorized him to tell the Israelis—in private—that he would never impose the Rogers Plan on them.

The plan eventually was dropped, but it did have some positive effects: While publicly on the table, it gave Israel and Egypt something to talk about, and the process helped end the War of Attrition between them. Shortly after the Six-Day War, fighting had broken out between Israeli and Egyptian armies separated by only the few hundred yards' width of the Suez Canal. It grew into almost nonstop artillery exchanges, hit-and-run attacks, and aerial dogfights.

The undeclared but bloody war led to a much closer connection between the military and intelligence complexes of the United States and Israel. Egypt's army and air force were bolstered by Soviet advisors, so it was no problem for America to choose sides.

The small staff of the hitherto unnoticed Israeli "defense purchasing mission" in New York moved to a bigger office, and its staff was tripled. Israeli army officers, salesmen, and purchasing agents were roaming the United States from Texas to Michigan, and from New Jersey to California, to visit defense facilities and industries.

Still, the first encounters were marked by suspicion and mistrust. To many American companies, the Israelis were no different from the other Middle Eastern customers.

"The Americans we were dealing with at that time," says an Israeli general who was involved in establishing the contacts, "had a very bad experience with the Arabs and the Iranians. They were bribing them and entertaining them lavishly in order to ensure the best contracts. For these American executives, we Israelis were the same.

"I remember a senior executive from a leading defense contractor in Texas who was dealing with Iran, Saudi Arabia, and now with us. He was telling me that his company would rebuild my house in Tel Aviv.

"I said, 'This is a bribe!' And he said, 'No, this is a loan.' I exploded and immediately told him, 'Don't dare treat us this way! We are different!' " It would take American-Israeli defense deals another fifteen or twenty years for things to change—when the first moral cracks appeared, with deep chasms of fraud and kickbacks.

The American and Israeli partners in military and intelligence projects did overcome their cultural gaps. Driven by Israel's needs during the War of Attrition, which Nixon's administration understood, the two sides extended their cooperation. On top of the established Mossad-CIA link, now Israel's military agency—Aman—forged new ties with American counterparts.

The most significant link was between Aman's Unit 8200 and America's ultra-secret National Security Agency. Both organizations are in charge of bugging telephones, eavesdropping on radio transmissions, breaking codes, and other electronic spying. To acquire the most information it could on the Egyptian forces across the Suez and on Israel's Syrian enemies in the north, Unit 8200 set up powerful electronic listening posts in the occupied Sinai and Golan Heights.

Most of the equipment, including electronic countermeasures against missiles and planes, was purchased in the United States. Israel, for its part, had very good coverage of the Arab world and provided the NSA and CIA with audio tapes and transcripts of some of its discoveries relevant to American interests in the region. Israel even managed to intercept conversations between King Hussein of Jordan and the U.S. ambassador to Amman, Thomas Pickering, who would later be posted to Tel Aviv. To impress the Americans, Israel sent a copy of this intercept to the NSA.

Israeli intelligence experts went to the United States for training with specialized equipment, while NSA and American military experts went to Israel to study the huge haul of Soviet-made equipment and armaments captured during the Six-Day War and the War of Attrition.

The most spectacular catch, for Israeli and U.S. intelligence cooperation, was Israel's capture of the newest Soviet radar installation—until then unknown in the West. In September 1969 Israeli commandoes made a daring assault on an Egyptian post across the Gulf of Suez and stole the radar. It was airlifted by Israeli helicopters, disassembled, and then flown to the United States for further study. The same radars were in use by North Vietnam, and the knowledge gained helped the Americans improve their tactics in the Vietnam War.

A further step in proving Israel's strategic importance to U.S. interests in the region came in September 1970, one month after Egypt and Israel signed a cease-fire mediated by Secretary of State Rogers. Now there was trouble in Jordan, where King Hussein declared a war against the Palestinian guerrillas who had created a state of their own in his kingdom and were threatening his throne. Syria, which supported the Palestinians, invaded Jordan with an armored column of 250 tanks heading south to Amman.

Nixon and Kissinger were concerned that if Hussein fell, Jordan would become a pro-Soviet stronghold. In relations that were perceived as a zero-sum game, they could not allow the Soviets to score such a gain. Thus they decided to defend the king. But with the war in Southeast Asia ever escalating, America was not about to send its own troops.

The White House team considered the Israelis the only efficient, reliable force that could be trusted to fulfill the American mission. Kissinger—who by now had outmaneuvered Rogers as the chief foreign policy architect—was ordered by Nixon to contact the Israelis. Using Ambassador Rabin as his central conduit, Kissinger said the United States would look favorably on Israeli attacks against the Syrian tanks.

Prime Minister Meir happened to be in the United States on a fund-raising visit for Israel Bonds, and she consulted with cabinet colleagues in Jerusalem by telephone. The strategic picture was clear, if unexpected: The United States was offering the opportunity of checking a power drive by Syria, Israel's enemy, with a pledge to fend off any Soviet intervention and to replace any lost planes or materiel.

The decision may have been easy, but still, by responding in the affirmative, Israel scored a lot of points in Washington. Rabin delivered the reply to the White House, using a side door so as not to be seen when he arrived for a meeting with Kissinger and some Pentagon generals. With what the Israelis assumed to be Jordan's secret assent, Rabin and the Americans coordinated a military plan in case the Syrians advanced deeper into Jordan. It was a very detailed scheme, relying in part on U.S. intelligence, but Israel would have to do the dirty work. The Israelis agreed to conduct air strikes against the advancing Syrians, with a follow-up attack if necessary by their ground forces.

As it happened, the Syrians and their Soviet backers noticed that the Israelis were obviously gearing up for battle. Syria backed down.

After acting together against a Soviet-Egyptian alliance in the southwest and then to rescue the pro-Western king of Jordan in the east, U.S. and Israeli decision makers felt they were now walking in step. Seeing eye to eye more than ever, the two sides reached a new stage. Truman and Eisenhower had treated Israel, at best, as equal to the Arabs; Kennedy and Johnson moved forward with Israel as a friendly partner without many deeds to back it up.

Now Nixon and Kissinger sowed the seeds of a strategic alliance. They saw Israel as America's only reliable partner between western Europe and the Far East. A significant branch of the budding alliance was the financial reward. The United States increased its loans to Israel, for the purchase of American weapons, to ten times what they were before. In the three years after the Jordan crisis, the military credits totaled over $1.15 billion.

The Jordan crisis of September 1970 would be the last crisis to occupy the U.S. administration in the Middle East for three years. Washington would be too busy with issues more urgent for Americans: from détente with Moscow, through relations with China, and on to the Watergate break-in.

The only major headline from the Middle East was the death of Nasser, later that month. While little that seemed critical occurred in the region, Israel used the time to fortify its position in Washington.

Ambassador Rabin took something of a gamble with his highly controversial step of taking sides in the 1972 presidential race. There was no formal endorsement, which would have not only bent protocol but shattered it. However, Rabin told almost anyone who asked that Nixon's Democratic opponent, Senator George McGovern, would be a weak leader, while a reelected Nixon would keep America and Israel strong. He was reflecting the true feelings of Golda Meir and her cabinet, but this blunt intercession in U.S. domestic affairs led to embarrassment in Israel and annoyance among American Jews, who were mostly Democrats opposed to Nixon's Vietnam policies.

Rabin's intervention may have influenced Jewish voters, for Nixon's share of their vote doubled to around 40 percent. But most likely this growth reflected widespread appreciation for Nixon's tangible support for Israel set against McGovern's deficiencies.

On Capitol Hill, meanwhile, pro-Israel lobbyists were strengthening their fortress. Having identified congressmen and senators most positively disposed toward the Jewish state, they promised to do everything they could to ensure their favorite legislators' reelections.

But the foremost senator in their camp, Henry "Scoop" Jackson, performed minor miracles on Israel's behalf even though he was not Jewish and did not seem to need Jewish electoral support. Through six terms in the House and six terms in the Senate, the Democrat from Washington state consistently showed his support for Jewish and Israeli causes.

He rewrote legislation to make it easier for the U.S. government to give more to Israel. He also put sharp pressure on the administration to withhold trade favors from Moscow unless Soviet Jews were allowed to emigrate. By linking the welfare of Jews to East-West relations, Senator Jackson helped to insert another dimension into the U.S.-Israel alliance: a new, humanitarian cause that would commit future administrations. The issue of free emigration would add a human face to the already established political, military, and strategic reasons to stand together.

Israel would benefit doubly. Its small population would be increased, and its image would be lifted, especially among Third World countries, to myths suggesting that Washington is heavily influenced by the combined forces of American Jewry and Israeli leaders. This impression would help Israel make more friendships among east European, Asian, and African states.

When asked whether "the Jewish lobby" was taking over Congress, Jackson laughed. "These people just don't understand," he said. "They refuse to realize that the *American people* support Israel. Americans, whether Gentile or Jew, respect competence. They like the idea that we are on the side which seems to know what it's doing."

Jackson certainly knew his way around the legislative process. By working the phones with a dedicated, anti-Soviet, pro-Israel staff of assistants, he would get as many as eighty out of one hundred senators to cosponsor his resolutions. At one point, when senators opposed to the Vietnam War blocked arms exports, Jackson pushed through an amendment that authorized the president to transfer—specifically to Israel— "such aircraft and equipment appropriate" to counteract Soviet aid to Arab nations.

The congressional blank check was put to the test in the crisis of October 1973.

With the absence of any serious peace initiatives by Washington, the Middle East was sliding toward war without anyone seeming to realize it. Nasser's successor, Anwar Sadat, repeatedly called for talks with Israel through international mediators, but the overconfident and complacent Prime Minister Meir and Defense Minister Dayan ignored him. "Our situation has never been better," said Dayan, referring to the occupied territories. Why negotiate their return to the Arabs?

The Israelis even shrugged off a warning from Jordan's King Hussein, who took the unusual step of flying secretly to Israel in mid-September 1973 for talks with Meir. Grateful for the assistance in saving his regime three years earlier, Hussein told the prime minister of an Egyptian-Syrian conspiracy—adding a promise that Jordan would not join it.

Yet when Egypt's Sadat decided to shake up the region and the world, Israel was still mired in the stubborn belief that the Arabs lacked the military capability to strike. Egypt and Syria made their secret plans, and Israeli intelligence and the CIA—dependent on Israeli analysis—were totally fooled.

On October 6, a Saturday, the armies of Egypt and Syria took Israel by surprise. Urgent intelligence reports that morning told Meir that the Arabs would attack within hours. Israel still had time to stage a preemptive air strike.

However, Meir and Dayan were utterly convinced, in the light of past experience, that they would need a green light from the United States before going to war. And last-minute consultations between Jerusalem and Washington made the Israeli leadership realize that America would not support a preemptive strike and might blame Israel for igniting the fighting. For the sake of good relations with the Nixon administration, Meir's cabinet made the tough decision to withstand the first blow.

In 1956 Israel had gone to war without checking for stop lights. Eisenhower had punished Israel for violating the traffic laws by forcing it to withdraw from conquered territory.

In 1967 Israel had looked for a green light from Washington

and had proceeded to war on the strength of a yellow light. So Israel was allowed to keep its territorial gains.

Now, in October 1973, there was a red light barring a preemptive strike and no time to wait—or lobby—for the lights to change.

The Arab attack came on Yom Kippur, the holiest day on the Jewish calendar. While that was an emotive date to worried friends of Israel in America, the fact that no Israelis were at work or on the road generally made mobilizing army reservists easier.

Rapid mobilization was needed, because on both fronts—in the Sinai and on the Golan Heights—Israel was sustaining heavy losses of men and aircraft. The defensive lines along the Suez and on the Golan had been broken by the Egyptians and Syrians, using Soviet-made surface-to-air missiles as their offensive shield. As always, the Israelis felt they would have to fight and win their own war. But this one looked rougher than the others, and Israel—accustomed to quick victories—quickly turned to Washington for help.

Before the Yom Kippur War was over, 2,700 Israeli soldiers would be dead—traumatic in a nation of just over 3 million people. More than 110 airplanes, almost one out of five of its fighter-bombers, and one-third of its tanks would be lost.

U.S. officials perceived a note of desperation in the official Israeli messages. Several Americans thought they could read, between the lines, an Israeli warning that if its back was against the wall, the Jewish state might have to resort to nuclear weapons.

In Israel, in fact, Defense Minister Moshe Dayan did panic, saying that the Jewish state could meet its end within a few days. He urged Prime Minister Meir to consider seriously the use of nuclear weapons. But she calmed him down. Despite the difficulties, Meir believed, Israel could win without its doomsday weapon.

But it needed conventional weapons to replace its losses. Israel was running out of ammunition. It also needed more tanks, more planes, and more spare parts. Golda Meir was clamoring for resupply by the United States. Nixon replied that once the war was over, America would replace all the losses. But Israel needed help now.

The American government's unsatisfactory reply alerted the Jewish community. Its leaders received urgent telephone calls from Israeli diplomats. American Jews also were shocked by radio and television reports that showed jubilant Egyptians and Syrians dancing on captured Israeli fortifications. Israel's friends, like the rest of the world, had gotten used to the notion of an invincible Israel that needed only hours or days to knock out the Arabs. This war, they realized, was different.

As in 1967, emergency fund raising began. But this time the Israeli embassy also was flooded with American volunteers wishing to fly to Israel to work or fight.

On the fourth day of the 1973 war, October 9, fund-raiser Max Fisher went to the Oval Office and found an exhausted-looking president. Nixon was under pressure from Watergate prosecutors, and his vice president, Spiro Agnew, would resign the next day because of unrelated corruption charges.

Fisher begged Nixon for attention. "I've worked hard for you and I've never asked anything for myself. But I'm asking you now. Please send the Israelis what they need. You can't let them be destroyed." The president repeated his willingness to help but made no specific commitment.

Finally, on Sunday, October 14, the help arrived, and Israel received it with cheers and tears. Golda Meir said she cried with relief. In an airlift setting the example for the Patriot-missile import that would lift Israeli spirits in January 1991, the United States was coming to the rescue. Thirty C-130 transports came in from the United States that day, and by October 16 the larger C-141s and giant C-5s were bringing in a thousand tons of weapons and munitions per day. Forty F-4 Phantom jets and thirty-six A-4 Skyhawks, so difficult to obtain during years of lobbying, were delivered to Israel that month, as were twelve C-130 transport planes for the Israelis to keep.

During and after the war, Israeli and U.S. officials would be dragged into endless debates over why the airlift had taken so long to get off the ground. Was there a deliberate delay? Were there mere problems of bureaucracy? Was Nixon too crippled by Watergate to act effectively? Was Henry Kissinger hoping to bring Israeli pride down a notch, to create a more pliant negotiating partner? Was Defense Secretary James Schlesinger reluctant to help Israel?

Some Israelis felt the delay may have been deliberate. Not only was the massive airlift slow in coming; lesser requests by Israel also ran into unexplained difficulties. When Israel's military attachés in Washington asked the Pentagon for satellite reconnaissance of the advancing Egyptian and Syrian forces, the Americans apologized but said the satellite was damaged so they had no photographs. "How could I know if it really was damaged?" one Israeli general recalls. "The bottom line was that we didn't get the information."

President Nixon, in his memoirs, says candidly that his goal was "a battlefield stalemate," even "an equilibrium of mutual exhaustion," so that no one would win and everyone would start talking peace.

And the fact is that even as Kissinger and Schlesinger traded accusations as to who had delayed the resupply, a U.S. goal differed sharply from Israel's.

When, in the first few days of the Yom Kippur War, the Israelis felt their backs were against the wall and they might lose, they demanded arms. But the United States did not believe them. On October 7 Nixon privately said Israel would certainly win and then "will be even more impossible to deal with than before." America had built up Israel as a strategic ally, but not the only ally in the Middle East. Nixon and Kissinger wanted Egypt, which had already expelled Soviet advisors in 1972, to join the Western camp.

The Israelis, once they repulsed the initial Egyptian and Syrian assault, wanted to continue pushing to outright, blistering victory. The Americans still wanted a stalemate.

It is true that bureaucrats wrestled with options such as using Israeli cargo planes with their markings painted out, chartered U.S. planes that could not get insurance, just a few air force transports, and then finally the entire U.S. airlift capability. And Nixon did settle the issue—by thundering to Schlesinger, "Whichever way we have to do it, get them in the air, now!"— and by snapping at Kissinger, "Tell them to send everything that can fly!" But he only thundered, and snapped, when the time was right for the deadlock he wanted.

Similarly, near the end of the war, when the "hot line" from Moscow brought a Soviet threat to send troops to Egypt, the U.S. response was based on America's sense of timing: the need to demonstrate that the deepening Watergate scandal was not undermining military and diplomatic resolve. Kissinger and Schlesinger dramatically put U.S. forces worldwide on their highest state of alert, technically ready for nuclear combat. The president is said to have been asleep, but Nixon claims credit: "Have you ever read our Constitution? You think secretaries of state do nuclear alerts and airlifts? Those are presidential decisions!"

Nixon does not claim to have acted out of love for Israel. He points to the fact that the Soviet Union was flying tons of military materiel into Egypt and Syria. "Under no circumstances were we going to allow a Soviet airlift to Israel's enemies to lead to an Israeli defeat," he says. "Strategic considerations were crucial. The airlift was important as a measure of U.S. reliability."

Kissinger later joked to Israeli officials that he was prepared to go with them to the threshold of nuclear war—but not one inch beyond. From Eban's point of view, "Our heroes were Nixon and Kissinger. Our enemies were the Pentagon and Schlesinger. But the outcome was a great miracle, for a big bureaucracy to make a decision that is so far-reaching and innovative as an airlift to a country that is not a NATO ally."

The war wound down in the last week of October, with a cease-fire arranged by Kissinger, which added to the realization by the Middle East's warring sides that only America truly can deliver. Israel eventually had made some military advances, but politically the results could be defined as a draw—as Nixon had hoped.

Seeing an unparalleled opportunity to reorganize the Middle East along pro-American lines, Kissinger launched a unique diplomatic initiative: shuttle diplomacy. With the Watergate-shattered Nixon withdrawing into the wings, the secretary of state had an open stage to show his skill.

Starting in November 1973, Kissinger made eleven exciting and exhausting trips to the Middle East capitals. The shuttles resulted in three interim agreements involving Israel, Egypt, and Syria. The accords enabled each side to heal some of its wounds and established an American-initiated pattern: Israel gave up some territory in exchange for security arrangements along the new lines, limited recognition from the Arabs, and greater U.S. reassurances for its political and defense concerns.

America would, in turn, boost its prestige among Arab countries as the only possible lever to extract concessions from Israel. This helped smooth relations with the Arabs, who had reacted to the Yom Kippur War by imposing an oil embargo against the West.

Along the way, there was much arm-twisting and tooth-gnashing in Jerusalem. Kissinger's many visits sparked emotional debates between right-wing Israelis, who rejected all concessions and tarred him as a self-hating Jew and liberals who welcomed him as a savior.

The visiting secretary of state quickly figured out how to manipulate the Israeli political system. In America, Israelis and their friends manipulated U.S. politics by playing government agencies—the White House and Congress, the State Department and the Pentagon—against each other. Israeli politics are much more personal and less structured, so Kissinger played politicians against each other. Knowing that decisions were made by three or four individuals, Kissinger might side with the prime minister against the army generals, or with the foreign minister versus the defense minister.

Israel was in turmoil, and the postwar traumas and investigations into the conduct of the Yom Kippur War forced Golda Meir to resign in April 1974. As if to underline the importance of relations with the United States, among other reasons, the Labor party chose former Ambassador Rabin as her successor.

Nixon was also on his way out. Hoping to survive on the strength of his being a world statesman, he made a pathetic trip to the Middle East, drinking in the adulation of huge crowds in the streets. To the bitter end, Nixon remained loyal to his unsentimental *realpolitik*. As he noted in his diary during the tour, "We would make Israel strong enough that they would not fear to negotiate, but not so strong that they felt they had no need to negotiate."

This first visit by a serving president to Israel was Nixon's final official trip abroad. One of the surprising aspects was his offer to both Israel and Egypt of nuclear reactors for generating electricity. Negotiations with the Israelis broke down later, but the offer—to a country that still had not signed the nuclear NPT—was a continuation of the Nixon-Kissinger acquiescence to Israel's nuclear ambitions.

Returning home, Nixon faced certain impeachment, and in

August 1974 he resigned. Gerald Ford, one of Israel's traditional friends on Capitol Hill, became the new president. But to
the disappointment of both Ford and the Israelis, the difference
between saying something as a congressman and doing something as chief executive quickly became apparent.

President Ford received a letter in January 1975 from an old
friend, Milton Hoffman, asking for what seemed to be a small
favor. He had donated thousands of dollars to plant a forest in
his beloved Jewish state, to be named the Gerald Ford Forest.
Would the president please send a message to be read at the
ceremony?

While in the House of Representatives, Ford would have said
yes without hesitation. As he explained in a handwritten memorandum to his White House staff, Hoffman had lost his wife
in an air crash, was "very active in Jewish organizations," but
did not promote "hard line" policies. Rather than going with
his gut, however, the new president asked his National Security
Council what to do.

The laborious decision process that followed showed the sen-
sitivity of matters pertaining to Israel—especially to its borders. In one of dozens of memos, NSC staffer Robert Oakley
wrote to his boss, the deputy national security advisor, Brent
Scowcroft: "It has become common for persons who have purchased and had planted one of these trees to dedicate it to someone. Several were dedicated to President Nixon, so it is not
unusual that one has been planted in honor of President Ford."

But, Oakley revealed, there was a problem. "The tree which
has been planted in President Ford's honor is, of course, in the
Judean Hills, south of Jerusalem in the Occupied West Bank. It
would be wholly inappropriate for the president to send a message to the dedication ceremonies of this tree which would appear to align him closely with Israeli policies on the future of
the West Bank. We have strictly avoided this in the past."

General Scowcroft accepted this recommendation, but came

up with a solution combining diplomacy with a personal style
of politics: The president could either phone or send a letter to
the donor thanking him for the honor without specifying that
the forest was in Israel.

This seemingly minor episode displays the danger of letting
the thick forest of Middle East policy be obscured by the
branches of human sentiment, basic support for Israel, and the
reluctance to offend political donors. Government bureaucrats
become the protectors of continuity and consistency partially
rooted in a wish to placate oil-rich Arabs.

A similar dilemma faced the Ford team, around the same
time, on the nuclear issue. The administration decided to proceed with the Nixon offer to provide nuclear power plants to
both Egypt and Israel. "Enrichment service contracts have been
completed between the Atomic Energy Commission and Israel," said a memo prepared for the treasury secretary, William
E. Simon.

But a longer sense of policy continuity dictated caution in
dealing with Israel on nuclear matters. So Secretary Simon was
advised by the White House to stress, in congressional testimony, that "these contracts are subject to the completion of
negotiation for nuclear plants and equipment under the safeguards of the International Atomic Energy Agency." In addition, all countries to receive nuclear material from the United
States "have signed bilateral cooperation agreements on the
civil uses of atomic energy." In talks with Israel, the United
States would insist that "additional constraints relating to the
storage, fabrication, and processing will be included in these
negotiations. The waste plutonium will not be processed in either country."

The willingness to extend aid, but not complete trust, also
colored the response to Israel's request for Pershings—ground-
to-ground missiles capable of carrying nuclear warheads. Defense Secretary Schlesinger did not give a straightforward no,

but he killed the Israeli plea with the explanation that "our Pershing line is closed, and equipment would have to be taken out of inventory," which the United States would not do to its own military without the demands of a crisis.

The challenges of diplomacy and defense overlapped with economics in the months and years after the Arab oil embargo and the quadrupling of petro prices that followed the Yom Kippur War. When key congressmen started a campaign to combat the Arab economic boycott of Israel—to make it more difficult, if not illegal, for American companies to comply with the boycott in order to do business with Arab countries—the White House downplayed the issue. Official U.S. policy was to discourage the boycott, but without endangering American economic interests in the Arab world.

The foreign policy elements of these and other debates, in the post-Watergate shock, were left to Henry Kissinger. As a cornerstone of continuity from the Nixon years, the secretary of state continued battling for peace, interim accords, and a *pax Americana* in the Middle East.

The third and final accord, which called for Israeli troops to give up more of the Sinai, led to a precedent-setting blow-up between the United States and Israel. In Jerusalem in March 1975, Kissinger and Rabin raged at each other when Israel refused to make further territorial concessions. The secretary of state sounded threatening when he told Israeli leaders: "I see pressure building up to force you back to the 1967 borders." Privately he spoke of Rabin's "lunacy."

A chill descended on U.S.-Israeli relations. Kissinger persuaded President Ford to announce a "reassessment" of America's relationship with Israel. The State Department commissioned study groups, for the sake of appearances, but the essence was a freeze on all arms deliveries. Just as Eisenhower had withheld aid to back up his demands, weapons were now being used as a negotiating lever for the first time. The United

States was refusing to send arms to Israel, unless it carried out specific instructions.

American Jews raised a storm of protest, but Kissinger had his mind on a global power struggle larger than domestic politics. Max Fisher tried to be a helpful bridge between Washington and Jerusalem, flying to Israel in early April for three long chats with Rabin. When he felt he fully understood the prime minister's position on the key mountain passes in the Sinai that Kissinger wanted Israel to give up, Fisher flew to Washington, wrote it all down with the help of former Nixon aide Leonard Garment, and got an appointment with Ford and Kissinger.

In the Oval Office on April 9, Fisher, in his low, quiet voice, read his notes on Rabin's arguments for thirty-five minutes. Ford listened; and Kissinger, too, was polite enough not to interrupt. But the secretary of state did not moderate his demands.

In fact, when AIPAC persuaded seventy-six senators to sign a public letter to Ford demanding the restoration of military and economic aid to Israel, Kissinger, suspecting Israeli orchestration, shouted at Ambassador Simcha Dinitz: "This letter will kill you! It will increase anti-Semitism! It will cause people to charge that Jews control Congress."

The outcome of a tense few months was Israeli capitulation. After Rabin, on a trip to Washington in June 1975, found Ford and Kissinger immovable, he agreed to withdraw from the mountain passes. The Ford administration reassessed its reassessment and unfroze previously committed military aid.

The United States agreed to around $500 million in extra military assistance to Israel as thanks for the Sinai accord. The old formula was now more blatant: After the Yom Kippur War, the Nixon administration approved $2.2 billion in military hardware for Israel, $1.5 billion of it as an outright gift at the insistence of Congress. That was understandable, considering the widespread sympathy for Israel's heavy losses in the war.

But while the postwar 1974 aid package was not directly linked with territorial withdrawal, the 1975 package was. Israel was being remunerated, to the extent of hundreds of millions of dollars per mile ceded, for obeying the American traffic lights.

The United States agreed to station a small number of American troops in several early-warning stations. U.S. aerial reconnaissance photographs would be given to both Israel and Egypt, to assure them that the mountain passes were indeed demilitarized. Although the honest supplier showed no preference for one customer over the other, the process of sharing information further consolidated and broadened the secret cooperation between America and Israel.

From the mid-1970s, the United States gave the Israeli military greater access to the intelligence data gathered by sophisticated, high-altitude SR-71 aircraft based in Cyprus. In addition to the earlier focus on immediate neighbors such as Egypt and Syria, the reconnaissance treasures now extended to more distant nations such as Libya and Iraq.

The interim disengagement accord also permitted the Israelis to keep manning their largest, NSA-equipped station at Umm Khisheiba in the Sinai, under an American flag. But as often occurs far below the level of international agreements, individuals made the difference that tipped the balance—this time in Israel's favor.

The Americans' role was mainly to see that the Israelis and Egyptians honored the restrictions imposed by the interim accord. There were limits on how many troops, weapons, and equipment could be brought to Umm Khisheiba, but the Israelis tried to bend the rules. Sometimes the American inspectors were sympathetic, notably one U.S. officer who was befriended by a senior Israeli military intelligence officer. The Israeli wined and dined the American in a Tel Aviv restaurant, and when they next saw each other in the field, the Israeli thought he would slip in some extra men and electronic monitoring gear and see what happened.

The American did not even bother to count, even though the Israelis were bringing in 260 soldiers rather than 200.

"What's that?" the American asked, pointing at crates of equipment.

"It's something you wouldn't like to see," the Israeli replied.

"Oh, I see," said the American, but he pretended that he didn't.

Rabin and Ford were only transitional leaders of their respective countries. In his first three-year term as prime minister, Rabin had few accomplishments to show off to the Israeli public. The only true point of pride was in July 1976, when Israel displayed its unrivaled expertise in antiterrorism by flying a crack commando force to far-off Entebbe in Uganda to rescue a hundred hostages who had been taken from a hijacked French airliner. They handily won a firefight against Arab and German terrorists and Ugandan soldiers, and the grateful passengers were then flown in American-built transport planes to a song-and dance-filled celebration in Israel. The daring and successful operation astounded the world.

The titanic image of Entebbe was a return to the heroic Israel of days gone by. It captured the imagination of the United States above all other countries, even though America was obsessively distracted by a huge bicentennial celebration on the day the news broke: July 4.

The administration, however, found some difficulty in publicly reflecting the delight felt by the American people. While U.S. officials privately expressed their admiration for Israeli courage, innovation, and determination to fight terrorists, a military operation that appeared to violate international law was officially unendorsable.

But as with the Gerald Ford Forest episode, White House

bureaucrats came up with a solution. Oakley and Scowcroft drafted a letter, to be sent by President Ford to the parents of the sole Israeli officer who died in the Entebbe raid—justified by the fact that Lieutenant Colonel Yehonathan (Jonathan) Netanyahu was "American by birth." His father was a professor of Semitic languages at Cornell.

While the condolences were ostensibly personal, Ford left no room for doubt on his own view of the Israeli raid. "By his selfless sacrifice," the "private" presidential message to the Netanyahu family read, "he has set an example which must inspire all governments and peoples to put an end to barbarous acts of international terrorism."

Israel was again, at least briefly, popular, a cause to gather around and cheer. Hollywood, always quick to recognize a trend, commissioned several movies about the raid. Israel went out of its way to help the filmmakers by providing authentic military equipment, soldiers, airmen—and even tactical information. More unusual still, cabinet ministers were encouraged to play themselves in the movies.

Israel was willing to do almost anything to preserve its old image. But the new version of the *Exodus* factor could not last. Israel and the world had changed.

CHAPTER TEN

A New Israel

Samuel W. Lewis was impressed. All around him at a diplomatic party, like characters walking out of the pages of books, were Moshe Dayan with his black eyepatch, Yitzhak Rabin with his ever-present cigarette, and Shimon Peres acting calm and debonair as if he were not torn up by the fact that he had just lost in his run for prime minister.

Sam Lewis, the new United States ambassador to Israel, had only arrived in Tel Aviv that day, May 18, 1977, but he was quickly catching on: This was not the country portrayed in the State Department briefing books. This was a new Israel, with a new team in the driver's seat.

Ezer Weizman had just walked into the party, armed with his famous mouth. The former air force commander had just masterminded the election victory of Menachem Begin and the right-wing Likud party. Weizman was crowing, after shooting down the Labor party of Peres, Rabin, Dayan, Golda Meir, and the entire cartel that had ruled the Jewish state since its founding.

Weizman "was the most obnoxious person I'd ever seen," Lewis recalls, "the way he was humiliating Peres and the other Labor characters—in English, for the benefit of us foreigners, as well as in Hebrew."

The party was at the Canadian ambassador's house in Herzliya, a comfortable, tree-lined suburb along the Mediterranean shore just north of Tel Aviv. "Well, this'll be a good chance to see Israelis informally," Lewis thought at the time. "I haven't presented my credentials yet, so I can't talk to any officials officially, but maybe I can meet a few privately."

It was just the previous day, May 17, that Menachem Begin's Likud party scored its stunning election victory. The prime minister designate, otherwise engaged, was not at the party. But practically everyone else that Lewis had read about was.

"The scene of the victors and the vanquished," says Lewis, "engaging in this cut and thrust in the most nasty fashion imaginable, gave me a sense of what Israeli political life was going to be like. It was a very educational evening."

And there was more to come for the new U.S. ambassador. On his first morning in the embassy building on Hayarkon Street, overlooking the blue Mediterranean, he was faced with a diplomatic dilemma that revolved around the demonology surrounding Begin.

Lewis had heard terrible things about the Likud leader, and not only in summaries of the Arab press. Even the Israeli media had long treated Begin as a rank outsider, with a terrorist past and opinions on the fringe or beyond it. No wonder the embassy, always depending on the local press and conversations with the Labor elite, had thought he would lose the election.

And perhaps no wonder embassy colleagues, immediately upon his arrival, were urging Lewis not to meet with Begin—all except the public affairs officer, who not only knew Begin but had set up lunch with him for the coming Friday.

Lewis wasn't sure what to do. Whereas it seemed obvious that the new U.S. ambassador and the new prime minister ought to get acquainted, and the sooner the better, people were still acting as if Labor ran the country and Begin was a nobody.

The ambassador wondered if there was something peculiar about Israeli protocol. He had learned the rules of the game in very different places: born in Houston in 1930, schooled at Yale and Johns Hopkins, a diplomat in South America and most recently in Afghanistan. Perhaps it might cause offense for him to have lunch with Begin before he was formally installed as prime minister and before Lewis went through the accreditation ceremony in Jerusalem.

The ambassador called Israel's foreign ministry for guidance and was surprised to hear the advice of Eppy Evron, the former envoy to Washington. Here was a man who obviously believed in personal diplomacy—having befriended President Johnson—telling Lewis not to meet Begin. "You'll really be making a mistake if you do that," Evron implored, saying the outgoing Prime Minister Rabin would be annoyed.

Lewis was beginning to comprehend what an outsider Begin had been. This understanding would contribute to the U.S.-Israel alliance, because finally there was someone in the American decision chain who understood the new Israeli prime minister.

The ambassador defied the conventional advice and went to his public affairs officer's house that Friday. "The result was three and a half hours of private conversation with Begin, sitting at a little kitchen table in Herzliya. We went over Begin's life history, his approach toward the world, his ideas for his prime ministership, his hope to become a peacemaker and not the warmonger that he was being depicted as in the press all over the world. They were the most valuable three hours I spent in eight years in Israel."

Tense allies: When the nuclear aircraft carrier USS *Nimitz* visited the Mediterranean coast of Israel in 1979, Prime Minister Begin *(right)* sought to strengthen his country's image as a strategic ally of the United States by visiting the ship and witnessing exercises at sea with Deputy Prime Minister Yigael Yadin *(center)* and U.S. ambassador Samuel W. Lewis *(left). (courtesy of Samuel W. Lewis)*

U.S. ambassador Samuel W. Lewis *(right)* always addressed the Israeli leader as "Mr. Prime Minister," while Begin would vary between "Sam" when relations were good and "Mr. Ambassador" when they were strained. *(courtesy of Samuel W. Lewis)*

A golden era: Prime Minister Begin *(right)* chatted with President Ronald Reagan in the Oval Office on September 9, 1981, during a get-acquainted visit. Begin, from then on, felt free to call the president "my dear Ron." *(courtesy of Ronald Reagan Library)*

Caspar Weinberger *(right)*, Reagan's defense secretary, was considered by most Israelis to be a rare foe in the administration. Weinberger was plainly relieved when the former ambassador to Washington, Moshe Arens *(left)*, became Israeli defense minister in 1983, replacing the architect of the previous year's invasion of Lebanon, Ariel Sharon. *(official U.S. Army photo)*

The President and Nancy Reagan pay their respects to the 241 American servicemen killed in the October 1983 suicide bombing of the U.S. Marine headquarters at Beirut airport—an event that brought the United States and Israel closer in their joint fight against terrorism. *(courtesy of Ronald Reagan Library)*

Prime Minister Yitzhak Shamir *(right)* spoke at the White House on November 29, 1983, the visit in which he and President Reagan *(left)* announced agreements on strategic cooperation and duty-free trade between Israel and the United States. *(courtesy of Ronald Reagan Library)*

Prime Minister Shamir and his delegation *(left)* further expanded strategic cooperation in talks on March 16, 1988, with President Reagan, Vice President George Bush, and General Colin L. Powell *(at far end of American side, on right). (courtesy of Ronald Reagan Library)*

The Holocaust factor institutionalized: President Reagan *(left)* attended the groundbreaking ceremony for the Holocaust museum in Washington, underlining his own emotional tie to the Jewish people's tragedy and their triumphs in Israel. *(courtesy of Ronald Reagan Library)*

Access to the top: The Reagan administration was generally friendly territory for the American Israel Public Affairs Committee, and it was common for AIPAC executive director Thomas A. Dine *(left)* to sup with senior officials including James Baker *(right)*, who was Reagan's chief of staff and later President Bush's secretary of state. Still, the smiles could mask sharp disagreements over Israeli policies. *(courtesy of Washington Jewish Week)*

Steven J. Rosen, director of research for AIPAC through its high-growth decade of the 1980s and beyond, helped fine-tune the pro-Israel lobby's message to fit almost perfectly in the Reagan-era Cold War framework. Often considered the number-two man in AIPAC, Rosen *(left)* was photographed with the number-two official in the Israeli embassy in Washington in 1991, Oded Eran. The lobby and the embassy worked in close, although not absolute, coordination. *(courtesy of Washington Jewish Week)*

Extended family: Israeli government officials and other politicians frequently visited the United States, sometimes urging support for their country yet often seeking financial backing for their political parties. Moshe Arens *(left),* who served as minister of defense and of foreign affairs during the 1980s, was U.S.–educated, American-accented, and thus a popular draw during his many visits. Here Arens met one of California's most active supporters of Israel, AIPAC, and the Likud party, Jonathan E. Mitchell. *(courtesy of Jonathan Mitchell)*

Another Israeli who benefited from his American-accented English was Benjamin Netanyahu, who was a big hit in the United States as an embassy official in Washington, as Israel's ambassador to the United Nations, and then as Likud's leader and candidate for prime minister. *(courtesy of Jonathan Mitchell)*

George Bush *(right)* and Yitzhak Shamir *(left)* never got along, from their first meeting as U.S. president and Israeli prime minister on April 6, 1989, when Bush honed in on the issue of Jewish settlements in the occupied territories and felt Shamir misled him by saying "It won't be a problem." *(courtesy of Bush Presidential Materials Project)*

A Jewish academic from California, Dennis Ross was the key strategist for the U.S. government in Middle East peace talks, both in the Bush administration and later for President Clinton. *(courtesy of Washington Jewish Week)*

Three months after Iraq triggered a crisis by invading Kuwait, President Bush *(center)* and his wife, Barbara, spent Thanksgiving 1990 with U.S. troops in Saudi Arabia, conferring on war strategy with the coalition commander, General H. Norman Schwarzkopf *(right)*. After the Gulf War, Israelis would wonder whether Bush and Schwarzkopf wanted to defend the Jewish state or just keep it out of the war. *(courtesy of Bush Presidential Materials Project)*

Stephen Solarz *(second from left)*, a Democratic congressman from New York, also visited a Patriot missile site, photographed with *(from left to right)* an Israeli air force colonel, commander of the Patriot task force Colonel David Heebner, and chief chaplain to the visiting U.S. troops Rabbi Jacob Goldstein. *(courtesy of Rabbi Goldstein)*

Despite disagreements and distrust on the political level, relations between the military structures of the United States and Israel remained excellent. General Frederick M. Franks, one of Schwarzkopf's key infantry commanders in the Gulf War, held a gift from the Israel Defense Forces while visiting the chief of staff, General Ehud Barak, in June 1992. *(courtesy of Israel Defense Forces spokesman)*

A Jewish academic from California, Dennis Ross was the key strategist for the U.S. government in Middle East peace talks, both in the Bush administration and later for President Clinton. *(courtesy of Washington Jewish Week)*

Three months after Iraq triggered a crisis by invading Kuwait, President Bush *(center)* and his wife, Barbara, spent Thanksgiving 1990 with U.S. troops in Saudi Arabia, conferring on war strategy with the coalition commander, General H. Norman Schwarzkopf *(right)*. After the Gulf War, Israelis would wonder whether Bush and Schwarzkopf wanted to defend the Jewish state or just keep it out of the war. *(courtesy of Bush Presidential Materials Project)*

Seen on a visit to Israel in June 1990, trying out a new Israeli assault rifle, the chairman of the U.S. Joint Chiefs of Staff General Colin Powell often credited his boyhood among Jews in the Bronx to explain his sympathy toward the Jewish state. *(courtesy of Israel Defense Forces spokesman)*

In December 1990, when Prime Minister Shamir *(left)* visited the White House, President Bush *(right)* extracted a promise that Israel would not stage a preemptive strike against Iraq. Public smiles could barely conceal the underlying tension. *(courtesy of Bush Presidential Materials Project)*

One of two U.S. officials who made the offer of Patriot antimissile missiles to Israel, Paul D. Wolfowitz *(right)* of the department of defense visited a Patriot site on the southern outskirts of Tel Aviv after the first foreign troops ever to serve on Israeli soil arrived in

January 1991. Wolfowitz shook hands with Lieutenant Colonel Harry Krimkowitz *(left)*, who by coincidence was also Jewish. *(photo from Israel Air Force videotape)*

American dignitaries who had long identified with the Israeli cause flocked to the Patriot missile site, visited here by Senator Daniel Inouye *(center)*, the Hawaii Democrat who was a leader of pro-Israel forces on Capitol Hill. The commander of the Israeli air force, General Avihu Bin-Nun *(far left, in dark sunglasses)*, later publicly criticized the United States for an insufficient effort to destroy Iraq's Scud missile launchers. *(courtesy of Rabbi Jacob Goldstein)*

Stephen Solarz *(second from left)*, a Democratic congressman from New York, also visited a Patriot missile site, photographed with *(from left to right)* an Israeli air force colonel, commander of the Patriot task force Colonel David Heebner, and chief chaplain to the visiting U.S. troops Rabbi Jacob Goldstein. *(courtesy of Rabbi Goldstein)*

Despite disagreements and distrust on the political level, relations between the military structures of the United States and Israel remained excellent. General Frederick M. Franks, one of Schwarzkopf's key infantry commanders in the Gulf War, held a gift from the Israel Defense Forces while visiting the chief of staff, General Ehud Barak, in June 1992. *(courtesy of Israel Defense Forces spokesman)*

President Bush *(left)* patched up relations with Israel while running for reelection, meeting at his family home in Kennebunkport, Maine, on August 10, 1992, with Yitzhak Rabin *(right)*. To the delight of the United States, Rabin had replaced Shamir as prime minister after the Israeli election. Bush would lose his job three months later. *(courtesy of Bush Presidential Materials Project)*

On his first visit to the Middle East as President Clinton's secretary of state, Warren Christopher *(center)* was taken on a tour of northern Israel by the foreign minister, Shimon Peres *(right)*, chief of staff General Barak *(far left)*, and other generals. The summer 1993 trip was a parallel effort to the secret negotiations that Israel and the Palestine Liberation Organization had begun, mostly in Norway. *(courtesy of Israel Defense Forces spokesman)*

Historic handshake: On the White House lawn, President Bill Clinton *(center)* had the pleasure of sponsoring the signing—if not the actual negotiations—of an interim peace accord between Israel and the PLO. On September 13, 1993, Prime Minister Yitzhak Rabin *(left)* reluctantly shook hands with Palestinian leader Yasser Arafat *(right)*. *(The White House)*

Just before the famous handshake, President Clinton *(center)* and his vice president Al Gore *(second from left)* made a point of having separate discussions with Rabin *(left)* and his foreign minister Shimon Peres *(right)*, to underline a continued U.S. commitment to Israel. *(The White House)*

Lieutenant Colonel Harry Krimkowitz *(right)*, commander of the Patriot missile batteries that shot down Iraqi Scud missiles heading toward Tel Aviv, found it especially meaningful to defend Israel because both he and his wife have relatives in the Jewish state. *(courtesy of Rabbi Jacob Goldstein)*

Hands-on tour: American Jewish organizations frequently invite prominent politicians and their aides to see Israel for themselves. In 1991 B'nai B'rith had both Brent Erickson *(top)*, legislative assistant to Senator Alan Simpson, and Charles Brooks *(bottom),* foreign affairs consultant to Senator Arlen Specter, as guests on a tour that included the Golan Heights to survey its strategic importance as an already bloodied battlefield between Israel and Syria. *(courtesy of Charles D. Brooks)*

Lewis felt that his cable to Washington that weekend, reporting on his private chat, deserved a dramatic title—"Menachem Begin: Moses or Samson?" Knowing it would not be easy to dispel the images and prejudices in the State Department, especially in the Arab-oriented Near East and South Asia Bureau, the ambassador gave a lengthy description of Begin's attitudes on all major issues.

The new prime minister, who would have to wait another six weeks before taking office with a right-wing coalition, wanted good relations with the United States. But he doubted that Jimmy Carter—much as he respected the new president's strong religious beliefs—understood the complexities of the Middle East.

Begin suspected that Carter's commitment to human rights was making him favor the Palestinians over the Israelis. And Carter's opposition to the international weapons trade was already making it hard for Israel to sell its arms abroad, not to mention his reversal of Nixon's decision to provide Israel with a nuclear power reactor.

Begin resented the president's diplomatic initiatives, in his first four months in office, aimed at bringing the Soviet Union—a country Begin despised—into the Middle East peace process. And, in general, he believed that Carter was being too soft toward the Soviets.

Lewis says he also wrote "that Begin was determined not to be what everyone in the world thought he was going to be, which was a militant hawk. His ambition was to be a peacemaker, and to do what Ben-Gurion had never achieved: finally break through and make peace with the Arabs. He always had that sense of competition with Ben-Gurion."

But was he going to be a Moses or a Samson? Would Begin lead his people to the promised land of peace, or would his ambitious plans for a stronger Israel bring down the house of relative stability in the Middle East?

Lewis knew that most American officials were expecting the calamitous latter course. "Washington was horror-struck by the result of the election," he says, "and everyone was scurrying around to figure out what he would do next."

Thanks to that early lunch, Lewis and Begin were able to communicate honestly—though not always pleasantly—throughout the Likud leader's more than six years in power. Lewis would always address him as "Mr. Prime Minister." But Begin played a little game. When relations with America were normal, he would call the ambassador "Sam." But when he was angry at the United States, he would sternly address him as "Mr. Ambassador."

There were tense moments from the start. The prime minister took Lewis to task every time President Carter spoke of the need for a "homeland" and "representation" for the Palestinians. Those sounded to Begin like code words for a PLO state.

He cringed when Carter said, "I don't believe there is any other nation with whom we've had better friendship and a deeper sense of cooperation than we've found in Saudi Arabia." What about Israel?

Begin pointed bitterly at Carter's public reference to "substantial withdrawal of Israel's present control over territories" and "minor adjustments in the 1967 borders," even though these were established U.S. policies by then. The president did not think the Israelis should keep the West Bank and Gaza Strip, and he demanded that Israel stop building Jewish settlements that might prejudice negotiations over the territories.

Lewis was present, in July 1977, when Begin and Carter argued over these issues in person. The Israeli leader had flown to Washington, shortly after taking office, for the traditional Israeli-American get-acquainted summit. Begin lectured Carter on Jewish history and on Israel's need to keep the West Bank— using the biblical names, Judea and Samaria—for security's sake. Even though Carter urged Israel not to build settlements, the talks were friendly—full of what Lewis calls "warm, reassuring statements about shared values and special relationships."

Begin, knowing Carter's great interest in human rights, got the president interested in a new humanitarian project: saving black Jews from starving in Ethiopia. The Israeli initiative was a new stage in a process that began with Nixon helping extricate Jews from the Soviet Union, and Begin asked for U.S. aid by drawing parallels with the Holocaust. Carter responded enthusiastically and ordered the CIA and other agencies to help Israel in its secret evacuation of Ethiopian Jews to the Jewish state.

Israeli agents were already in East Africa, instructing Jews to make their way from Ethiopia to Sudan, where Mossad men loaded them onto boats bound for Israel. Thanks to Carter, an official in the U.S. Embassy in Khartoum, Jerry Weaver, would soon be taking an active role. It was an important, emotive mission for Begin. When he and his cabinet ministers watched Mossad videotapes of the clandestine refugee route, Israel's leaders were in tears.

Begin was pleased with Carter's enthusiasm for the project and praised him as a "statesman" on the order of Ze'ev Jabotinsky, whom Begin revered as the founder of his right-wing political movement.

Lewis could see, however, that the proud and defiant Begin was not going to adjust his policies to accommodate America. Begin's cabinet authorized more settlements, and the White House branded them "illegal" and a serious "obstacle to peace."

Carter, while fascinated with Israel's history and supportive of its security, seemed to be trying to shock the Israelis into recognizing that the other side of the conflict had to be considered. "I see over and over a reluctance to face the troubling question of what to do about the Palestinians," he wrote later. "Many choose to pretend they do not exist."

Begin kept hoping that he could convince Carter of the justice of Israel's case. He had fewer hopes for the secretary of state, Cyrus Vance, although he did appreciate him as a gentleman—a quality always important to the courtly Begin. However, he considered the national security advisor, Zbigniew Brzezinski, almost a lost cause from Israel's point of view, although the two Polish-born men did enjoy competing at chess.

Brzezinski, for his part, remembers advising Carter that "precisely because Begin is so extreme," the president should be able to get the support of many American Jews in putting pressure on Israel to make concessions in peace talks. There was no sign of early success on this front, as the AIPAC lobby mounted what Brzezinski calls "a large-scale campaign" against Carter administration policy.

Sam Lewis was in the classic diplomat's position: in the middle, between the relatively mild Cy Vance and the often perturbed Zbig Brzezinski, delivering good news and bad. But the round-faced, balding Yale graduate in his late forties, usually found chomping on a cigar, tried to enjoy the learning process during his first few months on the job. As if following a textbook of diplomacy, Lewis injected himself into Israeli society: from 1,536 parties that made him a regular item in the social columns of Israel's newspapers, to scuba diving in the Red Sea and tennis matches against Israeli celebrities and politicians.

The ambassador was so well plugged in that Israelis took to calling him, behind his back, the "High Commissioner," referring to the British colonial governors who used to rule the Palestine mandate. When he finally heard that, the mocking respect made Lewis laugh.

But diplomacy was not all fun and games. Through Lewis and through a Vance visit to the Middle East in August 1977, President Carter applied pressure on Israel and Egypt to come to a Geneva peace conference under U.S.-Soviet sponsorship.

The effort collapsed, but Lewis was still smiling because an alternative route to a solution was found.

He is fond of remembering the day in November, just after President Anwar Sadat stunned the Egyptian parliament by announcing that he was willing to go to Jerusalem—to the lion's den—for the sake of peace. Begin summoned Lewis and handed him a large envelope, saying "Please get this to Sadat as quickly as you can."

Reporters had gathered outside, and when they asked what he was doing, Lewis held up the envelope and beamed: "I'm just a happy postman!" It was the formal invitation to Sadat, who changed Middle East history by flying to Israel on November 19, 1977. It turned out that both Israel and Egypt were fed up with Carter's attempts to arrange a Geneva conference with the Soviets.

The United States did not back away from the process, however. As Lewis recalls: "I had to get the Israelis to look kindly on Egyptian views, and to accept American compromise suggestions. The overriding theme was that we are an engaged third party, bringing them gradually toward a settlement."

Israeli officials had long wished for direct talks with their Arab neighbors, and the Sadat visit was a revolution born with high hopes. But Israelis also had wished that when a peacemaking stage would finally be reached—as it was in 1977—they would have the full support of the United States.

The United States, however, was following a pattern developed by Kissinger in his mid-1970s disengagement accords: When Americans act as mediators, they should be even-handed. As always, Israel did not care for the concept that its concerns should be considered equivalent to those of the Arabs.

Still, despite occasional clashes with Begin and being greeted with a frosty "Mr. Ambassador" quite a few times, Lewis says U.S.-Israeli interests coincided. "We were trying to help Israel make peace," he says. "It was all a matter of arguing about tactics."

The arguments were sharp enough, however, to endanger the peace process, and the White House played a dangerous game by finally taking up Brzezinski's suggestion of creating a wedge between Israel and Jews in the United States.

Lewis recalls the administration's "conscious effort in the spring of 1978 to sharpen U.S. differences with Israel" over settlements and other issues, so as to rally Congress and the American Jewish leadership "against Begin's recalcitrance." A number of Jewish activists took the opportunity—for the first time—to peel themselves away from what some called "the party line" and publicly call for a halt to settlements in the West Bank.

But the U.S. effort largely failed. Even Carter admits that while the pro-Israel lobby is powerful, "there is also widespread support for Israel among millions of U.S. citizens who are not Jews and who have no relationship at all with lobbying groups."

And AIPAC was not lying down and playing dead. It waged a strong fight against Carter's sale of advanced F-15 warplanes to Saudi Arabia. The administration did get the sale through Congress, by cleverly turning it into an all-or-nothing package of aircraft to the Saudis, Egyptians, and Israelis.

The White House privately warned Israel not to lobby against the deal because, as Brzezinski has written, "they would profoundly irritate the President and he might even have to air publicly the nature of the present security situation in the Middle East, including the sensitive question of who had what kind of weapons. This was meant to be a hint regarding Israel's efforts to obtain a small arsenal of nuclear weapons."

Lewis says the thought that Israel's secret weapon caused a perilous imbalance in the region "was only in the background of a lot of officials' thinking, but it was almost never discussed and never would appear in official papers." The nuclear shadow always added some extra impetus to American efforts for peace—"just kind of an implicit backdrop to your concerns"— because the U.S. government would never want Israel to feel that its back was pushed up against a wall. Lewis says Israel had no reason to feel so insecure in 1978.

As ambassador, he kept learning about Israel's complicated local politics and looked for possible wedges in Begin's cabinet. He identified officials who seemed more flexible and enthusiastic about a peace agreement—notably Defense Minister Weizman and Foreign Minister Dayan—and ministers who seemed less so, such as Ariel Sharon. Just as Israel and its supporters in the United States divided the world into pro- and anti-Israel categories, American policy makers came to see Sharon as the naughty boy of Israeli politics.

The retired general was a particular focus for Lewis, who concluded that the war-hero-turned-politician was an influential force that, if left unchecked, could lead the Middle East into terrible dangers.

"In the first four years, when he was minister of agriculture, Sharon courted me," Lewis recalls. "He was a big champion of the West Bank settlements and tried to persuade me. He tried to sell himself and his policies in the West Bank, took me on tours, and had me and my wife down at his ranch." The Lewises made a point of being cordial and often invited the Sharons to their Herzliya home.

But the peace process, in the months after the excitement of Sadat's visit to Jerusalem, seemed unable to progress to a breakthrough. Egypt was reluctant to shatter Arab unity by signing a separate peace treaty, and Begin was hesitant to give back the entire Sinai peninsula when his party ideology committed him to an Israel that would be more secure and larger based on biblical proportions.

By late July 1978, having run out of other ideas, President

Carter unveiled "his last card," in Lewis's words—"a long shot indeed." Carter invited Begin and Sadat to the presidential retreat at Camp David, Maryland, for a summit like no other: designed to bring peace to Israel and Egypt.

Carter sent Begin a letter of invitation replete with references to Jewish history and the peaceful destiny of all the religions in the Middle East. Ambassador Lewis knew that the tone was just right, and the Camp David summit was set for September 5. The conference was intended to last only two or three days, but the three delegations ended up spending thirteen days in their huts in the secluded Maryland hills. Like Moses atop Mount Sinai receiving the Ten Commandments, the deeply religious Carter was showing an almost messianic zeal—with more personal devotion than any president had displayed—to bring peace to the Holy Land.

Carter, Vance, and Brzezinski, with Lewis and their other diplomatic firefighters, refereed the many disputes between the two delegations. "Begin and Sadat were personally incompatible," Carter has written, "and we decided after a few unpleasant encounters that they should not attempt to negotiate with each other."

The Americans tried to engender a casual atmosphere of short sleeves, walks in the woods, bicycle rides, and chess games. But both sides threatened walkouts, and the peace process almost died. Begin, at one point, said: "My right eye will fall out, my right hand will fall off, before I ever agree to the dismantling of a single Jewish settlement."

But he did, on September 17, sign the Camp David accords, which committed Israel to a full withdrawal from the Sinai in return for a peace treaty with Egypt. The signing ceremony in the White House was cemented by the invention of a three-man handshake, a human triangle of goodwill broadcast and published worldwide as a symbol that age-old conflicts could be resolved.

Hearing the call of history, and seeing also the threat of a complete falling out with the United States should Carter's efforts fail, Begin did what most everyone had thought he would never do. Sinai settlements were dismantled, Sinai oil fields were handed back to Egypt, and Sinai airfields were abandoned.

There was, from the Israeli point of view, a hefty bill to be paid. And Israel felt only America could afford it. The United States guaranteed, in writing, to sell oil to Israel should supplies from elsewhere ever be impossible to obtain. And the United States agreed to pay for three new air force bases for Israel in its own Negev Desert, to replace the lost Sinai facilities. The total redeployment cost would be $3 billion, and Washington was offering outright grants. But—with a display of pride and honor that shocked his economic advisors—Begin insisted on loans instead, saying Israel was a sovereign nation and would pay back every penny. Later, under pressure at home, he realized his mistake and sent top officials to renegotiate the deal. The Israelis managed to salvage $800 million as grants, and the remaining $2.2 billion was a loan.

Carter, despite repeatedly insisting that he was not going to "buy" Middle East peace, ended up spending more than $5 billion to cement the Camp David accords. He was acting along the same lines as the two previous presidents, responding to an emergency—like Nixon after the 1973 war and Ford with the 1975 disengagement accords—by spending unprecedented sums. In addition, annual military and economic aid to Israel grew steadily: from less than $500 million a year before Nixon, to around $1 billion in his time, to $2 billion under Ford and Carter. These figures became new reference points, never falling, in the annual ritual of aid negotiations between Israel and the United States. "Those talks were on automatic pilot," an Israeli diplomat who served in Washington recalls.

The Camp David payoff also made Egypt a partner in the ritual. From then on, U.S. administrations and Congress would always discuss raising aid to the two countries together: Egypt receiving less than Israel, but reaping the financial benefits of peace nonetheless.

America's guiding hand had achieved the seemingly un-achievable. But Lewis watched as the new spirit of understanding between Carter and Begin unraveled as 1978 turned to '79. From a U.S. point of view, the Middle East seemed to be going mad, with the pro-American Shah of Iran falling from power. Carter hoped that, at least, his Camp David accords would work.

They did, to the extent that Begin and Sadat signed a formal peace treaty in March 1979, Israel gave up all the territory as promised, and peaceful relations with open borders, diplomatic links, and demilitarized zones were established. However, what Carter saw as the crowning jewel—an autonomy plan for the Palestinians—was coming to nought.

In messages sent through Lewis, Carter kept asking Begin to make moderate pronouncements on his intention to grant self-rule to the Arabs of the West Bank and Gaza. Yet as Lewis tried to explain to Washington, Begin was facing "noisy dissent in his own party" and had to talk tough. The Israeli leader made public statements that minimized the concessions he had made, "stressing the narrow limits" of Palestinian autonomy.

Begin's attitude was disappointing to a president who had spent another six around-the-clock days, in mid-March, flying to Jerusalem and Cairo to negotiate personally the final details of the peace treaty. Only the second serving U.S. president to set foot in the Holy Land, Carter spent so much time focusing on the Middle East, rather than other policy matters, that it contributed to his losing his bid for reelection. This was far more attention than Israel wanted, especially when it was based in the pro-underdog, pro-Palestinian terms embraced by Carter.

Carter says American officials "know that their influence on the policies of Israel in moments of crisis is sometimes embarrassingly slight, and often it seems that the Israeli leaders relish the domestic political popularity that comes from tweaking the superpower's nose."

It would be wrong to think that U.S. ambassadors, however well plugged-in like Lewis, could change Israel's domestic politics. But there was an expectation that Lewis could control or contain Begin, who was seen as a malevolent force by the majority of the State Department's experts on the Middle East—known as Arabists.

The Arabists, in turn, have been viewed by American Jews and Israeli officials as an enemy camp within the U.S. government. While they are not in fact uniform in their views and perceptions, these diplomats do share some common traits: They have studied Arabic. They have made the rounds of diplomatic posts in the many Arab capitals. And some have pursued the British role model of romanticizing the Arab world.

Whatever his background and previous career, Lewis could never again fit in with this group. There was the bureaucratic problem that U.S. diplomats, after serving in Israel, usually found it difficult to be posted elsewhere in the Middle East. There was the case of an American, formerly based in Tel Aviv, who did get a post in Jordan, where he was derisively described as "the Israeli ambassador in Amman."

Lewis found himself in a no-win situation. Not only was he unlikely to be promoted within the Near East division of the State Department, but he was also dismissed by the Arabists as too soft on Israel.

Lewis, who went on to serve for almost eight years in the Jewish state, recalls that Carter's was a unique four-year term in U.S.-Israeli relations. Motivated by his faith in the Bible and his interest in the Third World, Carter "put Middle East peacemaking at the top of his global agenda." Lewis says the president saw Israel "as a crucial player in that game, sometimes as partner, often as antagonist, and frequently as roadblock to be surmounted."

CHAPTER ELEVEN

THE FIVE-CARAT GOLDEN ERA

It was because of the time difference—Israel being seven hours ahead of Washington—that Prime Minister Menachem Begin could afford to go to bed at 10 P.M., as was his habit. When, as usual, he woke at 5 o'clock the next morning, November 3, 1980, he turned on the radio and listened intently to the reports coming into Israel Radio and the BBC. This was the pre-CNN era, and Israel had no overnight television, so the best way for the prime minister to learn who would be his alliance partner for the next four years—who was being elected president of the United States—was to keep his ear to the radio.

By the time he reached his office, at 8 A.M., Begin could not conceal his pleasure. At least, he said to a close aide, Jimmy Carter won't be sitting in the White House. This was the main thought in Jerusalem's political corridors: no more Carter.

When Begin's premiership began, in 1977, he had called Carter a great statesman, but with time the relations between the two men turned sour. The president's insistent demands to stop the building of settlements in the occupied territories, his public support for the Palestinian people's right to a homeland, and his personal interest in the human rights situation in the territories were a nuisance to Begin—whose policies were aimed at tightening Israel's grip on the lands he called Judea and Samaria.

Carter was a person that Begin and his Likud party came to hate. They had heard that the new president, Reagan, was a friend of Israel. But all that really mattered, that day, was getting rid of Carter.

Many American Jews also were unhappy with Carter's performance, at home and abroad, and one out of three Jews who had voted for Carter in 1976 now voted against him. His bitter relations with Israel overshadowed the fact that his efforts had led to the Jewish state's only peace treaty. Ronald Reagan's landslide victory included four out of ten Jewish votes, an unusually high proportion for a Republican.

However, when Israelis and their friends in the United States surveyed the new administration's list of appointments—as they do whenever a new president comes into office—they found a mixed picture: no signs of great interest in the Middle East, but many indications that all that would matter in foreign policy would be standing up to the Soviet Union.

As secretary of state there was Alexander Haig, Nixon's former chief of staff and a veteran military man who saw Soviet conspiracies around the globe but also leaned clearly in Israel's favor.

But the Jewish state's allies were concerned about the defense secretary, Caspar Weinberger. An old crony of Reagan's in California politics, Weinberger came to government service from his senior post at Bechtel, a construction company owing its prosperity to huge projects in Saudi Arabia.

On the other hand, the Israeli leadership and American Jews

could not overlook the very promising personal, ideological, and political background of the president himself. Ronald Wilson Reagan, born and raised in Illinois, became a middle-level movie star in Hollywood. During World War II he remained in California to work on training and propaganda films for the military. There, he says, he became "one of the first Americans to discover the full truth about the horrors of Nazism." He and his colleagues were able to watch classified films showing the liberation of Hitler's death camps, and those "engraved images on my mind that will be there forever."

Reagan had many Jewish friends in Hollywood, an early bastion of pro-Israel sentiment. After going into politics, his ties to California's Jewish community—second largest in the United States, after New York's—were very strong. Many Jews helped him get elected governor.

During the presidential campaign, candidate Reagan defined Israel as an important "strategic asset." Emphasizing "Israel's geopolitical importance as a stabilizing force," he said the Jewish state "has the democratic will, national cohesion, technological capacity and military fiber to stand forth as America's trusted ally."

Never had a candidate who turned president expressed himself so forcefully about the link between the two countries—words that were sweet music to Jewish and Israeli ears.

"The Holy Land is the Holy Land to a great many of us," Reagan said. "All of us in America go back in our ancestry to some other part of the world. There is no nation like us. Except Israel."

Add to that Reagan's visceral hatred of communism—something he shared with Israel's prime minister—and there is little surprise that Begin and the Likud party leadership were buoyant on January 20, 1981, the day that Reagan moved into the White House.

But, as always in politics, everything is easier said than done.

Like any new administration, Reagan's was faced with the diverse promises and inherited policies of its predecessor. His first two years in office proved to be much more complicated than expected, in terms of U.S.-Israel relations, and were marked by rapid twists and turns.

Reagan was lucky not to inherit Carter's crisis of fifty-two American hostages held in Iran, for they were released on inauguration day. But there was a pressing Persian Gulf security issue that Carter did bequeath to the Californian who had beaten him: the AWACS controversy.

When the Shah of Iran—whose government had been the most powerful U.S. asset in the Gulf—was overthrown in 1979 by Ayatollah Khomeini and the Islamic fundamentalists, Washington needed a replacement: the pro-American regime in Saudi Arabia. The start of the long Gulf War between Iran and Iraq was even more unsettling. The Carter administration decided on a massive series of arms sales to the Saudis: F-15 fighter planes, tanks, and five of the converted Boeing jets that serve as Airborne Warning and Control Systems (AWACS)— flying radar stations that can spot incoming aircraft and missiles up to 350 miles away.

Reagan picked up the AWACS ball from Carter and ran with it. The new president was told by Weinberger and other advisors that the planes would not dramatically affect the balance of power in the Arab-Israeli conflict, while they would be perceived by the Arab world as a gesture proving American readiness to be even-handed in the Middle East.

The arms sale was not, however, based merely on concern about America's image in the Arab world, or the reliability of oil exports from Saudi Arabia. The new administration had a definite wish to keep U.S. defense industries busy and prosperous. The AWACS sale and associated contracts meant money, and a lot of it: $8.5 billion.

Furthermore, the United States developed plans with the

Saudis that would see them spending $150 billion in America for construction of a modern military infrastructure. Mammoth, U.S.-style bases were designed to house American troops in a future war that Soviet aggression might spark. If Israel and the pro-Israel lobby tried to fight those plans, they would be contending with something very, very big.

The administration's final decision to proceed with the AWACS sale came in the first week of April 1981, when Reagan was in a hospital recovering after being shot by a would-be assassin.

In Israel, a serious debate erupted in senior political circles over how they should react to the proposed AWACS sale. The Saudis, like all major Arab countries except Egypt, were officially in a state of war with Israel. In the past they had sent small army units to join in battles against the Jewish state, and Israelis feared that in future conflicts the most up-to-date American military systems could be passed on from Saudi Arabia to confrontation states such as Syria, Jordan, or Iraq.

The decision makers in Jerusalem were aware, however, that Saudi Arabia was a moderate, pro-Western power in the region, which—despite its belligerent rhetoric—had secretly been in contact with Israel. In the field of intelligence, Mossad operatives had met with security and intelligence experts from the Saudi royal family on several occasions, exchanging views on how to weaken the forces of radicalism and fundamentalism in the region.

U.S. intelligence had always been aware of the clandestine Israeli-Saudi contacts and encouraged them. A striking example of American-backed secret cooperation followed a simple navigational error in the Red Sea in September 1981. An Israeli navy missile boat, on routine patrol, ran aground just off the Saudi coast. Begin's government, concerned that the crew might be captured by Arabs, relayed a firm request to the Saudis via the U.S. embassy in Tel Aviv: "Do not touch our men.

Any harm done to them will be seen as an act of belligerence."

The Reagan administration, fearing a flare-up of tension, intervened by persuading the Saudis that the Israeli ship had not landed on their coastline with hostile intentions. They agreed to the U.S. suggestion that Israeli rescue teams be permitted to operate on their coast as long as the entire event remained secret. It took sixty hours to dislodge the ship, which was then towed to the Israeli port of Eilat. Only after the vessel's safe return did the administration leak the story to the American media as an example of Saudi goodwill—a leak aimed at making the Saudis look moderate and wise, so that Congress would approve the AWACS sale.

Whatever it thought of the royal House of Saud, Israel could not still a reaction so automatic that it was a reflex: When the words "arms sale" and "Arab state" are uttered together, Israel starts protesting.

The Israelis did think long and hard about it. They knew that Reagan and his administration saw their support for Saudi Arabia as part of a grand, anti-Soviet world plan. And many Israeli officials were hesitant to get into a fight with a new, friendly president.

General Menachem (Mendy) Meron, Israel's military attaché in Washington at the time, recalls: "I was of the opinion that Israel should not fight the administration, for a number of reasons. I did not believe it was possible to win, with a president as popular as Reagan. I also thought that Israel ought not to enter into a conflict with a president who expressed such warm feelings towards us."

Ephraim Evron, now Israel's ambassador to Washington, agreed with Meron. They flew to Israel to participate in secret discussions on how Israel should respond to the proposed AWACS sale. During these consultations, it became clear that the commanders of the Israeli air force—the officers most directly concerned—were willing to live with AWACS flying over Saudi Arabia. They did not see them as a serious threat to Israel's security, and they did not demand that their country's diplomats and friendly American lobbyists try to block the sale.

In the air force view, if Israel could be compensated appropriately—with the United States providing weapons systems to ensure the qualitative edge that Israel's military enjoyed over the Arabs'—then the whole controversy could be forgotten.

Prime Minister Begin, however, did not think so. When Evron and Meron went to see him, he seemed short-tempered and said that he had no time for them as he was on his way to visit his wife in the hospital. Meron dared to sound a little annoyed: "Sir, I came ten thousand kilometers to discuss this issue with you. I urge you to hear me."

Begin agreed to listen to the Washington-based attaché but did not change his mind: The Israeli government would oppose the sale of U.S. arms to Arab states—to defend a principle—and would express its opposition loudly and clearly.

Among other reasons, Begin's determination stemmed from the fact that he and his party were at the height of a high-intensity political campaign. Public opinion polls indicated that in the election set for June 30, 1981, the Likud could well lose to the Labor party, and Begin believed that he could not afford at this crucial stage to look like a wimp. He had already conceded the Sinai to Egypt; he did not have to start agreeing to an Arab arms buildup.

Begin's position was on the same wavelength as AIPAC. The U.S. pro-Israel lobby felt certain that through its influence on Congress, it could gain the majority votes needed in both the House and the Senate to block the sale to the Saudis. AIPAC managers turned the affair into a test case, a kind of congressional *High Noon*, a duel of political muscle with the new administration. If AIPAC could make Reagan flinch now, this would surely make him gun-shy in the future.

Israel and AIPAC do not always have identical interests.

There have been times when AIPAC acted independently, ignoring Israel's position. Sometimes AIPAC has its own agenda, inspired by American considerations of no interest to Jerusalem.

But when it came to AWACS, Israel's premier and AIPAC were on the same flight path. While Begin and his people loudly protested the deal, the AIPAC activists were working behind the scenes, on the Hill, to block it.

But Reagan did not back out of the duel. He wanted to win for the very reasons that AIPAC and Begin were trying to break him. "I believed," Reagan says in his memoirs, "that it was a battle that had to be won. If we lost on AWACS we might undermine our ability to persuade Congress to approve our domestic programs and the rearmament of the Pentagon."

As Reagan recalls, the AWACS battle began to heat up in the first few days of his term. "I started getting calls and visits from the leaders of American Jewish organizations and their supporters in Congress voicing opposition to the projected sale," Reagan writes. "By the middle of April, while I was recuperating from the shooting at the Hilton, I was receiving so much flak on the AWACS issue that it was taking up almost as much time as the economic recovery program."

Reagan had difficulty understanding why Begin and American Jews were so worked up about the issue. "It must be plain to them, they've never had a better friend of Israel in the White House," he wrote in his diary.

The president even expressed his commitment to Israel and the Jewish people in such a way that Menachem Begin could not have put it better. "My dedication to the preservation of Israel was as strong," he writes. "The Holocaust, I believe, left America with a moral responsibility to ensure that what had happened to the Jews under Hitler never happens again."

Reagan sent his Jewish liaison, Jacob (Jack) Stein, who was on the staff of the National Security Council, to see Begin in Jerusalem and offer one last chance to settle the AWACS dispute amicably. Stein recalls that NSC staffers referred to the duel as "Reagan or Begin." He was worried that posing such a blunt alternative raised dangerous, hidden questions about American Jews, suggesting they might have divided loyalties between Israel and the U.S.

"I want you to know that in our legislative office at the White House, we've counted fifty-two senators to approve the sale," Stein told Begin. "The president would like very much for you to understand United States concerns about the Saudis and to low-key your opposition. He's prepared to make further significant commitments to Israel's security." Stein cautioned the prime minister that "This is your opportunity to work with the president."

Begin replied that his advisors told a different tale: that a majority of senators were willing to block the sale.

Such was the Israeli-Jewish pressure that the White House saw itself forced to trade in its silk gloves for boxing gloves, scoring counterblows on senators and members of the House of Representatives. Vice President George Bush led the administration's lobbying drive, working closely with the Saudi embassy.

The battle ended in a narrow loss for AIPAC and Israel. First, on October 14, they did win in the House, where congressmen voted 301 to 111 against the AWACS sale. But on October 28, the vote in the Senate was 52 to 48 in the administration's favor. When asked to choose between Reagan and Begin, Congress had almost gone for the Israeli. But not quite.

The president was as angry as his predecessor, Harry Truman, had been when he refused in 1948 to meet Jewish lobbyists. Reagan has written: "I didn't like having representatives of a foreign country—*any* foreign country—trying to interfere with what I regarded as our domestic political process and the setting of our foreign policy."

The AWACS battle was to become a watershed in the fragile relations between the two countries. Reagan, basically sympathetic to Israel, now realized how powerful the pro-Israel lobby was and how high feelings ran when the country's security seemed imperiled. In Israel, on the other hand, the reaction among many officials was to encourage AIPAC to get stronger. And for AIPAC, the lesson was not to count on Congress alone, but to begin lobbying the White House intensively.

However, the most important lesson that the Israelis and their supporters did not learn was: Never fight a president, unless Israel's life really depends on it.

The Israelis were getting some compensation, as is the usual pattern immediately after U.S. arms sales to Arab states. As well as an additional $600 million in military loans, President Reagan began to talk about new arrangements to formalize strategic cooperation with Israel—steps that he said would be substantive, not "cosmetic."

A positive effect of the AWACS fight was the increased understanding of how domestic politics impact on foreign policy in both countries. One of the reasons that the issue had grown to such proportions was the fact that the nations were undergoing opposite experiences at the same time. While the U.S. administration was shaking itself free from preelection rhetoric and lifting off with a tough new foreign policy, the Israeli government was getting ready for touchdown toward the next elections. Jerusalem might not have been so adamant had it not been for the June elections to the K'nesset. And once Begin decided to fight against AWACS, he was not going to call off the battle.

His successful reelection campaign was capped off with a bold military move: the destruction of Iraq's nuclear reactor near Baghdad on June 7, 1981. Begin, deeply rooted in the Holocaust trauma, had decided that he would do anything to prevent Arab enemies from gaining the most awesome weapons of mass destruction. Israel tried to warn the world about Saddam Hussein, and the Mossad used threats and bombs to frighten foreign scientists who had been hired by Iraq. But Saddam's nuclear program was not stopped.

Begin ordered Israel's air force to stage its longest-range bombing raid. It was a complete success, but while Begin was thrilled, the entire world condemned the attack. Secretary of Defense Weinberger was particularly livid, insisting that overall U.S. policy toward Israel should be reassessed. President Reagan ordered that the U.S. endorse the UN condemnation and that deliveries of F-16 warplanes be suspended—an echo of the arms freeze during President Ford's 1975 "reassessment."

On the day after the Baghdad air raid, Israel's ambassador Evron and his military attaché were summoned to the Pentagon to receive a formal protest. It was General Meron's first encounter with Weinberger, and he remembers it as a "peculiar" one: "While we tried to explain our motives and the reasoning behind the strike, the secretary repeatedly stressed that Israel had violated the air space of a friendly nation." Weinberger was referring to the fact that on their way to Iraq, Israeli warplanes had crossed through Jordanian and Saudi airspace without permission.

He was very formal, the Israelis say, without any small talk or social niceties. He merely repeated the laconic wording of the diplomatic protest. When the Israeli officials emerged from the meeting, their feeling that Weinberger was no friend of Israel was reconfirmed. Privately the defense secretary and Vice President Bush called for a cutoff of all U.S. aid to Israel.

In the days to come, more U.S. officials expressed their dissatisfaction with Israel, this time on the grounds that it had used American F-15 and F-16 aircraft without U.S. consent. Their sales contracts stipulated that Israel was provided with these arms for *defense* only.

Behind the scenes, however, Israelis were hearing a different tune. Secretary of State Haig was privately pleased and sympathetic. So were senior officers in the U.S. Air Force, who were impressed by the daring and accuracy of the raid, and said so to Israel's air force attaché during a cocktail party held a few days after the attack. This double-talk confused Israelis, who were hurt by the public condemnation and criticism.

The feeling in Jerusalem in the few months before the strike had been that Washington shared Israel's concern about Iraq's nuclear capability. Indeed, Ambassador Sam Lewis had sent a long and detailed report in January 1981 on Israel's case against the Iraqi reactor.

The Mossad and military intelligence were steadily passing on information about the supply of materials from Western nations as well as assessments about the pace of Iraq's nuclear development.

"The Americans were in agreement with us about most of the data, so we got the impression that they were understanding us," General Meron recalls. "It's true that we did not let them know about our intention to bomb the plant, and for operational reasons we kept the timing of the attack secret, but they could have read between the lines and come to the conclusion that we were running out of patience."

Whether the Americans were genuinely surprised and angered by the Baghdad raid or not, the official hostility quickly diminished. Privately a State Department official with many close friends among pro-Israel lobbyists told them: "The system made the president yell about the attack on the reactor, but personally he thought it was great."

Ambassador Lewis recalls that Reagan was, at first, angry at being surprised, "until he discovered something he wasn't aware of: that throughout the last six months of the Carter administration, we had been talking secretly with Begin about the problem of the Iraqi reactor. Begin had been warning us—over and over again—'You've got to get that thing stopped, diplomatically.' And we were saying 'Give us time! Give us time!' "

After thinking about it for a few days, Reagan let his forgiveness publicly slip out, saying it was hard for him "to envision Israel as being a threat to its neighbors."

The presidential pardon was the first sign of what was to become a pattern in the Reagan administration's attitude toward Israel. The chief executive would always be more understanding and considerate toward the Jewish state than most of his cabinet secretaries. It also became noticeable, in Jerusalem and among American Jewish leaders, that Reagan and his old friend Weinberger did not see eye to eye when it came to Israel and the Middle East.

The big thaw in the briefly chilly U.S.-Israel relations came when the two leaders met. Reagan and Begin, quite simply, got along. The Israeli prime minister's visit to Washington in early September 1981 was a get-acquainted session. Since the meetings between Levi Eshkol and Johnson and between Golda Meir and Nixon, Israeli leaders had made it their habit to aim for an early introduction to new residents of the White House.

Begin's visit was surprisingly friendly, considering that the duel over AWACS had not yet been settled. The prime minister was in an elated mood because of his victory in the recent elections and the successful raid on the Iraqi nuclear reactor. Begin was a man of moods, and occasionally he would sink into profound melancholy that could last for long periods of time. Now he was euphoric.

After a formal welcoming ceremony on the South Lawn of the White House, Begin and the president adjourned to the Oval Office. Reagan told his guest that he wanted "the two of us to be on a first-name basis." Begin was flattered, and from then on he referred to the U.S. president as "my dear Ron."

The tensions of recent months seemed to have been swept away during the Begin visit. He got a sincerely warm reception from the president, who went out of his way to show sympathy. He poured praise on Israel and repeated preelection phrases, such as "Israel is our friend and ally."

Reagan also returned to his political element: anti-Soviet rhetoric. He stressed how highly he rated Israel's strategic position in the containment of Communist expansion.

Begin, who felt that the conversation was taking a better course than expected, picked up on the reference to Israel as an ally and, with his legal inclinations, suggested the concept become a contract. "Mr. President, we're good allies," he said. "We share the same views. Why don't we formalize this in some kind of agreement?"

"That sounds pretty good," said Reagan—quickly, and almost casually.

The next appointment for the prime minister and his entourage—which included Defense Minister Ariel Sharon and Foreign Minister Yitzhak Shamir—was with Defense Secretary Weinberger. Begin met him, still beaming with happiness from his White House lovefest, saying to Weinberger: "Mr. Secretary, your president and I have just decided to formalize a defense agreement."

Recalling Weinberger's reaction, Ambassador Lewis says, "Cap almost swallowed his gum!" Weinberger, feeling ambushed, replied that he was not aware of this and promised he would clarify the matter with the president. That, however, was not all he actually did.

Concluding Begin's visit, Reagan ordered Weinberger to work with Sharon to set up teams that would put meat on the bare bones of the strategic cooperation concept.

In the months to come, Weinberger and his Pentagon staff would do all they could to try to torpedo the understanding that had been reached between Begin and Reagan.

The result, instead of a new policy, was new confusion. Howard Teicher, then a Middle East analyst in the White House, recalls: "For a senior bureaucrat like me, it was like being in a washing machine where sometimes things went very smoothly and the water was warm. Then suddenly cold water could come pouring out of nowhere and you'd be turned the other way and get hit across the head with some unexpected action or development. It was a funny time: On one hand, things were done at the president's direction that were unprecedented, but they would be undone by his secretary of defense."

Israeli officials would long wonder about the roots of Weinberger's unfriendly perspective, and they would place them in his years at Bechtel—building Saudi Arabia and proud of it. One of his aides has said that the Bechtel connection does not explain all, and there seemed to be a psychological, personal background to his attitude. The Israelis and many American Jews speculated that Weinberger had identity problems because one of his recent ancestors had converted from Judaism to Christianity.

But other Pentagon aides saw his attitude to Israel as honestly based on a calculation of American interests in the world. "He's not anti-Semitic," says Dov Zakheim, who worked closely with Weinberger. "He was close to the Saudis and thought they were very important to us. He really believed that the United States couldn't just rely on Israel in that part of the world, and he knew that Ronald Reagan had a weird visceral reaction in favor of the Israelis, so he balanced that."

Because the brief agreement between Reagan and Begin on the concept of formalizing U.S.-Israel relations did not extend to specific details, it remained open to various interpretations. In fact, from as long back as the early 1950s, with the shift in Israel's international orientation under Ben-Gurion's leadership, successive governments had been hoping for a formal defense treaty with the United States, something along the lines of the North Atlantic Treaty Organization (NATO).

Premiers from Ben-Gurion through Eshkol and Meir had amused themselves with dreams—which they occasionally voiced—of America committed, in writing, to rush to the salvation of the Jewish state. It would add an extremely important dimension to their country's security. The Arabs would never dare to attack an Israel linked to the strongest power on earth by a formal defense pact.

But over the years, the United States never went for the idea. Now, with Reagan, the Israelis believed they finally had their opportunity. The idea was first brought up, in the new administration, by two State Department officials who for many years would work for strategic cooperation with Israel: Paul Wolfowitz, the director of policy planning who in 1991 would talk the Israelis into weathering the Scud storm, and his senior deputy, James Roche.

Wolfowitz and Roche reported to Haig in January 1981 on the quiet but steady cooperation between the military establishments of the two nations under the Nixon, Ford, and Carter administrations. In April 1981 Haig visited Jerusalem and discussed future prospects for strategic cooperation in his meetings with Begin and senior cabinet ministers.

Haig and his top aides would continue speaking with Israeli strategic planners right up to the September summit, searching for areas of broad agreement that might somehow be set down on paper. The Americans were interested in reviving the kind of joint ventures the two countries had in the Third World in the 1960s: Israeli diplomats, agricultural experts, financiers, and spies might lend a hand to American interests in Central America and Africa. To Haig, Israelis could be U.S. surrogates, just as Cubans were fronting for the Soviets.

On the simpler, bilateral level, Haig also wanted advantages offered by Israel: combat experience with weapons systems, on-the-spot intelligence in the region, and the ability to store materiel for America's military in case of emergencies. However, there was a basic misconception between the two sides.

On surrogacy, Israel—while willing to help the United

States—did not, openly and formally, wish to match the already negative portrayal that it was America's lackey. More sensitive was Begin and Sharon's insistence that strategic cooperation should add to Israel's freedom of action. They argued that the United States should trust Israel to protect Western interests in the Middle East—adding that the United States might well be spared embarrassment if Israel did not turn to it for permission every time action was needed. The destruction of the Iraqi reactor, in June, underlined the Israeli point.

Haig, however, wanted the opposite. He hoped that a new set of formal undertakings would require the Israelis to consult with America before taking any major action—in effect, restraining Israel's freedom. The Baghdad attack was his case in point. The new "true partnership," said Haig, "means that actions taken by one side must always consider the vital interests of the other."

After the Reagan-Begin summit, Haig stepped back—bowing to the president's bureaucratic instructions—and left the detailed negotiations to the Pentagon and Israel's defense ministry. The American negotiators, however, behaved as if their mission was damage control. The president and prime minister wanted a piece of paper—a Memorandum of Understanding, or MOU—but Pentagon officials did not wish it to be worth the paper on which it was written.

The United States did not need the MOU, they believed. Israel was already on America's side, and a formal document would only irritate the Arabs, harming American relations and interests in the region. If there had to be a piece of paper, the most they would accept was a noncommittal statement that would express in the vaguest and most obscure terms the new Reagan-Begin spirit in relations between Jerusalem and Washington. The Pentagon wanted a hollow MOU, with empty words and no concrete deeds.

The talks continued, at an intensive pace between officials

and military men from both sides, for two months. "The atmosphere during these discussions was tense," recalls an Israeli participant, "and looked more like the sad conversation between mourners than the excitement about the impending birth of something new."

The mood also was adversely influenced by the fact that the Americans were convinced that Begin's government had misled them on the AWACS issue. Administration officials believed that Begin had agreed to drop his active opposition of the sale to Saudi Arabia, but then—on Capitol Hill during his September visit—he did speak out against the arms deal and even suggested it was an example of anti-Semitism.

Weinberger also railed at having to deal with Sharon—the famous Israeli "superhawk" whose ambitious plans in the Middle East seemed to imply that the United States was incapable of protecting Western interests.

Eventually Reagan and Haig realized that the defense teams were not getting very far, so they stepped back into the process. They were helped by the fact that the AWACS duel with Israel had been settled, with the pro-Israel lobby shot down by the Senate.

By late November an agreed MOU formulation was hammered out. Israel saved face by portraying it as a document of mutual concession. But in fact the Pentagon had won the day. The MOU was hollow, reflecting the original desires of the Department of Defense.

The document carefully defined the only threat that would trigger cooperation as one caused by "the Soviet Union and Soviet controlled forces from outside the region introduced into the region." In other words, Israel was being added to the list of nations that would have to help the United States when the United States chooses.

This, naturally, was a long way short of what Begin and Sharon had hoped for. Sharon wrote later that he "believed that Israeli-American cooperation could be mutually beneficial on a larger regional stage and even on the global stage." But he and the prime minister wanted coordination within the Middle East for any potential danger to Israel—not just the Soviet Union. The Israelis were thinking more of threats from Syria and Iraq.

The MOU specifically stated that cooperation "is not directed at any state or group of states within the region."

A worse disappointment for the Israelis was that the document did not delineate even one area of defense or military cooperation. The document clearly stated that collaboration, in whatever field, would be subject to further agreement between the two sides. Who needed an agreement that calls for negotiating another agreement? To the Israeli cabinet, it all began to look worthless, and ministers were not at all sure whether to ratify the MOU.

Some, led by Foreign Minister Shamir, expressed reservations about Israel explicitly naming the Soviet Union as an enemy. Israel was becoming the first country to sign an agreement with the United States in which the Soviets were literally named as the foe. In the end the cabinet decided not to pull out, fearing that tearing up the MOU would aggravate things, domestically and with Washington.

But Weinberger's Pentagon had further humiliations in mind. Sharon went to Washington for the signing of the MOU, in the full expectation that a ceremony would be held at the Pentagon. Weinberger, however, refused to host the event there and had it transferred to the national Geographic Society building. The ceremony, on December 1, 1981, was brief, and media coverage was not permitted.

General Meron, who was present at the occasion, remembers that Secretary Weinberger simply signed the MOU and left. No niceties, no cocktails. In the end, he had succeeded in orchestrating the event to give it the least possible significance and attention. Sharon was annoyed and decided to cut short his U.S. visit and return home.

"The agreement was dead even before it was born," another Israeli participant recalls. "The only question was when its death certificate would come through."

The coroner's pronouncement came nearly three weeks later. Begin at the time was confined to his Jerusalem residence because he had slipped and broken his hip, and was living on pain-killers and tranquilizers. It would seem, to some of his cabinet ministers, that one side effect of the drugs was the surprise— and political crisis with the United States—that followed.

Begin convened his cabinet in an emergency session at his home, astonishing them with the announcement that he had decided to extend Israel's civil laws over the occupied Golan Heights, captured from Syria fourteen years earlier. This made no practical difference in the thinly populated but strategically important heights.

The United States, responding to howls of protest from the Arab world, saw the Begin declaration as outright annexa-tion—unprovoked, unacceptable, and unhelpful to efforts for Middle East peace.

By way of protest and punishment, the United States sus-pended the MOU that had been so painstakingly negotiated. America's condemnation included, for the second time in six months, the withholding of a military favor—a brief slap on the wrist, but now becoming a pattern. The delivery of seventy-five F-16 fighters was suspended.

And so it came to pass that in the first year of the presidency of a self-declared great friend of Israel, relations between the two countries had sunk so low that they could be put on a par with the tensions that had characterized the Eisenhower and Carter presidencies.

The great expectations of a happy marriage with the admin-istration of Ronald Reagan and Alexander Haig had miserably dwindled to a sense that the United States—rather than marrying its interests with Israel's—was treating Israel as a mistress, bought on the sly with a cheap, five-carat gold-plated ring. Begin's Israel felt as insulted as a jilted lover.

CHAPTER TWELVE

MADE IN AMERICA

From his modest office on the lowest level of the K'nesset building, Israel's parliament, set among the green hills of Jerusalem, Moshe Arens kept his finger on the pulse of Israeli policies on war and peace. As the Likud-appointed chairman of the prestigious Foreign Affairs and Defense Committee, he chaired a constant round of hearings and enjoyed being part of the government's policy-making deliberations.

It was obvious to him that the U.S. suspension of the strategic MOU was a further blow to relations with the United States, a subject near and dear to him. Arens's committee had heard testimony from all the senior ministers, on their high hopes for strategic cooperation with the United States, now dashed.

Knowing Menachem Begin for many years, Arens understood the prime minister's anger, but even he was surprised by Begin's unusual reaction. On December 20, 1981, Begin—still recuperating in his bedroom—summoned U.S. Ambassador Lewis. He coldly addressed him as "Mr. Ambassador" while Defense Minister Sharon and Foreign Minister Shamir sat in as if attending a lesson in how to deliver a diplomatic dressing down.

Begin pulled out some papers, but without looking down at them he launched into a classic tirade: "Are we a vassal state? Are we a banana republic? Are we fourteen-year-olds who, if we misbehave, get our wrists slapped?"

Begin preached to the ambassador for fifty minutes, uninterrupted. "The people of Israel have lived 3,700 years without a memorandum with America and will continue to live without it another 3,700 years."

A verbal assault, however long, colorful, and harsh, was not sufficient for Begin—even though he was a lover of rhetorical flourishes. He wanted to send Washington a stronger message, through Lewis: that the United States might punish Israel; but Israel could, at the least, annoy the United States. If Washington did not wish to coordinate strategy any more, let the Americans guess what Israel was up to!

When the ambassador went downstairs in the prime minister's residence, he found the entire cabinet and the heads of the Mossad and military intelligence milling around. It took Lewis quite a few weeks to find out what that gathering was about, but he says Begin was trying—that very day—to get cabinet approval for an invasion of Lebanon. An operation to clear out Palestinian guerrillas, says Lewis, "was to be his response to the suspension of the strategic cooperation agreement with the U.S."

Begin did not get the cabinet vote he wanted that day, but he and Sharon kept raising the issue and within a few months they did.

Begin's fury subsided, however, and the prime minister understood that Israel's relations with America were in trouble.

Surely something more positive could be done with an administration that was fundamentally well disposed toward Israel and agreed with it in many ways.

So Begin decided that a supreme effort must be made to pick up the pieces—and immediately. With this in mind, he decided that the situation required more than just a career diplomat in Washington, not that he had anything against Ambassador Evron. To the contrary, Begin was even fond of him.

But what he needed now was a person who subscribed to Likud party ideology and understood thoroughly the American mentality and way of life. Begin called Moshe Arens and asked him to be Israel's seventh ambassador to Washington.

It was far from a random choice. Arens had the two requisite qualities, and Begin hoped that his soft manner and familiarity with America would get relations between the United States and Israel back into working order.

Being sent to Washington at the age of fifty-six was the closure of a circle for Arens. He was born in Lithuania, on the Baltic Sea, in 1926 to a Zionist family. His father was an affluent industrialist who did business with the United States, traveling back and forth between America and eastern Europe. In September 1939, after World War II broke out, the family flew to Sweden and then crossed the Atlantic by ship. Arens—still nicknamed "Misha"—recalls: "Although we left behind everything we owned in Lithuania, my father was also established in New York and possessed quite a lot of property." Emigrating to the States was natural for Misha and his family, because "all my life we were expecting to go there." Unlike most European Jewish immigrants, the Arens family found the adjustment quite easy.

The young Arens, who had learned fluent English with private tutors back in Lithuania, had no trouble fitting into American society. He went to school in upper Manhattan's posh

Washington Heights neighborhood and "felt completely like an American kid."

Although he received some Jewish education and was a member of a Zionist youth movement, Arens did not feel any conflict of identity by living in America. When he graduated from high school in 1943, he enrolled at MIT to study mechanical engineering. A year later he was drafted into the U.S. Army Corps of Engineers.

"I felt good in the army," Arens says. "I didn't feel any anti-Semitism." His military career appeared promising. Within less than two years he was promoted to the rank of sergeant-major. He and his unit prepared for what was supposed to be the invasion of Japan. However, the dropping of the atom bombs on Hiroshima and Nagasaki put an end to that plan and, indeed, the war.

Arens—who later would be involved in various Israeli arms projects—recalls: "Back then, we didn't know what the atomic bomb meant. All we knew was that within two or three days, the war was over, and we were happy about it. Only later books suggested that Japan was about to surrender anyway. If this is true, dropping the bombs was a tragedy."

Arens returned to MIT. Financed by the GI Bill, which subsidized army veterans' education, "I completed four years in less than three years" and in 1947 qualified as an engineer.

The prospects for a young, intelligent MIT graduate were bright. He was offered jobs, but just then his Zionism was re-emerging. Late that year the UN approved the creation of a Jewish state, and Arens decided his place was there.

Involved since high school days with Begin's right-wing brand of Zionism, Arens decided to move to the new nation. Begin's political movement asked him, on the way, to stop over in North Africa to work with Jewish youngsters there for a few months. He finally reached Israel in March 1949, after the War of Independence. The fact that he never served in the Israeli army would give his political opponents some ammunition in the future.

Together with other young Jews from the United States, Arens joined a kibbutz—but a right-wing commune—on the border with Jordan. He was reunited there with his New York sweetheart, his future wife, Muriel. She had gotten to Israel early enough to serve in the army.

Having won the War of Independence and now building its society, Israel became a magnet for young American Jews. Many quickly found interesting jobs—some, at the top of Israel's nascent military industries. But Arens—because he was a right-winger—could get neither a security clearance nor a job with the defense manufacturers controlled by Ben-Gurion's Labor party.

For two years the American engineer tried to be an Israeli pioneer and farmer. "It was an interesting experience," he says, "but it didn't work." This was a period of extreme austerity in Israel, and it was tough for a young couple—especially from America—to survive the hardship. Misha and Muriel decided to return to the United States.

He completed a master's degree at Cal-Tech in Pasadena and easily found work as a mechanical engineer at Curtis Wright, a small company in New Jersey. In 1957 Arens got a job offer from Israel: an offer to join the faculty of Haifa's technical university, the Technion—Israel's own MIT.

By now the bitterness of ideological divisions had subsided, so Arens was allowed to join Israel Aircraft Industries, where he was involved in missile and aviation projects aimed at making Israel an independent military manufacturer. Israel eventually succeeded in producing its own sophisticated systems, mainly based on technology acquired from friendly nations such as France and, occasionally, the United States. This left

Arens an enthusiastic supporter of Israel's military industries.

Now, in February 1982—sent by Begin, his political mentor—as ambassador to the United States, Arens thought he would have a once-in-a-lifetime opportunity to achieve the goal he had developed in his varied career: to make Israel stronger, and closer to America, by fostering the technological collaboration of the two countries' defense industries.

"I was very excited when I arrived in Washington," remembers Arens, bespectacled and with a crewcut making him look like a cross between a physics professor and a U.S. Marine. "It was a strange feeling to return to the country in which I grew up and went to school and whose political system I admired, as the representative of my state, Israel."

The new ambassador, however, had little time to devote to nostalgic reflections. There were burning issues on the agenda. "It was a difficult time," says Arens. "The issues of the bombing of the Iraqi reactor and the AWACS fight were supposedly behind us but still embittered the relationship. I arrived during the Americans' freeze of the F-16s, after the Golan move. Our main effort was to defuse the tension and defreeze the planes and the suspension of the MOU."

In contrast with Begin and Sharon, who were deeply disappointed by the failure of the strategic MOU, the new ambassador saw the bright side of the fiasco. For the first time in the history of U.S.-Israeli relations, military-defense links had been established and contractually formalized. Unlike the 1951 intelligence collaboration agreement, the MOU was published, with most of its details open to public inspection.

Arens's diplomatic challenge was aided by many American officials—and a majority of members of Congress—who were uneasy about the strained relations with Israel and felt they should be straightened out. Bill Casey, the director of the CIA, was among them—although not for sentimental reasons, but rather because Israel was anti-Soviet and a trailblazer in the fight against international terrorism, which the Reagan administration had high on its list of priorities.

Another member of this pro-Israel faction was Secretary of State Haig, who seemed to relish the role of main challenger to Defense Secretary Weinberger's frost toward Israel.

The leading pro-Israel light in the Reagan administration was the chief executive himself. "My heart went out especially to Begin," Reagan has written. "I had many difficulties with him while I was President, but he was an Israeli patriot devoted above all to the survival of his country." Reagan was impressed that Begin thought constantly of the Holocaust, "the depth of the hatred and viciousness that can be directed at Jews simply because they are Jews."

Arens was also helped by the goodwill that surrounded Israel's return to Egypt, on April 25, of the last part of the occupied Sinai. For the sake of peace, the Israelis were abandoning airfields, oil wells, and strategic strongholds. U.S. officials had begun to fear, in their months of high tension with Israel, that Jerusalem might cancel the closing chapter of the Camp David peace accords. The White House announced in May the lifting of military sanctions imposed on Israel after Begin annexed the Golan Heights, thawing the frozen sale of F-16 jets to the Israeli air force.

"At the embassy," Arens recalls, "we had the feeling that it was only a matter of time until the relations would heal." He felt he was making some headway by speaking in public to Jewish and Gentile groups, to senators and labor unions, on television and through the op-ed columns of newspapers.

Arens, who still speaks English at home in Israel, knew how to speak to the Americans—in their own accent, their own language. "I tried to deliver an Israeli message in a recognizable form," he recalls. "Unlike for us Israelis, ideology is less under-

stood by Americans. Stating Israel's security concerns, I tried
not to base them on ideology."

That approach had worked for him in his earlier days as a
politician in Begin's Likud party. In late 1977 he visited Washington as chairman of the K'nesset foreign affairs committee—
and attended a lunch hosted by the similar committee of the
U.S. Senate. Several senators had heard that Arens was an extreme right-winger, and although they were pro-Israel they
had not yet made the mental adjustment from three decades of
Labor rule in Israel.

Committee staffers, even more pro-Israel, had written briefing papers for the senators but were afraid that Arens "would
blow it." They gathered around a small table in Room S116 of
the Capitol, and within minutes the Israeli had gripped their
attention with a party-line talk on Israel and why it had to keep
the territories—a completely new line to the Americans.

By now the staffers were fearful for Israel's reputation on
Capitol Hill. But to their amazement, committee chairman
John Sparkman popped up and said to Arens: "Son, you're
wonderful! You speak American!" That was it. The bottom line
was, Arens's style had won them over. They did not seem to
care about the content of what he said.

Despite his American accent, in both English and Hebrew, he
says, "I am an Israeli. I have more friends in Israel, where we
have a frankness and freshness that derive from our collective
experience. We are all together, and that of course is a result of
the dangers we are facing. Our national pride over what we
have achieved is something you rarely find in other countries.
It reminds me of something you used to find in the U.S. for
many years: the pride of doing things together. In that sense,
the U.S. was a unique country like Israel still is, and being
proud of your uniqueness is—in a way—one of the common
elements that bind the two countries."

But by the middle of 1982, they were again unbound. Arens found there is a limit to what common traits of two nations, familiarity, perfect English, and hard work, can accomplish in international relations. Four months of his high-intensity diplomacy were undone by higher politics—when Israel invaded Lebanon in June.

It was not that the United States was infuriated with the operation itself. The problem, in the final analysis, was with the size of the invasion, and how it appeared.

Israel had begun warning the United States, long before Arens arrived as ambassador, that Palestinian guerrilla activities in Lebanon were intolerable and that Israel would have to "neutralize" the Palestine Liberation Organization. Surprisingly, that verb was first used in Washington, with regard to Yasser Arafat's organization, by Haig's inner circle at the State Department. At a meeting of American experts in May 1981, a senior official suggested that U.S. policy in Lebanon had to help bring about the "neutralization" of the PLO.

"It is important to recognize the gravity of the statement about neutralization," says Raymond Tanter, who was then on the National Security Council. "Neutralizing the PLO is a euphemism for destroying that organization. Ironically, State's circumlocution on neutralizing the PLO mirrored Israeli Defense Minister Sharon's concept of the 1982 war." Tanter contends, "One can surmise that the neutralization statement was an expression of the views of Secretary Alexander Haig himself."

Encouraged by what he heard of the American attitude, Sharon outlined his ambitious plans for Lebanon in a December 1981 meeting with Ambassador Lewis and another U.S. official who was visiting the Middle East. The Israeli minister spared no time, explaining in great detail his offensive strategy to destroy the military and political infrastructure of the PLO, to drive the organization out of Lebanon, and to install a pro-Israel, pro-American regime in Beirut.

The plan, code-named Big Pines by the random selection of an Israel Defense Forces computer, stemmed from a document approved by the Israeli army as long ago as 1979, before Sharon became defense minister. It was a typical contingency plan, tentative and designed to be filed away with hundreds of similar documents drafted and circulated by military planners. But Sharon, as he told his American visitors, intended to make Big Pines a reality.

A month later Israeli and American officials met secretly at the U.S. Embassy in London—ostensibly looking for ways to revive the strategic MOU. The Israelis spent a good deal of the time telling the Americans not to be shocked should Israel go to war against the PLO.

U.S. officials understood what was coming—"sounds like war to me," said one to another, in London—and also understood Israel's motives. Begin and Sharon planned a military action designed to destroy PLO guerrilla fighters and their military and political infrastructure in Lebanon. But, equipped with past precedents and experience, they did not wish to take America by surprise. They hoped to coordinate with the United States and even hoped for support. At the least, they never wanted it to be said that they had not informed Washington.

Israeli and American newspapers, meanwhile, were providing fairly precise details of Israel's military planning—predicting a large-scale invasion. These reports left no doubt in Washington that the Israeli government inspired the leaks, and officials assumed the source was "the big dripper himself, Israel's Defense Minister Sharon."

So in May 1982, when Arens's efforts seemed to have cleaned up the polluted atmosphere of U.S.-Israel relations, Sharon flew to Washington to take selected Americans into his confidence. At a State Department meeting with Haig and top aides, the Israeli gave a lecture on the Palestinian buildup in Lebanon and accused the PLO of violating an American-mediated cease-fire. Sharon has revealed that he delivered his message to Haig "in even more explicit terms" than he did to Defense Secretary Weinberger that same day. "We do not like the idea of war," said the visitor, but "at the same time we don't want you to be surprised."

Sharon pounded the table, and, as one U.S. official who was present notes, the Israeli defense minister "left no doubt that he was itching for war."

Both being military men, Generals Sharon and Haig took to each other. But Sharon admitted later that Haig had not given Israel a green light for the Lebanon invasion. Ambassador Arens and his military attaché General Meron, who were present during the meeting, agree that Haig never indicated to Sharon that he would sanction a war. And Howard Teicher, who sat on the American side, goes further, saying Haig "expressed his firm opposition to an invasion."

But Arens adds that Haig refrained from warning Israel. He did not inform Sharon that if Israel invaded, the United States would do this, that, or anything. Teicher adds that Haig "pointedly" credited the Israelis with the right to make their own decisions about self-defense—although Haig "expected Israel to act with a response proportionate to the provocation."

"The whole argument was really on this question of proportionality," Ambassador Lewis recalls. "Neither Haig nor Reagan would ever say that Israel had no right to defend itself. They took defense very seriously for the U.S., so they weren't going to say that an ally or friend didn't have the same right. So an ultimatum, 'You must not cross the border,' was never issued. I don't think it ever entered their minds."

The White House and State Department should have known better. As Tanter of the NSC admits: "It is a standard operating assumption in the United States government that Israeli officials have a penchant for reading vagueness and ambiguity in American communications as a sign of informed consent to some preferred Israeli action. An American nod acknowledging that an Israeli suggestion has been heard and understood could be reported, not only as an agreement to the substance of the idea, but as a Washington proposal.

"Washington officials charged with the conduct of U.S.-Israeli relations must play by explicit rules of the road, lest they leave an opening through which Israeli tanks might rumble."

The result was more implicit than explicit, but the United States chose, once again, to withhold an out-and-out green light. "There was a clear, strong amber light," says Lewis; the same kind of yellow for caution that was enough, in 1967, for Israel to stage the preemptive air strike that won the Six-Day War. Fifteen years and one day later, whatever the traffic signals, Israel took the wrong road.

As Israeli troops poured across the border on June 6, 1982, the American government understood that their aim was to advance twenty-five miles into Lebanese territory and expel the PLO. The United States believed that Operation Peace for Galilee would last only a few days, as Begin himself reassured the Israeli parliament.

By June 21, with Lebanon a battlefield for a third week, Begin found himself having lunch with Reagan at the White House. Now he assured the president that Israel had no intention of invading the Muslim, western half of Beirut.

To apply pressure on the Israelis not to try to conquer the capital of an Arab country for the first time, Reagan had already decided to return to the zigzag course of wrist slapping. He again delayed the sale to Israel of seventy-five F-16 fighter planes that had been unfrozen only the previous month.

Begin also had a difficult session on Capitol Hill with legislators who felt that Israel had betrayed them by going far beyond its declared war aims. Secretary Haig warned the Israeli delegation that the "continued bombing of Beirut would destroy what remains of the goodwill of your friends in the United States."

The invasion did go out of control and caused real damage to U.S.-Israel relations. What was supposed to be a short, sharp strike escalated into a three-year war. Instead of stopping at twenty-five miles, Israeli soldiers ended up in Beirut. Israel's air force and artillery pounded an Arab capital, day after day. Syrian aircraft and missile launchers were destroyed, and the United States suddenly saw the threat of all-out war.

Israel's Ambassador Arens had something of a fright when Haig suddenly resigned on June 25, fed up with Weinberger and other rivals and bureaucrats blocking his foreign policy initiatives. "Haig was a 100 percent supporter of Israel on all issues," Weinberger has written, "and many felt he left because our policy in the Middle East was becoming more even-handed." The loss of such a friendly secretary of state came at a bad time for Israel, when its invasion looked so ugly on American television and was widely questioned by U.S. politicians.

"I remember vividly how tense and difficult it was for me during the bombardment of Beirut," says Arens, who acknowledges that as a former American he knows how important television is in the United States. "I had a lot of meetings with the Americans, and they were irritated by our military actions, which they saw on TV. And ninety percent of American politics is TV.

"Television carried disturbing pictures of civilian casualties. I read a book describing the president as a film actor who looked at life as one big movie. So the television pictures from Beirut had a terrible impact on him. He was warm-hearted toward Israel, but the same warm heart was hurt when he saw the TV pictures."

President Reagan's choice of George Shultz as Haig's replacement did nothing to cheer up Arens and the pro-Israel lobby in Washington. They feared that they would have another Weinberger with whom to contend, because Shultz was the president of the same Saudi-involved company, Bechtel. But unlike Weinberger, Shultz eventually proved himself to be a sympathetic listener and then a strong supporter of Israel's case.

Shultz told only a few friends of a personal link he felt with the Jewish state and its fight for survival. He was dean of the University of Chicago Business School when war broke out in the Middle East in 1967. One of his students was a brilliant young Israeli, Yosef Levy, who left his courses and his pregnant wife to rush home and fight. Levy was killed in a tank battle on the Golan Heights, and Shultz—moved by the tragedy—visited the young man's grave and kept in touch with the family in Israel. This was private, however, and, with the Lebanon War still raging, it was hard for Israel's friends in America to read Shultz as the new secretary of state.

There were many unpleasant moments for Arens, with hostile questions from the American media and from officials. However, in reality, according to Shultz, "President Reagan was more hesitant than anyone else about cracking down on the Israelis." Shultz says he and Vice President George Bush wanted more pressure on them, to stop the aerial bombing and artillery shelling of Beirut. "Cap Weinberger was at the extreme; he seemed almost ready to sever relations."

Reagan would never do that, but he did feel the need to try to stop the chaos—in Lebanon and in U.S.-Israel relations. In a televised speech on September 1, the president announced a peace plan, which called for Israeli-Arab negotiations based on the idea of exchanging land for peace and a freeze on Jewish settlements in the territories. Although there was nothing revolutionary in the Reagan Plan, Begin branded it as a deviation from the Camp David Accords. The Israeli premier had wrongly expected that Reagan would never return to the old formula. In addition, Begin was miffed at not having been consulted beforehand.

Arens recalls: "There were people in Jerusalem who thought I failed, because I didn't know. So what if I had known? Even then, I wouldn't have been able to influence Reagan. He was a good friend of Israel, but during the war the Arabs believed the U.S. was Israel's ally. He was motivated by trying to demonstrate that the U.S. was also out to advance the peace process."

More bluntly, Arens raised his voice directly at Shultz at one point: "You want Israelis to clean up the mess, while you Americans stay clean with the Arabs!"

Less than three weeks later, with the Reagan Plan going nowhere, more calamity ensued. On September 17 and 18, in a section of Beirut controlled by Israeli troops, Lebanese Christian militiamen butchered nearly eight hundred men, women, and children in the Palestinian refugee camps of Sabra and Shatila.

The world, as well as hundreds of thousands of Israelis who opposed the war, held Begin and Sharon responsible for the massacre. Although Israeli soldiers were not directly involved in the killing, Israel's top commanders had been informed that the Christian militiamen were entering the Palestinian camps for a "mop-up" operation. Israeli troops provided logistical assistance, such as firing flares for lighting. And the commander of the Christian assault squad had been trained by the Mossad.

Even the tolerant President Reagan had severe doubts about Israeli behavior, privately telling the Israelis that their siege of Beirut was like another "Holocaust." The president expressed the view that Begin made it very hard for America to be his friend.

As if to stiffen the Reagan administration's backbone, former President Carter phoned Shultz with advice obviously colored by his own disappointments with the Israeli leader. "You have to throw the book at Begin," said Carter. "Tough talk is the only talk Begin understands."

Arens's embassy was, by then, worried about the break in communications between Begin and the White House. Feeling normal channels were blocked, embassy staffers looked for alternative means to revive the link. The old contacts with American unions proved reliable, as always. The Israeli embassy's labor attaché knew Jackie Presser, international vice president of the Teamsters' union.

"What can I do for Israel?" Presser offered. The Israeli asked him to make it possible for Begin to be on speaking terms again with Reagan. The American trade unionist pulled some strings, called a top aide to Reagan, and within a few days returned with a positive reply: Reagan doesn't want to hold a grudge, and when Begin next comes in person the two leaders would meet. Arens was able to send Begin the reassurance that despite the crisis, the United States and Israel would resume their friendship.

The immediate fear, that summer and fall, was that the entire region could catch fire. Reagan sent U.S. Marines to Lebanon. The State Department helped mediate the withdrawal of Israeli troops from Beirut and the departure by sea of the PLO, including Arafat—the first substantial political contact between the United States and the Palestinian leader, starting a process that would lead to a formal dialogue six years later.

The Americans sank deeper into the Lebanese quagmire, becoming the targets of Shiite Muslim terrorism—for which they blamed Iran and Syria. The U.S. Embassy and the U.S. Marines' base in Beirut were both destroyed by a terrifying Shiite weapon, suicide bombers. When Shultz tried to hammer out a peace treaty between Israel and Lebanon, Syria sabotaged his efforts. Months of intensive negotiations went down the drain. Shultz became disgusted with Syria, hastening his shift from even-handedness to firm friendship with Israel.

Arens was being pulled in the opposite direction. The Likud loyalist became more flexible, faced with the barrage of criticism and disintegration of Israel's stature in the United States. He suggested to Begin that he consider the Reagan Plan and its proposed freeze on Jewish settlements—as a gesture of goodwill. Arens's cable enraged Begin.

Angry and in a militant mood, Begin convened his cabinet and rejected the Reagan Plan. Begin intended to speak about it in person with the president, flying to the United States in November for their second meeting in five months. But while in Los Angeles, Begin got the bad news that his wife, Aliza, had died. Emotionally shattered, the prime minister returned to Israel for the funeral and canceled his date at the White House.

Perhaps it was too late anyway. Middle East reality would never be the same. The Lebanon war brought about changes, some of them slow and barely perceptible. But the most dramatic of these changes occurred in Israel.

Following the Sabra and Shatila massacre, a state inquiry commission was set up and ruled, in February 1983, that Defense Minister Sharon bore indirect responsibility and should give up his job. Sharon resigned. U.S. officials did not attempt to hide their pleasure. And Begin urgently summoned Ambassador Arens home to take Sharon's place.

Arens had mixed feelings about leaving Washington after only a year. He admits that he loved working in America, where he felt so at home, and he was sorry to leave before managing to repair all the damage in U.S.-Israel relations. But being promoted to defense minister would give him more opportunities to work on it.

CHAPTER THIRTEEN

THE
SOLID-GOLD
ERA

It was in late November 1983, during a visit by the Israeli prime minister to Washington, that Israel unwittingly struck gold. In September, Menachem Begin had shocked his cabinet by announcing his resignation. Two factors had led to his decision: the death, the year before, of his wife; and the unexpectedly large Israeli death toll, over 650, in the seemingly unending war in Lebanon.

His party, the Likud, moved quickly to appoint Yitzhak Shamir as the country's new leader. Shamir then embarked, with Defense Minister Arens, on the traditional get-acquainted trip to see the U.S. president. The visit signaled a real change, with Ronald Reagan's surprise declaration of a new strategic partnership. For the Israelis it was a recurrent dream finally come true.

On the White House lawn, on November 29, Reagan offered a free-trade agreement between the two countries and added: ''I am pleased to announce that we have agreed to establish a Joint Political-Military Group to examine ways in which we can enhance Israeli-American cooperation. This Group will give priority attention to the threat to our mutual interest, posed by increased Soviet involvement in the Middle East."

"I was totally surprised," Shamir admits. "We had very few indications that the U.S. would make such an overt offer of the strategic cooperation that we had been so badly wanting for so many years."

Reagan's idea was that the consultative group, immediately dubbed the JPMG, would consider specific areas such as combined planning against mutual threats, joint military exercises, and the prepositioning of U.S. war materiel in Israel.

What was unique in this proposal? After all, defense contacts between the two countries had already become solid. And the intelligence cooperation between the Mossad and other Israeli agencies on one side, and the CIA, FBI, and NSA on the other, was almost a matter of routine—with permanent liaisons and analysts on both sides exchanging ideas, estimates, and secret information. Soviet-made weapons that Israel captured had been sent for study and inspection by U.S. experts since 1967.

In addition, most of the American military equipment that Israel's army purchased came with instructors and technicians. Israel, in parallel, sent out its own military personnel for training and study in the United States. Israeli pilots regularly visited American air bases to practice flying in jets and on simulators.

Yet despite this large number of small exchanges on the various levels of U.S.-Israel defense and military relations, something bigger and stronger was missing. The cooperation was potentially unstable, dependent on capricious bureaucrats and officials from too many agencies and departments.

As long ago as Ben-Gurion's premiership in the early 1950s,

Israeli leaders had considered the advantages of having a formal defense pact with Washington. And in the United States, Jews and other friends of Israel wished for even more, with some wishing longingly that Israel could be America's fifty-first state.

Only after the 1973 Yom Kippur War, however, did this idea lift a few inches off the ground. At that time Israel was pulled down from the unbridled optimism of 1967's Six-Day War to the confused pessimism that followed a near loss.

"Israel won in 1973, but Israel destroyed its leaders," says Nicholas Veliotes, a senior member of the State Department's Middle East team for over a decade. "And after the war Israeli leaders recognized their very, very severe overdependence on the United States. Not just for tax-free treatment of UJA contributions; but for economic and military subsidies. This was a tough thing for them to face."

As number-two man at the U.S. Embassy in Tel Aviv, Veliotes "began to hear from the Israelis, for the first time, their need to be recognized by the United States as a strategic partner. There was this nervousness that unless that happened— unless Israel and its friends in the United States could point to what Israel was doing for the U.S.—given the heavy dependence, which no Israeli liked, the basis of American support would be weak.

"It suddenly wasn't enough to have the moral considerations, the cultural and historical motivations. There was a constant effort by the Israeli government, during the Carter administration, to turn the consultations between our defense ministries into something more formal—something that could be portrayed, in both countries, as an alliance."

To Veliotes, the bases of America's strong support for Israel were "the consensus that the Jews deserved a homeland" after the Holocaust, admiration for Israel as "one of the first democracies in the Third World area," and the cultural affinity that made "Americans more comfortable with the Israelis than with the Arabs."

Among the first to lay the ground for the extra, strategic element in Washington were two Jewish lawyers, Max Kampelman and Richard Schifter, who would both serve later in the Reagan administration. "I was struck," Kampelman has written, "by the intensity of rhetorical support for Israel by some members of Congress, particularly some Jewish members, who then voted against domestic defense budget items with equal intensity. They were hawks in the Middle East and doves back home—or at least, an infertile hybrid."

Kampelman and Schifter found financial backers and formed the Jewish Institute for National Security Affairs. "Our prime purpose for JINSA was to persuade Jewish members of Congress and the Jewish community to support a strong American defense," says Kampelman.

They were helped by changes in U.S. public opinion, as the Vietnam War faded in people's memories. Antiwar sentiment gradually gave way to a realization that America still needed the ability to project power in distant reaches of the globe, and the Middle East seemed a prime example. Even a liberal president, Jimmy Carter, understood that the United States needed strongholds to ensure the flow of oil to the Western world.

The need seemed all the more acute as the pro-American Shah of Iran's power slipped away during 1978. Thinking both of the Ayatollah Khomeini's Shiites and of the Soviet invaders in nearby Afghanistan, the Carter administration developed the concept of a Rapid Deployment Force that would enable U.S. troops to fly immediately to any place where American or pro-Western interests were threatened.

The U.S. Army installed part of the rapid force in Egypt, but local security arrangements seemed imperfect and—politically—Egypt was isolated from other Arab countries because of its peace treaty with Israel.

Israel shone brightly as the only Middle Eastern country with the necessary infrastructure and willingness to accept the Rapid Deployment Force, with overt cooperation where necessary and long experience at covert arrangements when preferred.

Carter's secretary of defense, Harold Brown, initiated a secret strategic dialogue with his counterpart, General Ezer Weizman, in 1978. Brown assigned one of his most trusted advisors to write assessments of the changing balance of power around the world, primarily between the Soviet Union and the United States. To examine the Middle East balance, he worked with a navy commander, James Roche, and Dennis Ross, a Jew from California who was a junior official at the State Department but would have great influence during the Bush presidency. Both men believed that the United States and Israel should cooperate strategically, the non-Jewish Roche perhaps even more so. Roche says that one reason he loves Israel is probably his childhood in a largely Jewish neighborhood of New York City.

Roche and Ross visited Israel, met with military officers and strategists to exchange views, and found that U.S.-Israeli military cooperation was shallow. It was the classic half a glass of water: To some the glass seemed half full, but for Roche and Ross it was half empty. Aside from a regular exchange of intelligence, mainly comparing notes on the Arabs' military capabilities and occasional Israeli tips on Arab political intentions that were of interest to the United States, the two countries' relations had no operational strategic dimension. Roche and Ross wanted to deepen these contacts. But their efforts produced nothing tangible.

Carter and his senior Pentagon officials were not prepared to go any further than an intellectual, abstract, and theoretical dialogue—practicing strategic exclusion of Israel, rather than Reagan's later strategic cooperation. They had no wish to commit themselves to anything substantial. When there was a rare display of military cooperation—such as port calls in Haifa by the USS *Eisenhower* and then other aircraft carriers—the administration linked it to the peace treaty with Egypt. Ambassador Lewis explains that these symbolic expressions of a special strategic relationship were "rewards for good behavior" by Israel. In other words, the Carter administration perceived defense and military benefits as a lever to extract further diplomatic concessions from Israel.

Defense Minister Weizman, moreover, came up with what at the time struck the Americans as extravagant demands. Among other things, he requested that the United States should give Israel ground stations linked directly to satellites providing real-time intelligence on Arab enemies without American editing or filtering. Even in the 1990s, Washington would still be refusing to grant this advantage.

Of course, the U.S. strategic perception underwent a sea change when, in January 1981, Carter was replaced by Reagan. Reagan had said, in the campaign, that the Jewish state was a strategic asset. He tried, late that year, to do something about it; but for various reasons—including Menachem Begin demanding Israel's right to be unfettered in its own defense—the original Memorandum of Understanding had collapsed. Late 1983 seemed, finally, to be the right time.

It was not that Shamir was a soft leader who would bow to whatever pressures Washington might exert. In fact, a psychological profile written by CIA analysts described the new prime minister as "tough, a hardliner, and uncompromising." But compared to the argumentative and eloquent Begin, the laconic Shamir was perceived in Washington as a welcome change. The CIA predicted that Shamir would rely less on rhetoric and would likely be pragmatic and businesslike.

Even more encouraging, from the U.S. point of view, was the changing of the guard at Israel's defense ministry earlier that year. Moshe Arens was seen as pro-American, a man in search of understanding and reconciliation with the United States; this contrasted with the confrontational approach of his predecessor, Ariel Sharon.

But it was not only a matter of personalities. American interests were being recalculated, mainly because the deepening U.S. involvement in Lebanon had become a nightmare for President Reagan. In May 1983 seventeen Americans were among the sixty people killed when the U.S. Embassy in Beirut was bombed by Shiite Muslim terrorists. And in October 1983, just five weeks before Shamir's visit, more than 240 U.S. Marines were killed by a Shiite suicide bomber.

America's broader Middle East policy was sustaining damage too. The Lebanese-Israeli peace accords, brokered by Secretary of State Shultz, collapsed under heavy pressure from Syria. U.S. intelligence reports showed that the Soviets were arming the Syrians to the teeth, and the Syrians in turn helped Iran sponsor the Shiite groups that would later kidnap Americans and other Western hostages. In the Iran-Iraq war, Iranian troops were showing their fundamentalist determination—a danger not only to Iraqi territory but also to pro-Western Saudi Arabia.

Reagan concluded that the United States was not benefiting in any way from the strain in relations with Israel, dating back to the invasion of Lebanon and before that to the bombing of the Iraqi reactor, the AWACS fight, the Golan annexation, and the abortive strategic memorandum of 1981. The search for solutions disintegrated into intelligent, but vehement, arguments between the two former Bechtel stablemates: the president's old friend, Secretary of Defense Weinberger, and the increasingly pro-Israel Secretary Shultz.

To the disappointment of both Weinberger and the generals of the Joint Chiefs of Staff, Reagan returned to his personal pro-Israel roots and sided with Shultz. The result was a classified document, National Security Decision Directive 111, signed by the president at the end of October 1983.

Within days Shultz sent his undersecretary for political affairs, Lawrence Eagleburger, to Israel to explain the change. He was already seen as a sincere friend of the Jewish state, and now he made the Israelis an offer they would be foolish to refuse. "The President and everyone in the administration want to sit down with you and really talk about strategic cooperation in the future," Eagleburger said. "We like Israel and want to establish the closest relationship. You and we have a long-standing special relationship. This is the time for defining it."

"We were taken by surprise," says General Menachem Meron, who, as military attaché in Washington, had participated in the ill-fated Memorandum of Understanding of November 1981.

"When the administration took the first opportunity—in December 1981—to scrap the MOU, we were so hurt that we decided we would not volunteer any more ideas about institutionalizing our defense relations. We said to ourselves that there's no point in going on pushing. If the Americans are not interested in having us as formal allies, then no amount of pressure will help." Meron, by November 1983, was director-general of the Ministry of Defense, and thus was a member of the Shamir-Arens delegation at the White House.

If there was any disappointment for Shamir, it was the U.S. insistence that "Soviet involvement" be the only specified enemy shared with Israel. But he was willing to pay that price.

The Americans demanded an immediate installment payment. They asked Israel to sign an agreement to build, in the Negev Desert, a large transmission facility for Voice of America radio broadcasts beamed at the Soviet Union. Arab countries had refused to play host to the transmitters. The first Israeli instinct was to say no, even though the project would create several hundred jobs, because Shamir preferred not to irritate Moscow when the emigration rights of Soviet Jews were a major concern. His cabinet was also under heavy pressure from environmentalists who claimed that the high-voltage station would destroy bird life in the Negev.

But Shamir did agree, in 1987, to build the radio facility. The deciding factor was the desire to please the Americans and to show that Israel was indeed a trustworthy strategic partner. To the relief of most Israelis, the Clinton administration would later cancel the transmitter project for environmental and budgetary reasons.

On the American side, some members of the National Security Council, working on injecting substance into strategic cooperation, understood that Israel could be more useful as a whip against radical Arab countries such as Syria and Libya than against the Soviet "evil empire."

"There was a broad range of potential benefits for the U.S. military posture in the Middle East," Howard Teicher of the NSC later wrote, "if America and Israel could have undertaken genuine strategic cooperation. In the eastern Mediterranean Sea, for example, the Israeli Air Force and Navy could have conducted operations in coordination with the U.S. Forces."

In a crisis, Teicher thought, Israeli forces could be employed to keep open strategic waterways in the region. And finally, well-equipped Israeli facilities could be used for "acclimatization exercises, bombing ranges, equipment maintenance, and to support B-52 aircraft."

These were the great expectations with which the first JPMG meeting took place in Washington, in January 1984. The Joint Political-Military Group was an umbrella committee composed of senior national security officials, military planners, and analysts of both countries led by General Meron and America's

Rear Admiral Jonathan Howe, director of politico-military affairs at the State Department. To their credit, Meron recalls, they showed great patience, goodwill, and frankness, setting the tone for future meetings in a "constructive and no-nonsense atmosphere."

Yet to their disappointment, the Israeli and American supporters of genuine strategic cooperation found that there was still a long way to go—a path strewn with obstacles. The main hurdle remained the secretary of defense, Weinberger, and a coterie of Pentagon officials who feared Arab reactions. As they had done with the first strategic memo with Israel in 1981, they now got to work on emptying the new understanding of any substance—or at least keeping the flame of strategic cooperation burning at its lowest possible flicker.

Weinberger and his staff decided to reduce the level of cooperation from imaginative joint operations, which they felt would spoil America's standing in the Middle East, to hospital beds and bandages. The Pentagon had been criticized, by congressmen and American Jewish groups, for turning down an Israeli offer to provide medical care to U.S. Marines wounded in the Beirut barracks bombing of October 1983. The Israelis thought a short helicopter flight to Rambam Hospital in Haifa, which specializes in victims of car-bomb attacks, would be perfect. But previously set plans were not altered, and many of the wounded Americans had to suffer a four-hour flight to U.S. hospitals in Germany.

After the first JPMG meeting, Weinberger sent an assistant secretary of defense to negotiate a memorandum of understanding on medical cooperation. During the official's visit to Tel Aviv and in subsequent meetings, Israel and the United States reached a series of agreements, including joint exercises simulating a future scenario in which U.S. and Israeli helicopters would ferry wounded Americans from naval vessels in the eastern Mediterranean to Rambam Hospital. The new route was tried in a June 1984 simulation, marking the first time that military forces of the two nations had ever engaged in maneuvers together.

It was also agreed that the makings of a large American military hospital, fully equipped, would be prepositioned in central Israel, ready to serve hundreds of casualties in case of an emergency involving U.S. troops. Thanks to a third agreement, American and Israeli doctors began a series of exchange visits aimed at increasing their mutual understanding of medical techniques, terminology, and equipment used by the two armed forces.

Later AIPAC, B'nai B'rith, and other Jewish organizations lobbied the Bush and Clinton administrations and Congress to establish a "national trauma system" in Israel. It would help Israel, of course, but would also be prepared to treat the physical or psychological wounds of U.S. military personnel in the entire Middle East and eastern Mediterranean. The cost would be relatively low for the federal budget, $15 million spread over several years, to build the trauma center at Rambam Hospital. In peacetime, it would treat Israelis wounded in terrorist attacks and the true Israeli epidemic, traffic accidents.

Weinberger's original intention was to use the medical channel to lower the level of joint U.S.-Israel action, but by the early 1990s the degree of medical coordination reached such heights that it, ironically, has become one of the cornerstones of strategic cooperation.

But this was not enough for the Israelis, who wanted much more from their special alliance with the Americans. They thought the subject of terrorism would be sufficiently compelling—even for Weinberger—to accelerate cooperative ventures.

As early as a decade before Reagan decided to formalize strategic cooperation, there was clandestine teamwork between Israel and the United States in the war against terrorism. As the primary target for Palestinian and other Arab guerrilla groups, Israel had been forced to develop an expertise in fighting back. It was the first country to devise military tactics for storming hijacked airliners and to train special forces in this craft. The Israeli techniques had been tested and proved successful during the raid on Entebbe on July 4, 1976.

Officers from Sayeret Matkal, the Israeli commando force that led the Entebbe operation, visited U.S. special units, including Delta Force and the Navy Seals, in the 1970s to share experiences. The Israelis had done so much more in the field than had the Americans. Israel's intelligence agencies, the Mossad and the military branch, occasionally gave the United States information on terrorist schemes to attack American installations in the Middle East or western Europe.

But it was only after Reagan's announcement about stepping up the strategic cooperation that Israel and the United States truly joined forces and minds to combat terrorism. The first opportunity arose on June 14, 1985, when a group of Lebanese Shiites hijacked a Trans World Airlines plane to Beirut. Most of the 113 passengers and crew were Americans, and the terrorists threatened to execute them unless Israel released 766 Shiite prisoners and Kuwait, another seventeen.

Colonel Oliver North, in charge of counterterrorism at the National Security Council, saw no barriers—political or tactical—to consulting with Israel. He turned to the prime minister's advisor on terrorism, Amiram Nir, who was able to supply information on the identities of the hijackers, all members of the fanatical Hizbollah—the Iranian-backed Party of God.

"Israel's ability to gather human intelligence in the Middle East was widely respected," North has written, "but even our own government often underestimated their technical abilities." The frequent contacts between North and Nir during the sixteen days of the TWA hijack crisis would prepare the ground for more joint activity in future terrorist incidents.

At the same time, Secretary Shultz called Benjamin Netanyahu, Israel's ambassador to the United Nations, who had made his name as an ardent advocate of tough measures against terrorists. Netanyahu, a former officer in the Sayeret Matkal unit whose brother had been killed in the Entebbe raid, was already a familiar spokesman for his country on American television. But in private, he was even more hard-line than in his public appearances.

Netanyahu recalls: "The secretary asked me how they could prevent the hijackers from executing the hostages, and I told him that the only weapon that would work would be to reciprocate by directly and publicly threatening to hold the Shiite leaders in Lebanon responsible for any killings, and to kill them in retaliation."

Shultz went for the idea and the president publicly warned the terrorists, "for their own safety," to free the passengers and crew. Still, the official, behind-the-scenes line from Jerusalem was near-total willingness to please the Americans: by making concessions, even if violating the official U.S.-Israeli policy of not giving in to terrorism. According to Shultz, "The Israelis were virtually inviting us to ask them to release all, or nearly all, of the many Lebanese Shiite prisoners they were holding in exchange for the release of TWA 847 and its remaining passengers." Israel feared that if it did not free the prisoners, and if the hostages were killed, the media and world public opinion would blame it for the deaths.

Shultz, as advised by Netanyahu, kept telling President Reagan to play it tough and offer no concession. But after a few days of consultations between U.S. and Israeli experts on counterterrorism, no option for an operation to rescue all the hostages could be found. So the decision was to bring the long, televised, and embarrassing crisis to an end. Israel let its Shiite prisoners go, while claiming that it had intended to free them anyway.

The clumsy handling of the TWA affair only encouraged the Israelis and the Americans to improve their coordination. Professionals in intelligence and commando techniques like to believe that there is a solution to every challenge, and they were not going to fail again. During a meeting of the JPMG, the two sides agreed to design contingency plans for the next terrorist incident. Experts on terrorism from both countries met face-to-face to plot possible scenarios. In the fall of 1985, advance planning had its test.

It was on October 7, 1985, that terrorists from a radical faction of the Palestine Liberation Organization hijacked an Italian cruise liner, the *Achille Lauro*, on its way from Genoa to the Israeli harbor of Ashdod. About one hundred passengers and crew, at least half of them Americans, were held hostage on the ship. The seajackers, while cruising between Syrian and Egyptian waters, announced that they would start killing Americans unless Israel released fifty jailed Palestinians. To underline their seriousness they murdered one of the passengers, Leon Klinghoffer, a sixty-nine-year-old American Jew in a wheelchair. After the Palestinians shot him, they dumped his body and chair into the sea.

"It was time," Reagan says, "to strike back at the terrorists, even though we all agreed that attacking the ship would be a high-risk operation." The president ordered that a rescue be mounted, although this would certainly be easier said than done, because America's special forces had no preset jumping-off points in the Middle East.

"The Israelis had time and again offered to make their own bases available for such prepositioning," Colonel North has written, "but Cap Weinberger wouldn't hear of it." A combined team of Delta Force and Navy Seal commandoes made a long flight from the United States to a NATO base in the Mediterranean, with orders to board the *Achille Lauro* at sea.

At the same time, the U.S.-Israel intelligence channel went

into action. Depending largely on Israel's radio intercepts, the Americans tracked the movements of the hijacked cruise ship—up to the time that the terrorists negotiated their surrender to Egyptian authorities, in exchange for safe passage out of the country. The Palestinians left the ship on October 9, only hours before the U.S. commandoes were going to clamber aboard.

Having such good Israeli intelligence, Colonel North was not willing to give up the hunt. Nir and General Uri Simhoni, Israel's military attaché in Washington, worked closely with the White House to provide the tail number and take-off time of the Egyptian airliner that was to take the hijackers to safety at the PLO's Tunis headquarters.

North and his boss, the national security advisor Robert (Bud) McFarlane, secured President Reagan's go-ahead to intercept the airplane, force it to land at a NATO base on Sicily, and arrest the hijackers. U.S. Navy jets and the special forces carried out the plan perfectly, but Italian authorities let the terrorist leader go and sentenced the other four to short stays in prison. Despite the less-than-perfect ending, Israeli and American officials were pleased with their intelligence cooperation and inspired to continue in the same spirit.

North and Nir convinced their governments to give them secret approval for a range of counterterrorism projects, mostly in Lebanon: the kidnapping of terrorists and possibly their relatives to exchange for U.S. hostages, and formation of a force of Lebanese Druze who would be paid to rescue hostages.

A parallel covert track began in 1985: an arms for hostages deal involving McFarlane, North, and others in the United States; Nir and others in Israel; and shadowy Iranians who seemed to have enough influence over Shiite kidnappers in Lebanon to procure the release of American captives.

Why did Israel cooperate so willingly in swapping U.S. weapons for U.S. hostages? First, despite the Muslim revolution in Iran, Israeli strategists always sought to keep contact with the country as a potential non-Arab asset in the region. In addition, the Israelis wanted to be part of such high-stakes ventures so as to prove their status as America's best strategic ally.

The plan worked fairly well for eighteen months, until anti-Western extremists in Iran leaked the story in November 1986. The American public was astonished by President Reagan's apparent hypocrisy. After insisting for years that he was tough on terrorists, here he was making deals with them. And of all people, the Israelis, even tougher on terrorists, were helping him.

Reagan fired McFarlane, North, and other officials after it emerged that profits from the arms sales were diverted to the anti-Communist Contra rebels of Nicaragua. For six years investigators would probe the roles of Reagan, Vice President Bush, Weinberger, and their underlings. The charges of cover-up and lying to Congress were complicated and rarely stuck, but they inevitably spilled over to make Israel and its strategic ambitions look bad too.

Israel argued that its involvement in the affair was marginal. It had been asked by the Reagan administration to deliver arms to Iran, and as a friend and strategic ally of the United States it had done so. Israeli spokesmen said they had nothing to hide and would cooperate with American inquiries, stressing that none of the Israelis involved knew that congressional bans on aiding the Contras were being violated.

New findings in the early 1990s, however, cast doubt on these Israeli claims. It appears that the diaries of General Hagai Regev, then military secretary to Israel's defense minister, Yitzhak Rabin, included some references indicating that Israeli officials were aware that Colonel North met with Contra leaders and financed them.

President Reagan was never ashamed of what his administration did to combat both communism and terrorism. And he was happy to have Israel as an ally in both struggles.

Yet Israeli leaders were wondering whether their strategic

cooperation with the United States was as valuable as it could be. Intelligence cooperation had already been in place for decades. Counterterrorism, while exciting, yielded only short-term fruits. Military medical cooperation was nice, but mainly for the Americans. And now, while the United States was beginning to preposition ammunition in Israel, as urged by JINSA and pro-Israel lobbyists, the host country was far from impressed by the level of commitment.

On the one hand, the Israelis were pleased that the United States could never again claim that it did not have ammunition or medical supplies available, should they go to war and urgently need resupply. Congress passed a U.S. military construction bill in 1987 that authorized nearly $70 million for prepositioning military hardware in Israel, and while this was officially for use by American troops in case of emergency, the Israelis were certain that they could get their hands on it if needed. They vividly remembered almost running out of bombs and bullets in the first days of the 1973 Yom Kippur War.

"But joint medical exercises, intelligence exchanges, and American ammunition fell short of what we saw as genuine strategic cooperation," says Ehud Olmert, a cabinet minister and close advisor to Prime Minister Shamir. "We asked ourselves, where's the meat? We wanted more tangible results from the alliance. They wanted symbolic gestures."

Problems arose in the differing concepts and perceptions of the two sides in the twice-yearly meetings of the JPMG. General Meron, the chief Israeli participant, said it was difficult to define more specifically the three broad areas of cooperation announced publicly by Reagan: combined planning, joint exercises, and the prepositioning. Plan what? And against whom? Were the Soviets the only enemies, or radical Arab states too? How closely would the United States be working with moderate Arabs?

"One of the problems was that we couldn't really decide who the enemy was," veteran U.S. diplomat Veliotes recalls. "For us Americans, the enemy was the Soviet Union. But many Israelis saw the strategic notion as aimed at Syria. The American focus in that region was on defending the oil in the Gulf. And try as we might, we couldn't come up with a role for Israel."

Since the tug-of-war was not between equals, the U.S. definitions prevailed. Strategic cooperation has been confined to the parameters that the Americans set. In 1986 they conducted a small-scale naval exercise with the Israeli navy in the eastern Mediterranean. In theory, Israel's ships and—far more important—its potent air force could be used in a future air and sea battle against the Soviets.

A wave of anti-Americanism was sweeping through the two important NATO allies in the region, Greece and Turkey, so the United States felt a need to practice joint action with Israeli forces. Already with more combat experience than any country's army would want to have, the Israel Defense Forces would make a formidable right flank in any U.S. offensive. "The Israeli air force alone could destroy the entire Soviet fleet in the eastern Mediterranean," said a U.S. Navy report. And there was hardly any fear of a wave of anti-Americanism in Israel.

While the Israeli navy was tiny, it had modern and fast missile boats that, with air cover, could challenge Soviet ships up to three hundred miles from Israel's coast. To test this capability, the United States and Israel conducted joint exercises in antisubmarine warfare in December 1984.

The secretary of the navy, John Lehman, made three visits by April 1985 and ordered the Sixth Fleet to become a regular caller at the port of Haifa. By the end of the 1980s, Haifa was the second most frequently visited port for the U.S. Mediterranean fleet, next to Naples, Italy. To manage the almost constant presence of sailors on shore leave, the U.S. Navy and the USO opened facilities in Haifa.

"The Israeli port became the most popular," says Jim Roche, one of the originators of strategic cooperation and a navy man himself. "For the kids who are religious, history students, those who want a good time, or just to feel safe, this was the place to be."

The Israelis were far friendlier than townspeople in Italy, Greece, Turkey, and other harbors, who had become tired of seeing U.S. sailors. People seemed to recognize the fleet as a great boost for the Israeli economy, which took in almost $300 million in spending by the navy's tourists.

Another financial side benefit of the broader naval cooperation was the Americans' willingness to have some of their vessels repaired at the Haifa shipyards. The U.S. Navy also recommended, through the Pentagon, that the United States help Israel deepen and upgrade its port so that it could receive bigger ships, including aircraft carriers. Haifa's harbor is shallow, and whenever carriers visited they had to anchor some distance offshore. The crews were ferried into port by small boats, which occasionally had accidents.

With some encouragement by AIPAC lobbyists, Congress agreed in the late 1980s to allocate $15 million to conduct a study on the feasibility and value of deepening Haifa harbor. Its conclusion was affirmative, but Israel's friends in Washington then found it difficult to win a $100 million grant needed for the project itself.

From the first meeting of the JPMG in 1984, Israel has been encouraging the American side to send military delegations and experts to come, see, and ask questions about Israel's military capabilities. The hope is that when Americans examine the areas in which Israel excels, they will help think of ways to close the few gaps where the defense interconnection could be improved.

As early as January 1984, General John W. Vessey, Jr., became the first chairman of the Joint Chiefs of Staff to visit Israel. It no longer seemed to matter much that Vessey had sided with Weinberger in opposing deep strategic cooperation. The commandant of the U.S. Marine Corps, General P. X. Kelly, had a useful visit a few months later. Many other generals and admirals followed, often discovering that Israel offered unique training opportunities for all branches of the U.S. armed forces.

On the beaches north and south of Haifa harbor, the U.S. Marines practiced amphibious assaults. They often used live ammunition, and occasionally Israeli troops took part in what thus became joint maneuvers to prepare for ground combat.

In the Negev Desert, the Americans were happy to find a large area in which to practice aerial bombing and other skills. Pilots based on Sixth Fleet aircraft carriers dived low, spitting machine-gun fire and explosives at the same target ranges used by Israel's crack air force. The topography and climate were similar to those of the Persian Gulf oil fields, and the desert has a good system of roads to ease military transport. It was also helpful that the three major air bases in the Negev were built by the United States, as compensation to Israel for surrendering the Sinai to Egypt in the Camp David Accords.

The Israelis were pleased when their own aircraft and tank units took part in joint Negev exercises with American warplanes. The American defense secretary, Frank Carlucci, was there to observe U.S.-Israeli war games in November 1988, and it was at such times that Israelis felt almost totally satisfied with strategic cooperation. They were out to prove their worth, in a crisis that might threaten the flow of oil from the Gulf to the West.

The American officials in charge of Middle East policy, however, saw the strategic relationship as a hollow set of slogans. "Politically, the leadership of both countries believed it was important," Veliotes says. "But militarily, it was always empty. There wasn't really anything there. Lots of people came up with a lot of ideas, but finally we saw none of them would be of great importance. If we had to go to war in the Gulf, as we would against Iraq, the Israelis weren't going to be too effective."

General Meron, who sat directly across the table from the Americans, disagrees. "While port calls by the U.S. Navy, desert training, and military exercises are not formally part of the strategic cooperation," he says, "those other things do add further dimensions to the strategic notion, because a new environment of positive attitudes is developed."

The Israeli general recalls that a JPMG meeting was scheduled for two weeks after the embarrassing exposure, in Washington, of a spy working for Israel inside a U.S. Navy intelligence department. Thinking back to December 1985, Meron says: "I thought the Americans would call off the meeting, but they did not. They knew how to make a distinction. Of course, they were angry at us over the arrest of Jonathan Pollard, but they knew how to restrain themselves and make the separation between short-term events and long-term developments."

At many levels, the number of U.S. officers and servicemen personally rubbing shoulders with Israelis was rising constantly. Since the leap in defense cooperation under the Nixon administration, thousands of Israeli military men and women had been visiting America each year. Whether pilots, tank gunners, or intelligence officers, they benefited from courses and training programs arranged by the Pentagon, and the bills were paid out of the U.S. military aid to Israel—$1.4 billion in fiscal 1985, the first year that it was all granted without any loans to be repaid, rising to $1.8 billion per year by the end of the 1980s.

Still, for the average American officer, Israel was an enigma. The formal strategic cooperation was changing that. Along with the twice-a-year JPMG sessions, a military-to-military group was established to direct the day-to-day workings of new joint projects.

"In these human encounters, both sides benefit," says

Roche, a retired navy commander. "We train them, and they train us. We learn from them, and they learn from us. And the more the two sides work together, the more they like each other."

There were also dividends for President Reagan and some of his pet projects. To his delight in 1986, Israel stepped forward as the third nation to join his controversial "Star Wars" concept—the Strategic Defense Initiative, which aimed at inventing a system that could reliably destroy enemy ballistic missiles in space.

But in its desire to please and thank the president who had finally replaced his cheap, gold-plated engagement ring with a solid-gold wedding band, Israel was endangering its delicate attempts to restore relations with the Soviet Union. Added to the Voice of America transmitter plan, and the strategic cooperation announcement itself in 1983, joining SDI meant Israel was throwing all caution to the wind. It seemed that the Kremlin might never forgive, and Israel could only hope that the possible risk to the emigration of Soviet Jews was worth it, for the benefits that could come from the happy ally Reagan.

At that time, in 1986, the Israeli decision—promoted by Defense Minister Arens—was seen as only a symbolic gesture. But two years later there were some extraordinary financial rewards for Israel when its own project to build an antimissile missile, the Arrow, became part of SDI. From 1988 on the United States was financing around three-quarters of the estimated $600 million cost of the Arrow.

Another by-product of secret U.S.-Israeli cooperation, in the framework of Strategic Defense, was the joint development of an electrothermal antimissile gun. Financed by Pentagon grants of $20 million, American and Israeli teams have been working together in Arizona and in Nahal Soreq—site of the nuclear reactor that President Eisenhower gave to Israel in 1955. Even a firing accident in Arizona, which killed three Israelis and injured several Americans in 1989, did not stop the high-technology, high-velocity gun project that includes one of the world's most sophisticated radars.

Israel also discovered that strategic cooperation could generate financial gains for the country's defense industries. One profitable deal was the agreement by Navy Secretary Lehman in 1985 to lease two squadrons of the Israeli-built Kfir jet, complete with Israeli maintenance services, for use in simulating the Soviet MiG-21 in *Top Gun*–style dogfights.

In an American administration that was like heaven for Israel, the navy was turning out to be its guardian angel. Lehman supported Israel's unusual request to use some of its U.S. military aid money to purchase two diesel submarines from Germany—because American manufacturers make only nuclear-powered submarines.

It was also the navy that bought an innovation in aerial photography from Israel Aircraft Industries: the remotely piloted vehicle, or RPV, that was first used successfully in the 1982 invasion of Lebanon. Equipped with a television camera and a transmitter, this small airborne drone can photograph enemy positions without any risk to pilots. The RPV sold itself when Caspar Weinberger visited Israel and saw what this "fascinating little gadget" could do. It had taken pictures of him.

The Israelis, he discloses, "showed me tapes they had made the previous day of me, in Beirut, conducting a ceremony for some of our marines. This was an interesting example of the capabilities of this plane. Not just for this reason, our navy has now bought some."

Weinberger was truly impressed, but it did not change his basic view that strategic cooperation with Israel was more of a burden than an asset for the United States. He stood almost alone, in a pro-Israel administration constantly pressed by a pro-Israel Congress to do more for the Jewish state.

But the defense secretary did manage to make matters difficult for Israel in two very sensitive areas. Sticking with the policy set by his predecessor, Harold Brown, Weinberger refused to let Israel have a direct link from U.S. spy satellites. The refusal simply pushed Israel—much to America's annoyance—to embark on its own space program.

This was one of the few areas of disagreement in U.S.-Israel strategic planning. Washington told Jerusalem that satellites are an extremely expensive business, perhaps too expensive for Israel. U.S. officials were also concerned that—as in the nuclear field—an Israeli space monopoly in the Middle East would only push wealthy Arab states to work on rockets and satellites of their own. This could add another level of tension in the region.

Congress, so pro-Israel by 1987 that it embraced almost all the legislative initiatives suggested by the AIPAC lobby, did obtain a special status for Israel: the official label of MNNA: a "Major Non-NATO Ally." Although not a part of the North Atlantic alliance structure, Israel had already been receiving many of the same weapons and technology that the United States was selling to NATO members such as Britain, Norway, Spain, and Italy. But now Israeli defense contractors would be eligible for American funding for research and development—for the good of the alliance.

"Obtaining that status through the legislation in Congress was one of our biggest achievements," an Israeli diplomat who served in Washington at that time says proudly. "We were looking for ways to increase U.S. military aid, with the $1.8 billion annual assistance on something like 'automatic pilot.' It was approved year after year, but we also knew that it would be difficult to ask for an increase. So we initiated the idea of turning Israel into a Major Non-NATO Ally. We told AIPAC, which started rolling the idea up and down Capitol Hill corridors until it was accepted."

The MNNA status was especially significant in opening the American market to a wide range of Israeli military and security products. It turned out to be an extra money machine for some of Israel's key industries. By the end of the 1980s there were 321 joint ventures and programs in defense research and development, with a combined value of over $2.9 billion.

The growth in Israeli military exports, to American and other markets, was an economic necessity for the Jewish state and was encouraged by President Reagan and Secretary of State Shultz. They were publicly committed to helping Israel gain more economic independence. But many American businesses—especially rival manufacturers who saw the world arms market shrinking—took a very different view, and they were often in close touch with Pentagon officials. Why, they wondered, should the United States help the Israelis become America's commercial competitors?

Some in the Pentagon also expressed concern that sensitive American technology, obtained by Israel with its MNNA status, might be transferred to third countries as part of Israeli products. Weinberger's defense department had set up a special unit—the Defense Technology Security Administration—with the aim of preventing the unauthorized transfer of "dual use" technology. This was know-how that could be used either for civilian industries or in weapons systems. Of particular concern was the sale of technology that could help in the manufacture of missiles and weapons of mass destruction.

Stephen Bryen, who headed the special Pentagon unit, recalls: "We chose fifteen countries to watch, on two criteria. Either they were fairly advanced industrialized countries that had their own technology and were a source of problems for us in reexport, or they were 'bad guy' countries that were dangerous to our interests. It was up to me to make up the list."

Scribbling on the back of an envelope, Bryen wrote the names of advanced nations such as Sweden, Finland, and Austria, and the "bad guys" such as Iran, Iraq, Libya, Syria, and Pakistan. Despite accusations by other agencies that Israel was engaged in the transfer of U.S. technology to "pariah" states such as South Africa and China, Bryen—perhaps because he is Jewish and a supporter of Israel, and perhaps not—found no room on the envelope for Israel.

"It was a close call," he says. "They could've been on the list. They'd still be on it!" Indeed, several "good guy" countries reached agreements with the United States to limit technology transfers and thus had their names crossed off the list. With Israel, negotiations went on for several years, but Ariel Sharon—by then the minister for trade and industry—refused to sign the deal.

The web of cooperation between the United States and Israel was so complex that even insiders found it difficult to understand. Calling the U.S. relationship with the Jewish state "extremely complicated," Senator Robert Byrd, a staunch opponent of foreign aid, made a point of revealing extra items that generally escaped public attention. For instance, he said on the Senate floor, there is "a petroleum reserve of 4.5 million barrels, worth $180 million," that is available for Israel's use in case of emergency. This had been guaranteed by the Carter administration when Israel surrendered the Sinai oil fields in Egypt in 1979.

To gain better understanding and control of such items, Secretary of State Shultz was persuaded by Israeli officials that the best way to clear the entanglement would be to have yet another agreement.

This was supposed to be an agreement on all the agreements in the fields of defense and strategy. The text was drawn up by the two countries, and on April 21, 1988, President Reagan signed the "Memorandum of Understanding Between the United States of America and the State of Israel Regarding Joint Political, Security, and Economic Cooperation."

The importance of the new MOU, initially valid for five years but then renewed, was that it institutionalized the special alliance between Washington and Jerusalem. All of the meetings of the various military, economic, commercial, industrial, and strategic groups now had a formal basis. They were legally binding.

The U.S.-Israel relationship had certainly traveled a long, historic road. But some Israelis saw it as an irony, rather than a tribute, that President Reagan presented the MOU as a gift to Israel on its independence day. After all, wasn't this fortieth birthday present going to limit Israel's freedom, on the very day that symbolized Israeli liberty?

CHAPTER FOURTEEN

CHANGE FOR A DOLLAR

Judith Gottfried has never met President Reagan, nor has she had any other contact with him. Still, she says: "We thank him, from time to time, in our hearts." The Gottfried family firm is Gottex, Israel's famous swimwear manufacturer. And it is largely thanks to Reagan that tens of thousands of American women wear Israeli bikinis.

The Gottfried family's company tops the list of hundreds that have benefited from the president's decision to eliminate all duties on trade between Israel and America. "Because of the agreement," she says, "50 percent of our exports today go to the U.S."

Although both sides agree that the Free Trade Area (FTA) agreement—a landmark document signed in April 1985—was Israel's brainchild, the precise identity of the Israeli parent is a matter of dispute. The Labor party claims that it came up with the notion as early as 1975, during a conversation between

Prime Minister Rabin and President Ford. Likud politicians, however, argue fiercely that the idea was theirs, pointing with pride to the fact that FTA became reality on their watch in government.

"Despite all claims to the contrary, there is no doubt in my mind that the agreement is my child," says Gideon Patt, former minister for trade and industry. Sounding like a proud father in a custody dispute, Patt knowingly points to his fifteen years in Likud cabinets.

Even before FTA, Israel enjoyed favorable trading terms—but only under the same system of preferences as many other countries. So while Israel's exports to the United States totaled around $1 billion per year in the early 1980s—half of them in polished diamonds—the Israelis felt they could do better.

"We wanted some special arrangement for Israel," says Dan Halperin, who at the time served as the nation's commercial attaché in Washington.

Ex-minister Patt recalls his yearly visits to the United States to negotiate details of Israeli-American trade: "The talks we had with Robert Strauss, President Carter's trade representative, and later, under Reagan, with William Brock, seemed quite ridiculous to me. They focused on issues like 'Can Israel expand its cheese export from seven to seventeen tons per year?' or, 'What will happen to the export of tomato puree?' They were really dealing with trivial, marginal matters that should not be considered on the ministerial level."

So in a mid-1981 meeting Patt said to Brock, "Bill, look what peanuts we're dealing with. Let's do something really big!"

"What do you have in mind?" Brock wondered.

"I have an idea," said Patt. "Let's come up with a free trade area between our two nations that will get rid of taxes and levies on goods and commodities." The Israeli minister explained to Brock that his country had a similar agreement with the European Community. "It's time for something like this between Israel and the U.S. For you, it will mean hardly anything; it will be unimportant. To Israel, it's vital."

Brock hesitated a few moments before replying. "Gideon, give me two good reasons why I should bring this to the White House."

The Israeli minister had lived in the United States for several years before going into politics and found the experience helpful when negotiating in Washington. "I refrained from preaching to the Americans, as some of my Israeli colleagues would have done, and decided to focus on issues close to their hearts," Patt explained later. "So I ended up giving my American counterpart more than two 'dishes' of food for thought."

Patt's argument to Brock was based on interlocking assumptions—almost a Rube Goldberg mechanism of U.S.-Israeli economic relations. If Israel's exports to the United States could be increased from $1 billion, said Patt, "to six or seven billion, that will give us a push toward economic independence. And economic independence will make Israel into a more stable and a stronger country. It is in your, American, interest that we should be a strong power in the Middle East. And as we grow stronger, we shall be able to decrease our dependence on your contributions and gifts. You know that because of the Jewish lobby and your historical commitment to Israel as a Jewish homeland and a Western democracy, you can't possibly dodge supporting my country's economy. If you give us less money, you'll have more left to spend on your national problems."

In the more tactical short term, Israeli officials also suggested, American companies could exploit Israel's special trade preferences in Western Europe by using Israel as a way-station for tax-free export into Europe.

It took a few months for Patt to get the good news from Brock that President Reagan had given the go-ahead for negotiations aimed at a free trade area. "However," Patt remembers, "Brock urged me to keep the matter strictly secret.

He said, 'Over there with you, everything gets leaked; and if the rest of the world finds out that we're negotiating a deal with you, they'll all be asking for similar arrangements.' " The American cabinet secretary was especially concerned that Canada, Mexico, and the countries of South America—next-door neighbors to the United States—would demand the same concessions as far-off Israel.

In April 1982 the two governments set up working teams and started to exchange ideas and position papers. For the first year and a half negotiations moved along slowly. "We were disappointed with the pace," says Dan Halperin, who became Israel's chief negotiator on the trade deal. "So we looked for ways to speed up the process. Our break came toward the end of 1983. This was when the U.S. was entering an election year, and we took the opportunity to tighten the screws on the administration—by means of friends in Congress and influential Jews."

In 1983, during the same visit to Washington by Prime Minister Shamir that resulted in the agreement on strategic cooperation, Reagan announced that Israel would also benefit from a trade agreement—couching it in terms of free market economics. "I had hopes of making international trade freer and fairer," he wrote in his memoirs.

His secretary of state, George Shultz, was a former professor of economics and thus had a special interest in making Israel a real-life example of what the free market could accomplish. "I started to push for a U.S.-Israel free trade agreement," he wrote, "which would give Israel access to the U.S. market."

Despite such high-level interest, the talks dragged on for eighteen months. Various American pressure and interest groups raised objections to giving Israel nearly unlimited access to the U.S. market. Groups of farmers and industrialists lobbied senators and congressmen to block the FTA. They argued that Reagan's free trade policies were already opening America to enormous competition—especially from Japan. They did not want Israeli competitors undercutting their prices too.

Says Halperin: "It was only through the support of our traditional friends from AIPAC and on the Hill and thanks to the help of union leaders that we managed to persuade the opponents that the giant U.S. economy really had nothing to fear from little Israel."

AIPAC's lobbying was a big help in Congress, clearing the way for the 1985 ratification of the FTA—"this historic agreement," as Reagan termed it. When fully implemented in 1995, the agreement would eliminate most restrictions on all trade between Israel and its principal benefactor.

Both sides refrained purposely from explicitly stating whether the agreement would also cover goods from the West Bank, Gaza Strip, and Golan Heights, held by Israel since the 1967 war. Official U.S. policy was always that Israel's settlements in those territories were illegal—which would seem to make their produce and factory products unacceptable as well. The Reagan administration, however, did not attempt to draw a distinction—choosing, as always, to turn a blind eye to settlements as a point of friction with Israel. Only later, when George Bush's successor administration began to have strained relations with Israel, did Washington officials become punctilious—demanding that Israeli companies based in the occupied territories be excluded from FTA status.

President Reagan called the agreement an "important milestone in our efforts to liberalize trade" throughout the world, while his negotiator Brock said: "I do not believe that this trade agreement is any gift. I think, in so many words, that it is very much in the interest of the United States."

"Since signing the agreement, U.S. exports to Israel have nearly doubled," AIPAC says in a summary of the FTA's advantages to America. "In fact, Israel is second only to Canada in terms of per capita imports of U.S. products."

But the truth of the matter is that Israel was, and remains, the main beneficiary. To the Israeli leadership, the two agreements signed during the Reagan era—for strategic cooperation and for the free trade area—were the "ultimate expression" of the friendship, cooperation, and alliance between the two countries. In the eight years after the signing of the FTA, Israel increased its exports of goods and services to U.S. markets from $1 billion to $4 billion.

And the future appears bright. "Because of the free trade agreement," swimwear manufacturer Gottfried enthuses, "we got offers from non-U.S., non-Israeli companies to take part in joint ventures." Countries in Asia and even in Europe discovered that Israel could serve as an economic gateway for their own exports to America. These countries sell unfinished goods to Israel, where they are processed so they can be marketed in the United States without the usual restrictions.

Over and above the economic advantages, the FTA gave Israel political benefits that are harder to quantify. Just as Bill Brock had feared, the trade agreement with Israel did prompt Canada and Mexico to plead for similar deals. When Washington seemed reluctant, Canadian and Mexican envoys approached Halperin and other Israeli officials to ask what the "secret" might be: How did Israel get the FTA? Within five years the United States signed similar agreements with Canada and Mexico.

But while organized labor, in league with many on Capitol Hill, strongly opposed the North American Free Trade Agreement, there had been no such opposition to the deal with Israel. This can be explained partly by the relatively small effect the Israeli FTA has on the gigantic U.S. economy, but also by the fact that Israel is a special case. This small country, as the world saw it, somehow managed to receive from America what no other nation could get.

Another example is the antiboycott legislation passed by Congress. Israel needed a way out of the economic choke-hold by nearly two dozen Arab nations, whose well-organized black-list included not only Israel but companies outside the Middle East that did business with Israel.

Most Western corporations put their profits ahead of morality. The Arab world was such a huge market, and it seemed to make no sense to endanger it for the sake of trade with tiny Israel. As a result, Israelis for years were unable to enjoy the products of many multinational corporations—such as Pepsi—that avoided being on the list of sinning companies compiled by the Arab Boycott Office in Damascus.

The economic damage to Israel was enormous, and when Israel asked foreign governments to ban the boycott only the United States seemed to be listening. AIPAC, the American Jewish Congress, and other Jewish organizations waged a public relations campaign stressing the immorality of helping the Arabs strangle Israel. Congress then passed a law prohibiting U.S. citizens and firms from participating in the boycott against Israel, and President Carter's Commerce Department in 1978 set up an Office of Antiboycott Compliance.

But the U.S. desire to help Israel fight the boycott really got off the ground when President Reagan's pro-Israel administration took over. Since 1982 the Office of Antiboycott Compliance has imposed penalties for violations, including hefty fines assessed on leading American companies for refusing to do business in Israel and, sometimes, for signing declarations to that effect in order to win contracts in the Arab world.

Israeli diplomats, in coordination with AIPAC and other Jewish organizations, occasionally went on tour to tell American Jews not to buy the products of companies colluding with the Arab boycott. The antiboycott boycott included a 1985 instruction from Israel's foreign ministry to its diplomats in the United States to get in touch with Jewish organizations to spread bad publicity about Hyundai, a South Korean automaker. The manufacturer refused to export to Israel, for fear of losing sales to the Arabs.

The combination of civil penalties and Jewish lobbying was a success, and large corporations were increasingly willing to invest in Israel. Sara Lee, for instance, became a partner in an Israeli textile company. Coca-Cola and the Ford Motor Company felt vindicated in their decisions, after the 1967 war in the Middle East, to buck the boycott. Henry Ford II's willingness to do business with Israel is especially intriguing, because his grandfather's anti-Semitism was well-known.

"Henry Ford and I became good friends in the late 1950s," recalls Max Fisher, the Detroit industrialist and leader of Jewish philanthropies. "Then, in 1967, he was on a boat with me in the Greek Islands when the Six-Day War was about to break out. I flew to Israel, promised to help raise money, and when I returned to Detroit I told him what I'd seen there. Henry later wrote me a letter that said, 'Dear Max, I'm enclosing a check for $100,000 for the cause you're so actively involved in. I'm doing it because I believe in it.' And he sent me a personal check every year until he died in 1987."

Ford was enchanted by the spirit of Israel and, during a visit in 1972, decided to sell automobile components to a businessman there. Knowing that Arab countries might cancel their contracts with his company, Ford told Fisher: "Nobody's going to tell me what to do. As long as I'm the chairman of this company, I'll be shipping to Israel." Ford was on the official Arab boycott list for fifteen years.

All of Israel's past accomplishments on the business battlefield were dwarfed by the economic gains of the 1980s. It was more than just the FTA or simple statistics. The Reagan administration did raise the floor level for aid to Israel by 60 percent, to a total of $3 billion. And, thanks largely to AIPAC lobbying Congress, none of the $1.8 billion in military aid and $1.2 billion in economic assistance had to be repaid: all grants, no loans.

With Israel firmly in place as the largest recipient of U.S. foreign aid, the Jewish state and the American lobbyists who supported it took on a new aura of power in Washington. Before any important vote on assistance to any countries abroad, Secretary of State Shultz and other members of the administration would ask Israeli diplomats to use their influence with key senators and congressmen to pass the bill.

"Israel became a locomotive," says an Israeli diplomat in Washington, "which was pushing the entire train of U.S. foreign aid." Countries such as Egypt, Pakistan, and Turkey, which also receive generous U.S. aid, are aware that they get their billions only so long as Israel gets its. State Department officials, building foreign policy on foreign aid, seem also to accept that Israel must top the list.

"We became the darlings of anyone in the administration or Congress who favors foreign aid as a tool for advancing U.S. interests," explains an AIPAC activist. "They use us to push ahead general foreign aid policy."

Israel finds extra profit in the method by which economic aid is disbursed. When sending money to other countries, the United States designates specific projects to be supported—such as the sewer system in Egypt. This is then supervised by the Agency for International Development and other arms of the U.S. government, and the recipient country is required to submit regular progress reports to Washington.

Israel—in contrast—is free to do almost anything it wants to with the grant and is under no obligation to submit interim reports to the United States. And unlike other nations, which receive aid in quarterly installments, Israel receives the entire sum—all at once—every October. The funds are deposited in an Israeli government bank account in New York and are usually invested in U.S. Treasury bonds, which some years have yielded over $100 million in extra interest.

In fact, most of the economic aid finally circulates back to where it came from: the United States. There is a requirement that Israel, when using its aid money to buy grain, buy only from American farmers. Israel is America's eleventh biggest wheat customer. But unlike most large importers, Israel pays in cash: originally federal government money, but its availability pleases the growers. In addition, grain shipments must be made on U.S. merchant vessels.

American banks also benefit from Israel's cash flow, courtesy of Washington. Depending on interest rates, Israel pays over $1 billion a year in interest on old loans, dating back to the pre-grant days of the early 1970s. Israel has never defaulted on a loan, thanks largely to friends in Congress ensuring that there has always been enough cash to make the payments.

With increasing regularity, third countries began to treat Is-raelis as if they held the key to Washington, D.C. It was no longer just a few interested questions, as posed by officials of Canada and Mexico before the FTA. Now nations were actively approaching the Israelis for permission to climb aboard their Washington bandwagon.

"There's no doubt about it," says embassy veteran Halperin. "We managed to gain the reputation of being all-powerful in the U.S." If diplomats of other countries came to think—like the anti-Semitic but bogus book *The Protocols of the Elders of Zion*—that Jews controlled the world, Israel's representatives made no real effort to disabuse them of the notion. On the con-trary, they tried to exploit the impression.

Romania was one of the countries that activated the Israel connection to approach the U.S. First the Romanian economic attaché in Washington went to Halperin, "asking us to help him get U.S. aid." Then, in 1986, Romania's ambassador to the U.S. contacted Israel's, Meir Rosenne, with a more specific re-quest: Would the Israelis and their friends lobby the United

States to grant "most favored nation" trading status to Romania? This would ostensibly be to reward President Nicolae Ceausescu for permitting his country's Jews to move to Israel and allowing Soviet Jews to use Romania as an outward transit point—an emigration route, in fact, paved by Israeli cash bribes to the Ceausescu family amounting to millions of dollars.

Ceausescu's human rights record was frowned upon in Washington, but Israel and some of its leading supporters in the Senate put in a few friendly words on his behalf. This was not true sentiment, but rather a calculation of Israel's own interests. Romania was the only Communist country that maintained diplomatic relations with Israel after the 1967 war, a situation Israel liked, and there was concern that saying no to a Romanian request could shut the gates for Jewish emigrés. The Israeli lobbying helped, and Ceausescu got the trade advantages he sought.

Less successful were Israel's efforts on behalf of Zaire. Israel felt a certain obligation to the central African country and its dictator, General Mobutu Sese Seko, because he was the first leader on the continent to restore diplomatic relations with Israel in 1982. The relationship was cemented by arms sales and military advice from Israel, but what Mobutu dearly wanted was for Israel to help improve his poor image in Washington. In coordination with the Israeli embassy, members of AIPAC and other prominent Jews started whispering a few nice words about Zaire into the ears of U.S. officials and legislators. Israel's friends even helped General Mobutu find a public relations company in Washington, and Israel paid $3 million for a publicity campaign on Zaire's behalf. What it all accomplished is somewhat murky, although Israel kept a friend in Africa and Mobutu continued into 1994 as dictator of his country.

In another case, Israel was not able to translate its image in the Third World as an unstoppable Washington wheeler-dealer into tangible results. This was in 1989, when Turkey approached Israel with a request to help prevent official U.S. celebrations of a Day of Remembrance for Armenians massacred by the Turks in World War I.

Israeli diplomats, anxious to preserve good relations with Turkey, one of the few Muslim countries willing to maintain links with the Jewish state, quietly reminded senators and congressmen that Turkey was a NATO ally and not worth offending.

The Israelis found that they, however, were offending a senior Republican senator, Bob Dole of Kansas. He was working on a memorial to the Armenians, and what the Israelis did not know was that after being wounded in battle during World War II Dole's life had been saved by a Chicago surgeon of Armenian origin. The two men became great friends, and Dole became interested in the tragedies of Armenian history. The senator was also annoyed by the arrogance of Israel and its Washington friends, who appeared to believe that they could intervene in almost any issue.

The United States did, in the end, mark Armenian Remembrance Day. The Israelis had to face the unpleasant fact that there was a limit to their power. Although the Reagan administration was generous, it had no intention of handing Israel a blank check.

Even the financial aid from the United States could be a double-edged sword, as Israel learned after obtaining American support for its ambitious project to develop an advanced fighter plane of its own.

The "Lavi"—Hebrew for "lion cub"—was to be the Israeli air force's great silver hope. The warplane would, it was believed, reduce Israel's dependence on U.S. military hardware. But the Israelis had neither the technology nor the money to do it on their own. In the early 1980s, they turned to President Reagan for special help in constructing the Lavi. The guiding spirit behind the project was Ambassador Moshe Arens, and the former aeronautics engineer at Israel Aircraft Industries treated the fighter as if it were his own supersonic baby with wings.

Arens asked the United States to pay for the Lavi, a startling suggestion considering the standard requirement that U.S. military aid be spent on buying U.S. products and services. There was, however, a precedent that worked in Israel's favor: a modern tank, built with American help.

It was in 1975 that Israel had asked the United States to finance the "Merkava"—Hebrew for "chariot"—with a suggestion that the technology could help America too. "I'm very proud that I played a major role in the Merkava project," recalls Stephen Bryen, who at the time was a senior staffer with the Senate Foreign Relations Committee. On a visit to Israel with another Senate aide, Bryen heard about a new tank being developed and asked to see it. "I was very taken by it and said: 'What can I do?' "

The Israelis approached Bryen a few months later with a request for his help. "We were told they had financial problems: They really wanted to do the tank but they were stuck." Bryen, who as a Jew felt attached to Israel and concerned with its security, also believed that the Merkava's thermal sleeves and positioning of the engine in the rear "could make sense" for U.S. arms manufacturers.

"So with the cooperation of friends in the Pentagon at the time—though that's never been revealed—we drafted an amendment" that would give Israel money to develop the Merkava. "The Pentagon was divided on this," says Bryen, "and the White House threatened a veto."

But the traditional pillars of Israeli support in Washington— sympathy from congressional staffers, including many Jews, and the active support of outspoken senators such as Henry Jackson—made the unthinkable possible. President Ford was persuaded to finance the Merkava. And the amendment's passage meant that foreign aid money was, for the first time, used to fund a domestic Israeli development. The special assistance for the tank system added up to $104 million, spent in Israel. Bryen believes the American generosity really "saved the Israeli program while the U.S. also got something out of it." Israel Tal, the Israeli general in charge of the Merkava program, became a major consultant on America's Abrams battle tank.

The Merkava precedent was not enough to guarantee that, almost a decade later, the United States would pay for the Lavi. The fighter plane project was much larger and would require billions of dollars. There were some extraordinary considerations, however, that tipped the balance.

It was during this period, around 1983, following Israel's Lebanon debacle and the death of his wife, that U.S. officials noticed Prime Minister Begin's flagging interest in politics and his increasing tendency to become depressed. Begin's potential heirs in the ruling Likud party were beginning to jockey for position, and the Americans began to take an interest in the succession struggle.

After the tension caused by the Lebanon crisis and the resignation of Ariel Sharon as defense minister—which the Americans welcomed—they favored Sharon's replacement, the old hand in Washington Moshe Arens, to be the next prime minister.

"It appeared to me," Howard Teicher, the Middle East expert for Reagan's National Security Council, has written, "that the emergence of Arens as a friend of the United States could prove essential to any effort to improve our relations." Unlike the other contenders for the Likud throne who were "prone to approach U.S.-Israeli relations from a confrontational stance, the tough-minded Arens was a realist who understood the importance of the U.S.-Israeli security relationship. The challenge for Washington was to find a way to take advantage of the opportunity created by Begin's passivity, the probable leadership vacuum, Sharon's demise and Arens's potential ascendancy, in order to influence Israeli leaders and policy in a direction that would advance and support American interests."

This could crudely be termed interference in the domestic politics of a foreign nation. Yitzhak Rabin, as ambassador in Washington, had done it in failing to hide his preference for Nixon's reelection; and Israel had worked with AIPAC on Capitol Hill for favorable legislation. Now the United States had a favorite candidate for Israeli prime minister and was ready to pour in financial incentives that might affect the outcome.

Teicher's pro-Arens advice was accepted by the White House NSC in April 1983, with a decision to improve Arens's standing in Israel's cabinet and among the public by helping the Lavi project, to which he had become ardently devoted.

Using the Merkava tank subsidy as a model, the administration announced that approximately $250 million could be diverted to the Lavi project from the annual $1.8 billion in U.S. military aid. Congress, heavily lobbied by friends of Israel, then passed an amendment that permitted an investment of $400 million in the Lavi. Of this money, $250 million would be converted into Israeli currency, to be spent in Israel, while the rest would have to be spent in the United States to enable American manufacturers and contractors to participate in constructing the new advanced tactical fighter.

Secretary of State Shultz, with his strong economic orientation, has written that he "favored U.S. approval of the licenses required to enable Israel to design and build the next generation fighter" because this also "helped keep some high-tech jobs in Israel at a critical time" for the Israeli economy.

Secretary of Defense Weinberger and the Pentagon, however, were against the Lavi project from the start. As in other clashes between Shultz and Weinberger regarding Israel, President Reagan ruled in favor of the secretary of state. But the Department of Defense continued to look for an opportunity to reverse the decision, and a Pentagon troubleshooter, assistant undersecretary Dov Zakheim, was assigned to analyze and liaise with the Lavi project.

Arens and many other Israelis working on the new fighter were delighted by the Pentagon's choice, for it was obvious from his name that Zakheim was a Jew. As always, Israeli officials went for the Jewish angle: Who's Jewish in the administration? Who can be counted on as pro-Israel? The Israeli press was quick to publish features on Zakheim, fed by Israeli diplomats in Washington who stressed his being an Orthodox Jew who eats only kosher food.

"I was a trained economist and got my doctorate from Oxford," says Zakheim, "but the Israeli focus was that I was working on Lavi because I was Jewish."

The project was "soaking up too much money," Zakheim's professional analysis soon established. "We were forking out the money, and obviously every dollar spent on the Lavi meant another dollar not spent on a ship or tank or whatever. It was not really just Israel's problem. We were providing this money and at one point we thought they'd be soaking up 60 percent of all the military assistance just on this project."

Zakheim also recalls that even though some American companies did benefit from the project, the defense industry on the whole was "very upset because they thought the Israelis were building a competitor to their programs. The international market was going to be glutted with aircraft, which also raised some questions."

Zakheim and the Pentagon ended up giving a lot more answers than posing questions. And in 1987 they finally made their point that U.S. money for the Lavi was a waste. Reagan and Shultz reluctantly accepted the verdict that the project was too ambitious for a tiny state such as Israel. The president also became convinced that the American economy would benefit more if Israel had to acquire its future aircraft in the United

States—so that American companies could profit from the U.S. taxpayers' foreign aid money.

In April 1987 the Reagan administration dispatched an official statement to Israel to the effect that funding of the Lavi would henceforth stop. The Shamir cabinet, especially Arens, was bitterly disappointed. Israel Aircraft Industries, forced to fire thousands from its development team, organized a large demonstration by workers outside the U.S. Embassy in Tel Aviv.

In Washington, Israeli diplomats put pressure on Zakheim. "I remember," he recalls, "there was a number of instances when I was asked by Israeli embassy officials, 'But how can you do this?' I think they knew that I was basically sympathetic to them. And the fact of my background, that my dad was friendly with Shamir, knew Begin from Europe, and knew Arens since he was a little boy didn't help matters. I mean, I was considered a special kind of traitor. The feeling was that I had betrayed my background, my roots, my family connections. I kept throwing up numbers that were going to bring the Lavi crashing down on its own."

Officially, the decision to stop production of the Lavi was made by the Israeli government. In practice, its death warrant was signed the moment the U.S. administration announced it was pulling out. Arens has never forgiven the Americans. He believes that the Lavi was finally grounded by a coalition of opponents: the Israeli finance ministry, elements of the air force, and Americans at the Pentagon led by Weinberger and Zakheim—whom he disparagingly labels "this little civil servant."

Arens did not become prime minister anyway. Even if the Lavi had survived, it would not have brought him the nation's leadership. Teicher and other Americans should have known that Israeli politics are much more complex than the success or failure of pet projects—even when the United States pours in a billion dollars.

Israelis have a saying "The master of the hundred is the master of opinion." It rhymes in Hebrew, and its nearest English equivalent is: "He who pays the piper calls the tune." Israel was realizing the basic truth of the concept. Even with its fundamental sympathy toward Israel, the Reagan administration showed that it could be a very difficult paymaster when waste was perceived.

When Israel annexed the Golan Heights in 1981 and the United States protested, Prime Minister Begin had shouted at Ambassador Lewis: "Are we a vassal state?" But the Lavi affair suggested to many Israelis that the answer was yes. Now, however, there was no Begin to shout back. Since 1987, though reluctant to admit it publicly, Israel has been increasingly aware of its reliance on America.

But still, when the United States exploited the dependence by insisting that Israel change, in order to earn its dollars, America presented itself as a caring friend rather than as an adversary. George Shultz's assiduous attempts to reform Israel's economy offer an excellent illustration.

In the early 1980s Israel's economy had declined to a condition best described as a real mess. Inflation had soared to an annual rate of 1,000 percent, and the consequent mockery of Israel's currency and pricing threatened to spiral into chaos. Shultz has blamed the economic disorder on two factors: first, the obsessive preoccupation of Israel's leaders with issues of security at the expense of their economy; and second, their adherence to a "socialist tradition" imported from central Europe.

But there were additional reasons. In Israel's early years, the country had been an economic success story, with an annual growth rate of 10 percent and inflation never over 10 percent. And that was well before any substantial aid from the U.S. government.

A White House memorandum prepared for President Kennedy on the eve of his May 1961 meeting with Prime Minister Ben-Gurion went beyond the usual dry bureaucratic language in admiring the Jewish state's economic achievements. "Israel's Bar Mitzvah," the memo reads, "or entering into manhood in the Judaistic tradition, is an appropriate time" to "take great pride" in "a substantial and remarkable rate of economic growth.

"The figures are striking: In 1960 exports were up 25 percent, industrial growth 14 percent (highest in the world), GNP per capita was at $1,145, which is several times that of its neighbors and even above that of the Netherlands and Italy."

But prosperity bred an appetite for consumption. Starting in the 1970s, Israelis were unwilling to tighten their belts, and their leaders refused to introduce austerity when the costs of national defense went sky high.

Instead, Begin's government adopted policies that were described as populist while in fact creating false prosperity. Taxes were cut, but four-digit inflation was created along with record levels of foreign debt. Shultz, combining his skills as economist and diplomat, was concerned that the imminent collapse of Israel's economy would endanger its security and, eventually, would also weaken it as a regional ally of the United States.

"Shultz had a real and sincere concern with where the economy was going," says Uri Savir, who at the time worked at the prime minister's office in Jerusalem, observing the personal interest the secretary of state took in Israel's economy. "In the months between March and July 1985, Shultz was strongly involved. We had the clear feeling that he was a man who cared about Israel."

Shultz was also concerned that to keep Israel afloat, the United States might have to pour more funds down a bottomless pit. He first managed to persuade President Reagan—and then Congress—that a one-time shot of money was needed to put the Israeli economy back on course. If they waited any longer, he said, even larger sums would be needed. Thus was born the special grant of $1.5 billion that the United States gave to Israel in 1985 and '86.

There were a lot of American strings attached, however. Israel had to introduce economic reforms to be suggested by America, to change Israel from a socialist society into a free market economy based on capitalism. Shultz set up a team of U.S. economists to oversee the reforms, headed by professors Herbert Stein and Stanley Fisher.

Stein and Fisher were American Jews who knew Israel very well. They had visited the country, had taught at its universities, had studied its economy, and had good friends there. With Shultz's full backing, the U.S. team devised an economic plan that rested on three central elements: privatization of the Israeli economy by forcing the state to sell its assets to the public; budget cuts; and monetary reform.

The American plan got a mixed and highly emotional reception in Israel. Some government ministers were concerned about what they saw as increased U.S. intervention, and they feared that Israel was losing its already declining independence. Some mourned the potential loss of power that they used to wield through government-owned companies and agencies. Others feared that Shultz's plan, with its reduction in the average standard of living, would be a certain vote-loser.

Another strain of Israeli opposition was based on economic analysis. Here the argument was that U.S. aid was bad because it was enslaving Israel. The Jewish state, these analysts reasoned, was turning into a U.S.-financed experiment in which the laboratory rats—the Israeli people—were forgetting how to fend for themselves. This school of thought mixed its metaphors by comparing Israel's dependence on the United States with an addict who must wean himself away from his drug pusher. So if America would withhold the one-time injection and the annual habit of massive aid, it might be doing Israel a favor. But politicians looking for votes were unlikely to champion any kind of withdrawal pains.

Another minority—mainly Israel's political left during the years of Likud rule—suggested that the United States should use foreign aid as leverage to force policy changes. This analysis, often including the notion that "America can save Israel from itself," contended that a cash-rich Israel would be more self-confident to the point of arrogance, refusing to make any concessions in return for peace. Some Israeli politicians and economists actually approached the American team with advice to try the political-pressure approach.

At the other end of the political spectrum were Israelis who feared that if their country was too economically dependent, it would be unable to repel the kind of American political pressure that the Israeli left was hoping for. This right-wing Israeli concern was echoed by right-wing American Jews. Columnist William Safire counseled Israelis to protect their "political freedom" and "diplomatic independence" by sorting out their economy.

Some of the most original and provocative arguments were made by Ariel Sharon. Since the humiliation he felt at the hands of Weinberger when the first strategic Memorandum of Understanding collapsed in late 1981, Sharon had become very hostile to the United States. Ambassador Lewis says that "Sharon's whole theory of how to deal with the United States was to stick a thumb in our eye and make the U.S. like it."

Sharon, out of defense but still a minister now focusing on industry, told his cabinet colleagues that Israel owed nothing to America. In fact, he preached on several occasions during the mid-1980s that "they owe us." He computed that Israel's strategic value to the United States since 1967 was worth over $80 billion, measured largely by intelligence sharing and the huge savings made possible by inside information on Soviet weapons systems.

Anti-American and antiaid voices, however, represented only a small minority of Israelis. The majority simply wanted the U.S. aid. The government seemed quite willing to make the changes recommended by the American economists, and Shultz's involvement was welcomed. "There was no paternalism or quasi-colonialism," says Savir.

Indeed, within only two years, Shultz, his team, and the Israelis working with them performed a near miracle. By the end of 1986 inflation was down from 1,260 percent to a manageable 13 percent, and the crisis crippling Israel's foreign exchange reserves and its currency had blown over.

The stabilization of Israel's economy was a source of relief for Shultz and the administration. But the secretary of state wanted to go further by enhancing private enterprise. "I hoped to open up the Israeli economy to American investment," he has written, "and that American private enterprise would take the lead." Shultz asked Max Fisher, not only a philanthropist but a Republican, to work on the issue.

Fisher formed "Project Independence" to encourage American investments in Israel. He enlisted more than one hundred successful U.S. businessmen, mainly Jews, including the top people in several Wall Street investment firms. The project's managers hoped to sell shares in Israeli companies with bright, new ideas that could be exported to America and around the world. This, Fisher insists, would not be charity: "When you ask a guy like me to make a contribution to Israel, that's one thing. I give. But when you ask Max Fisher the businessman to make an investment, that's a completely different matter. I want to see my way to a reasonable return, and I want to operate my business in a way that has been successful for me in the past."

Some investments were made, but after some long and difficult months, Project Independence foundered. American entrepreneurs who tried to take part said they had been defeated by
Israeli bureaucracy: endless forms and officials who were less
than competent.

In some cases—as happened to Melvin Ross—they even fell
prey to Israeli criminals. Ross, a Jewish philanthropist from
Boston in his early seventies, who had a successful packaging
plant, had in the past given money to various Israeli causes, including universities. Now, in 1986, he was urged by an Israeli
official to invest in the Jewish state. Ross was introduced to two
young Israeli businessmen, whom he fully trusted. He put
hundreds of thousands of dollars into setting up two projects in
Israel—a packing plant and a medical center. But he remained
in Boston, without involving himself in the daily running of his
Israeli business.

A few years later, on a visit in Israel, he discovered to his
dismay that his enterprise had failed. Even worse, he was in
debt to Israeli banks to the tune of several million dollars. His
Israeli partners denied any responsibility. And the worst of his
humiliations came when Ross was legally prevented from leaving the country for a brief period—a miserable end to what had
seemed a good idea for Israel's sake.

There are also some success stories. The principles of Project
Independence did sink in, and an increasing number of American Jews have been willing to do business in Israel. One of them
is Alan Greenberg, chairman of the Bear Stearns brokerage
house. During the late 1980s Greenberg and his partners acquired assets in Israel by spending a few million dollars here
and there, in property, agriculture, and industry. By 1993 his
Israeli investments had risen in value to about $500 million,
making Greenberg one of Israel's largest and most enthusiastic
U.S. investors. "Israel," he said, "proved to be a good invest-

ment for us. We've had a good experience in dealing with the Israeli government.''

Still, private investment makes up only a small portion of total U.S. financial aid. There seem to be limits, for several reasons: the official state of war with Arab neighbors, the perceived instability of the Middle East in general, the unchangeable geography that leaves Israel over five thousand miles and at least seven time zones away, publicity surrounding past failures in doing business with Israel, lack of familiarity with recent successes, the bureaucratic mound of paperwork for imports and exports, and the perception—by now incorrect—that Israel is a socialist state. All of these keep potential investors away.

Most U.S. assistance still comes from two traditional sources: the federal government and private donations—mainly from Jews. There is a huge difference, however, between Israel's first years and its most recent economic assistance. From modest beginnings in 1948, amounting to no more than $200 million in both federal economic aid and Jewish charity collections, all forms of American aid to Israel have increased and have mounted up to a total—since the start—of almost $100 billion.

In addition to the highly visible economic and military aid, institutionalized as irreducible during the Reagan years, the estimate for total aid includes special interest rates applied to old debts, guarantees for housing and oil, sales of Israel Bonds in the United States, American-funded research projects in defense and other fields, the Free Trade Area agreement, entrepreneurial investments, and private donations.

Official federal aid accounts for about three-quarters of the grand total, which means that for every three dollars Israel receives from the U.S. government, it gets an additional dollar in private American contributions channeled through organizations such as the United Jewish Appeal, Hadassah, and the Jewish National Fund.

The grand total exceeds the amount of money that the United States put into the Marshall Plan for the rehabilitation of devastated Europe after World War II. Europe, at the time, had a population of some 300 million people; Israel has a little over 5 million. An oversimplified long division would suggest that every Israeli has received about $20,000 from America since the establishment of the state. But, as Israelis ask each other, "Where's the money?" It was mostly spent on defense, and mostly in the United States.

Still, it is a lot of money. And naturally, there have been dissenting voices. Two chairmen of the Senate Foreign Relations Committee, William Fulbright of Arkansas and, later, Charles Percy of Illinois, suggested the United States should not bankroll a country that acts so independently that American interests seem ignored. Like them, former Republican congressman Paul McCloskey of California is a frequent speaker against Israeli policies. McCloskey antagonized the pro-Israel lobby by proposing that U.S. aid be cut, and campaign contributions to his rival from Jewish Americans helped unseat McCloskey in 1982.

Years later mainstream U.S. politicians again dared to suggest that aid be slashed. A former Senate majority leader, Robert Byrd of West Virginia, complained, "We have poured foreign aid into Israel for decades at rates and terms given to no other nation on earth. And we are the only nation to have done so." Senate minority leader Bob Dole suggested, in February 1990, that the five top recipients—led by Israel—have their assistance cut by 5 percent so that the money could be spent on eastern Europe instead. Dole's office received a flood of letters, mainly disagreeing with his proposal.

"Israel is still a special case, and you don't abandon old friends," says a Senate aide who has worked closely with Dole.

"But it's not a static relationship. We live in the real world, and the real world is changing. And the relationship, in some ways, is going to change.

"What is frustrating is that when someone like Senator Dole raises some legitimate, budgetary questions, in some quarters there's a tendency to make a huge quantum leap and he's labeled 'anti-Israel.' Now that's absurd!"

But equally absurd is the thought that Israel could receive a huge amount of aid, in the face of tightened U.S. budgets, with no questions asked. America has always demanded some explanations of how the money is spent by Israel, but even more questions would be asked in the years to come.

"It's a unique situation, there's no doubt about that," says former president Jimmy Carter. He does believe that the United States should help pay for Israel's defense, but the levels of aid—and dependence—have been boosted by well-organized lobbyists, whom Carter calls "very astute people" who "assessed the potential."

"I don't think it is wholesome for either country," the former president adds, "but it has become a way of life."

True, the U.S. and Israeli economies became so intertwined that they sometimes seemed like a married couple with a joint checkbook. But the more frequent, and apt, analogy was with a parent who gives a child a generous allowance in the hope—but not the assurance—that the result will be a family with no complaints and no trouble.

CHAPTER FIFTEEN

FAMILY SCANDALS

In the summer of 1979, while being briefed prior to his departure for Washington, General Yoel Ben-Porat received a clear warning: Stay out of trouble. Espionage is not part of your job.

These were his instructions from General Yehoshua Saguy, the director of Aman, Israel's military intelligence agency, to the man who was being sent to serve as Israel's deputy military attaché at the embassy in the United States. Both men were professional intelligence officers, intimately familiar with the craft of espionage. General Saguy explained that spying or stealing secrets from Israel's best ally could be very risky and counterproductive.

Similar briefings are conducted and warnings issued every year to the three hundred Israeli diplomats, officials, and military personnel who are assigned to the embassy in Washington and to the nine Israeli consulates in major U.S. cities.

The large size of the staff is a good indication of the importance the State of Israel attaches to the United States. Ever since the Nixon administration, Israel's has been one of the most visible of diplomatic presences on American soil. Relative to its own population, a mere 5 million, Israel sends a greater proportion of its own citizens to the United States as diplomats than any other nation.

Most Israeli envoys have made the Foreign Ministry their careers: counsels, secretaries, and clerks, supervised by an ambassador who is often but not always a career diplomat. But in addition there are representatives of other parts of the Israeli government machinery—including a labor attaché, who liaises with American unions, and a commercial attaché to keep an eye on the latest technological developments.

A large section at the embassy—situated at Van Ness Street, off Connecticut Avenue in northwest Washington—represents Israel's military-security complex. Internally referred to as the "Prime Minister's extension," Mossad operatives work at the embassy primarily as liaisons with the CIA. Officers of the General Security Services, Israel's counterespionage and antiterrorism agency also known as Shin Bet, form close ties with their counterparts at the FBI.

The United States, for its part, has a more than respectable representation on Israeli soil. With its 550 American and local Israeli employees, the U.S. Embassy is not just the largest in Israel but is also considered fairly large among U.S. diplomatic missions and institutions worldwide. The embassy, on Tel Aviv's Hayarkon Street along the sea, is a mirror image of Israel's embassy in Washington: housing State Department career diplomats; personnel from the U.S. Information Agency; and attachés for labor, commercial affairs, and science. Moreover, each branch of the U.S. armed forces is represented, as are the various agencies of American law enforcement and intelligence: the CIA, the FBI, the Drug Enforcement Administration, and the Customs Service.

However friendly the relations, there is an undercurrent of distrust. Every host country tends to consider all the accredited diplomats in an embassy—especially the military attachés and the envoys of the intelligence community—as potential, if not actual, spies. This is the tradition in international relations, and the U.S.-Israel link is no different.

Whoever it is in any embassy who might be engaged in some spying, most of his or her efforts center on the gathering of information from open and public sources. This does not fall under the usual definition of espionage, but the fact is that the files of intelligence agencies contain mostly unclassified material. Israel's science attachés acquire almost every scientific or technological publication that comes out in the United States, so as to stay up-to-date on topics from which Israel may benefit.

At the same time, American diplomats make intensive efforts to collect data on Israel's domestic politics. Several employees, including a former Israeli journalist, busy themselves in the political section of the U.S. Embassy, reading everything written in the Israeli press and monitoring every radio and TV broadcast. They can frequently be seen in the K'nesset cafeteria, trying to pick up the latest parliamentary gossip or to get an angle on the latest moves in Israel's Byzantine politics. These open collection activities are internationally legitimate and accepted.

Diplomats and other embassy personnel are extremely cautious not to cross the very thin line separating permissible from inadmissible.

Of course, General Ben-Porat was aware of all these finesses when, in January 1980, at the end of the Israeli embassy's normal Washington workday, an American walked into his office unannounced. "You don't know me yet," the man said, "but I'm very familiar with your bosses." He identified himself and went on to drop the names of several prominent Israeli leaders. He explained to the astonished general that he had met them all, as U.S. sales representative for Israeli arms manufacturers.

The man then opened his briefcase, pulled out a sheaf of documents, and smiled. "I have something for you!" he said, handing the papers to Ben-Porat, who quickly scanned through them. They were plans and drawings for airbases and military camps in Saudi Arabia, built by the American construction company Bechtel.

Ben-Porat went pale and immediately handed the papers back to his uninvited visitor. Giving them up was not easy, as this kind of information about an enemy state was obviously the dream of any Israeli intelligence officer. But he had never met this American before, and he had not even heard of him. Ben-Porat's intelligence intuition told him that the man could be a trap, sent by U.S. counterespionage or some other country to compromise him.

The Israeli called for a security guard and ordered that the stranger be removed from the embassy premises. As he was taken out of the room, the American managed to leave a business card with Ben-Porat and snapped: "You'll come back to me yet!"

A quick background check discovered that the American had not only violated embassy security, but he should never have been allowed in under any circumstances. A few years earlier he had tried to recruit an Israeli embassy employee to work for Syrian intelligence, leading to his name being put on a "blacklist" kept by the Israelis. The file showed the man was Jewish, and Ben-Porat found his seemingly conflicting activities very puzzling.

But one of the basic rules of the intelligence game is that no potential source should be spurned. He should be handled cautiously, perhaps, but his information should not be lost. So Israel found another way to contact the American, despite his dubious past, and the reward was a great deal of material about military installations in Saudi Arabia.

Months later, when General Ben-Porat returned home from work one evening and switched on the television, he was shocked when the evening news announced that the American—the very same man who had offered the Saudi blueprints—had been arrested in a mob-related bribery and kickback scheme in the United States.

Ben-Porat and some of the heads of Israeli intelligence now went through a few tense weeks. They assumed that the FBI had put the American under surveillance before his arrest. He must have been secretly photographed and his telephone conversations recorded—so they feared his contacts with Israel might be uncovered. In addition, the Israelis knew that the FBI tapped phone conversations made to and from the embassy.

When Israeli embassy staff about to be posted in the United States are briefed not to involve themselves in spying, they also are warned that telephones in the embassy and possibly at their homes are being bugged. The Israelis knew that American wiretapping is so sophisticated that it can be done from a distance. Israeli security men noticed that opposite their embassy, on a small hill, a van—disguised as belonging to a utility company—was parked almost night and day. They were sure that the vehicle was there to operate the espionage equipment.

Israeli diplomats therefore use scramblers on some of their phone and fax lines, and the embassy has a secure room electronically outfitted to counter any attempts at eavesdropping.

The caution and suspiciousness, even between friendly countries, is nothing exceptional. The staff of the U.S. Embassy in Tel Aviv also assumes that Israel is monitoring its telephone and fax messages.

The Israelis were relieved that they were not even mentioned at the trial of the American with the mysterious Saudi blueprints. But over the years there have been other such scares. However, the benign outcomes made many Israelis feel they could get away with anything. They thought they had the Americans in their pockets.

The perception of freedom to bend the rules is part of the average Israeli's psychology. While most Americans are reared on notions of order and planning, Israelis grow up in an atmosphere of improvisation: trying things and assuming that somehow they will work out.

Israelis also are educated to believe that anything goes, if it is for the sake of the country's security: lies, of course; but even violations of other countries' laws.

The unprecedented heights reached by U.S.-Israel relations during the golden era of President Reagan only contributed to the cockiness of many Israelis. It seemed the sky was the limit when it came to their activities in America. But when the Israelis pushed their luck too far, they were proved wrong. The illusion exploded in their faces with the Pollard affair.

Jonathan Jay Pollard was born on August 7, 1954, to a Jewish family in Galveston, Texas, and grew up in South Bend, Indiana. Mainly through his own reading and thinking, Pollard became a Zionist zealot. In 1979, after attending Tufts University near Boston, he was hired by the U.S. Navy as a civilian intelligence analyst. He was among the chosen few working in the new and ultra-secretive antiterrorism alert center of the Naval Investigation Service in Suitland, Maryland.

In May 1984 a Jewish businessman in New York introduced Pollard to Aviem Sela, an Israeli air force colonel. This was no casual chat for Pollard. He told Sela of his deep concern for the Jewish state, how he felt terrible working in U.S. intelligence and knowing that Israel was not being given all the information that America had that could help Israel's defense. Pollard offered to provide the secrets that he claimed the United States was withholding.

Sela dutifully reported back through the chain of command, to air force headquarters in Tel Aviv. After a short while he was ordered to recruit the frustrated intelligence analyst.

For reasons of spycraft, the Israelis preferred to use Pollard as a paid informer rather than as a volunteer. When you pay, you have leverage over your agent: You can apply extortion or can generally use him or her as you like. If, on the other hand, the person operates on a voluntary basis, it is the walk-in who sets the rules. The agent can quit anytime.

Israel did not, however, use the Mossad to run Pollard. Intelligence chiefs did not want to jeopardize the Mossad's good relations with the CIA, based on the 1951 agreement not to spy against each other. Instead, Pollard was operated by a unit named Lakam, a Hebrew acronym for Science Liaison Bureau, one of the smallest but most efficient sections of Israeli intelligence.

Initially, at its beginnings in the 1950s, the unit's function had been to guard the secrets of the nuclear reactor in Dimona and to procure special materials such as enriched uranium for the project. Over the years, however, Lakam's activities expanded and the unit came to be, in effect, a theft contractor for advanced technologies that would then help the Israeli military complex. It was Lakam that appointed the science attachés to Israel's diplomatic missions abroad, including the Washington embassy.

Colonel Sela helped arrange a trip to Paris for Jonathan Pollard and his fiancée, Ann, and there and in Tel Aviv they were given jewelry and $10,000 cash. Pollard also agreed to accept a monthly stipend of $1,500 plus bonuses, to be deposited on his behalf in a Swiss bank account.

Whether for money or only out of concern for Israel's security, Pollard became Israel's best-ever asset in Washington. Nearly every Friday he brought piles of documents to an apartment occupied by a secretary working for Israel's science attaché. For a year and a half, until his arrest, he provided thrilling details on subjects ranging far beyond his work for the navy. His high security clearance enabled him to borrow from several restricted archives, including those of the Defense Intelligence Agency at the Pentagon. He handed over maps, military plans, and reconnaissance photos taken by American satellites of installations in the Arab world.

Israel was now learning a great deal more about Syria's chemical weapons and Iraq's efforts to revive its nuclear program. There were even lists of recent arms purchases by Egypt, Jordan, and Saudi Arabia. Because those three Arab states were seen as pro-American moderates, the United States had generally refused to share its intelligence on them with Israel. And when Israel's air force planned its October 1985 bombing raid on Palestine Liberation Organization headquarters in Tunisia, Pollard's handlers first asked him for detailed information on all the antiaircraft facilities along the coast of North Africa.

It was only then that Pollard's boss at naval intelligence begin to have doubts about him, after catching the young analyst lying about some trivial matters. Navy and FBI agents started watching Pollard and eventually called him in for questioning. Three days later, on November 21, Pollard, his wife, and their cat got into their five-year-old Mustang and drove to the Israeli embassy, hoping that they would be given asylum there. The embassy's security staff, however, turned them away. With an FBI surveillance team plainly on their tails, any other Israeli response would have provoked a nasty, public showdown.

Once the Pollards were arrested and the story broke, there was plenty of outrage anyway. The White House, Congress, the media, and the public were all shocked that Israel, already the recipient of so much American aid, was stealing American secrets.

American Jews were more than astonished; they were put in

an uncomfortable bind. Jewish community newspapers offered the justifications that Pollard had not damaged U.S. security interests; that the documents he had transferred related only to the Middle East; and that he had done so only after discovering that the United States had not been warning Israel of military threats from the Arab world.

But the American public, at large, seemed now to have cause to question the loyalty of their Jewish neighbors. Were they true American citizens? Did they divide their allegiance between the United States and Israel? The media unearthed cases in which the FBI had investigated Jews in prominent positions—aides on Capitol Hill and government officials—on suspicion of transferring information to Israel.

"It was a dark time to be a Jewish official anywhere in the U.S. government," says Howard Teicher, then the National Security Council's Middle East expert. Several journalists told him that they had received tips from FBI sources suggesting that Teicher was a Mossad agent.

Another official who had experienced such harassment was Stephen Bryen, a former senior staffer on the Senate Foreign Relations Committee who later worked in the Pentagon. An Arab-American lobbyist lodged a complaint that he had heard Bryen, who is Jewish, discussing U.S. military secrets with Israeli officials at a Washington restaurant.

As Bryen recalls the 1978 breakfast, he was chatting with half a dozen Israeli embassy employees—carrying out his senators' wishes by pressing the Israelis for more information on their complaints over U.S. arms sales to Arab countries. Teddy Kollek, visiting from Jerusalem, even came over to chat, "so it was not exactly an invisible meeting to hand out secrets," says Bryen.

A short while later Bryen found himself under investigation by the FBI, which may have been thinking that the elderly mayor of Jerusalem was still an Israeli spy.

The case was dropped, but it came up again when Bryen joined the Department of Defense in 1981. He had been invited into the Pentagon by Richard Perle, also a former pro-Israel stalwart among Senate staffers. Bryen said: "Look, Richard, they're going to give me hell over the past, and they're going to start arguing that the Arabs think I'm a Mossad agent." Bryen was concerned that Weinberger, with his anti-Israel reputation, would veto him.

Perle said, "Why don't we find out?" To their surprise, Weinberger personally directed a reinvestigation and after six weeks accepted Bryen.

But some officials, notably in part of the FBI, believed there were hundreds of "Bryens" in Washington. Far worse, after November 1985 they would hint darkly at there being dozens of "Pollards." American Jews in public service grew tense and fearful. "I arrived in Washington after Pollard's exposure, and the mood was anti-Israel," a female Israeli diplomat recalls. "Non-Jewish acquaintances of mine, but especially the Jewish ones, who had always been pleased to welcome us in their offices and also socially at cocktail parties in their homes, suddenly were concerned about meeting with Israelis. I was especially close with a Jewish official who worked for one of the U.S. intelligence agencies. We lived in the same Washington neighborhood, we prayed at the same synagogue, and we used to visit each other at home. Now he was telling me he would be embarrassed by a visit from me—that it might cost him his job."

Most American Jews concluded that Israel had been wrong, that Pollard had broken the law and deserved to be punished. Even Pollard, in his prison cell, wrote: "I regret the adverse effect which my actions had on the United States and the Jewish community." He said he should have understood "the ammunition provided to anyone who might want to accuse American Jews of having dual loyalties."

In the post-Pollard witch-hunting season, even non-Jews became targets—even Jerry Weaver, a so-called Arabist in the State Department. A native of Newark, Ohio, he was wild about football and guns, indulging the first passion at Ohio State University and the second in the National Guard and the U.S. Army.

He managed to study, too, earning a doctorate in political science at the University of Pittsburgh and teaching for a while before applying to the State Department in 1977 for a job. He was sent to Sudan the following year to work on refugee issues, taught himself Arabic, and made many friends while enjoying the wilds of East Africa, which most diplomats would consider a hardship.

Weaver added to his gun collection and went lion hunting with all types of people, from government officials to smugglers. These contacts provided him with excellent information, and thus he learned that secret agents from Israel were encouraging Ethiopian Jews to leave their villages and move to refugee camps in eastern Sudan.

Weaver reported the Mossad's presence, as part of his many reports on the flood of refugees from drought and civil war in the entire Horn of Africa. Washington asked him to keep monitoring the Israelis, but in mid-1984 his orders changed. He was to become the coordinator, on the U.S. side, for cooperation with the Israeli agents in spiriting the Ethiopian Jews to safety.

Liaison work with the Mossad would usually be the CIA's job, but the Agency did not want it for fear of annoying the Arab governments that without doubt would eventually learn from the Sudanese about the operation. "I assume the job was given to me," Weaver says, "because if it had failed, the CIA would have blamed me; and if it succeeded they could still take the credit."

Between October 1984 and January 1985, he met with a Mossad officer, whom he knew as Ephraim, in Athens and Geneva. The Israeli gave Weaver huge sums of cash in suitcases, needed to rent safe houses, to pay salaries and bribes to Sudanese state security agents who provided escorts, and to buy bus parts and communications equipment in Saudi Arabia and elsewhere.

Occasionally, the Mossad would ask him to use the money to buy personal gifts for Sudanese officials—such as Rolex watches and, once, a Magnum pistol on which the Israelis had engraved a personal dedication to an army general.

During these three months, buses ferried Jewish refugees from camps in eastern Sudan to an airport where they were flown to Europe and Israel by Belgian airliners the Mossad had chartered. Eight thousand Ethiopian Jews were taken to an ancient homeland of which they had prayed and dreamed.

Sudan's vice president Omar el-Tayeb, who was head of the security service, asked that a special fund be established. He claimed that this would serve to fund his pet project: a huge building complex for his security service "like the CIA's headquarters in Langley."

Weaver told the Israelis about it. Ephraim responded by asking whether $1.5 million would be sufficient. Weaver said yes, and the Israelis opened a bank account in London and gave the account number to Weaver, who then provided it to the Sudanese general.

In January, news of the clandestine refugee route leaked from a talkative Israeli official. It was immediately headline news around the world, and the Sudanese stopped the project. Weaver received death threats from radical Muslim students and fled the country in March 1985. U.S. Embassy security officials went to his home to pack up his belongings and shipped them to Washington.

He took a desk job at the State Department, but when more stories appeared in the media about the U.S. helping Israel's secret rescue operation, Weaver found himself being questioned sharply by department officers intent on plugging the leak. Even worse, the subject shifted suddenly to guns and marijuana—both found in his Khartoum home by the Americans who packed up his property.

The interrogators then zeroed in on the contents of a safe in Weaver's home: money and a lot of receipts. This line of questioning caught fire in November 1985, just around the time that Jonathan Pollard was arrested for spying on Israel's behalf in Washington. U.S. investigators pressed Weaver: What was the money for? What were those receipts?

Assuming that the investigators in Washington did not know about the refugee operation with the Mossad and were not supposed to know, Weaver refused to answer and referred them to his superiors. "You people find out!" he snapped.

According to Weaver, the U.S. officials then became downright aggressive. "They started telling me that I'm an Israeli agent, a second Pollard, paid by the Mossad." The chief investigator, he recalls, was "an inexperienced highway patrol officer, and she didn't know what kind of work I was involved in. But I sensed hostility toward Israel, with questions like 'what does America get from helping Israel?'"

Top officials of the State Department did finally assure the security personnel that Weaver had been on an authorized mission. But he quit government service in disgust, returning to Ohio where he raises cattle and horses.

Suspicions that Israeli and American interests clash rather than coincide were explosively revived by Pollard's arrest. There should be no conflict, because Israel has been a friend of the United States and Jews are loyal U.S. citizens.

Yet Israeli officials were not truly concerned with the dilemmas of their American brethren. Clearly, they had made a grave mistake in recruiting a local Jew for the benefit of their intelligence gathering. But they were not too worried about the problem their actions caused American Jewry. What bothered them was the price that Israel was going to have to pay, given the fury of the administration and of the president in particular.

President Reagan first heard of Pollard's arrest aboard Air Force One, flying back to Washington from his summit with Soviet leader Mikhail Gorbachev in Geneva. Of the Israelis, whom he had nourished with juicy financial and military aid, promoting them into major allies of the United States, he said: "I don't understand why they are doing it!"

Israel had no real answer. Three days into Pollard's arrest, Israel admitted that he had worked for one of its agencies, but, the announcement continued: "It was a rogue operation."

To demonstrate how seriously it took the matter, the government agreed to cooperate with American investigators who went to Israel to gather evidence for Pollard's trial. Although it would emerge later that this cooperation was not wholehearted and that there were attempts to deceive the U.S. inquiry team, unprecedented results doomed the defendant. Israel's cooperation made the prosecution far easier, and—largely on the strength of a stern recommendation to the judge by Defense Secretary Weinberger—Pollard was sentenced to life in prison in March 1987.

In the annals of modern espionage, there had been no case in which a country ran a loyal spy in another country and then cut him off, while helping the other country in bringing criminal charges.

Israel also tried to mollify the Americans by claiming that the senior political echelons had not been aware of Pollard's activities. The Israeli government also announced that it was disbanding Lakam. Neither of these statements was completely accurate.

It was true that Israel's political, military, and intelligence leaders had not personally seen Pollard's name. Indeed, they were not supposed to know—given the secrecy and compartmentalization of espionage. But they clearly did know that Israel was receiving excellent material from an American source, and they also knew that these were data that the Americans had refused to give when Israel officially requested it. So they must have been aware that the information was reaching Israel via dubious channels.

As for Lakam, even when the agency was shut down, Israel continued—and still continues—to operate, though in a different framework invented by the army and the Mossad, a unit tasked with gathering technological information.

Israel also publicly apologized to the American government. But this was false contrition. Behind closed doors, Israelis were arguing that the Americans had overreacted. Senior Israeli leaders said privately that notwithstanding the seriousness of the incident, it should be viewed in perspective.

The wider context, Israeli officials claimed, included the fact that American spy satellites and listening posts kept a constant watch on Israel's defense structure. The officials added that the United States had been sending spies into Israel on specific missions to learn about military, economic, and scientific projects.

Immediately after Pollard's arrest, Yitzhak Rabin—then defense minister—revealed that Israel had discovered five American spies in the late 1970s and early 1980s in sensitive nuclear and industrial facilities. One had been caught gathering information on the premises of the state-owned arms development company Rafael, in Haifa. Another was an American scientist working on an exchange program at the Nahal Soreq nuclear research reactor. The American spies were arrested and questioned, but the less rigid Israeli legal system made it possible for the government to release and expel them for the sake of avoiding conflict with the United States.

The problem with these Israeli accusations about American espionage was that they were never backed up with publicly available information and documentation. According to what the Israelis themselves leaked, these were borderline cases, people who had engaged in activities that were considered semiacceptable among friendly nations: seemingly not much more serious than the data-gathering by U.S. diplomatic staff from overt sources.

These cases—although Israel considered them very serious indeed—were entirely different from that of Pollard, which was a blunt breach of prior understandings between the two countries. Israel did not merely spy against the United States, and not only did it do so on U.S. territory, but it used an American citizen and recruited him for money.

Even worse, the spy belonged to the U.S. intelligence community. Worst of all: The spy was caught, and his connection with Israel was fully exposed.

There is only one confirmed case that the Israelis could have pointed to in which U.S. intelligence acted in a manner remotely similar to the Pollard affair. Israel, for its own reasons, kept tight-lipped about it.

Yosef Amit was arrested by several plainclothes officers of the General Security Services, the GSS, along with uniformed police, on March 24, 1986, in the parking lot of his apartment building in the northern port city of Haifa. He was forty-one years old at the time of his arrest. The son of a well-known police officer, he followed in his father's footsteps by deciding on a career in uniform after his three years of compulsory military service ended in 1966. He stayed in the Israeli army, serving in the special forces, and was wounded during a border clash with Palestinian guerrillas in 1972. Amit then joined a supersecret unit of military intelligence, where he reached the rank of major.

That same year, however, he was court-martialed for the alleged cold-blooded killing of a wounded Palestinian guerrilla in Lebanon. Amit was acquitted, however, and was permitted to remain in the army.

In 1978 Major Amit was in trouble again, in a case that Israel would rather not discuss. His special intelligence unit was in charge of running Palestinian and Lebanese Arab informers. In return for the information they provided the Israelis, the Arab agents were paid with illicit drugs that had been seized by the Israeli police in day-to-day law enforcement. The drugs-for-espionage operation was one of Israel's most closely kept secrets.

The police and military security personnel discovered that Amit and some of his colleagues were cutting their own "commission" by selling drugs on the Israeli market. Amit himself was arrested in his army Jeep while making a sale to a local Israeli pusher in a small town south of Tel Aviv. When police searched his apartment, they found classified documents related to his secret military unit.

The major, then thirty-three years old, was again brought before a court-martial, this time charged with drug trafficking and possession of classified material with the intention to sell it to foreign agents. But a psychiatric examination found Amit unfit to stand trial, and instead of facing years in prison he was discharged from the army and secretly hospitalized for four years in a mental hospital.

After his release from treatment in 1982, Amit got a job with a private security firm in Haifa. It was from there, according to investigators, that he contacted American intelligence, offering secret documents about Israeli intelligence and information about his fifteen-year army service. Perhaps he sought some personal vengeance after his run-ins with the military justice authorities.

Amit's capture, indictment, and trial were not announced to the public, and it seemed only a coincidence that he was arrested a mere four months after the arrest of Pollard in Washington. Under interrogation, the former army major confessed to the charges, which included "serious espionage" and "contact with a foreign agent," but in his subsequent trial he pleaded not guilty. Nevertheless a civilian court of three judges convicted him on four counts and sentenced him to twelve years in prison. The sentence was handed down in Haifa in March 1987, the same month that Jonathan Pollard was sentenced to life.

After his arrest, Amit disappeared. His family and friends refused to talk about him, and the media were threatened with prosecution by Israel's military censor should they dare to publish a word about his case. Nevertheless, in a small country like Israel where everyone knows nearly everyone, rumors concerning a "Prisoner X" serving a long term in the psychiatric wing of an Israeli prison surfaced from time to time. Again, there was the irony that Pollard, too, was compelled to spend part of his imprisonment in a federal facility usually reserved for mental patients.

Also like Pollard, Amit filed an appeal to his country's supreme court. Amit's appeal was rejected in 1988. He then began sending hundreds of letters to journalists, lawyers, and politicians, complaining that he had been mistreated. One letter, dated January 2, 1990, was sent to the U.S. ambassador in Tel Aviv, mysteriously warning him not to believe the official version of the case.

Adding further mystery was the discovery by Israeli investigators that some of the documents leaked by Amit had come from the GSS, the counterintelligence agency, leading them to believe that the Americans might have organized an extensive spy ring in Israel. It turned out that Amit had obtained the papers from a friend in the GSS, and this Shin Bet man told authorities that he had been unaware of Amit's intentions. An internal GSS tribunal sent Amit's friend to jail for three months.

Less surprising was the discovery that, to avoid detection, American intelligence had not used operatives based in Israel to maintain contact with Amit. The Americans had been in touch from Germany and other countries and had met him in Europe. The entire case had received only one brief and inaccurate mention in the press. A small Hebrew-language newspaper in New York reported in 1986 that an Israeli intelligence officer was facing trial charged with "spying for Syria."

The next time part of the story came up was in early 1991, when a group supported by intelligence veterans and some government officials in Israel, the Public Committee for the Release of Jonathan Pollard, informed a few Israelis that a spy swap was possible. A leader of the committee even called the U.S. Embassy in Tel Aviv to suggest an exchange: Amit for Pollard. An American diplomat seemed surprisingly well briefed on the matter and had an immediate reply: "I don't know what you're talking about. There is no American spy."

When, in March 1991, Amit learned about this in his prison cell, he wrote a letter to a senior lawyer at the state prosecutor's office to ask for clarification. He also claimed to have been beaten up by police officers during his arrest, and he accused the Israeli authorities of bringing false charges against him purely because the spy for Israel—Pollard—had been caught in Washington. He was, he argued, the victim of an orchestrated Israeli attempt to avenge Pollard's arrest.

Amit added in his letter that it was he himself who had informed the authorities that American spies had initiated contacts with him. The prisoner contended that he was not interested in a prisoner exchange, because he had no reason to want to live in America.

The state prosecutor rejected Amit's accusation that the authorities were behind the leaks about a possible swap. She assured him that there were no such plans and that he would not be forced to leave the country. Amit continued, however, to smuggle worried letters to friends and journalists.

Despite Amit's pleas of innocence, Israeli authorities are convinced that he was a genuine spy. However, they have no compelling reason to point fingers of blame in public. This is partly because unlike the Israelis in the Pollard affair, the American spyhandlers ran Amit professionally and at a distance. They used methods that are known in the craft of intelligence as "false-flag recruiting," posing as NATO operatives rather than just Americans. Israel's security services also may be reluctant to publicize specific charges, so as not to expose their methods of investigation and confidential sources.

In addition, with the strain in relations with the United States caused by Pollard's arrest, Israel's political leaders preferred not to cause aggravation by announcing that an American agent had been caught. Amit and his case were swept under the carpet, even as he was paroled in October 1993. As part of the reaction to this news, Israeli and American Jewish leaders who had been reluctant to mention Pollard began calling more vociferously for his early release, insisting his life sentence was excessive.

In any event, the United States denied engaging in espionage in Israel. Senator Dave Durenberger, soon after stepping down as chairman of the intelligence committee in 1987, reacted to the arrest of Pollard by saying that the CIA had already "changed the rules of the game" by employing an Israeli military man as a spy after the invasion of Lebanon in 1982. Defense Secretary Weinberger condemned the senator's statement as "very damaging and very wrong."

Israel decided not to use the Amit ammunition to fire back at the United States and was left to handle the Pollard ricochets. The Washington espionage case, useful to Israel but ultimately harmful, led to an unprecedented falling out that haunted American-Israeli relations for the rest of the 1980s.

"After the Pollard affair," recalls Alon Pinkas, who worked in the military attaché's office in Washington, "the atmosphere between us and our American counterparts became suspicious." Even without Pollard, the attaché—General Amos Yaron—had a hard time. In 1982 he had been among the senior Israeli officers near the Sabra and Shatila refugee camps, and his name was mentioned during the official Israeli inquiries held after the massacre.

Israel's decision to send Yaron to the United States became a source of embarrassment for the Pentagon. The Canadian government had earlier refused to grant him diplomatic accreditation, and Palestinian-Americans protested near Yaron's house in Washington. Slogans against him were even spray-painted near the tracks of the Washington metro.

American officers, on the other hand, had no problem with the appointment of General Yaron, who had studied at a U.S. military academy. They admired Yaron's impressive battle experience and respected him as a fellow general. But now, after Pollard's arrest, even this sense of fraternity ceased to work for the general and his staff at the embassy.

"In telephone conversations and during face-to-face meetings, we received very strong hints that they were apprehensive about us," Pinkas says. "In the past, if we asked to see some paper or document, we would usually get it without going through the routine procedures. Now we were being told: 'Sorry, you can't have this document; file an official request with the foreign liaison office of the army.'

"Our access to army bases was also restricted. Every year hundreds of Israeli officers and pilots visit the U.S. for training courses and just to exchange ideas with colleagues. In the past, before Pollard, we could send them almost anywhere, to any U.S. base, to any military maneuver. All it needed was a quick phone call. In '86 and '87 things changed. If there was some Israeli colonel who'd come for a visit and wanted to be at such and such a base or observe this or that exercise, we got evasive replies. The bad smell of the Pollard affair fouled the atmosphere."

The smell became a stench, with a series of revelations by various U.S. government agencies about Israeli individuals and companies suspected of breaking American law. Even before the Pollard affair, suspicions occasionally had been raised against Israel for sponsoring the theft of American technology to be smuggled to that country.

In a CIA report about Israel's intelligence community dated 1976, the United States was mentioned as a "target." Israeli spies, the CIA said, focused on "collection of information on secret U.S. policy or decisions, if any, concerning Israel" and the "collection of scientific intelligence in the United States and other developed countries."

However, this U.S. government interest in the Israeli interest in America was not confined only to theoretical CIA reports. There was also the practical side of things. In May 1985, six months before Pollard was captured, an American Jew, Richard Smyth, was charged by a federal grand jury in California with smuggling 810 krytrons to Israel. Krytrons are electronic devices that can be used as detonators in nuclear bombs. A special license was required to export them, but had Smyth applied for one, the U.S. government would certainly have refused on the grounds that Israel had not signed the nuclear Non-Proliferation Treaty. FBI investigators found that Smyth owned a small company called Milco, and 80 percent of its business, dating back to 1973, was with Israel. Acting as a go-between was Arnon Milchan, an Israeli entrepreneur and Hollywood producer. He was not charged, while Smyth was freed on bail—but never turned up for his trial. Later reports claimed that he escaped to Israel and was living in an affluent suburb north of Tel Aviv. Israel apologized to the United States after the case hit the headlines, stating that the krytrons were destined for medical purposes and had not been used in the nuclear program. America demanded that all "unused" krytron detonators be returned.

As embarrassing as the apparent nuclear smuggling might be, the United States forgave Israel, accepting the apologies and the returned equipment. But as more dishonorable headlines appeared, the Israeli diplomatic corps in Washington and the ministry of defense representatives in New York felt as if they were facing an orchestrated campaign.

On December 12, 1985, three weeks after Pollard's arrest, U.S. Customs raided three East Coast sites where authorities charged that weapons technology was being smuggled to Israel. Customs officers said a Connecticut-based firm, Nafco, had shipped equipment for coating steel with chromium—destined for the guns of Israel's newest tank, the Merkava. Searches at an Israel Military Industries office in New York yielded evidence that the machinery—worth $2 million—had been dispatched to Israel without an export license. To make things worse, it also emerged that the deal had been funded by U.S. military aid. Nafco eventually paid a fine and damages of $750,000. No Israelis were charged.

A similar case arose in suburban Chicago, where Recon/Optical claimed that Israeli air force officers stole its aerial reconnaissance technology on behalf of an Israeli company. After years of arguments and arbitration, the Israeli government paid Recon $3 million for "abuse" of its information.

Israel was now getting the terrible reputation of a ruthless arms dealer that flaunts international regulations. Every visit by an Israeli defense minister to Washington seemed to be preceded by leaks to the media about Israeli weapons sales—allegedly behind America's back—to South Africa, China, or other nations of ill repute.

The tense relations between the Bush administration and Yitzhak Shamir's government helped create an atmosphere that turned quiet questions into public scandal. In April 1992, on the eve of a visit by Defense Minister Arens, a report by the inspector-general of the State Department was leaked to the press, charging that the United States had failed to control exports of arms and military technology.

Many of the findings, spread over sixty-nine pages, dealt with indications—allegedly ignored by U.S. officials—of unauthorized resales to other countries by "a major recipient of U.S. weapons and technology." Officials confirmed that the alleged culprit was Israel.

"The violations, cited and supported by reliable intelligence information, show a systematic and growing pattern of unauthorized transfers by the recipient," the inspector wrote, "dating back to about 1983."

Being a State Department report, it did not deal with the Pentagon, but hinted at the Reagan administration's lax atmosphere that inspired Stephen Bryen's decision to keep Israel off the technology watch list.

As if that were not enough for beleaguered Israeli officials, a separate leak from the Pentagon exposed unsubstantiated suspicions that Israel had given China some of the technology used in the Patriot missiles sent by America during the Gulf War. The Israelis said they were being smeared, and a team of U.S. experts who flew to Israel to investigate concluded the story was untrue. General Avihu Bin-Nun, who had just left the air force, snapped: "Those who are saying all those things either want to disrupt the special relationship with the United States or don't know what they are talking about."

More specifically, the Israelis point out, they are not the only ones engaging in technology transfers. Arens says, "When we buy weapons systems, and especially aircraft, in the U.S., we have them modified to our specifications. Occasionally we discover that these modifications find their way into the weapons systems our Arab enemies get from the Americans."

Israel's image in the area of defense cooperation sank to its lowest point when the names of some Israeli generals were linked with bribery and payoffs in the United States.

While investigating a widespread corruption scandal in the Pentagon in the Reagan-Weinberger period, the Department of Justice exposed a web of bribery spun around Melvin Paisley, an assistant undersecretary of the navy who had become a private consultant. Investigators said some of America's leading defense manufacturers had paid bribes to win contracts, but they also named an Israeli company: Mazlat.

Mazlat manufactured remotely piloted vehicles—RPVs— that had been sold to the U.S. Navy for unmanned aerial reconnaissance. The investigation alleged that Paisley and an accomplice conspired with two retired Israeli generals—Mazlat's director Zvi Schiller and a former military attaché in Washington, Uri Simhoni, to lubricate sales of the Israeli drone to the United States. In return for Paisley helping Mazlat win a $100 million contract, the two Americans and two Israelis planned to share $2 million of Mazlat money put into a Swiss bank account.

While the federal government brought charges against Paisley and other Americans, Israeli authorities were very slow to do anything. Since Mazlat is owned by Israel Aircraft Industries, the largest defense contractor in the country and a huge exporter to the United States, the Israeli fear was that investigations would lead to more revelations. IAI was concerned that word would emerge of a slush fund specifically for bribing American officials.

Americans had found, long before, that their own sales to Third World countries often required bribery. But it was an entirely different story to have U.S. officials accepting bribes. Conversely, Israel's defense officials used to profess—in the early 1970s—total cleanliness in their business practices, rejecting the payoffs offered by Americans accustomed to Iran and Saudi Arabia. Now Israelis were wallowing in the middle of the military-industrial mud puddle.

After all, Israeli society had changed in the ensuing twenty years. The austerity of devoted pioneers that had led many Americans to adore Israel had given way to opportunists profiting from their country's military predicament. Israel had become no different from other countries swept by corruption and greed.

An even worse case involved Rami Dotan, an Israeli general on active duty in the air force. Head of the technical and logistics section, Dotan was arrested in Israel in October 1990 and charged with corruption, theft, and deception. He cooperated with investigators, to some extent, paid back part of the money, and was jailed for thirteen years—Israel's harshest sentence in a case of corruption in the military.

A simple reading of the charges made it clear that someone in the United States had paid millions of dollars to Dotan and his subordinates. Naturally, American investigators wanted to know who had bribed the Israelis.

Dotan's tainted deals had begun in 1984 and continued until the day of his arrest. His status as the air force's supreme expert on engines had enabled him to determine which American manufacturers could sell their products and services to Israel. He would sign bogus contracts and sometimes even flew worthless junk from Israel to the United States and back again to establish the fiction that some engine maintenance had been performed. U.S. government funds, part of the annual $1.8 billion in military aid, were allocated for the American companies—to perform services for Israel—but some of the money went to Dotan.

The U.S. criminal investigations centered on General Electric, the company that in the 1980s clinched a $500 million deal to supply engines for Israel's fighter planes. American authorities have estimated that at least $40 million was stolen by Dotan and accomplices. In July 1992 GE finally admitted making payoffs to Dotan and defrauding the U.S. aid system. GE paid fines and compensation amounting to almost $70 million.

A congressional investigation then found that a GE competitor, Pratt & Whitney, was involved in diverting $12.5 million in a five-year overpricing scheme organized by General Dotan. The investigators for the General Accounting Office also found that Israel's ministry of defense had a role in mishandling the funds, the strongest evidence that federal authorities had to confirm their suspicions that the Israeli government knew about the diversion.

The broader suspicion was that Israel systematically exploited the U.S. military assistance program by violating laws and restrictions.

Congressman John Dingell, chairman of a House subcommittee on energy and commerce, bitterly commented on an "uncooperative" Israel. "We have a very extensive program to give them substantial funds, and they are alleging that their national security precludes us from looking into something that they admit is a crime." Dingell called for a cutoff of military aid to Israel, unless it permitted U.S. investigators to question Dotan.

Israeli officials were reluctant to give foreign authorities free rein on Israeli soil. The elementary issue was of national sovereignty. But they also feared that Dotan might reveal other abuses of U.S. military aid, which would further damage relations.

But the Americans had the right to intervene, because Israel had given them that right—without noticing. In the agreement for the Foreign Military Sales aid program for 1989, America had inserted a clause giving the U.S. authority to investigate cases of fraud involving FMS money in any country. Not a single Israeli official had read that year's contract before signing it, much to Israel's regret later. And Israel had already set a precedent by allowing U.S. investigators, in the Pollard case, to question Israeli citizens and to view documents.

Feeling squeezed between the pressure of American paymasters—as usual, difficult to resist—and Israeli interests and pride, Jerusalem agreed to a compromise. U.S. Department of Justice investigators would be permitted to go to Israel and interrogate Dotan and ten other former air force officers—but only in the presence of Israeli security personnel able to stop the questions or answers if secrets were about to be revealed.

In June 1993 the Pentagon decided to crack down on the unusual degree of freedom that Israel had enjoyed in its use of FMS money. Israel had been one of the few countries permitted to use U.S. military aid without bureaucratic delays: purchasing arms and materiel from American·manufacturers without placing orders through the Pentagon. Two-thirds of the money in recent years had been spent on direct purchases. From now on, the Department of Defense decreed, it would have to be the conduit for all orders. This vote of no confidence, after the abuse of FMS funds, could slow down Israel's procurement of weapons.

All these scandals, touching on defense and intelligence, rocked the U.S.-Israel relationship as reminders that beneath the alliance's surface lurk some shady practices that—if left unregulated—threaten goodwill, cooperation, and the military lifeline that America represents to the Jewish state.

In any multibillion-dollar enterprise, corruption at some level might be expected. And while the Israeli defense ministry sharpened its control over purchasing procedures, it is impossible to certify that all the abuses are over. But for those busily widening the bridges between America and Israel into an extended family, the positives in the relationship must be seen as outweighing the negatives of family scandals.

CHAPTER SIXTEEN

THE AIPAC DECADE

Ronald Reagan was calling the American Israel Public Affairs Committee—known by Washington shorthand as "the Jewish lobby"—to say thanks. "You know," said the president, "I turn back to your ancient prophets in the Old Testament and the signs foretelling Armegeddon, and I find myself wondering if we're the generation that's going to see that come about."

Thomas A. Dine, listening carefully, was flattered by the call. His reign as executive director of America's pro-Israel lobby had begun two and a half years earlier, in 1981, along with Reagan's presidency. And if Reagan's worry about the state of the world was one reason for his support of Israel, that was just fine with AIPAC.

"I don't know if you've noted any of those prophecies lately," the president continued, "but believe me, they certainly describe the times we're going through."

It was October 1983, and the United States and Israel were

finally acting in broad concert again after the tensions of the
Israeli invasion of Lebanon. In fact, when Reagan needed help
to lobby key legislators who threatened to limit his power to
station U.S. Marines in Beirut, the president had asked for
AIPAC's assistance. And Dine had complied.

Senators and congressmen who had doubts about the Marines' mission received a flurry of calls from their own constituents—who happened to be AIPAC members—urging
them to give Reagan the authority he sought for the sake of
stability in the Middle East and in the world. "Frankly," Dine
told the president, "we fought very hard because we thought
that the U.S. was being tested."

Reagan replied: "I certainly appreciate it. I know how you
mobilized the grassroots organizations to generate support."

Ronald Reagan, long familiar with Jewish political activists
and always working at luring them away from their traditional
nest in the Democratic party, recognized the key to AIPAC's
success under Dine. The organization was merging with America's heartland.

When founded as the American Zionist Council by I. L.
Kenen in 1951, it was registered as a foreign agent for Israel.
Transformed into a clearly domestic group in 1954, as the
American Zionist Committee for Public Affairs, it quickly
identified lobbying Congress as its great mission. And by the
time Kenen renamed his group AIPAC in 1959, he was learning
that the best way to approach members of Congress is through
their own constituents—preferably through political activists
who contribute both time and money to the members' election
campaigns.

Still, Kenen's AIPAC was small. And when he handed the
leadership to Morris J. Amitay in 1974, the organization was so
little known that Amitay and his tiny staff had to explain—
even to Jewish audiences—that AIPAC was not OPEC, the oil
cartel.

When Amitay was replaced by Dine at the end of 1980, the lobbying organization had eight thousand members providing an operating budget of $1.4 million. Within seven years Dine and a growing staff swelled the membership rolls to over fifty thousand. After another five years AIPAC's annual budget had grown tenfold to $14 million while the number of employees more than quadrupled.

"In some far Western state, I'd get maybe four or five people who knew the senator or congressman very well," Amitay recalls. But Dine's superlobby of the 1980s "would try to get two hundred AIPAC members way out there, using more mass support to approach the member of Congress."

Like Amitay, Dine was a former congressional staffer. But Dine's experience, as an aide to three Democratic senators, taught him that a lobby could be a lot more than stationing a small number of individuals in the corridor outside a committee hearing. He had a fascination with the process of government and believed—although not a religious Jew—that it was in keeping with the ethics of Judaism to do everything possible in the American political system to help Israel.

"I didn't come to this job thinking Israel, Israel, Israel," Dine said. "I came to this job thinking American foreign policy and how to strengthen America's position in the world. At the same time, I thought a lot about Israel because I am Jewish." He did not have any relatives in Israel, and his primary personal reward was the satisfaction he felt from plotting a political strategy that worked.

The first challenge that faced him, in 1981, was figuring out the new Reagan administration. As Dine's chief lobbyist on Capitol Hill, Douglas M. Bloomfield, recalls: "We had heard that Reagan would be a friendly president, but for a while we didn't see the evidence. Weinberger seemed to be looking for ways to build up his pro-Arab credentials by pissing on Israel. There were ups and downs, and everyone in this town knew that the president wasn't running things."

The first "up" was nowhere to be seen when AIPAC faced a massive "down" in 1981: the Reagan administration's insistence on selling the AWACS reconnaissance aircraft to Saudi Arabia. Not yet a large, coast-to-coast, grassroots organization, AIPAC failed to stop the sale—but the vote in the Senate was so close, and the arguments so bitter, that lessons were learned on both sides. Reagan was reluctant to tangle with the "Jewish lobby" again, and Dine determined that AIPAC would have to become even stronger so as not to lose should there be a next time.

There were, indeed, more clashes. From AIPAC's point of view, it was fortunate that it was sharpening its skills on Capitol Hill and adding new members around the country, because Israel's invasion of Lebanon in June 1982 made it difficult for Reagan to pursue the pro-Israel policies that his heart and his Hollywood history would have preferred.

Bloomfield, the AIPAC legislative director, recalls receiving a telephone call from a friend on the White House staff who warned of rough times ahead. He said Reagan had stood alongside Israel during the war, but now "we owe the Arabs one."

The Reagan peace plan of September 1982 was only part of the new balancing act. It caught AIPAC and Israel by surprise, to the point that their frequent consultations could not prevent differing outlooks. AIPAC's leaders often meet with the Israeli ambassador in Washington, and the Israeli embassy has one diplomat concentrating on the U.S. Senate and another talking full time with House members.

"There is very good cooperation with AIPAC," says one Israeli who used to lobby Capitol Hill, "but we try to avoid the embarrassment of anti-Israelis accusing us of intervening in U.S. domestic affairs and accusing AIPAC of working for foreign diplomats."

In any event, Jerusalem sets its own policies, and often they are not what AIPAC recommended. The lobbying organization thus said publicly that the Reagan plan had positive elements that were worth considering. But Prime Minister Begin firmly rejected both AIPAC's advice and the Reagan plan.

The administration refused to give up on its outline for Middle East peace. Hoping that Arab countries could be persuaded to support the plan, the White House attempted a show of force—against Israel. If aid to Israel was cut, perhaps the Arabs would be impressed that America could be even-handed.

For AIPAC, as for Israel's Abba Eban many years before, the notion of "even-handedness" was a call to arms. When, in December 1982, the White House urged a Republican senator to propose a cut of $250 million in military assistance to Israel, he ran into a brick, AIPAC-built wall. Daniel Inouye of Hawaii, one of Israel's greatest non-Jewish champions in the Senate, rounded up unanimous Democratic support for the full aid package. As a soldier in World War II, Inouye had been touched deeply by Jewish suffering in the Holocaust. He has studied Judaism, has even considered converting, and keeps a Menorah candelabra in his office. But Inouye also insists that helping Israel is in America's interest. "I've yet to see any country in that part of the world that is as reliable, as far as our strategic requirements are concerned, as Israel is."

On the Republican side, while some senators naturally went along with their president, Robert Kasten of Wisconsin—acting largely on his Christian faith—strengthened the pro-Israel wall. As senior members of the foreign operations subcommittee making the initial decisions in doling out federal money overseas, Inouye and Kasten—from opposite sides of the political aisle—frequently teamed up to support increases in aid to Israel.

Bloomfield was the lobbyist on the spot, in and around the committee room, sowing dissension between Republicans favoring the aid cut—at least one complaining to AIPAC that

Jews don't vote Republican anyway—and others feeling the president was wrong. AIPAC would never let such a discussion take place on Capitol Hill without one of its half-dozen full-time lobbyists on hand to answer questions, to cajole, and to remind legislators that there is a politically active group of voters interested in the outcome. AIPAC won that committee battle.

"I was astonished and disheartened," Secretary of State Shultz wrote later. "This brought home to me vividly Israel's leverage in our Congress. I saw that I must work carefully with the Israelis if I was to have any handle on congressional action that might affect Israel, and if I was to maintain congressional support for my efforts to make progress in the Middle East."

Tom Dine and his staff at AIPAC could see that whatever they were doing, it was working. True, the American public had elected overwhelmingly pro-Israel candidates in 1982. And as his predecessor Amitay puts it, "I've always felt comfortable lobbying on behalf of Israel, because basically I feel I'm on the right side and I'm talking about America's interests." But the ability to defeat a president does not come merely from righteousness.

The power to win on a foreign policy issue—always seen as the executive branch's territory—was the result of rapidly transforming a small, intelligent, and well-run lobby into a muscular behemoth with roots planted in all corners and all levels of U.S. society.

AIPAC membership drives began, full force, in cities where many Jews lived and in towns where only a few did. The official policy was still to stay out of the spotlight, almost never to be quoted, and—in founder Kenen's words—"to stand behind legislation, not in front of it." But the word was getting around the Jewish communities that there was a new way to be politically active: to band together, whether Democrat or Republican, in support of their one, true consensus cause—Israel.

With an eye on the future, AIPAC decided to create a young cadre of activists to take the pro-Israel case into the decades ahead. The task of building this legacy was put in the hands of Jonathan S. Kessler, a dynamic activist then still in his early twenties. For the first seven years of the 1980s, he led AIPAC's Political Leadership Development Program—focusing its efforts on 350 college campuses from coast to coast.

Many of his alumni, including AIPAC college representatives hand-picked by Kessler to counter anti-Israel propaganda by Arab students and others, went on to influential positions in Washington. As the years wore on, former "AIPAC reps" increasingly popped up in congressional offices, presidential campaign staffs, and even in the White House and the State Department.

"AIPAC empowered thousands of students," says Kessler. "When these people acquired political skills, they developed confidence. The campus program was an integral part of the politicization of the American Jewish community. It was the final component of a political revolution which took place in stages after the Holocaust, the Six-Day War, the Yom Kippur War, and the AWACS battle of 1981."

For Kessler and his young generation of pro-Israel activists, it is natural and comfortable to believe that they are fighting for both the United States and Israel. They can hardly imagine, save for a brief flurry over a UN vote or a disagreement over an Israeli bombing raid, a serious clash between U.S. and Israeli interests. That, he says, is why the espionage affair involving another Jonathan—Pollard—was "so problematic; psychologically, it was devastating." And yet they remained loyal to the Israeli cause.

Kessler and many other Reform and Conservative Jews in America also had their faith challenged in 1988 when Israel toyed with restricting its definition of "who's a Jew." Israeli religious parties were insisting that the only converts to Judaism that should be recognized—and thus be approved for immediate citizenship in Israel—were people converted by Orthodox rabbis. The implication that Reform and Conservative rabbis were not good enough was deeply offensive to the majority of American Jews, who were not Orthodox. In the end, Israel's government gave in to the protests by U.S. Jews.

"A whole generation of people came of political age during the 'who's a Jew' controversy," says Kessler, explaining that the religious dispute added to other doubts that some Americans born to pro-Israel families were beginning to harbor: doubts related to the Lebanon war, the continuing occupation of the West Bank, and the intifada that began at the end of 1987. That Palestinian uprising, coupled with television coverage of an Israeli army harshly trying to suppress it, made it seem far more fashionable to criticize rather than to support Israel.

But Kessler was still solidly pro-Israel as he decided to leave AIPAC, after seven years, for a new level of activism. He honed his political skills in an ill-fated presidential campaign, learning how to raise money en masse, and then found himself in a part of the Jewish political scene that was at least as controversial as AIPAC. He became one of the leading officials of a PAC.

Despite the similarity in name, AIPAC is not one of the PACs—the controversial "political action committees" authorized by Congress after the 1973–74 Watergate scandal to clean up campaign finance. AIPAC does not give contributions to or even endorse candidates. Yet many senators and congressmen have forgotten the difference. They see AIPAC as "the leader of the PACs." They feel it is the lobbying organization that acts as "judge" of who is pro- and who is anti-Israel.

Legislators, by the end of the 1980s, sometimes went out of their way to be close to AIPAC, asking euphemistically what "the community" thought—even on issues that only remotely touched upon the Middle East and Israel. One congressional aide remembers her boss querying AIPAC on aid to Sudan, as if avoiding a run-in with the lobby were the top priority in deciding how to vote on a low-priority question.

Another senator, Bob Packwood, was considered by AIPAC to be a sincere friend of the Jewish state. The Oregon Republican was a great supporter of Israel, but he seemed to think that by portraying himself as Jewish he could get even more support when he sent a campaign fund-raising letter to a Jewish mailing list. "You and I must help Israel resist pressure to trade our historic Jewish homeland for Arab promises," Packwood wrote. "Only during the diaspora, when we were dispersed to other homelands, did the Jewish people become a minority in our own homeland. It was not our fault that we were kicked out by the Babylonians." The senator, a Unitarian, later denied that he was trying to fool anyone into thinking he was a Jew.

The true measure of friendship is a legislator's voting record. And solid friends quickly learned that they could count on campaign contributions from supporters of Israel—often pooling their resources in the almost one hundred pro-Israel PACs that sprouted up during the 1980s. By the end of the decade, they were giving a total of around $4 million per campaign cycle to around five hundred congressional candidates, mostly incumbents who consistently supported foreign aid. It proved that Jews were among the quickest Americans to understand the campaign-finance reforms and to embrace them.

The fact that some of the most successful PACs had many Jewish members united by the single goal of helping Israel triggered envy, suspicion, and condemnation from those who claimed there was undue influence on behalf of a foreign country. Critics of pro-Israel PACs insisted that something must be wrong when American Jews—just over 2 percent of the U.S. population—are making campaign contributions far larger than that tiny proportion might suggest.

Among them were two politicians from Illinois who blamed

AIPAC and Jewish campaign funds for their downfall: former Congressman Paul Findley, who writes and lectures against "Israel's lobby" since his defeat in 1982; and Senator Charles Percy, who was indeed targeted by pro-Israel activists in 1984 because they saw him, as chairman of the Foreign Relations Committee, taking a harsh turn against the Jewish state. "Who is running the foreign policy?" Percy asks. "Can Israel and the prime minister have more power than the entire Senate of the United States or the president?" Findley, Percy, and others bitterly rail against being labeled as "anti-Semites" just for being critical of Israel and its PAC-based supporters.

Kessler contends, however, that some critics of Jewish activism do deserve the label. "It may be appropriate to speak of certain people as anti-Semitic, if they specifically single out Jews for attack; if that's what their complaint comes down to—'The Jews are too influential! They're too involved!' But what is democracy, without involvement? Do they favor involvement in politics, but not to the point of influence? Do they take offense at my passionate concern for Israel's security—for my brethren, for my family—or simply at my effectiveness?"

The Federal Election Commission did, in 1988, investigate a complaint made by critics of Israel—former U.S. government officials—who claimed that AIPAC was violating campaign laws by directing the contributions made by twenty-seven PACs. The case was dropped a year later, and this, too, the critics ascribed to the lobby's great power.

"The word 'power,' when it's used for AIPAC, is a myth," said Rabbi Israel Miller, longtime vice president of the lobbying organization. "It's baloney. AIPAC is powerful only because the American people are behind Israel."

And what of the widespread assumption that the pro-Israel PACs change congressional voting patterns? "Anyone who thinks you can buy votes doesn't understand the process very well," says Kessler, who worked for The National PAC, the largest of the pro-Israel action committees, for four years, during which time it contributed well over $1 million to campaigns. "You can't buy votes. But you can earn access. And if your cause has merits, and you've got access, and you work hard, and you stay involved, and you show that there's a commitment to remain involved—that does make an impression. I believe members of Congress look upon money as a barometer of passion. The question politicians ask is, 'Are they putting their money where their mouth is?' "

There is also the fact that both AIPAC and the various PACs are extraordinarily adept at reminding elected officials that Israel has support in their constituencies. It often takes barely half an hour from the time that a member of congress expresses even the slightest doubt about an Israeli policy, until a high-rolling campaign contributor calls the legislator to explain why the policy is just. The contributor is, most likely, a member of AIPAC.

Politicians can be forgiven for confusing AIPAC and the PACs when their membership lists largely overlap. A notable example is Amitay—the former executive director of AIPAC—who immediately set up a PAC. Like others who see no particular benefit to having the words "Zionist," "Jewish," or "Israel" in the names of their political action committees, Amitay chose to call his "Washington PAC," and it became the second largest in the large pro-Israel pack.

Legislators were accustomed to seeing him, but now he became a PAC man with a checkbook. Amitay's policy line was the same—every one of his campaign contributions was accompanied by a note that said: "We thank you for agreeing with our view that a secure Israel is in the best interest of the United States."

The Jewish lobbyists ask American legislators and decision makers to listen. Then they ask them to visit. A trip to Israel, they find, is worth a million words.

AIPAC sponsors trips to Israel for members of Congress and their staffs, and so do B'nai B'rith and other Jewish organizations. Says Amitay: "Any congressman or senator, with very few exceptions, who goes to Israel has been impressed by the Israelis. Why? 'They're like we are!' they say, and, 'It's like the United States must have been in frontier days.' Israel sells itself, to 95 percent of the people who go there. And even if Joe Public doesn't go to Israel, congressmen do." Out of 100 senators and 435 members of the House, Amitay estimates that 99 and 350 have visited the Jewish state.

When the legislators themselves are unavailable to travel, a senior aide may be invited. Wyoming Senator Alan Simpson's legislative assistant, Brent Erickson, was at the Israeli embassy in 1991 asking some tough questions about Jerusalem's policies when an embassy staffer—realizing that Erickson's boss was Senate minority whip and therefore important—suggested the aide might wish to visit Israel. Erickson agreed, because "I had some questions in my mind," and the embassy passed his name to B'nai B'rith, which was organizing a tour for senior Senate aides.

"The visit was an eye-opener," says Erickson. "I had been pretty adamant that Israel should give up the West Bank, but afterward I wasn't so sure. And I had always thought Israel should give the Golan Heights back to Syria—until I visited it. There's some very strategic high ground there, and when you see it in person it becomes vividly clear why it is so important to the security of Israel."

With Simpson—and every senator—being busy with so many issues, an on-the-spot report by a trusted aide can be highly influential. If a vote for foreign aid is won or assured, then AIPAC's mission is accomplished. In the case of B'nai B'rith, basically a social service organization, the objective is to find broader acceptance for Jews in American society—by encouraging Gentile neighbors to understand the special connection with Israel.

Some Jewish groups have occasionally gone too far. The Anti-Defamation League of B'nai B'rith, with the broad aim of collecting data on anti-Semitic and neo-Nazi groups, worked with private investigators who also gathered intelligence on pro-Arab and anti-Israel activists. While ADL officials found this perfectly natural, since some radical Islamic and Arab organizations did engage in anti-Jewish propaganda, it caused offense to Arab-Americans who might disagree with Israeli policy but held no grudge against their Jewish neighbors.

In at least one case the ADL was accused of obtaining information by illegal means and transferring it to the Israeli government. FBI and police raids on ADL offices in San Francisco and Los Angeles in 1993 discovered that the League possessed classified FBI reports on Palestinian terrorist groups and Louis Farrakhan's Nation of Islam, as well as driver's license information on members of neo-Nazi and Arab-American groups.

Even on Capitol Hill, there are Jews who feel a need to pull out all the stops, because Israel faces unique needs and dangers. Says Charles D. Brooks, foreign affairs consultant to Senator Arlen Specter of Pennsylvania: "Jews tend to be involved in liberal politics, but they tend to be very assimilated. They're involved with the environment or women's rights. But for me, Jewish survival and Jewish identity count. No one's looking out for the Jews if we don't look out for ourselves."

With the support of his senator, a fellow Jew and Republican, Brooks organized the "Senate Caucus for the U.S.-Israel Strategic Alliance," which holds hearings on the mutual benefits of the partnership. He sees his Capitol Hill career as a follow-up to his early work with AIPAC, B'nai B'rith, and "neoconservative" think tanks that linked Reagan and Israel as twin causes to support.

On the House side, among many staffers making no secret of

their support for Israel is a Democrat, M. J. Rosenberg. A former writer and editor at AIPAC in the 1970s and again in the 1980s, Rosenberg has been an aide to three members of Congress serving on key committees affecting foreign aid.

His introduction to the world of pro-Israel activism was unusual. Rosenberg was thrust into prominence in 1969, when as a campus radical he wrote an article demanding of his fellow members of the political Left: "If we march for all the good causes, why are you anti-Israel? Why do you walk away from Jews and their cause? When the barricades are erected, I will fight as a Jew."

"It catapulted me from not being in Jewish life at all," Rosenberg recalls, "to, while still in college, speaking all over the place and exhorting students. I became a celebrity, invited to synagogues." He had long hair and spoke against the Vietnam War, but "all they cared about was: 'Here was this kid who loves Israel anyway and makes Israel his number-one issue.' "

He seemed a perfect fit for AIPAC, and after working on a presidential campaign and for B'nai B'rith he was hired by Si Kenen just before the 1973 Middle East war. "There were only eight people working at AIPAC at that time," says Rosenberg. "So I was really vital. I was sent up to Capitol Hill. I was lobbying!"

By 1976 he was on the Hill full time, working for a congressman. Legislators usually know whom they are hiring, and they know that love of Israel does not wear off. If anything, it rubs off; and the politicians often share their staff's pro-Israel sentiments. As a result, in many offices along the long corridors of the Senate and House office buildings, there are staffers who stay in touch, sharing information—professional gossip—about legislation affecting Israel.

But Rosenberg laughs at the notion they make up a Jewish cabal manipulating Congress. "They may be on the phone to each other a lot, but they're not all Jewish," he says. "What we have are a lot of key aides who care a lot about Israel." He believes they reflect general public opinion, heightened by the fact that almost all have been to Israel and have found it a moving experience.

The core of supporters on Capitol Hill do not have to be truly lobbied by AIPAC, but instead enjoy a frank give-and-take with the lobbyists. When Israeli settlers took over a Greek Orthodox hospice in Jerusalem, Rosenberg—then chief of staff for Ohio's Edward Feighan—recalls being called by a friend in AIPAC who asked, "What're you hearing?"

"I'll tell you what I'm hearing," he replied. "People are appalled! I work for a Catholic! This is the first time the congressman's ever said to me, 'I can't believe what you guys just did!' "

"Oh, it's that bad," the AIPAC staffer said glumly, "that even Feighan's upset?"

Rosenberg explains: "Then she's able to go back and say to Tom Dine or whomever, 'Hey, even Feighan is appalled by this! We'd better put out some explanation, but don't expect anyone to jump to their feet on the House floor and defend the storming of the hospice!'

"To me, most things *are* defendable. And AIPAC says to everyone on the Hill, 'Okay, wait a minute. I know on first blush this seems really bad, but in context . . .' And then it turns out that people like me can very easily be brought around. It would never occur to me, in any context, to ever do anything that would be harmful to U.S.-Israel relations."

Doug Bloomfield, as AIPAC's chief lobbyist for most of the 1980s, found Capitol Hill to be fertile and familiar territory. He had spent ten years in the office of a New York congressman, learning how the legislature works and making friends with other Jews concerned for Israel's welfare.

Years later, best known as a columnist for Jewish newspapers nationwide, Bloomfield has concluded that AIPAC made a mistake in the 1980s by diverting energies away from Capitol Hill. He is one of many former employees of the organization who feel that—as part of Tom Dine's impressive expansion in the eight years of the Reagan presidency—AIPAC expended excessive efforts on lobbying the White House.

"What AIPAC can do is work with Congress, the legislative branch that controls the purse strings," says Bloomfield. "The truth is that a board largely made up of affable millionaires can't influence the executive branch of government. Not even a large corporation can do that, except two or three that the president is predisposed to being influenced by."

Similarly, the Reagan White House was predisposed in Israel's favor. Having lobby members call, write, and visit simply makes it easier for politicians to do what they would have done anyway. The same analysis applies to Congress, where it is unlikely that the prospect of receiving campaign contributions changes anyone's vote. On the Middle East issue, the only partisans who care enough to contribute and to unite are the pro-Israel Americans. They get the entrée to the legislators. Everyone's life seems easier when high levels of aid to Israel are approved, but that is not to say that such votes run counter to America's interests.

Still, as basic and successful as these lessons seemed to the AIPAC of the 1960s and '70s, the lobby leadership of the 1980s seemed to want more. Board members had become jaded by meetings with congressmen and senators. Now they wanted to be impressed by meeting the president or the secretary of state. And Tom Dine hired a new "director of research and information," former political science professor Steven J. Rosen, who believed that working with friends in the executive branch could give the U.S.-Israel alliance a resilience it had never had.

Rosen began issuing memos that described the executive branch as "proactive" and the legislative branch as "reactive," as if influencing the proactive body made the reactive Congress far less important. Says one of his colleagues: "A group of us talked, in jest, about quitting and starting an organization and calling it 'the Old AIPAC.' The new AIPAC was executive-oriented."

Amitay recalls that in the 1970s he would avoid the executive branch, except to discuss developments on Capitol Hill and how best to get the foreign aid bill passed. "Executive lobbying is utterly stupid—an oxymoron! You lobby a member of Congress, because you have something he wants. To political appointees or the secretary of state, you're going to talk policy? You're going to send in lamp salesmen and real estate developers to talk about Middle East policy?

"But you can send in a salesman or developer, who's raised X number of dollars, to talk to a senator or a congressman about the Middle East. That's because these congressmen or senators don't follow the issue that closely, don't know that much about it, and basically have to vote 'yes' or 'no' or sign a letter or not sign a letter. So that makes sense.

"But in the White House or at State, they can't be bamboozled or co-opted. And they're negotiating things that involve Israel's security." Amitay says, "it was ridiculous for AIPAC to start on that course."

Moving AIPAC closer to the executive branch also meant moving it to the political right, and the shift added to the rapid growth in financial support for AIPAC because Jewish millionaires tended to love the Ronald Reagan agenda. Ironically, Amitay's successor—Dine—had been known in his Capitol Hill career as a liberal Democrat. But as the 1980s wore on and it seemed vital to guarantee President Reagan's goodwill, the lobby's director forged a new alliance with Cold War conservatives in the administration.

Dine and Rosen published the *AIPAC Papers on U.S.-Israel Relations*, a series of mostly academic monographs that perfectly reflected Reagan-era concerns: focusing on the strategic value of Israel to an America determined to defeat the Soviet Union. Whether this was pandering to Reagan or an honest embrace of conservatism, Jews in the liberal mainstream began to feel uncomfortable with the lobby that in Washington was often regarded as their mouthpiece.

A warning emerged when three larger organizations—the American Jewish Committee, the American Jewish Congress, and the Anti-Defamation League—wrote to AIPAC in 1988 to complain that it "pursues policies that are at variance with the consensus of the organized Jewish community." The three groups tried to jolt AIPAC by declaring that they had set up "a joint political committee for Israel in Washington," hinting that it could be a rival lobbying mechanism.

"More consultation is always desirable," AIPAC responded, and its leaders began to hold monthly meetings with the three organizations and others—dubbed the First Tuesday Club—so that a broader spectrum of the Jewish community could influence the strategy of its sole congressional lobby.

There is no doubt that the AIPAC agenda, professionally fine-tuned and reaching out in fifty states, was tremendously exciting for a new generation of Jews. AIPAC veteran Bloomfield saw the effect: "that the greatest growth in American Jewish political activism came during the Likud's stewardship meant many new leaders were trained, educated, and indoctrinated with Likud policy. They frequently tended to be wealthy, conservative, and Republican."

One, in California, was Jonathan E. Mitchell. A real estate developer based in Beverly Hills, Mitchell—in his forties—has become one of the leading advocates for Israel in the nation's largest state. He is always rushing off to a meeting in support of an Israeli university, a Jewish charity, or AIPAC, where he served as one of twenty-six national officers.

"My grandfather, Edward Mitchell, was a great Zionist, very friendly with Ben-Gurion and all the Israeli pioneers in the

'40s. He lived here in L.A., but he believed very strongly that the Jewish people needed a safe harbor."

The elder Mitchell helped launch Israel's shipping line, Zim, but involvement with the new nation was much more philanthropy than investment. Jonathan Mitchell, ironically, grew up "resenting the whole charity thing, because my parents were so active working for the UJA and other Jewish organizations that they were out of the house and away from me a lot. I said I would never do that."

It was his marriage to an Israeli-born woman that changed his mind. "Amie was looking for something that the two of us could get involved in together, something that we'd have a mutual interest in. So she took me to an Anti-Defamation League meeting, and I went reluctantly. There was one speaker after another, on the various problems facing Jews both in Israel and in the U.S. And I started to think, 'Wait a minute, those problems affect me too!' "

He became so interested that he joined the ADL board, and that "started all of my juices going: about Jews, protection of Jews, the future of our people, and Israel was definitely a part of it. It was probably 50–50, between Israel and domestic issues."

His wife then became active in Hadassah, the worldwide Jewish women's organization, and Mitchell again tagged along. "I found my focus shifting almost entirely from the plight of Jews in America to the plight of Jews in Israel. I saw that Israel is the only place: the last salvation."

A close family friend suggested that he might enjoy AIPAC, and within a short while his willingness to contribute both time and money made Mitchell one of AIPAC's national decision makers.

"I've always been interested in politics," Mitchell says, "and I'm also active in Israeli politics as a contributor to the Likud party. If you think it's been a challenge raising money for AIPAC, go out and try to raise money for Likud!"

Ego-boosting can be part of the allure for pro-Israel activists. After all, how many Americans can speak of hosting prime ministers and defense ministers in their homes? By political involvement with Israeli causes, Jews can enjoy access, as Mitchell did, to top-ranking Israeli politicians.

But his own political commitment went much deeper. Unlike most American Jewish activists, Mitchell and his family hope to move to Israel within a few years. "So I want the country safe. I want it secure. I want it strong."

He believes trends in America are running against the Jewish state. "I see more people are coming out against Israel and calling for cuts in aid. This is of great concern to me! People don't realize what the U.S. is buying for that money—one of the great values of all time. We've spent a lot more money, a lot more, on NATO allies like Belgium and Holland. So to say that Israel is some supported child, that continues to eat up our money here and then crap all over us, is a lot of garbage. The U.S. wants stability and can rely on Israel."

In even-numbered election years, he spends a lot of time reading about races from coast to coast. "AIPAC, when asked, supplies its members with the voting records of elected officials. From the voting records, you can draw your own conclusions."

His commitment to Israel, almost nonexistent in 1982, has become consuming. He ravenously reads all the publications that AIPAC sends him, while skipping many of the property prospectuses that are the bread and butter of his real estate business. "I've taken a big financial sacrifice, because there are a lot of deals that I didn't do because I just didn't have time to work on them. Because I have felt I should devote more of my time for the sake of my own people than for the sake of my own pocketbook."

When asked how many other Jon Mitchells he has met in his pro-Israel travels, tears come to his eyes as he says there must be some but admits he has met none his age. "As a percentage of their time, no. I know people who are older, who've retired and give almost 100 percent of their time. They're some of the same people who were our leaders twenty years ago, only they're older now. Those are the people who lived through World War II and saw what happened in Nazi Germany.

"It makes me sad. Most people are more selfish now. And today the people my age, who were born after the war, don't see that there is risk for Jews in America. I don't know what it's going to take, but I sure wish there was something that would get Jews to become aware that they're a little more fragile than they think they are.

"All the leaders of the Jewish organizations—at least the ones that I've met, for the most part—are wealthy people, and they're very comfortable. They have businesses; they have families. They go home at Thanksgiving and carve the turkey in the nice dining room in their nice palatial homes. They don't feel at risk!"

Mitchell and other senior members of the lobby are avid readers of a weekly AIPAC newsletter, *Activities*, which chronicles public comments, speeches, and articles that are hostile to Jews or Israel. Arab-sponsored publications are often quoted, but so are American politicians—and even some Jewish critics of Israel, such as Woody Allen—who later complain that they have been put on an AIPAC "enemies list."

While research director Steve Rosen has written of the need to "reward friends and punish enemies," he and other senior members of AIPAC very rarely speak publicly of its work. They generally accept two nuggets of Rosen's advice: "hostile ears are always listening" and "a lobby is a night flower—it thrives in the dark and dies in the sun."

Israelis tend to react to their country's supporters in the United States with muted thanks, at best. They would prefer that Americans offer less advice, and certainly stop talking about moving to Israel, and instead actually move there.

To Israeli politicians holding left-of-center views, Mitchell represents what they feel was characteristic of AIPAC and most major Jewish organizations: that they drifted not only toward Reagan but also in the direction of Israel's political right, which ruled the country for fifteen years.

A left-wing cabinet minister, Yossi Sarid, complains that during his years as an opposition member of parliament, "I was considered by many American Jewish organizations to be persona non grata," using the jargon of international diplomacy for an undesired person.

"American individuals and some liberal-progressive Jewish organizations who had invited me to express my views were subjected to tremendous pressure and even intimidation by AIPAC and other Jewish activists who wished to cancel my speaking engagements. AIPAC thought that my calls for an Israeli-Palestinian reconciliation should not be expressed on American soil.

"I retaliated by refusing to brief AIPAC-guided tours of American groups to Israel. AIPAC wanted to use me only in Israel, as an example to show how democratic and pluralistic is Israeli society."

Sarid adds: "For me, the AIPAC of the '80s was standing more to the right than the Israeli right. It seemed that they wanted to be more Catholic than the pope."

Tom Dine, head of AIPAC for over a decade, denied that his lobby was politically partisan—either in Israel or in America. "AIPAC takes positions," he wrote, "only on issues on which a broad consensus exists in the constituency it represents, such as foreign aid. It does not take positions on issues like the land-for-peace debate, on which this constituency is in fact deeply divided."

CHAPTER SEVENTEEN

ALL IN THE FAMILY

Sitting at his usual table in Café Tamar, one of Tel Aviv's most fashionable hangouts, Robert Rosenberg, with his full mustache and abundant, graying hair, looks like any other middle-age Israeli. It is late Friday morning—the most easygoing and social day of the Israeli week—and like tens of thousands of Israeli men and women who escape the mundane pressures of life, he is chatting, arguing, and laughing with his friends.

Rosenberg, a journalist and thriller writer in his mid-forties, is not, however, a typical Israeli. Neither are most of his friends around the table. As can be perceived from the accent of their Hebrew, they came from America—a large group often labeled as "Anglo-Saxons."

Born in Boston in 1951 but living in Israel for the last quarter of a century, Rosenberg does not think of himself in the broad context of international politics, not realizing that he and his ilk are symbols of the special relations between the United States and the Jewish state.

But Rosenberg has contributed to the cultural link between the two countries: if only when he was a columnist for the *Jerusalem Post*, read worldwide, portraying the vitality of life in Tel Aviv. American readers could feel a kinship with the yuppies of the Promised Land, the new class of young, upwardly mobile professionals who peopled Rosenberg's columns. He shed a new light on Israel by adding dimensions unknown abroad, even to the relatively informed Jewish reader.

The cultural link stands behind the family ties that bind the United States and Israel. In the literal sense, there are tens of thousands of Jews in America who have grandparents, uncles, or cousins in Israel. In the broader sense, the astoundingly free interchange of ideas, products, and people makes the American people and the Israeli people one large family.

The value of such contacts can be neither quantified like military hardware nor measured in dollars like government aid or UJA contributions. Yet Rosenberg's life story is an example of the many personal tales that contribute to the unique friendship between Uncle Sam and Israel, the favorite nephew.

"I was born into a typical family of Conservative Jews, which means they went to *shul*—the synagogue. One of the things which at that time differentiated Conservative Jews from Reform Judaism was our great emphasis on identifying with Zionism and later Israel. While my father was a scientist, but not a Zionist, my mother had a very strong Jewish background. She was a Hebrew teacher and involved in all kinds of Zionist causes. She was even arrested after World War II, outside the British consulate in Boston, demonstrating for a Jewish state."

At their home in the Boston suburb of Newton, the Rosenbergs often played host to visiting Israelis. Most were scientists and politicians—the privileged few who, in the austere Israel of the 1950s, could afford the luxury of traveling to America. The Rosenbergs themselves traveled to Israel as early as 1950, before Robert was born. "My father," he says, "was employed by an American R&D company which did some work for Israel's largest industrial corporation, the Dead Sea Works.

"Woven into my life as early as I can remember was being Jewish and Israel. It was a little bit more tangible to me than to my schoolmates and Jewish friends. But I rebelled against all that, with everything else in the sixties. I wasn't infected by the Zionist bug."

Rosenberg, like many young Jews, was instead bitten by the political bug of the counterculture, "which began for me with the Kennedy assassination in 1963, through to the Nixon resignation in 1974." He joined Students for a Democratic Society, the SDS, and "became a political hippie, a freak, a student demonstrator. I was one of those who were not going down the straight course through life as defined by the rhetoric of middle-class suburbia."

And yet somehow Rosenberg could not shake off the impact of his Zionist home. "I remember the Six-Day War, when I was in high school, and I was almost oblivious to it. But unlike me, my parents were like most American Jews and were very worried about Israel. The war made Israel even more a part of their life. So it was very natural for them to send me, right after the war, to a kibbutz for the summer."

Even before that, he spent a few weeks in a Jewish summer camp. "It turned out to be a mythologization of the war in the minds of all these kids. We had a few Israeli counselors who taught us all the songs about 'Jerusalem of Gold,' the victorious Israeli army, and even about the new territories, and most of the kids loved it—but not me. We raised the American flag and the Israeli flag every morning, but I was much more interested in what was happening in America. It was a summer of love, and the Red Sox were going to be in the World Series, and here they have me singing about some obscure place halfway around the world!"

And yet, Rosenberg admits, "the Zionist indoctrination had some effect on me." And going to a kibbutz with a friend, as volunteer workers, sounded like "a fun thing to do."

For tens of thousands of American kids who did what Robert Rosenberg did that summer and in the summers to come, touring postwar, victorious Israel was an exotic and heady experience. Most simply had a good time for a few months and then returned to their families. Only a few, whether consciously deciding or aimlessly drifting, stayed in Israel. Rosenberg was one of the few.

"Israel was at that time both appealing and not appealing. It was very colorful but also noisy and smelly. I didn't like what the Israeli government was doing, but I didn't accept the anti-Israel arguments used by my friends in SDS. They were trying to say that the southeast Asian model of U.S. imperialism against the Vietnamese people also applied to the Arab-Israeli conflict. I disagreed with the New Left, and that ideological battle eventually shaped me as a Jew and helped me to decide to stay and live in Israel. I did not see any contradiction between being a liberal, left-wing American and an Israeli."

Whatever his views, there was room for Rosenberg in Israel because the country is built on the principle that all Jews—from every corner of the globe—can enjoy instant citizenship. Israel, like the United States, is truly a society of immigrants. Having absorbed Jews from nearly eighty countries, Israelis are justly proud of their "melting pot," and the American ingredient is but a drop in the pot.

Although there are no official figures, the size of the American expatriate community in Israel is estimated at sixty thousand, barely 1.5 percent of Israel's 4.4 million Jews. The communities of Russian, Moroccan, Romanian, Iraqi, Polish, or Argentine immigrants who have arrived in Israel since independence in 1948 are much larger than the American contingent. Yet the input of American Jews who adopted Israel as their homeland is as noticed as any other group's—and probably more so. Ex-Americans are in all walks of Israeli life: politics, government, the military, business, and among artists, lawyers, doctors, and writers. Israel has had a prime minister, a supreme court judge, members of parliament, a cabinet minister, and many university professors who started out as Americans. They all brought their own little piece of American heritage with them, adding to the diversity in Israeli society.

On one hand, there is Joshua Schoffman, a champion of human rights in Israel who fights mainly against their violation by the Israeli army in the occupied territories. He was born in Brooklyn and graduated from Brandeis University. A committed Zionist, Schoffman moved to Israel in 1975, at age twenty-two, studied law at Hebrew University in Jerusalem, and after a three-and-a-half-year stint in the Israeli army went to Washington to study civil liberties law at American University. Upon his return in 1985, he became the first full-time legal director of Israel's Association for Civil Rights.

The association, trying to establish itself as an Israeli version of the American Civil Liberties Union, is financed primarily by the Ford Foundation and the New Israel Fund, a New York–based Jewish charity aimed at encouraging American-style liberal attitudes in Israel. Among Schoffman's issues are the rights of Reform and Conservative Jews and converts irritated by the state-sanctioned monopoly of Orthodox Jews in running Israel's religious affairs. The association challenges laws requiring the closure of businesses, entertainment, and bus services on the Jewish sabbath. It is ironic that Schoffman himself wears a *yarmulke*, the skullcap of an observant Jew.

He also litigates on behalf of women, prisoners, the disabled, and Israel's ethnic minorities as well as Palestinians. And he believes his work embodies the best values to import from the

United States. In Israel, a country with no written constitution and founded on socialist ideology, he wants to inject "more of the American spirit of individualism." Like Rosenberg, he is also a product of the 1960s and remembers how he and his classmates from a Jewish day school in Brooklyn would sneak out and join civil rights marches. In 1972 he worked for George McGovern's presidential campaign.

Miriam Levinger is also an Orthodox Jew born in the United States, but in most other ways a sharp contrast to Schoffman. In her late fifties, she is married to Rabbi Moshe Levinger, the spiritual and political leader of Gush Emunim, the "Bloc of the Faithful." The bloc is the vanguard of the Jewish settler movement, thumping the Bible in insisting that God promised the entire Land of Israel—including the West Bank—to the Jewish people.

She was born in the Bronx, New York, in 1937 to a family of Jewish refugees from Hungary. "We were poor, especially after the Depression," she recalls. "As an Orthodox Jew, my father refused to work on the sabbath, so he found himself with no work and penniless. To make a living, he used to sing on the street corner." Unlike her five brothers, who abandoned religion for secularism, she remained observant.

Her belief was only strengthened by the anti-Semitism she encountered in her youth. The Bronx changed after World War II, as Jews who managed to climb the social ladder moved to better neighborhoods, and new immigrant groups moved in.

"I still vividly remember how frightening it was to return home," says Miriam Levinger, adding that blacks and Puerto Ricans "cursed us Jews and harassed us." These incidents only made her more committed to her religion and Zionism. "I realized that my place is in my land, the land of Israel."

In 1955 she "made *aliyah*" and after studying at a nursing school in Jerusalem, she met Moshe Levinger, a young Israeli student in a *yeshiva* (a seminary), and married him. For ten years she followed her husband to the mainly rural religious communities where he served as rabbi. And then came the smashing Israeli victory over the Arabs in the June 1967 war. To the Levingers, as to thousands of other devout Israelis and Americans, those six days symbolized "a divine message."

The Levingers and their four children spearheaded a group of young zealots, inspired by messianic self-righteousness, who moved to Hebron, in the newly captured West Bank, in April 1968. According to Jewish tradition, Hebron was the hometown of the ancient Hebrew Patriarchs and is second only to Jerusalem in importance. The fact that Hebron is the West Bank's second largest Arab town did not deter the Levingers. They even violated Israeli regulations, though with secret government support, and clashed with Palestinians who contended their land was being expropriated.

The Levingers and their followers managed to create facts on the ground: a new Jewish town overlooking Arab Hebron, then reestablishing a Jewish quarter in the heart of the town. The Bloc of the Faithful members walk through narrow alleys bearing guns, for self-defense and to show the Palestinians who is really in charge.

"This is our land," says Mrs. Levinger in Hebrew still marked by a strong American accent. "It belongs to us. God promised the land to Abraham." She believes in "divine imperatives" that stand above man-made laws or a democratically elected government.

Miriam Levinger is not alone. Her determination and strong belief in a "Greater Israel" have made her a role model for many young American Jews who feel that life in America is impossible because of anti-Semitism, extant and still growing. Thousands have followed Mrs. Levinger's example, often moving not to pre-1967 Israel, but directly from American cities to the new urban and rural settlements dotting the biblical lands of Judea and Samaria. They believe that by living between, overlooking, and sometimes in the midst of Palestinian population centers, they find fulfillment as Jews.

For the more radical and angry among them, it sometimes seems that aggressive abuse of their Arab neighbors represents a form of revenge for the insecurity previously felt as Jews in America. There are probably no more than 10,000 immigrants from the United States among the 130,000 Jewish settlers in the territories, but because some of the ex-Americans are among the most quoted and most vituperative they leave a lasting impression. Whether it is Miriam Levinger or Rabbi Meir Kahane, the founder of the Jewish Defense League who moved from New York to Israel in 1972 to lead a political party calling for the expulsion of Arabs and then was assassinated by a Muslim extremist in New York, an American on the right-wing fringe of Israeli politics creates the impression that all Jews from the United States are alike.

"These extremists," says writer Robert Rosenberg, "are so vocal that liberal and moderate voices—like me—who support an Israeli withdrawal from the territories and the creation of a Palestinian state alongside Israel are rarely heard."

Usually reluctant to speak out is another group that crossed the binational divide: the Israelis who moved to America. Several hundred thousand have done so since independence in 1948, most settling in New York and Los Angeles. Many have become naturalized U.S. citizens, a step that does not entail giving up their Israeli citizenship. Among them have been government officials, former diplomats who served in the United States and decided to stay, army officers and air force pilots who wanted a break from nonstop war status, and workers and professionals of all kinds who feel America is the place to gain new skills and find greater profits. It is often the cream of the cream of Israeli society who are leaving for more comfortable, prosperous, or simply larger horizons.

During Israel's early days most of the people who left were

either failures or frustrated individuals who felt they could achieve their personal goals only in a bigger, richer country.

Twenty or thirty years ago the Israelis' reasons for moving to the United States were about the same as those offered by other groups of immigrants: the Irish, the Italians, the Poles, and even the nineteenth-century Jews from eastern and central Europe—mainly, the opportunity to prosper.

Over the years, however, some uniquely Israeli motives for emigration have emerged: escaping the fears of terrorism and war, and the reluctance to do army reserve duty at least once a year until well into middle age.

Most of the Israelis in America have also, unlike other immigrants, harbored an often-unspoken sense of humiliation. They were ashamed of having left their country, and some took every opportunity to apologize and explain that they were going to go back "very soon"—even if "soon" often stretched into eternity. The Israeli community in the United States is probably the only expatriate group that argues, in large numbers if not unanimously, that they are only temporarily in America and their true place is to be found in their country of origin.

Their situation is much more delicate than that of American Jews who became Israelis. While those who make *aliyah*—the *olim*, or immigrants—are appreciated both in Israel and among American Jewry and perceived as fulfilling what is expected from any Jew in the world, the Israelis who leave Israel are negatively depicted. In the first two decades of statehood, their fellow Israelis loathed them as "traitors." In the Israeli lexicon, they are derogatorily dubbed *"yordim"*—meaning those who are "going down" from Zion. Even Abba Eban, who in recent years spends most of his time in New York, has been lumped into this category.

At the same time, many Jews in the United States were reluctant to accept *yordim* as equals because of cultural discomfort. People moving in from Israel were a living example to Jews that, despite their fondest hopes, the Jewish state was not in fact heaven on earth. There have been exceptions, to be sure: Israelis who shamelessly merge into American Jewry, sometimes as Hebrew teachers in religious schools and often considering themselves unofficial ambassadors for the Israel they left behind.

Whether doubly rejected or amiably joining U.S. Jewish culture, Israelis in America do play a role in helping to build the alliance. And so do the ex-American Israelis. Though lacking the official status of an AIPAC or Conference of Presidents, they make up an informal lobby promoting bilateral relations. The *olim* and *yordim* have become ambassadors at large, promoters, and cheerleaders wherever they travel or reside. Whether they are happy or unhappy, proud or ashamed of their Israeli experience, they are a living example of how the two societies have become interwoven.

Both groups, those who emigrated from and those who immigrated into Israel, build a human-cultural bridge over the Atlantic and the Mediterranean. By now generations of Israelis and American Jews have been using the bridge for family exchanges. The bigger the human traffic is, the more relatives go back and forth to visit their loved ones, and the more marriages between Israelis and Americans, the better the mutual understanding of the two countries. There is still a long way to go, because out of 5.5 million Jews in the United States, nearly 3.5 million have never been to Israel.

As the numbers grow, American Jews get to know Israel and Israelis; while Israelis come to comprehend and like America. Not always did Israelis look affectionately upon America. When their state became independent, they still felt attached to British culture and institutions that had ruled the area for thirty years. Utilities and government agencies such as police, broadcasting, and even the military were based on British mod-

els, and London was considered the cultural capital of the world.
But from the mid-1950s, Israel discovered France. This was a
natural and popular reaction to the tight political and military
relations that developed between Jerusalem and Paris. Israeli
radio broadcast a lot of French music, and French food and films
were the favorites. But the moment that diplomatic and defense
relations cooled, French cultural influence waned.

To fill the gap left by the French, Israel looked to the United
States. But it took time. At first, in the 1960s, American music,
food, sports, and consumerism were not widely liked by Israelis—although the government was happy to receive financial
and military aid from the United States. Many Israelis saw
Europe as the great repository of culture and tradition, while
America was dismissed as shallow and plastic.

But Israelis did eventually succumb to the exciting attrac-
tions of Americana. Their BBC-style radio networks started
running commercials in 1960. Television broadcasting began in
1968, first in black and white and free of advertising, but later
in color and with ads. Coca-Cola bucked the Arab boycott and
sold its first distinctive bottles in Israel, also in 1968. And to
Israelis, it did not taste merely like a brown, caffeinated, and
carbonated beverage. It tasted like America.

From "Chicago" pizza to "New York" ice cream, Israeli merchants increasingly found that if they labeled their products as
"American" or "U.S.-style," they would take on a special
glamour that made people buy them. Refrigerators and other
appliances from the United States cost four or five times the
prices of their Israeli equivalents, yet many consumers were
willing to pay the huge premium for the sense of luxury.

The Israeli love of sports has also brought the two countries
together. National Basketball Association games are on Israeli
TV, and almost every schoolboy knows the names of the teams
and star players. In addition, more than a thousand basketball
players from the United States, mostly African Americans,

have gone to Israel during the past two decades to play for Israeli professional teams. In some instances team owners were so eager to recruit American players that they faked their conversions to Judaism. They were given Hebrew names and presented to Israeli fans as "Jews." When their contracts expired, they would often return both to the United States and to Christianity. Most had never been able to make it to the NBA; but occasionally, like Mike Mitchell, they were veterans of the big league.

Mitchell was born in 1956 to a poor black family in Atlanta and graduated from Auburn University. He was drafted in 1978 by the Cleveland Cavaliers, and three years later he moved to the San Antonio Spurs. He was even an NBA all-star, but after an injury ended his league career, he moved to Italy in 1988. After three years playing for Naples, he signed up with Tel Aviv's Maccabi team, Israel's champions for twenty-three years.

Like most professional basketball players, he came to play for the money. Yet because Mitchell is a "Born Again" Southern Baptist, he says: "Israel means something special." He and his wife were enchanted by the holy places of Jerusalem and Bethlehem.

"It's the realization of a dream for me to play in the same places where Jesus walked," says Mitchell. "Once, when we played a game close to the Jordan River, my wife and I were very moved. We went to the water, touched it, and prayed. This was the place where Jesus walked on water. It touched me straight in my heart."

Mitchell says he will treasure the experience, and "to my dying day, I'll be an ambassador praising Israel and a missionary spreading Israel's message in America."

While partly imitating America's taste in sports, Israelis have also adopted its food fads. Israeli entrepreneurs traveled to the United States, browsed for ideas, and imitated them back home. Some Israelis opened MacDavid's hamburger stands, and only years later did the authentic McDonald's decide to bring yet another American icon into the Israeli market. U.S.-style shopping malls have been popping up on the outskirts of large Israeli towns, and thanks to credit cards, plastic money is used almost as widely as the real thing.

Before long Israelis had made microwave ovens a fairly standard kitchen accessory. And soon they were consuming as much popcorn, potato chips, and beer per capita as Americans. Needless to say, aerobic exercises on videotape became popular items too. In fact, as more videos of all kinds were watched at home, health experts warned that Israeli children were getting less fresh air and reading far fewer books.

Television has been the great spreader of American culture. *Dallas* and all the other major TV series from the United States were big hits in Israel, especially when there was only one government-run channel buying entertainment from abroad. Even now, with cable service giving upscale and middle-class Israelis more than a dozen channels, a huge proportion of the programs are made in America.

The Israeli who best understands the importance of television is the highly visible politician and ex-diplomat Benjamin Netanyahu. He borrowed the knowledge from the United States and brought it with him to Israel.

Netanyahu was born in Israel in 1949 to a very politically minded family. His father, he says, "was an ardent opponent of Ben-Gurion's Labor movement and a supporter of Begin." But as nationalistic as he was, the elder Netanyahu did not stay put in Israel. With his family, he shuttled back and forth to the United States, where he taught Jewish history in several colleges. Benjamin and his two brothers were thus able to acquire both cultures, while mastering flawless English and perfect Hebrew—the keys to his becoming a media star in America and the political successor to Begin and Yitzhak Shamir in the Likud party.

Going to high school in Philadelphia, Netanyahu recalls, "I was near the top of my class, especially in writing." After graduating in 1967, he returned to Israel and followed his brother Jonathan's footsteps by joining the elite commandoes of the Israeli army, Sayeret Matkal.

Netanyahu served in the unit for five years but always remained in the shadow of his brother, nicknamed Yoni. In 1972 Benjamin—known to friends as Bibi—returned to the United States to study architecture and business administration at the Massachusetts Institute of Technology. But during his four years there, he learned the excitement of politics, the importance of marketing, and the magic power of words.

"I was shocked at MIT to realize that the best students in America didn't know how to compose words," says Netanyahu. He met other Israeli students while there and joined forces with some of them in trying to promote right-wing political ideology among Israelis.

His other activities were firmly in the American milieu, however. He got a job with Boston Consulting Group and seriously considered staying in the United States. He even contemplated changing his name to Nitay, which is shorter and for the average American easier to pronounce.

What changed the course of Bibi's life dramatically was the death of his brother Yoni, when he led Sayeret Matkal in the daring rescue of hijacked air passengers in Entebbe, Uganda, on July 4, 1976. Bibi returned to Israel to mourn his brother, and in his memory the family founded the Jonathan Institute for the Study of Terrorism.

Benjamin Netanyahu and his efforts there attracted the attention of foreign dignitaries, including George Bush and George Shultz, and Netanyahu established himself as an expert on terrorism. He made a living, in the meantime, as the marketing director for an Israeli furniture company. But increasingly, he became active in Likud party politics.

Ambassador Moshe Arens invited Netanyahu, even without diplomatic experience, to move to Washington as number-two man in the Israeli embassy in 1982. At that post and later as Israel's ambassador to the United Nations, he displayed his formidable skills as a communicator. He had an answer to every question raised about Israel; he felt comfortable expounding on the policies of a Likud-run government; and his replies were almost always tailored to the needs of American television: short, clear, and punchy.

All the ingredients of his younger life in America—his command of the language, his marketing experience, and even his fashion sense and relaxed manner—now helped to elevate Bibi Netanyahu to the modern-day Voice of Israel. American Jews adored him, as Israel's most eloquent spokesman since the glorious days of Abba Eban.

Netanyahu explains his rise to stardom in America in a pithy burst of self-analysis: "You can live in one culture and develop both empathy and criticism for another." After ending his diplomatic stint in the United States, he was elected to Israel's parliament by introducing American-style politics: campaigning with his family, distributing bumper stickers for cars, and placing a strong emphasis on the candidate rather than on his party or ideology.

Skeptical commentators predicted that Netanyahu's American tactics would be rejected by the Israeli public. But he was the right man, with the right style, for the 1990s. In Israel, as in America, TV commercials and party primaries are part of the political way of life.

But has the Americanization of Israeli society, in its daily life as well as its politics, truly added to Israelis' understanding of the United States? Are the present and former Israeli-Americans and American-Israelis, such as Benjamin Netanyahu, Robert Rosenberg, Miriam Levinger, and Joshua Schoffman, really building bridges and reducing tensions?

"Not necessarily," says Malcolm Hoenlein, executive vice chairman of the Conference of Presidents of Major American Jewish Organizations. "I'm surprised, but Israelis do not have a real sense of what's going on in the U.S."

Precisely the same sentiment—that they do not know and understand us—can be heard from the Israeli side, supplemented by an Israeli concern over the increasing efforts by American Jewish leaders to influence important decisions faced by Israel. For many years, even before statehood in 1948, Israelis perceived their relations with American Jewry in blunt terms: You, the Americans, provide the financial and political support; and we who spill our blood in wars and make other sacrifices will make the life-or-death decisions. You Americans should give us money and support not just because you want to help us, the Israelis, but because you want to help yourselves. The State of Israel and we Israelis, by our sheer existence, are helping you to find your own identity as strong members of American society.

The Israelis feel they have paid a price for smooth relations with American Jews. Israel has not pressed them to go and live in the Jewish state, as other Jewish communities around the world are constantly urged. There is a tacit understanding not to embarrass each other, and this may partly explain why only around sixty thousand American Jews have moved to Israel. Fewer than one in six American Jews have seriously considered living in Israel, and only one in ten believe they can live a fuller Jewish life in Israel than in America.

The unspoken deal, which most American Jewish leaders seem to have accepted, is this: Israel needs money and political support; and Jews in the United States need the psychological security blanket of knowing that there is an Israel—out there somewhere—always offering shelter.

But American Jews are rarely willing to give up the "American" label. Thus AIPAC's favorite slogan is: "American, Pro-Israel, and Proud." And the United Jewish Appeal and the Jewish Federations have not forgotten to spend a healthy proportion of the contributions they receive on community needs inside America.

Still, misunderstandings develop when key Israelis act independently in the United States—independently of local Jewish leaders, that is. When Israel's diplomats and visiting officials had direct contacts with a wide variety of minority, non-Jewish groups, American Jewish leaders complained that they were being bypassed.

Colette Avital, Israel's outspoken consul-general in New York, had to field the complaints—especially after she met with leading African-Americans without consulting the Jews. "Unfortunately, many Jewish leaders think that they are *machers*," she says, using a Yiddish term for "doers" with the added inference of "know-it-all wheeler-dealers."

"American Jews forget that I represent the State of Israel, which is a free country and has its own agenda. But in a way, it is our fault as Israelis. For many years we accepted this kind of relationship. American Jews were supposed to foot the bill, while we accepted their role as intermediaries with the U.S. government and other parts of American society." Avital says that she appreciates the support Israel has had from the Jewish community, but she adds that the rules of the relationship should be rewritten.

Other Israelis call for even more dramatic changes, including the abolition of the Jewish Agency and the United Jewish Appeal, which they label as outdated. They point out that the UJA, in an average year, raises less than $1 billion, with only one-third going to Israel and the greater proportion spent in the United States. Although $300 million is a substantial amount, it is less than 1 percent of Israel's budget. Some American Jews believe that were it not for their contributions of ten, a thousand, or even a hundred thousand dollars, the State of Israel could not exist. As time goes on, and the Israeli economy grows, the belief is increasingly unfounded.

There is also resentment on the American side, when some Jewish activists speak derisively of Israeli cabinet ministers, members of parliament, and generals—some with only rudimentary skills in English—enjoying the first-class travel and luxury hotels on the speech circuit in the United States.

Many Jews are also far from thrilled to see that when the Israeli government makes controversial decisions, it simply expects supporters in the United States to fall into line or at least keep their mouths shut. Israel would like to keep such disputes bottled up within the family.

But some American Jews, who insist that they love Israel as much as anyone else does, felt the need—especially during the Likud years—to tell the Israeli government precisely what they believed: that it was making some big, dangerous mistakes. These Americans were acting on their own opinions and emotions about Israel's behavior in the occupied territories and the almost automatic approval by many "establishment" leaders of organized Jewry. The dissenters were also influenced by left-of-center opposition politicians in Israel, who encouraged American Jews to speak out against the Likud.

Thus the divisions so deeply affecting Israeli society since 1967, threatening to break the fragile consensus in the Jewish state, finally reached American Jewry. The American side of the family was also divided, reflecting the political splits in Israel, further cross-cut by the slicing of U.S. politics. But for many years there had been a successful effort to maintain a solid front as far as Israel was concerned. In recent years the front has become shaky.

Eleanor (Elly) Friedman took a major step after a first visit to Israel in 1978. She and her husband, Jonathan Cohen, formed the New Israel Fund, the foundation that finances Schoffman's civil liberties group and more generally exports American, liberal values to the Jewish state. The NIF is an alternative to the United Jewish Appeal, because the UJA's broad funding for programs in Israel has freed a lot of capital to be spent on West Bank and Gaza settlements.

Friedman says that while the situation in the territories upset her, she also saw social problems in Israel that reminded her of the community-action work she was doing in San Francisco. She felt, "I'm a Jew. I can't walk away. And somehow I'm connected with Israel, even if I don't like what's going on. I need to do something, when I see something I don't like or when I see something hopeful."

She recalls introducing some causes that few Israelis were embracing: "Civil rights, women's issues, and gay rights. They were also not as concerned as we with the environment."

Another heartfelt effort to invest directly in a project in Israel, without going through the UJA, can be seen in the work of an American doctor whose name adorns the Sanford Kuvin Center for Infectious Diseases at the Hebrew University in Jerusalem. Traveling as an expert on malaria in the 1960s, he says, "My first experience in Israel was overwhelming, but I really didn't know how I could make a significant contribution other than writing a check."

A decade later, he raised $1 million—and then millions more—for a research center that he found easy to promote to the National Institutes of Health and other American backers. "Jerusalem has a mystical draw, and Jews especially know that the re-creation of Israel in our lifetime is a bona fide miracle.

Non-Jews are interested too, because Christians find their roots in the Hebrew Bible."

To help cement the peace between Israel and Egypt in 1979, Kuvin got the U.S. government to finance the only cooperative health program between the Jewish state and any Arab country. Progress was made toward eradicating diseases killing people and livestock throughout the Middle East and Africa. "Egyptians work in our labs in Jerusalem, and we have Israelis working in Cairo," he says. "Now we're putting together joint research projects teaming Israelis and Palestinians."

Promoting peace, as the prerequisite to prosperity and a stable society, was also a concern for Elly Friedman's New Israel Fund. When she noticed tens of thousands of Israelis demonstrating to urge their government toward peace with Egypt, Friedman encouraged the sponsoring group—Peace Now—to form a fund-raising arm in the United States.

Franklin Fisher, an MIT professor, became treasurer of both Americans for Peace Now and the New Israel Fund. "We provided a way for Jews who are left and left-center to feel good about their Jewish heritage," says Fisher, "because they were somewhat alienated from the Jewish community by Israeli government policies on the peace issue and a feeling that the things they really care about were not represented in this country they care about."

But Fisher insists he could never be labeled anti-Israel. "I was once a board member of the UJA, and my connections with Israel are very personal. I forged very warm relations between my department at MIT and the economics departments of Hebrew University and Tel Aviv University. In fact, my friends in Jerusalem got me together with the Peace Now group in Israel, and they told me, 'You have to do something.' It's as simple as that. They needed support from the U.S., including money."

Fisher denies that he and the New Israel Fund, which doled out over $14 million to nonprofit groups in Israel in the first three years of the 1990s, foist foreign values on the Jewish state. "These are the values that are held by a very large fraction of Israeli society, and I believe these values are not only American. They are deeply rooted in the Jewish tradition. The phrase that comes to mind is: 'The stranger who lives among you shall be as a citizen, and you shall not oppress him.'

"And anyway, we American Jews have the right to express ourselves on these issues! We don't have the right to vote, but the State of Israel and its people expect my money and my political support in the United States. In exchange for that, they also get my opinions—thank you very much."

Fisher and his wealthy family have contributed to Israel's Labor party and its leftist coalition partner, Meretz. And he recalls, in early 1992, having an angry argument with AIPAC's Tom Dine about it. "Dine was very big on how we should keep our mouths shut. I thought that argument was gone years ago! I had to say to him: We have more credibility in Congress if we don't automatically snap to attention all the time. We have an obligation to speak out on Israeli policies.

"And New Israel Fund helps Americans feel better about Israel and about the kind of American values that you'll find in Israel's Declaration of Independence."

CHAPTER EIGHTEEN

THE AMEN LOBBY

In the middle of a field along Israel's coastal plain, near the Mediterranean Sea, ten miles north of Haifa, an American geologist named Harris "Koop" Darcy stood by the tower of an oil well. His oil well. God's oil well.

Now, in the summer of 1983, he was praying to the good Lord to save him because his $13 million investment was stuck, four miles deep inside the Holy Land. The drill wouldn't budge. It wasn't going up or down.

What would his investors think? They were backing an audacious search for oil in Israel, on the strength of both geological surveys by mineralogists and biblical interpretation by theologians. Darcy's fellow believers, spread among Christian congregations all along the Bible Belt of the southern United States, had donated the money. Faith or no faith, the hundreds of investors wouldn't be pleased about a stuck drill.

"I believe that God will miraculously open the well," Darcy

said, "and it will just start flowing on its own." Hope springs eternal, even when oil doesn't, for people who read the Bible literally when it identifies the places where Jacob's sons would "dip their feet in oil" or find "the hidden treasures of the sand." Darcy had been hired to see if biblical promise could turn to petroleum reality.

The Christian oil drillers were interested in recovering their investments and perhaps even making a profit, if they could find some in the land of the prophets. Striking oil would also give them spiritual satisfaction, because it would mean that their reading of the Bible proved accurate. To evangelicals, revealing the truth through the pages of the scriptures—and relating it to today's reality—is very important.

For the State of Israel, finding petroleum could be the fulfillment of a dream. Envying their oil-rich Arab neighbors, Israelis are unable to understand why their land was not anointed with oil. As a result, the government is happy to support any and all foreign investors who come to drill for crude. Unfortunately, Darcy and several other evangelical oil prospectors were not successful.

His attempt illustrates, however, a much larger relationship between the Jewish state and Christians. Their religious beliefs may diverge. Their perceptions of heaven are quite different. But here on earth their interests occasionally coincide. The links between Israel and American Christians have become another factor that strengthens the U.S.-Israel alliance.

The attraction of the Holy Land is perfectly understandable. Jesus Christ was born, preached, and died there. So ever since the first pilgrims from Maine arrived in 1866, the land now known as Israel played a major role in the thoughts, writings, sermons, and dreams of American Christians. The group with the strongest interest in the land itself were the evangelicals—now usually dubbed fundamentalists.

They were generally supportive of the first Zionist settlers in

Palestine, who started arriving in the 1880s, and of the Jews' demand for a state of their own. To the evangelicals, watching from their homes and churches across the Atlantic, the return of Jews to their ancient homeland was a realization of biblical prophecy and a necessary step on the road to redemption for the world. Christian newspapers in the United States carried reports about the progress that Jewish pioneers were making in building their new settlements and lives.

William Blackstone, a Methodist who was a successful businessman in Chicago, was prominent in the early Christian, pro-Zionist movement. In 1891 he wrote a memorandum to President Benjamin Harrison, asking him to sponsor an international conference of governments to decide in favor of a Jewish state in Palestine. Forty-three prominent congressmen, governors, mayors, and leading industrialists such as J. P. Morgan and John D. Rockefeller signed Blackstone's petition.

Being more Zionist than the Zionist Jews, Blackstone was quickly spotted by the newly emerging Zionist movement in America. Encouraged by Louis Brandeis and others, Blackstone sent yet another petition to the White House—this time in 1916, urging President Woodrow Wilson to honor his own call for self-determination worldwide.

Fundamentalist views went out of fashion between the two world wars in much of America—after bitter debates over the teaching of human evolution. And as their standing declined, the evangelicals found themselves so busy defending their small patch of the U.S. ideological field that they did little for Zionism. In Palestine, lacking a high level of funding, their activity was also at a low ebb.

Mainstream Protestant Christianity was on the rise, however, and liberal theologians—such as Reinhold Niebuhr— gave their support to organizations that supported Jewish sovereignty in the Land of Israel.

Their support for Zionism did not stem from messianic expectations, but more of a change in attitude toward Jewish people based on the liberal notion of reconciliation and dialogue between religions.

Both fundamentalists and mainstream Protestants were among the first Americans to raise their voices against Nazi Germany, for its persecution of church leaders and Jews. But aside from going to war against Germany and Japan, the United States was in no mood to do anything specific for the Jews. The passivity of most Christians through the Holocaust would contribute to their guilt feelings later—pushing them toward more active support of Israel.

Fundamentalists viewed the establishment of the Jewish state as a sign that the fulfillment of their vision was drawing near. Various Christian congregations established cordial relations with the Labor party of Ben-Gurion and Eshkol—the Southern Baptists setting up their own "Baptist Village" near Tel Aviv. But there was no great warmth.

The Pentecostalist preacher Oral Roberts visited Jerusalem in 1959, and Ben-Gurion met with him. And when in 1962 the Pentecostalists held an international conference in Israel, the prime minister addressed them but upset quite a few by describing the Jewish state as the ultimate fulfillment of biblical prophecies. His words showed that he did not understand the fundamentalist view that Israel was only a step toward their realization.

It was the Six-Day War that led to a quantum leap in relations between Israel and the fundamentalists. For many of them, with their worldview of current events based on prophecy, the war was the most important occurrence since the French Revolution of 1789, for it made it seem that the coming of Jesus was nearer.

Those lightning events of June 1967 bolstered the faith of many fundamentalists that the holy scriptures would be realized—not just sometime, but very soon.

The world-famous American evangelist Billy Graham went to Israel in 1970 to make a film entitled *His Land*. He had no need for Hollywood set designers, for the actual sites of the life of Jesus were all around him. The State of Israel was much more than a mere extra, and was depicted in impressively positive terms. Prime Minister Golda Meir attended the premiere, in America, signaling that the Israeli government was now beginning to understand the importance of the Christian audience.

But the relationship was not easy for Labor party administrations, dominated by socialists brought up in antireligious households. They were suspicious of the zealotry that drove the fundamentalists who declared their great interest in Israel.

When students from Oral Roberts University in Tulsa, Oklahoma, spent a term on a kibbutz—as many did—it seemed a normal part of the enormous pro-Israel sentiment among American youngsters after the Six-Day War. But while many of the socialists on the kibbutzim were open-minded enough to play host to Christians, they were unhappy once they realized how religious were the volunteers.

To the kibbutz members, the Pentecostalists seemed like missionaries—trying to convert their children not necessarily to Christianity, but to religiosity. For many on the kibbutz, just talking about God was a foreign concept.

It was Menachem Begin, more than any other Israeli leader, who understood the huge potential that Christian goodwill represented. After his election overthrew the socialists in 1977, his own religious sentiments played a dual role: On one hand, as a Jewish believer and a man obsessed by the Holocaust, he might have every reason to be suspicious of Gentiles. On the other hand, he respected and understood religious feelings and rhetoric.

But above all, he realized it would be politically beneficial for Israel to forge links with Christians. They were rising in influence in the United States—with the Reverend Jerry Falwell forming his Moral Majority organization in 1977, coinciding with the presidency of an evangelical Christian, Jimmy Carter. Carter, as a devoted Baptist, read the Bible and prayed every day, and without a doubt his deep faith helped bring Israel and Egypt together in peace.

But Begin and his government felt that Carter's vision of a just Middle East would endanger their country. Some Israelis branded Carter just plain naive.

Ronald Reagan also called himself a born-again Christian and helped build fundamentalists into a powerful political force in America. They agreed wholeheartedly with his antiliberal domestic policies, which included opposition to abortion and moves toward allowing prayer and the teaching of the biblical Creation story in the schools. And overseas, fundamentalists adored Reagan's tough stand toward Moscow. It was only natural for the religious Right to support Reagan in his support for Israel as a bastion against communism.

Begin was the first prime minister to tell a top aide that while on a fact-finding tour of America, he should specifically meet with fundamentalist Christians to explore the depth of their pro-Israel sentiments. The results were excellent, from Begin's point of view, and later in 1977 full-page advertisements started appearing in major U.S. newspapers, declaring the support of Christian organizations for Israel—and often for specific Israeli projects, such as the dramatic immigration of Jews from the Soviet Union and other lands. The supporters called themselves Christian Zionists, and that was fine with Begin.

After Israel bombed Iraq's nuclear reactor in 1981, Begin—seeing that the United States was officially condemning the Jewish state—telephoned Jerry Falwell and asked him to do some positive publicity on Israel's behalf. Falwell agreed, and in his many television and personal appearances spoke in favor of the raid on Baghdad.

Begin paid Falwell the highest compliment in the lexicon of his Likud party, by awarding the Jabotinsky Medal—named for Begin's late political mentor—to the Moral Majority leader. In November 1982 Begin agreed to speak at a Baptist convention in Dallas, but had to cancel the appearance after his wife's death.

It was no wonder, in such a friendly atmosphere, that a plan to search for oil based on biblical clues could gain financial backers. Or that a campaign called the National Christian Leadership Conference for Israel (NCLCI) could get off the ground.

"Because Christianity owes so much to the Jewish people," says Sister Rose Thering, the executive director of NCLCI, "we reach out in a spirit of friendship and solidarity." Unable to bridge the theological gap, believing fervently in Jesus Christ but knowing that Jews do not, she has chosen Israel as her point of contact.

As fiery at age seventy as Begin was in defending Jewish rights to the Land of Israel, Thering is a Roman Catholic nun and educator who in 1978—to celebrate the thirtieth anniversary of Israel's birth—put together a small but media-savvy coalition of Catholics, mainline Protestants, evangelicals, and members of other Christian denominations "united in our common commitment to Israel's security and survival."

But NCLCI is mainly Sister Rose herself, traveling around the country from her New York base, telling Christians to love and support Israel and the Jews. "We are recognizing God's covenant with them," she says, "and we acknowledge the responsibility that Christians have for past injustices committed against Jews. Christians have to come to know Israel better, because Jews are our elder brothers and sisters."

Thering's organization is one of 273 similar groups set up in America after Begin's election. He and his successor, Shamir, would find that the fundamentalist base of support offered a no-lose situation. Whatever Israel does, the Christian believers see the hand of God in it—whether it is simply a new office building, a highway, or the bombing of an Arab nuclear facility.

Sister Rose Thering often leads tours of Israel, marveling at everything that the young country has accomplished. "I know Christians who can go to Israel and see nothing but the holy places," she says. "They wear blinders. They do not see the wonders—the miracles—of God's revelation taking place today within that Land of Israel."

Richard Hellman saw them. A Washington lawyer, he says he heard the voice of God telling him to move to Israel. He did so in 1976 and ended up staying for seven years, writing laws for the country's Environmental Protection Service. "I constantly looked at the Bible," he says, "and everything I was doing made perfect sense with the scriptures." Returning to the United States, he set up a lobbying group called CIPAC, the Christians' Israel Public Action Campaign, a small echo of AIPAC.

AIPAC employs a "Christian Zionist" as deputy legislative director. The lobby and other Jewish organizations form links with the Christians of America for two purposes: first, to live as good neighbors, sharing whatever values and experiences they can find in common; and second, to make support for Israel one of those shared values.

As part of the effort to generate Christian backing for the Jewish state, paths were found to powerful politicians through their personal religious connections. Jacques Torczyner, a Zionist activist since his Belgian childhood in the 1920s and later an active Republican, recalls stressing the Christian factor when he pressed the victorious Reagan campaign chief, James Baker, to go to Israel in 1980.

"I said, 'Mr. Baker, you know nothing about Jews. I would like you to meet some.' I arranged a long dinner with ten Jews, on many subjects. But he wouldn't go to Israel. I did send his wife, however. She's a fundamentalist Christian." In 1991, on several visits to Israel by Secretary of State Baker, his wife went along and revisited the landmarks of Jesus' life, including the Church of the Holy Sepulchre in Jerusalem where he was briefly entombed.

However moved Mrs. Baker may have been, did that really help Israel argue its corner with her husband? The political effects of President Jimmy Carter's faith were similarly questionable, as would be the influence of President Bill Clinton's Southern Baptist faith.

Clinton's official briefers, however, did tell journalists a touching story in September 1993. They said that on the eve of the historic peace accord between Israel's Prime Minister Rabin and PLO chairman Arafat, the president was so excited that he could not sleep. So at three o'clock in the morning, worrying about the speech he would have to deliver in a few hours, Clinton picked up a Bible and read the entire Book of Joshua—to review the part about the trumpets that toppled the walls of Jericho.

Just three days earlier the president had ruminated on the surprising breakthrough in the Promised Land and what it meant to him. "This whole thing is immensely interesting for Christians," he said. "Well, I mean, it's our Holy Land too. I never will forget the only time I went to Israel was with my pastor, who told me after I got back that he thought one day I would be president. And since at that time I was the youngest ex-governor in America—I was thirty-four—I didn't think he knew what he was talking about. And he said, 'Just remember, God will never forgive you if you turn your back on Israel.' "

For the average American, however, a visit to the Holy Land is expensive. It is a great distance and a jumble of languages for Americans unaccustomed to world travel. And it seems dangerous to most Americans, who get their images of the Arab-Israeli conflict from television news. But many churches and influential groups such as the National Religious Broadcasters and Bridges for Peace do organize tours, and Israeli envoys in the United States actively encourage them.

The visits of Christian pilgrims help Israel, not only because the circle of support for the Jewish state and its political case keeps enlarging, but also because of the economic benefits. Tourism is a principal source of foreign-currency earnings for the country.

Israel's eagerness to maintain this link with Christians is so great that the sensitivities of American Jews are sometimes ignored. When it was revealed that Pat Robertson, a former presidential candidate and a leading fundamentalist broadcaster, gave financial support to "Jews for Jesus," a missionary organization aimed at converting Jews, rabbis in the United States were furious. But Israeli officials did not bat an eyelash. For them, Robertson was a pro-Israeli bastion who in the 1990s began sending large tourist groups to the Holy Land. "If every rabbi in America would bring to Israel 10 percent of what Robertson is bringing," said one official, "it would be fantastic."

When Christian groups arrive in Israel, they are typically loaded onto buses and taken to the actual places where Jesus lived. It is tremendously exciting for most group members to walk in Christ's footsteps in Bethlehem, Nazareth, Capernaum, and Jerusalem.

And the most likely next step would be into the International Christian Embassy in Jerusalem. This is indeed a rare institution: not truly an embassy, in the juridical diplomatic sense of the term. It is more of a protest.

In 1980, when Begin was in one of his feisty moods, he pushed through parliament the "Jerusalem Law." It made a point of stating the obvious. In 1967 the Arab sector of the city had been annexed and a united capital of Israel established. Now Begin's law, declaring that Jerusalem was the united and eternal capital, only served to irritate foreign governments.

The few countries that had their embassies in Jerusalem now

changed their minds and relocated to Tel Aviv. The choice between the two cities had long been controversial because most governments do not recognize Jerusalem—its status officially unsettled—as the capital of Israel. Almost as an American election-year ritual, both Republican and Democratic party platforms promised to move the U.S. Embassy from Tel Aviv to Jerusalem. But once the campaigns were over, it remained an unfulfilled promise.

Fundamentalists, however, had a different idea. In what they billed as a gesture of solidarity with the Israeli cause, they sought and quickly got Begin's permission to open their own "embassy."

At their modern and impressive outpost, members of the Christian Embassy—supported largely by U.S. citizens—produce films, host conferences, and organize the largest annual gathering of Christians in Israel, with upwards of five thousand pilgrims from seventy nations. But this is not all. It is, in fact, a mission—in the old sense of a station for missionaries in Jerusalem.

In addition, on the remote fringes of the fundamentalist movement are groups that are not content simply to wait for the Messiah. Since the return of the Jewish people to their land, including from Russia, is being completed, their theology suggests what the next step must be to make the Second Coming come sooner.

The Jews, they believe, should rebuild their Holy Temple—a third temple—on its ancient site in Jerusalem. And since there are two big mosques on the Temple Mount, some extremists believe it is time for them to be cleared away.

That is what Dennis Rohan tried to do. An Australian staying on a kibbutz and associated with a fundamentalist church in America, he set fire to the Al Aqsa mosque. The silver-domed building was badly damaged, and the Muslim world went alight with anger and high rhetoric including calls for *jihad*, or holy war. Israel, not wishing to fuel the religious aspect of the political and national dispute with the Arabs, moved quickly. Rohan was arrested, charged, found guilty, and imprisoned. But the authorities also declared the Australian insane, a verdict that conspiracy theorists in the Muslim world had trouble swallowing.

Christian extremists, who persist in wishing that the Temple Mount mosques could be flattened, find unlikely allies among Jewish extremists, mainly settlers in the West Bank. But even for right-wing Israeli governments, the idea is repugnant as well as political dynamite. Israeli authorities have done what they can to keep the extremists in check, and in May 1984 they arrested a group of Jewish terrorists who planned—among other things—to blow up the mosques.

Even when there are not plans so violent, the connection persists. Spokesmen from the Jewish settlement movement occasionally go to the United States, to raise funds among supportive fundamentalist groups.

Israel's entire Christian connection, not just its extremist aspect, bothers many Israelis as well as many American Jews. The Israeli opposition to fundamentalists forms an unholy alliance. On one side, left-wingers and liberals are concerned that Christians wielding influence in Israel tend to support ultraconservative policies: stepped-up settlement drives, militarism, and a ban on abortions.

On the other side, Israel's Orthodox Jews keep their distance from the fundamentalists, believing that they have come to Israel only to convert Jews to Christianity. In the Orthodox view, the Christians do not like Jews for who they are, but rather as a religious vehicle—tools of Christian theology leading to Jesus' return. Under pressure from Orthodox parties, ironically, the same Begin government that solidified the link with Christians passed a law restricting their right to engage in missionary activities in the Holy Land. Begin wanted evangelists to visit but not to evangelize.

"Begin asked his foreign ministry for a report on the various Christian groups in the United States, so I was asked to write it," says Rabbi Yehiel Eckstein, director of the Chicago-based International Fellowship of Christians and Jews. "I explained the differences between mainline evangelicals like Billy Graham, fundamentalists like Jerry Falwell, and the Pentacostalists and Charismatics like the Assembly of God and Pat Robertson that have really become the core of Christian Zionists. Basically, though, Begin was very concerned that all this was a way to bring in Jesus through the back door." The prime minister welcomed their support for Israel, so long as they played down their religious mission.

The Israeli concerns are reflected among American Jews as well. Most Jews are liberals, favoring abortion rights and opposing prayer in public schools—the Jewish community feeling it needs the protection offered by the constitutional separation of church and state. "Our differences on school prayer and on a woman's right to choose cannot be covered up," says Robert Zimmerman, president of the American Jewish Congress for Long Island, New York, "because the fundamentalist agenda would threaten the freedoms that make Jews safe in America. And keep in mind that Israel's survival depends on a thriving and secure Jewish community here."

CHAPTER NINETEEN

IN HEADLINES WE TRUST

It takes a special cause to bring Dan Rather and Peter Jennings to appear together, even on videotape, yet in a hotel ballroom here was an audience of three hundred New Yorkers in black ties and evening gowns, watching the nation's two leading anchormen satirically bid farewell to an Israeli diplomat.

It was partly a personal tribute to Uri Savir, ending four years as consul-general in New York, but also a tribute to Israel and the incredibly disproportionate attention it receives from the media.

As the master of ceremonies, also a popular anchorman on a local television station, introduced the guests, the famous faces of CBS's Rather and ABC's Jennings entertained them with taped, bogus news bulletins.

Broadway stars and the city's mayor, David Dinkins, took part in the gala evening, showing that in the summer of 1992 Israel was still able to penetrate broad sectors of the Big Apple's diverse community. Everyone joined in singing, to the tune of "New York, New York's" climactic ending: "You'll be remembered here / by friends who hold you dear / Good luck Ambassador Savir." Movie stars Kathleen Turner and Ron Silver sang yet another salute, and two *New York Times* writers performed a skit on the impact Savir had made as Israel's representative.

The Jewish state's diplomacy had hit the heights of media, show business, sports, and politics—in short, everything that really matters in capturing the hearts and minds of ordinary Americans. Dinkins even celebrated the Israeli's center-court affection for the city's basketball team. "Uri now knows the difference between Knicks and knishes," said the mayor.

The laughter, the music, and the banquet underlined the effort by Israel's diplomats in the United States to walk in Teddy Kollek's early footsteps: his fascination with Hollywood, celebrities, and high society. But things had changed, a decade after the invasion of Lebanon and five years after the outbreak of the Palestinian intifada uprising. Israeli envoys now had to make extraordinary efforts to improve their country's image. They wanted to return to the good old days when the Jewish state was an adored newborn, a coddled child, and a respected nation reaching maturity. But the shootings and beatings by Israeli soldiers trying to suppress the intifada built up such a negative reputation that there was little hope of turning back the clock.

The Israeli diplomats could no longer rely on the good image that sprang forth from the pages of the Bible that portrayed the Israelites heroically liberating their land by smiting Philistines. And in the 1948 War of Independence they smote their enemies again, a victory with powerful resonance in Christian, Bible-reading households.

Israel's birth was welcomed, so soon after newsreels seen in movie theaters everywhere showed the Nazi concentration camps being liberated, revealing the crematoria where millions of Jewish corpses had been burned and the walking skeletons who were the survivors. It was General Dwight Eisenhower who urged that footage entitled "Nazi Atrocities" be shown nationwide. According to a researcher into the effect of World War II films on American culture, "audiences seem to have responded with an appalled solemnity. Some gasped, a few hissed obscenities at the Germans, but most sat in shocked silence." Americans—including newspaper editors and TV producers—were hooked on the story.

Israel's leaders and diplomats responded with delight. They craved attention. Harry Truman's recognition was one thing; now the Jewish state wanted to be talked about. American writers and broadcasters responded to invitations by visiting Israel, becoming wrapped up with the intriguing characters who were building the new society. Many would even send their children to Israel, much as upper-class English families would do in financing the "grand tour" of Europe for their offspring in the eighteenth and nineteenth centuries.

Teddy Kollek recalls that "one of the most unique men I have ever met," the CBS newsman Edward R. Murrow, was a frequent visitor to Israel after making a documentary there in 1957. Broadcast journalism and show business overlapped even then, with Kollek introducing Murrow to Marlene Dietrich and other movie stars—a reservoir of sympathy into which Israel would dip for fund-raisers and publicity. "Ed also brought his thirteen-year-old son, Casey, to Israel for an extended stay," says Kollek, "and I think he enjoyed that visit the most." Murrow's son even had an audience with the legendary Ben-Gurion.

The Arabs were upset. They couldn't seem to get their message into the American press. In March 1960, diplomats from ten Arab countries met with Secretary of State Christian Herter and complained about the media. "Not a week passes," they said, "in which American papers, especially Zionist papers, fail to pillory Saudi Arabia, United Arab Republic, Lebanon, etc."

As an example, they said that the United Nations had recently criticized Israel after a clash with Syrian forces. Yet "the subsequent press campaign [was] suggesting the Arabs had committed aggression." The ambassadors said they "had pleaded with American papers to publish the UN report. Not a single paper had done so." They also said they had invited CBS News to film the battle site "in an effort to enable the American public to learn the truth about the incident," but while CBS said yes, nothing was broadcast.

Now, to the Arab diplomats' annoyance, they claimed that "the Israeli anti-Arab campaign is intense and extends even to the field of literature. Thus, for example, it is regrettable that the book *Exodus* is now to be filmed."

The 1967 war brought another flood of attention. And Israel could not have written a better scenario itself. In an America still watching Westerns on TV, the Israelis certainly looked like the good guys wearing the white hats. The Arabs were the bad guys who started the trouble, and they would be stuck with their black hats for many years.

Life magazine was especially powerful, with cover photographs of smiling, handsome, and young Israeli soldiers liberating Jerusalem's Wailing Wall or wading in the Suez Canal. Almost everyone in America saw those pictures or similar stimuli that helped them share in the flush of Israel's victory.

Newspapers, magazines, and TV networks knew a good story when they saw it, and they stayed with it. Their correspondents opened bureaus in Tel Aviv and Jerusalem, and the number of foreign correspondents registered with Israel's press office soared to almost 400: rivaling Washington, Moscow, London, and Paris as a news capital. During times of crisis many more would come: 2,500 to cover the historic visit of Egypt's President Sadat in 1977, more than 1,000 at the height of the intifada in early 1988, and 1,700 during the Iraqi Scud attacks of 1991.

It was the Israeli invasion of Lebanon, in 1982, that changed the content of the reporting. This was the first military campaign—or, certainly, the first televised war—that Israel did not truly *have* to fight. As portrayed by the overwhelming majority of editorials in the U.S. media, the once lily-white self-defense force of Israel was now an aggressor, brutally shelling and bombing the city of Beirut. It was as if the Israelis and Palestinians had swapped hats.

Israeli officials could see the damage that media coverage was doing to their country's image. But there was no practical way of stopping TV crews from getting to the scenes of the action. When Israel's military censor tried to suppress stories, foreign reporters and crews found it easy to circumvent the system. Many, after all, were based in Beirut and beyond any Israeli control. Even the light application of censorship during the Lebanon war poisoned Israel's reputation every time the words were flashed on American TV screens: "Censored by Israeli Army."

"The war in Lebanon was a real killer," recalls an Israeli diplomat who served in Washington at the time. "The veterans among us could not avoid drawing a comparison. In the '67 war, American television showed us filling sandbags and preparing our cities for what was seen as our heroic last-ditch fight. And the Arabs were seen on TV shouting 'Butcher the Jews!' Now, night after night, TV showed Palestinians and Lebanese defending Beirut while Israel's air force heavily bombarded their houses. For most of us it was a lost battle."

But not for Benjamin Netanyahu, then Ambassador Arens's deputy chief of mission at the Israeli embassy. He searched desperately for image-builders with which to fight back. When Netanyahu heard that President Reagan had been deeply touched by a news-agency photograph of a Palestinian girl whose arms had been blown off and that Reagan had offended Begin by telephoning him to demand that he call off the "holocaust," the Israeli diplomat set out to prove that the photo was bogus.

"I managed to establish telephone contact with the Israeli headquarters in Beirut and suggested that the military try to find the girl," Netanyahu writes. "The Israeli army succeeded in locating her. Her arm had indeed been damaged, but years earlier during the Lebanese civil war; she had been the victim of Arab and not Israeli fire. But by then it was too late. The notion of Israel's brutality had penetrated a notch deeper into the consciousness of the American leadership and public."

And yet somehow Israel's cause was far from completely lost. When a Gallup poll asked Americans, "In the Middle East situation, are your sympathies more with Israel or more with the Arab nations?" the invasion of Lebanon appeared to have little effect. In August 1981 the public had supported Israel 44 to 11 percent. In November 1982 it was 48 to 17 percent.

This is partly because the Arab side of the Middle East dispute has never had effective spokesmen in the United States. The PLO's Yasser Arafat did not come across well on television—at least not until the historic White House handshake of 1993. Thereafter the Palestinians' image immediately began to change. Arafat was on all the major news and talk shows, from *Larry King Live* to the *McNeil-Lehrer NewsHour*. It suddenly became legitimate, even fashionable, to broadcast long interviews with the chairman of the PLO.

Nevertheless, as Uri Savir—who after returning to Israel was involved in the secret diplomacy with the PLO—rates his rivals: "While they have become more sophisticated, the image of the Arabs in America is still negative. It's only positive when they come into contact with Israel—like Sadat and the moderate Palestinians showing they're wise enough to talk to us. In all public opinion polls since '67, on the basic motherhood and apple pie questions, Israel has a four-to-one edge over the Arabs."

But what do Americans remember about Israel? The courage of rescuing hostages at Entebbe? The ordeal of being hit by Iraq's Scud missiles? Or the killing of Palestinians in trying to put down the intifada? Says Savir: "Things that fit basic images, they last. Things that contradict get rejected. Unless they contradict for too long a time—and then they become the new image." The positive aura of the Israel-PLO accords seemed set rapidly to replace the negative images of the intifada.

The uprising in Gaza and the West Bank was a good story for journalists, but a very bad one for Israel. "We'd been the blue-eyed boys, pioneers and conquerors like in the American Wild West," an Israeli diplomat in Washington comments. "Americans found it easy to identify with us. The intifada broke that image. Our army's behavior was perceived as a betrayal: the breaking of a trust, as though you'd caught your wife cheating with somebody."

Americans, often subconsciously, had developed such high expectations of Israel that anything unsavory seemed shocking. In 1988 it was common for U.S. newspapers to feature photographs that simply made Israeli authorities look ugly, such as an Israeli soldier or policeman shoving a Palestinian—and shouting at him, not even shooting. It did not seem to be real news, yet the players in the photo were so familiar to Americans that it worked as a piece of front-page drama.

Bloodshed that was much worse, in Asia, Africa, and even some parts of the Middle East, got barely a mention in the U.S. media. But stories featuring Arabs and Jews, especially with strong pictures, filled thousands of minutes on network news programs and tens of thousands of column-inches in major newspapers. These were easy stories for readers and viewers to comprehend. Everyone knew that the Jews, the biblical heroes, were tussling with the Arabs over a single piece of land. It seemed fascinating, to Americans, to see how the battle progressed. Of particular interest was how the Jews behaved.

"There's a tendency to single out Israel for special, negative treatment," says Richard Schifter, a longtime pro-Israel lawyer who was the State Department's chief human rights monitor from 1985 to 1992.

"I do share the concern of many Israelis and many American Jews about some of the actions of Israeli security forces in the occupied territories. Practices that run counter to the basic moral principles on which Jewish culture rests must end.

"And I know our media thrive on bad news. But why do they pay so much attention to Israel? Why, in a world in which interethnic strife abounds, this inordinate emphasis on day-to-day events in Israel?"

After studying the phenomenon, both in and out of government, Schifter has concluded that reporters based in Israel and editors at home are responding to a new "revealed religion"— as if suddenly discovering that the occupation of the West Bank and Gaza Strip can be a tough business.

"I don't think it's organized," Schifter says in describing the bias he perceives. "But there's a tendency to run with the pack, which is customary in the media. And the news that reaches the U.S. public also has something to do with where reporters are stationed. They're usually stationed where it's comfortable," as in Israel, and cannot easily get to Mauritania, Sudan, or Kashmir, where his official reports found some of the worst violence by governments against civilians.

When issuing the annual U.S. government compendium of torture and other rights abuses, Schifter found "the media were not inclined to identify the most serious human rights violations—or those affecting the most people—so as to supply the general public with a good overview of the state of human rights worldwide. The news accounts would focus special attention on Israel."

The annual report would be around 1,600 pages long, yet most reporters "would breeze past all the summary material to hone in on the 15 pages or so which dealt with the occupied territories."

Schifter is aware, he says, that "the general public is more interested in Israel than in India or Iraq," but he wonders whether major newspapers are not creating that interest. "A large percentage of *New York Times* readers is Jewish, and a significant percentage of the journalists is Jewish, so *they* may be especially interested in Israel. For some it may be a mark of professionalism to lean over backward and report negative news about Israel.

"The problem did not arise until after the '67 war," he admits. "As long as the country was an underdog, the media were very kind to Israel. After success in the '67 war, that's when things changed."

Israeli officials, who had so enthusiastically opened their country to the press and TV, could not go on selling the "land of milk and honey" slogans forever. They learned that the media tire of running the same story for years. The 1973 war, and especially the Arab oil embargo that affected every American who buys gasoline, made the world appear a lot more complicated to newspaper editors and readers.

Israel was also changing, especially after Begin's election victory toppled Labor's government monopoly in 1977. Life in Israel, as described by the many news correspondents assigned to cover it, was far from simple. Was Israel still fighting for survival, particularly in Lebanon in 1982? In the intifada since 1987?

The only continuous theme is that the media like stories from Israel. They are dramatic. They are picturesque. They often include biblical references. And they are usually easy to understand. Producers of television newsmagazine programs often call up Israeli journalists to ask, "Have you got any stories?"

Reporters and producers, including many Jews, have friends and relatives to visit in Israel. Reading *The New York Times*, which often sets the tone in foreign news reporting for the rest of the media, it often seems as if Israel were almost a local story. The space accorded events in and around the Jewish state sometimes exceeds the column-inches devoted to Queens or the Bronx.

The *Times* phenomenon might be explained by the numbers of Jews among the newspaper's readers, advertisers, editors, and journalists. Yet there are additional reasons. Israel has an interesting and open society. Its politicians are very accessible. Unlike in the United States or western Europe, journalists—not only the most famous, but almost all—can easily get the home telephone numbers of cabinet ministers or army generals and call them late at night. And there is a good chance of getting even the prime minister for an interview.

An American journalist based in Israel is more likely than his counterpart in the United States to talk frequently with a senior official or to meet with a top air force pilot. As in their early days of independence, Israelis still seem insecure, wanting to be loved, to get compliments, and to be seen as important.

The factors at play are more than psychological. There is also a strong political explanation. With the United States well established as Israel's foremost friend and ally, the American media are very important to Israeli politicians and strategists. Whenever visiting the United States—and they do it so often that occasionally half of Israel's cabinet can be found in New York's luxury hotels—they never miss an opportunity to appear on a morning talk show, on the evening news, or in a newspaper article, however small.

Aware of the special role of the media, especially at times of crisis, Israeli leaders unhesitatingly put their spins on controversial stories through leaks to foreign reporters. When, in November 1985, relations were badly strained by the espionage arrest of Jonathan Pollard, Prime Minister Peres's office initiated a special briefing for a select group of American journalists, to the annoyance of Israeli newspapermen who knew the truth but were stopped from publishing by the military censor. Led by *The New York Times*, the Americans were given the full Israeli version of the spy case with all the W's: who, what, when, where, and why. The aim was clear: to reach out, through the media and over the angry heads of Reagan administration officials, for "the real America"—the America that has always liked and supported Israel.

Israel also has the allure of good working conditions for journalists. There are comfortable hotels, bars open at all hours, people who are open and highly vocal when asked their opinions, and professional briefers always willing to bring the story to the hotel restaurant. That partially explains why the country gets so much coverage. It's perfect for television.

Yet recently Israel's high profile and tarnished media image worry some American Jews. Knowing that the overheated interest in Israel will not disappear, some of them have banded together in monitoring groups concerned, full time, with how their favorite foreign country is seen.

Andrea Levin is executive director of CAMERA, the Committee for Accuracy in Middle East Reporting in America. At their headquarters in Boston, she and her staff scan dozens of newspaper and magazine articles every day, while watching television and listening to the radio. Most times that Israel is mentioned, they wince.

A lot of coverage of the Middle East, says Levin, "gets the whole landscape wrong. It's not that a single tree or bush is out of place. It's not just a fact or two that's inaccurate. The whole works is wrong."

CAMERA was formed in 1982 as a small committee of pro-Israel activists, writing letters to the editor and protesting in other ways when the invasion of Lebanon seemed unfairly portrayed in the media. After the intifada began, Levin was hired, and she used a direct-mail marketing firm to swell the membership rolls from 2,000 to almost 25,000, including many of AIPAC's financial backers.

"We're articulating what a lot of people are feeling—a lot of anxiety," says Levin. "If our mission is to have an impact, and our way to do that is to document the problem and to educate and stimulate citizen action, then the more people we have the better."

CAMERA's biggest complaint is the narrow focus of reporting on the Middle East. "There is a certain rhetoric the media keep using," says Levin, "making the Palestinian problem seem the core of all the region's problems, labeling administered territories as 'occupied,' or speaking of 'Arab' East Jerusalem." Hardly any time or space is given, she complains, to mentioning that Israel is a tiny island in a huge sea of Arab nations, that radical Palestinian groups still vow to destroy the Jewish state, or that the Middle East has many violent conflicts that have nothing to do with Israel.

"Why is the context and history of the region usually absent?" asks Alan Dershowitz, a lawyer and author who calls on American Jews to speak out on their concerns. There is no anti-Israel conspiracy by the media, says Dershowitz, but budget-cutting and laziness lead to distortions and inaccuracies.

"Full and balanced reporting on Israel and the Middle East is critical in an American democracy where public opinion ultimately shapes public policy," Dershowitz adds.

CAMERA exchanges lively letters with editors and foreign

correspondents, often asking why they focus so heavily on a small aspect of the Middle East story instead of reminding their audience about the wider dangers faced by Israel and the West. The *Wall Street Journal* is the only major newspaper consistently praised by CAMERA members. The *New York Times* is considered to have a mixed record. Frequent targets for criticism include columnists Patrick Buchanan, Richard Evans and Robert Novak, National Public Radio, NBC's Bryant Gumbel, and ABC's Peter Jennings.

Jennings, for his part, says he is being scrupulously fair in his reporting on Israel and its neighbors. "People on this subject, more than any other, tend to see truth through their own eyes," he says. "There are some people who believe that if you are not 100 percent on their side, then you're on the other side."

Some American Jews worry about media coverage, in part out of concern that their own place in U.S. society can be undermined when Israel looks bad. "The intifada played on the American Jewish community's insecurities," says Abraham Foxman, national director of the Anti-Defamation League. "Jews watched the TV news, thought about their non-Jewish neighbors and wondered, 'Oh my God, what are they going to think?' "

Negative stories, even if legitimate, are used by professional Israel-bashers; and the tone of condemnation seems directed at the Jewish people as much as at a foreign government. Based on a lot of hate mail that he receives, Dershowitz warns: "Hostile reporting markedly increases the anti-Israeli theme in anti-Semitic incidents throughout the country."

When Jonathan Mitchell, the AIPAC activist in Beverly Hills, thinks of negative press, he is especially unhappy about articles written for the American press by Israelis who oppose their own government's policies. "If you have a problem in your family at home, isn't it better to work out your problem at home? Why take your dirty laundry outside and start discussing it with the entire neighborhood and let everyone know all the trouble going on at home?"

He finds that newspapers in the United States seem to delight in finding American Jews who will criticize Israel openly. "I think it's wrong," says Mitchell, "because it gives the president of the United States the license to do what he sometimes wants to do: to kick Israel in the butt, and favor the Arab position and say 'let's make a deal!' And people who don't like Israel get to say 'The Jews themselves don't like what Israel's doing.' "

The argument, whether from Mitchell or others, puts little store in the sophistication and complexity of democratic interaction in the modern age. The reality is that there is a price to pay for Israel's pride in being the only democracy in the Middle East. A free country produces a broad spectrum of views, and these are expressed every day in the highly active Israeli press and broadcast media.

Their reporters and analysts tend to dig and rarely accept official explanations, as they try to discover the core of the convoluted twists and turns of the region's politics. Sometimes what they find out can be embarrassing to the Israeli government. "There are more investigative reporters there than you had in the *Washington Post* in Watergate," said George Bush when he was vice president. Israel's newspapers feature many commentators who are critical of the government. That is what makes Israel gloriously different from its neighboring countries.

It is only natural, too, that in an international media market, Israeli journalists sell their books and articles abroad—bringing American readers into the controversial world of Middle East analysis. But it is not only that the United States is the place to make a good literary sale; it is also the only meaningful place abroad to make a political pitch.

Israeli leaders, whether in government or in opposition, have for many years been making their arguments on the op-ed pages of American newspapers. And in a world of instant communications and translations, it was irresistible for any U.S. paper to quote Abba Eban's stinging criticism of the Lebanon invasion in the summer of 1982: "These six weeks have been a dark age in the moral history of the Jewish people." It was written for an Israeli newspaper, but opinions now circle the globe more quickly than some supporters of the Jewish state might wish.

Israel's friends in America never demanded that the media be monitored in the years that the Jewish state was a media darling that could do no wrong. And most Israelis are unmoved by the issue.

"I find the American Jewish concern about the media rather unconvincing," says Yossi Sarid, a prominent left-wing member of parliament and cabinet member after mid-1992. "Where were all these people for twenty years? Why were they silent then? I'll tell you. Because when we, the Israelis, were liked by the media, American Jews liked it as well. To complain about the media only when they slap you, when you deserve to be slapped, is really a double standard." He believes that American reporters in Israel generally do an honest job and "occasionally are very considerate."

Although journalists from the United States did sometimes violate censorship, reporting on military operations in progress, they also have shown great restraint. In the first half of the 1980s, they censored themselves and did not report on the secret Israeli operation that was bringing tens of thousands of Ethiopian Jews to safety by sea and by air. Most of them knew what was going on but complied with an Israeli request not to mention anything that might disrupt the historic rescue.

Still, it is the job of journalists to find out what they can, to ask hard questions, and to share their findings with an audience. There is immense interest in Israel. Almost all Americans seem to care: whether editors searching for a good story, Ronald Reagan reaching out for a good ally, or his successor George Bush trying to accomplish some good—as he saw it—in the Middle East.

CHAPTER TWENTY

THE ULTIMATE CHALLENGE

On August 2, 1990, less than nineteen months after George Bush was sworn in as the forty-first president of the United States, one far-off Arab country invaded another. Iraq's seizure of Kuwait took him, as well as the world, by surprise and immediately dominated the global scene.

The Soviet Union was by now too weak to exercise any strong influence. The U.S. thus faced its first true test as the world's sole superpower. And America would have to choose how, if at all, to use Israel—the country long billed as its best and most reliable friend in the Middle East.

These complex realities struck one Israeli leader more than any other: the one who knew the United States better than the others. The defense minister, Moshe Arens, had spent nearly a third of his sixty-five years in the United States. Although born in Lithuania, he was raised in America, earned academic degrees at MIT and CalTech, and served as Israel's ambassador in Washington. His English, therefore, is perfect, and his style and body language could pass for those of a bureaucrat or politician in Sacramento, Tallahassee, or the nation's capital.

And the once-improbable fact that the United States was heading toward war against Iraq—as a response to Saddam Hussein's invasion of Kuwait—had a special resonance for Arens, for he had every reason to think or even to say "I told you so."

Washington had come to rely on Israel's inside knowledge of the Middle East since the glory days of June 1967, when pinpoint intelligence cleared the way for a six-day triumph over the combined forces of Egypt, Syria, and Jordan. The United States usually agreed with Israel's analyses of political and military developments in the region.

But on the Persian Gulf area, the two countries could not seem to agree—especially in the confusion sown by Iran's Islamic revolution in 1979. While Israel engaged in the wishful thinking that Iran, even under the ayatollahs, could continue to be a strategic asset, the United States quickly realized that when the Shah was toppled, one of the pillars of American strategy had crumbled. Now, to Washington, the Iranian Shiite Muslims were the growing menace.

Starting under President Jimmy Carter, and even more so under Ronald Reagan, the United States turned to Iraq as a replacement for Iran. American policy, since World War II, was based on finding local surrogates that would ensure U.S. interests—primarily the flow of oil to the West—without the need for U.S. troops to spill their blood.

America's needs clashed with Israel's most sharply after Iraq invaded Iran in September 1979. U.S. officials were annoyed that the prediction by Israeli intelligence, that Iraq would win within a few weeks, proved to be wrong. In fact, as the war dragged on for years, Iraq was on the defensive. Faced with a choice between two evils, Washington decided that Iran's was worse.

The Reagan team responded by ignoring Saddam's many sins: his brutality, his radicalism, his flirtation with Moscow, his territorial claims against pro-Western neighbors, and his support for international terrorism. The United States gave Iraq tactical intelligence, including satellite photographs of potential Iranian targets, plus loans and diplomatic support, hoping this would be enough to contain Iran's threat to Saudi oil.

Iraq, however, exploited the surprising U.S. generosity by diverting the funds to obtain some of the world's most lethal weapons. Iraqi purchasing agents circled the globe, buying parts and technology for nuclear, biological, and missile development. Washington looked the other way; Western Europe did most of the selling; and only Israel raised the alarm.

Not by coincidence, a flood of information on Iraq's global purchasing network began to pour out of Israel, trying to grab the attention of intelligence agencies in the United States and western Europe.

Israel was particularly frustrated with America's response. There was little reaction when a report by Aman, Israel's military intelligence agency, noted in 1988 that Iraq—having ended its war with Iran in a draw—could now pursue its territorial claims against Kuwait. U.S. Army intelligence did take part in a joint research project with Aman, in early 1989, on the capabilities of Iraq's armed forces. But the Americans were working from a wholly different set of assumptions, seeing a rational Saddam who could be a force for stability, so Israel's conclusions were rejected.

"We had hard and bitter discussions about assessing the potential Iraqi threat," recalls a senior Israeli intelligence officer who participated in the data exchange with the United States. "We were saying that the Iraqi army was not demobilizing. We told them that government funds were not being transferred to Iraqi reconstruction projects, but continued to be used for military purposes.

"American intelligence—both the CIA and the army—believed that Iraq, after the war against Iran, was a more moderate place. We warned them that Iraq's nonconventional arms plans were at an advanced stage. The Americans thought that we were supersensitive and inclined to overdo things—like a 'cry-wolf' syndrome. They treated us like a bunch of eternal paranoids. I also think that they were afraid that our view of things included some manipulation of intelligence facts, that we were sneaking in some political bias to serve our interests."

The Americans were stuck with their preconceived notion that Saddam Hussein, their brutal but reliable dictator, would not upset the Middle East balance by boundless aggression.

On July 20, 1990, less than two weeks before the Iraqi invasion of Kuwait, Defense Minister Arens flew secretly to Washington. He was accompanied by his nation's top intelligence officers, General Amnon Shahak, head of Aman, and Shabtai Shavit, director of the Mossad. As an experienced case officer who ran networks of Iraqi informers, Shavit was in a particularly good position to impress the Americans with his knowledge of the inner works of Saddam's regime.

The Israelis met with their American counterparts—Secretary of Defense Dick Cheney, Central Intelligence Agency director William Webster, and senior army officers—and tried to convince them that the Iraqi threat was not limited to Israel but was tangible also for Arab states such as Saudi Arabia and Kuwait. Did the United States take the Israeli warnings seriously? While an American participant in the meeting argues that "Cheney pressed the CIA to step up its surveillance of Iraqi weapons procurement in Europe," a disappointed Arens has a different recollection: "The Americans did not take our warnings seriously."

A few more weeks would pass before the chill between the crisis monitors in Washington and Jerusalem would warm up. The White House and State Department thought that now, more than ever, the United States would need support in the moderate Arab world and thus should behave as though Israel were not a friend.

Cheney and his undersecretary, Paul Wolfowitz, on the other hand, saw a necessity to work with the Israelis instead of isolating them. Only on August 28, after delays and unconvincing excuses, did the Bush administration decide on coordination rather than isolation. On that day, a defense ministry delegation from Israel was secretly received at the Pentagon.

It seemed to be poetic justice that the delegation was led by David Ivri, a former air force general who sent his pilots to destroy Iraq's nuclear reactor in 1981. Ivri told Cheney that Israeli analysts assumed that if war were to break out, Iraq would attack Israel. The defense secretary ordered that Patriot missiles be sold to Israel, on favorable terms, to counter either missiles or warplanes flying in from Iraq. Israeli crews went to the United States for training with Patriots.

Since then, knowing that the Israeli warnings about Iraq had been right all along, the Americans started giving the Israelis the impression that their long-held hope of intimate strategic coordination was becoming a reality.

"In the months leading up to January, when the war broke out, we Israelis in the United States had a sense of elation," recalls a senior diplomat at the Israeli embassy in Washington. "All of a sudden, the Americans let us know that the military, political, and strategic interests of both countries were more or less identical."

"From the start of the crisis," says the intelligence officer, "we were in the Pentagon and at navy, air force and army headquarters almost every day. We exchanged information and assessments about the Iraqi army, its capability, and its operative plans."

Running parallel to these discussions of Iraq's military power came contingency planning. Through liaison officers of the Mossad and the CIA, opinions were exchanged on the possibility of destabilizing Saddam Hussein's regime—and even on getting rid of Saddam himself.

Another channel for operational details ran between the Israeli and American air forces. Here, as was revealed in a slip of the tongue by the U.S. Air Force chief of staff, General Michael Dugan, the Israelis provided a list of recommended targets in Iraq. Israel's advice was to bomb Saddam, his mistress, his family, and his top aides.

The Mossad also handed over an English translation of a personality profile of Saddam, advising that he was Iraq's sole decision-maker and would not hesitate to start a war. The Israelis were aware of the presidential ban on the CIA taking part in assassination plots, so it was they who came up with the idea of trying to hit the president and his aides—right at the start of a Gulf War—by targeting a motorcade or headquarters building.

But whatever the Israelis did to help the United States, they were annoyed with the Americans for always insisting that it be kept absolutely secret. And in December 1990, when Prime Minister Shamir visited Washington, all that really mattered to President Bush was extracting a promise that Israel would not stage a preemptive strike against Iraq. Shamir agreed but stressed that should Israel be struck by Iraqi bombers or missiles, he would reserve the right to retaliate.

Bush and his advisors, long wary of Shamir's promises, still feared that Israel might attack. On January 12, three days before expiry of a United Nations ultimatum for Iraqi withdrawal from Kuwait, Bush sent State Department envoy Lawrence Eagleburger and Pentagon official Wolfowitz to Tel Aviv to make sure.

Immediately upon landing at Ben-Gurion Airport, the Americans and their aides stepped into the cars that awaited them near the runway for a half-hour drive to Jerusalem to see Prime Minister Shamir. During the three-hour meeting, the U.S. request was strengthened into a blunt demand, contained in a letter from Bush to Shamir: Do not get involved in the fighting, not even in response to Iraqi provocation.

Eagleburger and Wolfowitz tried to convince the Israelis that the war, without them, would be more beneficial to their interests. One of their principal enemies, Iraq, would be severely damaged; and Israel would not have to put its own forces at risk. Eagleburger granted the Israelis only one exception: if Iraq used nonconventional arms. "We all understood that if they got hit by chemical weapons," he recalls, "not only would they respond but they should."

The talks were tough, and the atmosphere was tense. Shamir and Arens bristled at the bluntness and insisted on more detailed discussion of specific scenarios: What if an urban area were hit, with a multitude of Israeli casualties? What if a vital military base or industrial facility were damaged? Didn't Israel have its elementary right of self-defense?

Even though Eagleburger understood that right, his mission was to prevent its being exercised. He told the Israelis that the U.S. Air Force could do a better job, because the Americans were geared up for flying extended campaigns with around-the-clock refueling. "We are a superpower," he said.

The Israelis, although acknowledging it might be true, found his saying it to be arrogant and even provocative. They argued that their approach would be different, more "microscopic" and fully focused on eliminating Iraqi missiles.

Eagleburger realized he had ruffled feathers and was pleased that he had a proposal in his pocket that would soften the harsh reality. He made the most dramatic offer ever in U.S.-Israeli relations: an "aerial umbrella" in case Israel was attacked by Iraqi missiles. "I offered them U.S.-manned Patriot batteries, until their own Israeli-manned batteries would be up and running," he recalls. "But I was turned down. And I understood why: because the Israelis have always had the view that they would defend themselves."

However, the Israelis did embrace the American offer of a direct communications circuit between Arens's office and the Pentagon, specifically to relay messages if and when Iraq launched missiles westward. Israel did not have its own surveillance satellites, so any launch seen by America's "spies in the sky" would immediately be reported to Tel Aviv over the new circuit.

The Americans assigned the code name Hammer Rick to this communications system, and they stressed that the electronics would add a symbolic dimension to the special relationship between the two countries. The impression made was that this relationship, by meriting a "hot line," was as important as the one between Washington and Moscow.

Yet the question remained: What would be done if Israel were hit? Eagleburger and Wolfowitz promised that the U.S. Air Force would then act quickly and decisively against the missile sites in western Iraq.

Shamir, as the Americans recall, was bitter, saying: "You are treating us like some black sheep of the family that you want to pretend doesn't exist, like someone with a social disease."

Wolfowitz responded that while some U.S. officials might be acting that way, "Here is the president of the United States, for the first time in American history, offering to deploy American troops to protect Israel. This is a very public connection."

The American delegation returned home only partly satisfied. Eagleburger says he had not expected an immediate commitment by Israel not to retaliate, "but we did begin to talk about the things we were prepared to do for the Israelis if they got hit." He and Wolfowitz felt that they did, at least, secure Israel's agreement to what they defined as their backup plan: that should the Israelis decide to act on their own, they would consult with Washington beforehand.

The Israelis, on the other hand, were left heavy-hearted. As far as they were concerned, the "hot line," the proposed aerial umbrella, the commitment to spring into action against Iraqi missile bases, and other bonuses served mainly U.S. interests—namely, to prevent anything that might upset President Bush's plans.

It had become clear to Defense Minister Arens that rather than seeing Israel as a strategic asset, the U.S. saw it as a liability—at least in terms of the situation with Iraq. His aides could hear the frustration as he remarked: "The delegation came here to tie our hands!"

The Israelis were left, like the rest of the world, to guess when the United States would start bombing Iraq—a waiting game that ended just after midnight on January 17 when a message reached the defense ministry in Tel Aviv to the effect that a phone call from the American defense secretary was about to come in. Arens rushed over from his home in the affluent Savyon suburb. After speaking with Cheney for a few minutes on the new Hammer Rick system, Arens turned to his aides and said, "That's it, they're starting."

Nearly everyone in Israel's defense headquarters watched CNN's coverage of the bombing of Baghdad. The American government, that night, was stingy with information transferred to Israel. But the next day, some detailed reports did come in from the Pentagon. These stated—as reassurance to the Israelis—that among the first targets of the U.S. attack had been an airbase in western Iraq and the Scud missiles stationed nearby. The Pentagon, reflecting Washington's general euphoria, said that Iraq's capacity to launch missiles toward Israel had been impaired.

But that capacity was real, and it was used, barely twenty-four hours after the first U.S. raid on Baghdad. At around 2 A.M. on January 18, Tel Aviv and Haifa were hit by a salvo of Scud missiles. Advance warning had hardly been helpful at all: It had been only around half a minute before the Scuds crashed into Israel's urban centers that civil-defense units received the Hammer Rick alert so they could sound the sirens.

Of course, the fact that missile launches could be detected at all was a technological miracle. Two American satellites equipped with infrared telescopes and flying twenty-four thousand miles above the earth, somewhere above the Indian Ocean, detected the heat of missiles being fired from western Iraq. These signals were transmitted to two ground stations in Australia and Colorado, manned by U.S. Air Force personnel. They reported the missile launch to Washington, where the Pentagon, in turn, relayed it to Israel via the Hammer Rick phone system. The whole process took up to three minutes, leaving Israel barely enough time to alert its citizens.

"The alarm found me at home in bed," Arens recalls. "I jumped out, got dressed and into the car. I didn't want to waste precious time, so I decided not to call my driver and just get there on my own. The roads were nearly empty, and the trip took about a quarter of an hour. As I was driving, I heard explosions and I got the impression missiles were falling everywhere around me. Today I can admit that, contrary to instructions, I didn't put on my gas mask.

"I got to my office, but the guard wouldn't let me in. Guards that night had been given very serious orders to step up security. The guard, who was wearing his gas mask, did not recognize me. So I went to another gate and got in through a side entrance. Meanwhile some of my aides and army officials had arrived, and they started to collect reports that were coming in from the field."

It was a tense night for anyone in Tel Aviv. In the south of the city, some residential gas cylinders exploded, and the monitoring equipment used by rescue teams picked up signals that they mistakenly identified as nerve gas.

Only a few minutes after the Scuds slammed into Israel, news agencies and live TV broadcasts were reporting that it had been a chemical attack, and retaliation by Israel was expected momentarily.

The Americans, naturally, were alarmed. U.S. intelligence detected Israel's air force apparently preparing for action. In Washington, Secretary of State James Baker and Defense Secretary Cheney placed calls to Shamir and Arens but suffered a few more minutes of concern when the lines were busy. But as it was becoming clear that Israel had actually been attacked "only" with conventional warheads, the two Americans urged again that Israel keep its cool.

In the hours that followed, Baker and Cheney exchanged several telephone calls with Shamir and Arens. Anxious to please the Israelis, the Americans promised to press ahead with efforts to locate both the mobile and fixed Iraqi launchers. Yet they were speaking without checking that the American commander of the war effort, General H. Norman Schwarzkopf, and his air force units felt the same urgency about Scud hunting.

Arens, for his part, pointed out the seriousness of the situation from Israel's point of view. For the first time since its independence in 1948, the nation's cities were under Arab attack. He dismayed Baker by telling him that there would be a retaliation, asking that the United States arrange with Israel's Arab neighbors—Syria, Jordan, or Saudi Arabia—that airspace be cleared for Israeli warplanes and troop-carrying helicopters.

Baker, in a mixture of imploring, persuasion, and arm twisting that would become a U.S. pattern during the war, asked Arens not to do it. There was the clear implication that Israel should not dare to incur America's anger. Baker's fear was that an Israeli attack would lead to rapid escalation of the war, with the Arab allies threatening to quit the coalition, so that the United States would have to rush into a ground offensive in which many Americans might die.

As a last resort, the Americans reluctantly suggested to Arens that if Israel felt no choice but to attack Iraq, ground-to-ground Jericho missiles should be used. Some U.S. officials thought this would satisfy the Jewish state's desire for revenge. They assumed that Israel had the capability, largely because in the previous thirty months it had launched two experimental satellites into orbit using a variation of the Jericho. U.S. intelligence estimated that Israel's homemade missile now had an extended range of 900 miles, nearly twice the distance to Baghdad. The Soviet Union saw that even its own territory could be targeted and issued a warning to Israel in 1989.

Arens, however, rejected the American suggestion out of hand. The United States did not seem to know that the new Jericho was not yet fully operational and thus Israel did not have a ready option for an unmanned strike on Baghdad, the only target that might satisfy a quest for vengeance. But in any event, the Israelis were not thinking in the bloodthirsty terms of extracting an eye for an eye. They were confronting the genuine need to suppress an enemy weapons system. Israel's military doctrine called for specific action against the Scud missile launchers; firing long-range missiles against launchers hidden in the sand dunes of western Iraq would be an absurd waste.

In a subsequent telephone call, Cheney was preparing to renew the offer to send Patriot missiles with American crews to Israel. But to his surprise, Arens had consulted with Shamir and was now asking for the Patriots. What had changed in the five days since Israel rejected the offer? Israeli leaders had known that their cities might be hit, but the reality felt harsher and less acceptable than the expectation—especially when Shamir concluded that retaliation would do little good. He was left feeling that he had to do something to appease the shock and anger of the public.

Although Israel's military was deeply dubious about the ability of the Patriots to defend cities against missiles, the intended effect was that of a placebo to calm the Israeli public. Arens had higher hopes for the Arrow antimissile missile, being funded by the United States as an ingredient in the military friendship, but the system was not nearly ready.

The prime minister may have understood that accepting the Patriots would also mean accepting America's advice not to retaliate against Iraq. But Arens and some of his top commanders still hoped for the opportunity to conduct a military operation, if only to preserve Israel's policy of deterrence and to remind Israeli citizens and Arab foes that the Jewish state cannot be attacked with impunity.

Shamir managed to calm them, however. And later in the day, after further discussions, it was decided to do nothing until the Patriots could arrive the next day. Israel would wait, in the hope that the Scud attack had been a one-time nightmare.

It certainly was not, however. Tel Aviv was hit again: on Friday night, January 18, when hundreds of thousands of Israeli families were sitting down for their traditional Sabbath meal; and then for a third time on Saturday morning. This one was worse. One missile came down on an air-raid shelter in south Tel Aviv and totally destroyed it. It was merely good fortune that the shelter had been empty. Another entire warhead fell into a Tel Aviv residential area but failed to explode. These miracles—and flaws in Soviet missile technology—helped to minimize the damage. After three attacks, there was only one fatality. But the psychological blow to Israel's society, politicians, and defense mythology was unprecedented.

Many of the one million residents of greater Tel Aviv—nearly one-fourth of Israel's entire population—panicked as their homes and businesses were turned into a war zone. Almost half left to seek shelter with relatives, in hotels, or anywhere else outside the main target area.

David Dinkins, who was then mayor of New York City, recalls being at Israeli consul Uri Savir's home for a gathering honoring the memory of Martin Luther King, Jr. "I was speaking at the lectern, and I noticed an aide handed Uri a note and he stiffened but didn't do anything. When I finished my speech, he told me and the others that Scud missiles had fallen on Tel Aviv. We were all concerned; and in that room filled with 100 percent African Americans and Jews, we all joined hands and sang 'We Shall Overcome.' It was a very, very moving experience, one that I shall never ever forget."

In Washington, American policymakers felt the war was going well. The bombing campaign against Iraq seemed to be a success, and one of the few fears was that Israel could ruin the whole shooting match by intervening. Therefore, the United States stepped up its intelligence-gathering focused on Israel.

Most of the surveillance was electronic, such as eavesdropping on Israel's radio, phone, fax, and other communication systems. That activity is in the purview of the National Security Agency, which uses powerful satellites, listening posts in Great Britain, and specially equipped aircraft and ships. At its secret British installations, NSA employs Hebrew-speaking specialists to intercept, transcribe, and when necessary decipher Israeli communications. Before and during the Gulf War, NSA intensified its attempts to find out what Israel's leadership was thinking and planning to do.

It was from such eavesdropping that the United States grew increasingly convinced that Israel was indeed on the verge of taking military action. And then the Israelis themselves informed Washington of that. It was early Saturday morning,

January 19, that the special Hammer Rick line was activated by General David Ivri at the defense ministry in Tel Aviv. Paul Wolfowitz took the call, stunned to hear Ivri say, "We will be going in with both air and ground forces, and I want to give you the coordinates."

"I'll take the information," the American undersecretary said, "but this should not be taken as U.S. agreement to what you're doing. That's got to be the subject of higher level consultation."

"Well then," said Ivri, backing off, "I won't give you the information." That was the closest the Israelis came to retaliating. Shamir had not made a definite decision, but his cabinet would be meeting within a few hours and the Bush administration decided intervention at the highest level was required.

The president himself was mobilized. Bush made two hurried phone calls to Shamir, calls that were transferred to the prime minister's home as he was not in the office at the time. The president repeated his concern that Israeli action could cause the anti-Iraq coalition to crumble.

"Shamir was under heavy pressure from some cabinet ministers who were pushing for military action," his aide Yossi Achimeir recalls. "On the other hand, he understood America's insistence on Israeli abstention. His heart told him to operate against Iraq, but his brain told him to desist. To the opposing ministers, he said: 'What's the use of Israeli action in Iraq? All you'll do is anger the Americans. And why should we be doing that if, after all, the U.S. is fighting our enemy and thereby helping Israeli interests?' Israel and the United States are allies, but such relations are put to the test when one side is asked to help the other in times of distress."

The Israelis—the side being asked for the big favor of passivity—felt they, however, were the ones in distress, a feeling shared by senior politicians and military men. Shamir called an emergency meeting of his war cabinet in Tel Aviv—one of the most important and dramatic meetings in Israel's history. It was January 19, a few hours after the third Scud attack on Saturday morning, and two religious ministers were granted special permission by rabbis to travel on the Sabbath.

The highest drama came when a small group of ministers and army officers demanded immediate retaliation. Some of them were even talking about possibly using nuclear weapons.

Israel has never defined what its nuclear strategy might be. The country has not even admitted possessing a nuclear arsenal. But most Israeli strategists assume that the secret weapon was developed as a weapon of last resort. The Jewish state's very existence would have to be in danger, before it would unsheath this most awful of all arms. In the meantime, selective leaks are meant to ensure that Israel's nuclear arms provide deterrence by frightening its Arab enemies.

The possibility of actually using the nuclear option had only arisen once before: during the first three days of the Yom Kippur War of 1973, when the Syrian and Egyptian armies had taken Israel by surprise. This time, during the Gulf crisis, Israel's existence was not under such threat, but the ministers who called for discussion of the unspeakable option were worried by the loss of Israeli deterrence.

They said the warnings that Israel had issued before the war—to the effect that Iraq would suffer severe punishment if it dared to attack Israel—had not helped. Now these ministers believed a nuclear strike should be considered so that the whole world would understand the message: No one can get away with attacking Israeli cities!

They were overruled, however, by Prime Minister Shamir, Defense Minister Arens, and other ministers who rejected the nuclear option outright. "Israel cannot afford to use nuclear power," said one of them. "You have to think about the day after the bomb. What will happen then? How are we supposed to live on as the only nation to have used this horrible weapon since the United States in Japan? The idea is inconceivable."

Israel did, however, heighten the alert status of its air force immediately after the first missile attack. Their bombs were conventional, but pilots in full flying gear sat ready in their cockpits, awaiting government decisions.

Army planners suggested two broad options. First, the air force could be used against strategic targets in Iraq. Hundreds of fighters and bombers would be needed, and they would have to fly through the air space of hostile Arab states—a mission that could be very costly. An even greater risk was getting into dogfights with U.S. pilots.

The second option was to fly Israeli commando units into western Iraq with the aim of locating Scud missile sites and destroying them. This could be even more dangerous, however, risking the lives of thousands of crack troops.

It was ironic that Shamir—the prime minister with the toughest and most irreconcilable image of all Israel's leaders—actually made one of the most surprising and fateful decisions of Israel's history: For the first time, after undergoing a serious attack, Israel did not respond.

What helped him in this decision—and the same dilemma kept bubbling to the surface throughout the war—was the fact that the casualties from the Scuds were far fewer than feared. "Shamir admitted," his loyal aide Achimeir recalls, "that if, God forbid, there would have been a hit causing the deaths of dozens of civilians, he would not have been able to keep his cool."

Just hours after the war cabinet met on January 19, Tel Aviv residents had something to cheer about in the sky above: forty huge C-5A Galaxy transports flew in from Germany, filled with Patriots and patriots. U.S. Army missile crews, commanded by Lieutenant Colonel Harry Krimkowitz, fanned out to locations up and down the Mediterranean coast. "We were told we were going to southwest Asia, and when we found out that meant Israel it was an awe-inspiring experience," Krimkowitz recalls. "I felt a tremendous amount of responsibility, because this was the first time Israel had allowed anyone from outside their country to assist in their defense."

Newly trained Israeli missile crews worked with the Americans, and without any publicity, Dutch soldiers were assigned to Patriot positions surrounding Jerusalem. But because the holy city was never attacked the Dutch spent the war watching the horizon while sipping beer.

The U.S. crews were far busier, firing for the first time on Tuesday night—and missing two incoming Scuds—and then scoring a hit on Wednesday. "It was a real feeling of happiness, exhilaration, and tremendous pride," says Krimkowitz. "The other soldiers and I were thrilled that our training paid off and we were allowed to make a difference in reversing Israeli fears of Saddam's terrorism. The mayor of Haifa brought us champagne and cake to celebrate." In the eight weeks of the war, however, the Patriots' record continued to be spotty.

In fact, later analyses by the United States and Israel found that from a military point of view—as opposed to the psychological value—the Patriots were nearly useless. As former defense minister Rabin said, "The Patriot has great PR, but its intercepting results are very poor." Senior military officers and most government ministers were well aware that the American-made weapon was designed to shoot down airplanes, not missiles. It could not cope effectively with high-speed trajectories.

When put to the test, although this was revealed only after the war, the Patriot caused a lot of damage—not only to the Scuds, however, but also to buildings and people on the ground. This was because the midair encounter usually ended up creating more debris, spread over a large radius. Some Pentagon officials, however, believe that the Patriots did destroy several Scuds and saved lives.

Whatever their success rate, the mere fact that Americans were firing these missiles represented a watershed in relations between the two countries. Give us political and moral support, plus ammunition—the Israelis always used to say—and we'll do the job ourselves. The Gulf War was the exception.

The extraordinary arrival of the Patriots was followed, the next day, by Eagleburger and Wolfowitz—on their second visit to ensure that Israel did not attack Iraq. They were greeted by "a lot of chest-thumping on the part of officials and military people," as Eagleburger recalls.

To enable Israel's planes to attack, Arens repeatedly requested the electronic codes—the IFF, or Identity Friend or Foe—emitted by modern warplanes so that other planes and ground monitors can distinguish between allied and enemy aircraft. He wanted the Americans to "deconflict," military jargon for stepping aside.

The commander of the Israeli air force, General Avihu Bin-Nun, tried to persuade the U.S. delegation by saying, "My nightmare is of an aerial *Liberty*," referring to the American spy ship mistakenly attacked by Israel in the confusion of the 1967 war. "I have problems sleeping at night because of one reason only: the absence of coordination. All I want is for us to sit down and coordinate."

General Bin-Nun asked what would happen if his planes did go into action. As Eagleburger recalls, "I told the Israelis this: That in the end we were not going to deconflict. We were not going to be prepared to have them say, 'We're going to be flying flights at such-and-such an hour or such-and-such a place; will you get your aircraft out of the way?' The danger was if we weren't prepared to do that, the Israelis run the real risk of getting shot down by our people.

"So that was the card that we had all along. And we, in the end, had to play it. But my sense of it is: There was not a lot of anguish when we said that was our position. I really don't think they wanted to do it. Shamir, Arens, all of them spoke as if they wanted to retaliate. But it is my belief that most of the really senior Israeli officials, in the end, didn't want to become involved. And I provided them with a reason not to be."

For the duration of the conflict, a syndrome was taking hold. And both sides identified the symptoms without curing them. The Israelis continued to cry in agony that they must act, but the United States knew they did not truly intend to. President Bush held them off by publicly promising "the darndest search and destroy mission that's ever been undertaken" for the Scuds in western Iraq. But both sides knew that it would not be possible for all launchers to be eliminated.

Knowing what was going on was not enough to keep the Israelis from getting angry. Much of their ire was directed at the allied commander, General Schwarzkopf. In one of his first daily briefings in Saudi Arabia, the general declared that his pilots had destroyed most of the Scud sites in Iraq's western sector, but this proved obviously premature to Israelis under attack. Then, commenting on the first few missile attacks on Israel, he said that the Scuds' damage was no worse than the havoc wreaked by thunderstorms over Georgia.

"From these words, together with the fact that the missiles kept coming down on us," says Dan Meridor, then minister of justice and a close aide to Shamir, "we got the feeling that the Americans related to our complaints like they would to a bunch of hysterics."

Defense Minister Arens felt the insensitivity in person. On February 11, he flew to Washington for a quick, half-day visit with President Bush, Secretary of State Baker, and Secretary of Defense Cheney. The now-familiar ritual was played out, yet again. Arens asked for clearance to act independently against

Iraq, and the Americans gave a firm "no" while promising to continue their bombardment of Iraqi missile launchers.

It was during a meeting with Baker that Arens received word that a Scud had hit Savyon, his neighborhood. "The message was that a missile had fallen in my street," Arens recalls. "I left the meeting and Baker's secretary helped me phone my wife. My wife told me that the Scud had not exploded in our street, though it had been nearby, causing cracks in our walls. Then I went back to the room and continued the talks. I had a hard time concentrating, and I kept thinking of my wife and home."

Baker, however, did not react in the slightest way to the fact that the house of his guest, Israel's defense minister, had been hit. It apparently made a difference that Baker had not shared the experience of his deputy, Eagleburger, who himself had to don a gas mask and sit in a sealed room during an Iraqi missile attack.

Israelis, who had all shared that experience, felt something must be wrong with their fabled alliance with the United States. The main reason they had kept out of the war was because America kept saying it would eliminate the Scud threat. But the missiles kept hitting Israel, even in the last week of the war at the end of February.

The recriminations began as soon as the war was over. Israeli officials and generals blamed the United States for not having done enough to remove the Scud threat. The main accuser was General Bin-Nun, the commander of Israel's air force. "The Americans did not manage to put a stop to the Scuds because they simply didn't try," said the Israeli general angrily.

Bin-Nun claimed that devoting 3,000 allied sorties to western Iraq, out of 110,000—less than 3 percent—was insufficient, and he claimed Israel could have done better. "It would have taken us about four days, not forty, to make three thousand sorties. But there was the problem of coordination with the Americans. We couldn't act freely there without coordination or, at least, their consent to leave our airspace." The United States never did consent.

What Bin-Nun did not reveal was that Israeli flyers, who had secretly practiced identifying Scud sites, had learned that it was no easy task. Dummy launchers were hidden at various locations in Israel's Negev Desert, and one pilot who participated in the exercises says: "It was like trying to find a needle in a haystack."

The Israeli tactic would have been either to bomb from low altitude or to send in commandoes. Behind-the-lines operations requiring surgical precision have been an Israeli specialty for over forty years. Twice during the Gulf War, once at the beginning and again near the end, the Israelis planned a commando operation: Helicopters and transport planes would carry special forces and drop them into western Iraq for a few days of locating launchers and destroying them.

They were held back, both times, by American pressure. "If you don't let us do this," Arens said to Cheney during their Washington meeting toward the end of the war, "then at least do it yourselves." U.S. and British commando activity was stepped up.

Once the war was over, various agencies of the Israeli government studied, from various angles, the enigma: Why had the Americans not paralyzed Iraq's missile capability? From the military point of view, the conclusion was that the United States and its allies had not tried as hard as they could have in western Iraq. Israel's air force believed that Schwarzkopf's staff gave Scud missile launchers only low priority. Some analysts found their explanation in the U.S. Air Force doctrine that "no target is worth an airplane." But others believed they saw evil intent.

There were suspicions that President Bush had signaled his forces not to worry about western Iraq because he wanted Israel to be reminded of its dependence. Israelis could even find circumstantial evidence for their theory in Bush's later contention that the Gulf War made Israeli-Palestinian peace possible. "By crushing Saddam's vaunted army," he declared, "we helped make Israel more secure and in the process we facilitated the direct talks in the Middle East."

Israeli skeptics speculated that, like Nixon in 1973, Bush wished to see a weakened Israel. Perhaps he felt that a partially humiliated Israel would be more likely to make political concessions in the future. Israelis raising this argument admit that while U.S. interests would not be served if Israel were heavily damaged and then retaliated, Bush might be interested in having Israel stripped of some of its confidence.

However, Bush administration officials insist that to pacify Israel—for the sake of a smooth victory over Iraq for everyone's sake—they kept putting pressure on the military to try harder to eliminate the Scuds. The president and his national security advisors urged General Colin L. Powell, the chairman of the Joint Chiefs of Staff, to make sure that Iraq's missile launchers were a high-priority target. "General Powell was very concerned," one of his aides recalls, and was constantly on the telephone with General Schwarzkopf.

However, allied commander Schwarzkopf strongly denies the allegations made by Israelis and some Washington officials that he did not share the worry over Scuds. "Washington was very, very concerned about the Scud attacks, and we were too. Some people said, 'Holy smokes! You're sending Patriots to Israel and allocating planes to search for every launcher?'

"But I was not annoyed," Schwarzkopf adds. "I clearly understood the strategic imperative of doing everything we could to defend Israel.

"I will never forget the first night those missiles were fired. 'Oh shit,' we thought, 'this will put additional pressure on the coalition in the conduct of the war,' which was already tough enough. I was more concerned when the first Scuds were launched at Israel than at Riyadh, and I was sitting in Riyadh. I realized the strategic impact of missiles hitting Israel could be much greater than the impact of missiles hitting on top of my head!"

Some senior Pentagon officials had the impression that Schwarzkopf resented having his arm twisted to spend more time and resources hunting for Scud launchers. "He kept complaining about political interference," one official recalls.

The general, now retired, does say that Washington made at least one suggestion that he found ludicrous: that Israeli liaison officers be stationed with him in Saudi Arabia to help direct the Scud hunt. And when Israeli night-vision goggles, mobile bridges, mine plows, and other military gear were shipped in to fortify Schwarzkopf's coalition, he made certain that all Hebrew labels were "rubbed off," because if the Saudis "had found the Israeli markings, they would not have used the equipment"—even if they discreetly knew about the help from the Jewish state.

He says he was also briefed by Washington on the conflicting opinions in Israel, both among the public and in the leadership. "The majority of the Israeli people did not want their military to retaliate, and the majority of the government didn't want to. Maybe there was a sector in the defense ministry that wanted to retaliate to justify the expenditures on defense, which is understandable."

His own analysis, as the supreme commander, of the overall battle plan persuaded him that Israel must be made to feel secure enough to stay out of the war. But he always remembered the central aim: to cripple Iraq. And his honest opinion was and is that "Scud missiles were not strategically significant; they were just a random attack."

So, Schwarzkopf explains, "there was a tradeoff. Hunting Scuds would slow down another part of the campaign. Our other time schedules were diverted by this." But considering that the war aims included keeping Israel out so as to keep the Arab allies in the coalition, Schwarzkopf was prepared for the tradeoff. It did, however, annoy the U.S. Air Force.

"It was always disconcerting to the air force when I called them up and said we'd have to direct more planes to the Scud hunting," he says, recalling that the commander of the air campaign, Lieutenant General Charles A. Horner, typically replied: "For Christ's sake, sir, we had those planes scheduled for the strategic missions."

The truth, somewhere between the Israeli suspicions and the American justifications, might be found in the Checkmate project. It was originally an air force unit planning air-to-air combat like playing chess against a computer. In 1990, before Iraq invaded Kuwait, this group of air force strategists was assigned to conduct a study on the effect of precision, high-technology bombing on ground targets. Some civilians, including Edward Luttwak of the Center for Strategic and International Studies, took part.

Luttwak suggested to the unit—pure luck, he says—that Iraq be chosen as the sample target. After the invasion of Kuwait, the Checkmate team was diverted to planning a real, rather than theoretical, bombing campaign. This group of analysts selected targets for General Horner, who was under Schwarzkopf's command.

Once the bombing began in January 1991, the planners faced a problem. Although the U.S., British, and other air forces mustered a huge fleet of planes, they had no more than two hundred state-of-the-art bombers for precision attacks.

Checkmate's main aim was to destroy Iraq's industrial and communications infrastructure, focusing on its military forces and nonconventional weapons program. Scud missile sites in western Iraq were a low priority for the basic mission: They posed no serious military threat, and many flight hours would have to be expended on finding each one.

"It looks as though there were a lot of sorties in the war," Luttwack explains. "But most of them were what could be called 'garbage.' Only the precision bombing was of real value."

After the second and third Scud attacks on Israel, the Checkmate planners, Horner, and Schwarzkopf were put under tremendous political pressure to make Scud launchers a high priority. Although all the fixed launch sites were hit and the mobile launchers were intensively hunted on the first weekend that Israel was hit by Scuds, Iraq kept firing missiles—although with decreasing frequency. The Checkmate team decided, without telling their political masters, that it would be useless to tie up sophisticated bombers in a fruitless search.

When Baker and Cheney repeatedly told Shamir and Arens that the U.S. Air Force was taking care of the Scud missiles, the reassurances were swelled by exaggeration. At least once, after Israel was attacked and Washington gave orders to step up the Scud hunts, the Checkmate team advised Horner to assign only two airplanes to the task. Even when presidents want something done, the chain of command can become kinked along the way.

Both U.S. and Israeli strategists knew that the best way to hunt for Scud launchers was by sending special forces and low-altitude Apache helicopters on search-and-destroy missions. American officers feared that Apaches could be shot down, but U.S. and British commandoes were sent into the area toward the end of the war. They suffered casualties, including several British dead, but their behind-the-lines daring did yield the destruction of some mobile launchers.

Perhaps because the truth about motives, action, and inaction would touch the raw nerves of both Americans and Israelis, it will never be aired fully in public. But the lack of understanding between the two allies during their ultimate challenge was stunning.

Despite acting as friends in deed, by going out of their way to cooperate with the United States, Israel's leaders felt that they had little to show for it. And they were surely friends in need. There were hundreds of thousands of Jewish immigrants to be absorbed, with more arriving from the Soviet Union even during the Scud attacks. Now, in addition, there was war damage. "Of course we are suffering," said Shamir's aide Achimeir, "and we expect we will be helped by the Americans."

Even the liberal newspaper *Ha'aretz,* usually a voice of opposition to the government, agreed that Israel's restraint "gives it the moral and practical right to demand a significant material increase from the United States." The problem was that the demander was the finance minister, Yitzhak Moda'i.

Eagleburger, while visiting Israel, was willing to meet with Moda'i and seemed open to rewarding Israeli behavior with some compensation. After all, the U.S. role as Israel's financial backer was another important layer of the alliance. Why exclude the topic during the Gulf crisis? Still, Eagleburger says he was "horrified" by the size of the invoice from Moda'i.

"He presented me with something like a $13 billion bill!" the American diplomat recalls. "It was taken very badly in Washington. Put it in the mind-set of the time: American troops are going to get killed. Don't ask us now—not only to take on that burden—but also to pay you millions or billions of dollars for the glory of getting our troops killed." Not to be totally negative at such a critical time, however, Eagleburger told the Israelis that their request would be considered after the fighting was over.

As the smoke of war cleared in March 1991, U.S.-Israel relations had done an about-face. Before the war, they had seemed to be at their finest hour, yet now they returned to a sour and ugly time.

A profound crisis was in the making. Operation Desert Storm and its aftermath proved to be a crossroads in relations between the two countries. By the end of 1991, it would be the United States *versus* Israel.

CHAPTER TWENTY-ONE

No Guarantees

Israel's best friends in America sent their human wave into action on the morning of September 12, 1991. Their deployment synchronized by all the leading Jewish organizations working together, over 1,200 citizens—mostly Jews, but also many Christians—fanned out through the corridors of the Dirksen, Russell, and Hart Senate office buildings and the Cannon, Longworth, and Rayburn House office buildings.

Almost all of them had appointments to see three or four congressmen and senators, almost always representing their own home states. The constituents would breakfast together at 8:30, start with a 10 o'clock meeting, hurry to another at 11, then stop to chat with friends and colleagues in the hallway before lunching on Capitol Hill and moving on to an afternoon session or two.

Working from briefing papers churned out by the various

organizations, they made nearly identical points in support of Israel's request for U.S. loan guarantees that would make it affordable to borrow $10 billion over the coming five years.

"It's a humanitarian project," one would say. "Almost a million Jews are leaving the Soviet Union for Israel, and we've all seen the pictures of the 40,000 Jews who've escaped starvation in Ethiopia by coming to their spiritual homeland. Homes must be built and jobs created for these refugees."

"And besides," another might chime in, "this won't cost the U.S. government a penny! Israel has always repaid its loans, so the guarantee will never have to be used." Their briefing sheets said Israel was even willing to pay the small percentage of the $10 billion—known as "scoring"—that federal regulations would require Congress to set aside in case of default.

What these amateur lobbyists, the front-line troops in the battle for U.S. aid to Israel, did not know was that their marching orders had been issued by Prime Minister Yitzhak Shamir—based on the mistaken notion that Congress would override President George Bush's refusal to grant the loan guarantees immediately and unconditionally.

That late summer day in Washington marked the beginning of a bitter dispute over Israel's settlements in the West Bank and Gaza Strip. Shamir accused the Bush administration of holding humanitarian aid hostage. The White House charged that Shamir was endangering hopes of a Middle East peace, for the sake of Jewish settlements. Within fourteen months the clash would contribute to the political downfall of both Bush and Shamir.

The Israeli premier made his September blunder on the advice of one of his loyalists in the U.S. capital, the Israeli embassy's liaison with the Senate, Yoram Ettinger. He had been in Washington for two years, and embassy staffers who had been there even longer feared that his unbending Likud ideology—

believing with every beat of his heart that Israel's security depended on keeping the West Bank—was blinding him to political realities in America.

Ettinger, in turn, was egged on in his belief that Bush would cave in to a pro-Israel Congress by an American with whom the embassy often coordinated lobbying efforts: AIPAC's research director Steve Rosen, who had become the power and the brain behind the throne sat upon by executive director Tom Dine.

Together, Dine and Rosen had turned the pro-Israel lobby into a bodybuilder strengthening its muscles by exercising them. Sometimes, they believed, it's worth having a fight just for the sake of keeping the organization fit and alert. AIPAC might not win them all, but it had to confront every test with the absolute certainty that it would.

Proud to be muscular, brimming with confidence, and increasingly well financed by an expanded roll of members as it entered the 1990s, AIPAC had learned lessons and adjusted tactics after the AWACS debacle of 1981.

The pro-Israel lobby now had offices and activists dotted around the country. It was training students; and it was both charming and pressuring politicians at the state level as well as national. But in one important tactical change—the "executive branch lobbying" that was largely Rosen's concept—AIPAC was finding it had to reverse course.

The idea of dropping in on the White House and State Department—a preserve that had previously belonged to the Conference of Presidents of Major American Jewish Organizations—worked fine for AIPAC when Ronald Reagan was president. Reagan was pro-Israel, and talking to his administration was usually pleasant and fruitful. But Bush and his secretary of state, James Baker, were perceived by Israel's supporters as very hostile.

In the eight Reagan years, says an Israeli diplomat intimately involved in talks with the United States, "you didn't have the feeling that he was a president who lost any sleep over the lack of a peace process in the Middle East." But now it had high priority—given new impetus by a sudden change that was effected, ironically, by Israel's two great friends, Reagan and Shultz.

After months of U.S. pressure, the head of the Palestine Liberation Organization, Yasser Arafat, finally said the magic words in December 1988: He recognized Israel's right to exist and renounced terrorism. Reagan and Shultz immediately recognized the PLO and launched political discussions. Why did they make this U-turn? Shultz explains in his memoirs: "We really have no choice. If the P.L.O. meets our conditions, we have to honor our commitment to start a dialogue. We win, I told the President. Once again in the Reagan presidency a firm policy has caused others to meet conditions set out by the United States."

But the Israelis lost and felt betrayed by their best friends. The truth of the matter was, as Shamir and his advisors saw it, that the United States certainly had a choice. It could have found excuses, as it always had since 1975, to snub the PLO. But even Israel's most ardent supporters in any administration saw that Shamir would not make concessions for peace—not with the PLO and not with any Arab state. He distrusted them all and was determined to keep the West Bank.

As lame ducks shorn of reelection concerns, Reagan and Shultz decided that the United States should talk to the PLO. They coordinated the move with the incoming administration. Bush and Baker were delighted, because upon taking office the very next month they rolled up their sleeves and got to work in the Middle East without feeling bound by old taboos.

Lawrence J. (Larry) Smith, a Florida Democrat and one of the most reliable pro-Israel members of Congress at the time, recalls that Israeli officials were shaken by the realization that Reagan's vice president would not be Reagan's clone. "They suddenly saw people like John Sununu, Brent Scowcroft, and Dick Darman in the White House, who are strongly anti-Israel. And Jim Baker started out as an unknown quantity to them, with no background in foreign policy and hardly any ties with the Jewish community. Israel probably would have been more comfortable if Michael Dukakis had won the presidency, coming from Massachusetts where there are a lot of Jews and having a Jewish wife."

It was against this already rocky background that Yitzhak Shamir made his first, get-acquainted visit to the White House in April 1989. Unlike Begin, who was happy to engage in unrehearsed verbal and philosophical jousting, Shamir prepared carefully by clutching the same kind of briefing cards favored by American presidents.

It turned out that Bush and Shamir, each with his set of typed cards, had a clash that set the tone for their entire relationship. "We were astonished by the power with which Bush raised the settlements issue," one Shamir aide recalls. "Settlements were a sleeping issue," says another, "and suddenly we were slapped in the face."

The president explained that it was his strong opinion that building settlements prejudged the future of the West Bank and Gaza. This, said Bush, gave the Arabs the impression that there was nothing to negotiate, thus dooming peace talks. So Israel, he said, had to stop.

Shamir became nervous and tried to explain, in effect, his party's ideology: "Mr. President, we are committed to the Camp David accords, but settlements are not an obstacle to peace. Just as Arabs are living among Jews in Israel, Jews can live among Arabs."

But Bush kept pressing on the settlements issue and said it was harming U.S.-Israel relations. Shamir then uttered five words that the White House would long hold against him: "It won't be a problem."

With a kind of wishful thinking that ignored Likud party ideology, Bush and his team assumed that meant that the pace of building Jewish outposts would decline. They interpreted Shamir's reassuring tone as respect for the views and sensitivities of the president. To Bush, being respected was very important. And he was livid when he concluded that Israel was not respecting him.

The Americans—by sending officials out from their Tel Aviv embassy and Jerusalem consulates, and also by using spy satellites to photograph settlements in the West Bank—found that construction continued apace. Now the Israelis and their alliance with the United States were in trouble. While Reagan had been disinterested in details and always thought the best of Israel, Bush was asking for all the data and came to believe the worst.

For Bush and Shamir, it was a case of hate at first sight. Never in the history of relations between the two countries was there such antipathy—true emotional dislike—between their heads of government. Even between Eisenhower and Ben-Gurion things were not so bad.

Underlining the misunderstanding after that first meeting at the White House, Shamir boasted to his aides that he had persuaded Bush of the necessity to hold territory. "Have you ever seen a prime minister talking like that with a president?" he asked proudly. "This is my way of representing Israel's interests!" Shamir was always puzzled as to why his personal chemistry with Bush was so bad.

The very next month the prime minister launched a diplomatic preemptive strike by announcing the "Shamir Peace Plan." Before the United States might try to compel Israel to talk to the Palestinians regarding the West Bank and Gaza, Shamir thought it better to offer to do so—on his terms. While refusing to speak to the PLO, rejected by Israelis as a terrorist group out to destroy the Jewish state, Shamir called for "free,

democratic elections" to choose Palestinian delegates "to negotiate an interim period of self-governing administration." From
Israel's point of view, either the intifada uprising would stop
for the sake of elections, or more likely nothing could be organized but the United States would have to credit Israel for
trying.

Secretary of State Baker responded, however, by personally
taking up the challenge of forming a Palestinian delegation.
Working with Egypt's help, after abandoning any hope of an
election, U.S. diplomats drew up lists of potential negotiators.
Shamir then found fault with almost every Palestinian on the
lists: Several were considered too close to the PLO, and others
living in east Jerusalem were not accepted by Israel as West
Bankers.

To the Israelis, who always felt their most vulnerable when
peace talks were nearest, Bush and Baker were downright insensitive. "All the time they were hurting us with declarations," recalls Ehud Olmert, a cabinet minister and confidant to
Shamir, referring to United Nations condemnations of Israeli
behavior and statements that designated the formerly Arab half
of Jerusalem as part of the territories. "Bush could be aggressive and cruel."

They were even insulting the one minister in the Likud party
who used to be the Reagan administration's favorite: Moshe
Arens. "They humiliated Misha," says Olmert, "as though he
couldn't understand what they were telling him." That was in
March 1990, when a mixed Likud-Labor cabinet was dead-
locked over U.S. proposals for selecting Palestinian delegates.
Arens, who had just been in Washington, declared that Jerusalem was waiting for the ideas in writing. The State Department
said Arens must have misunderstood, and as minor as the incident might have seemed it contributed to Labor's walkout from
the government that month.

Likud leaders even suspected that Bush and Baker had tried

to engineer the collapse of the Shamir-led coalition, in the hope that Labor could form a replacement government. The second National Unity Government did fall in March, but to America's disappointment Israel emerged with its most right-wing government ever. Shamir was still in charge, and relations with the United States plummeted.

The American and Israeli governments, for the first time since Eisenhower's post-Suez anger of 1956, had lost almost all trust in each other. To the Bush administration, Shamir was a close-minded, misleading, and maddening partner. But the United States seemed to be tilting toward the Arabs, in the view of many ministers in the new rightist and religious coalition formed by Shamir in June 1990.

A mere two days later Baker lashed out with unconcealed exasperation. The secretary of state was asked, in the House Foreign Affairs Committee, whether he was willing to give the new government a fresh start.

"You bet we are," replied Baker, but within seconds he proceeded to make the freshness seem positively stale. He told the congressmen that he had just seen news reports, quoting an Israeli cabinet minister who dismissed U.S. efforts to promote negotiations as "no longer relevant."

"Now, if that's going to be the approach, and that's going to be the attitude," said Baker, "there won't be any dialogue. And there won't be any peace. The United States can't make it happen."

As if to underline his frustration with the Israelis, the secretary of state treated them like teenagers who habitually forget to phone home. "When you're serious about peace, call us," he snapped. "The phone number is 202-456-1414," the White House switchboard listed in the public Washington telephone book. And, like a teen expecting an angry parent at the other end of the line, Shamir never felt like calling.

But in other areas the U.S.-Israel alliance was robust. Foreign aid levels, the most important barometer from AIPAC's point of view, continued to exceed $3 billion per year for Israel, but that was regarded mainly as a product of congressional goodwill. And the strategic relationship—with its labyrinth of defense contracts, research and development projects, and joint military ventures—was thriving, but that was seen as equally in America's interest and so institutionalized that it was almost taken for granted.

President Bush personally and enthusiastically pressed the Soviet Union to permit its Jewish citizens to move to Israel and secretly arranged for Ethiopian Jews to be flown to new homes in Israel. And even the cynics in Shamir's new cabinet found it difficult to dismiss the claim by American officials that they were helping in the historic mission of *aliyah* because "it's the right thing to do."

Therefore the "facts," as U.S. officials and AIPAC lobbyists were quick to point out so as not to consign the alliance to a trash heap, were still good. But the "tone" and the "music," they admitted, were terrible.

Israel had few alternatives, however, when it needed help in meeting the financial burden of providing homes, education, and jobs to all the newcomers from the Soviet Union and Ethiopia. The worldwide Jewish community would be asked to contribute hundreds of millions of dollars, matched by investments in State of Israel Bonds, but there was little doubt that assistance of superpower proportions would be required.

So in early 1990, over a year and a half before the mass citizens' lobby on Capitol Hill, Israel approached the United States with the idea that would come to dominate and poison their relations: asking the American government for guarantees that would make it much easier for Israel to raise money in worldwide financial markets. Since the 1950s, the Jewish state had never had trouble on Wall Street, as long as the bankers and brokers knew that the federal government would stand behind Israel.

After lobbying by AIPAC and many other Jewish groups, the Bush administration and Congress agreed in April 1990 to guarantee $400 million in loans that Israel would take to pay for immigrant absorption. Despite the gathering storm on U.S.-Israel horizons, Bush was willing to accommodate Israel's request.

The guarantees enabled Israel to borrow funds from commercial banks at far more favorable terms, saving around $25 million in interest and extending the loan terms to thirty years rather than five or seven. It was a relatively small sum, but Israel's planners knew that the first set of U.S. guarantees would likely set a precedent for larger deals.

But, unlike the no-strings-attached ease of other aid programs to Israel, Bush and Baker insisted on a condition: full details of Israeli expenditures on settlements.

For the first time since the Eisenhower years, a U.S. administration was conditioning its financial support on Israeli policies. Never mind that the connection between the controversial outposts and humanitarian assistance to immigrants was tenuous, at best. Hardly any Soviet or Ethiopian Jews were being placed outside the pre-1967 borders. But, pressed by the United States, Foreign Minister David Levy wrote a letter that pledged "No special incentives exist to encourage Soviet Jewish immigrants to settle beyond the green line."

Positively outrageous for some cabinet colleagues was Levy's further promise to "use his best efforts to provide annually as complete information as possible on the Government of Israel's financial support for settlement activity." The United States proposed to be an auditor, checking Israel's books.

"It is a matter of great importance to the United States," Baker told congressmen, "that these funds not be used for the construction of housing in the occupied territories."

In private consultations at the White House, President Bush—while stating his firm conviction that the Israelis were diminishing peace prospects by building settlements—told his advisors that he could "accept the fact that they were not going to stop settlement activity, because this Israeli government has an ideological belief in it.

"I accept that," Bush added. "I'm not going to change that. But what I want to know is, if I go ahead and provide loan guarantees, will those guarantees contribute to a policy I oppose? I want to know it's not doing that."

One administration official explained to another about the intent of Levy's letter: "The mere fact that they were informing us on settlement activity would have a somewhat inhibiting effect. And if they would give us the financial information, then we'd know that if we're giving them $400 million in loan guarantees when they were spending 'X' on settlement activity, that spending shouldn't go up to '2X' or '3X.' But instead, we saw ourselves that it soared to around '3X.'

"And it went to 3X without them telling us! They didn't provide the information we asked for, but their actual behavior was to triple the housing starts." By then there were 100,000 Jewish settlers in the West Bank and Gaza, living amid 1.7 million Palestinians. The U.S. Embassy in Tel Aviv reported to Washington that the Shamir government hoped to increase the number of settlers to 150,000 within a year or so.

The White House and State Department were livid, especially when Levy insisted that the statistics the United States was seeking were "not available." The Americans seriously considered never issuing the actual guarantee document covering $400 million, but in early 1991 it was wartime in the Middle East and Israel was—for a while—behaving well, by U.S. standards. After Shamir bent to American demands and refrained from retaliating against Iraq's Scud missile attacks, it would have been difficult for the Bush administration to deny Israel the loan guarantees already promised.

So despite its half-hidden feelings, and after Israel's friends in Congress put pressure on Baker during the Scud strikes, the administration handed over the guarantee document in February 1991. U.S. officials felt cheated, however, and vowed never to be fooled again.

When, in March 1991, Israel requested and received a grant of $650 million for repairs and military resupply after the Gulf War, some Bush administration officials were tempted to make that aid conditional on a slowdown in building settlements. But AIPAC's Tom Dine and sympathetic congressmen spoke to Baker, and no conditions were attached. That would come a few months later, when Israel's wartime restraint—portrayed by the American media as heroic—began to be forgotten.

First, in June, came a trial balloon in Congress. A Democrat, John Bryant of Texas, proposed that aid to Israel be reduced by $82.5 million—the amount the State Department estimated that Israel was spending on settlements. This was a more precise effort than the first aid-cutting balloon floated in 1990 by Senator Dole.

Just as Dole had experienced, Bryant found an extraordinary lobbying effort running in high gear just outside the House chamber. The congressman said: "AIPAC has been in the hall all day long, working members one by one against this amendment, which they should be supporting. But it is wrong to continue to remain silent, when we know that to remain silent is not in the interest of our country or of Israel."

Both AIPAC lobbyists and Israeli diplomats were stunned. They realized that the administration was serious, for the first time in thirty-five years, about punishing Israel in its purse. However, the many responses from pro-Israel members of Congress were not only from the expectable states with large Jewish populations. Richard Stallings, a Democrat from Idaho, said: "With this amendment, foreign aid to Israel becomes the tool of individual policies, rather than the product of a strong relationship between two nations. Doing this sets a dangerous precedent for U.S. policy." The vote was 378 to 44 to defeat Bryant's proposed cut.

On the entire foreign aid bill, providing the now-standard $1.2 billion per year to Israel in economic assistance, plus $1.8 billion in military financing, the vote was 301 to 102 in the House and 74 to 18 in the Senate.

It was no wonder, with such massive majorities for aid to Israel, that AIPAC and the Israeli embassy felt ready to proceed to the next request: the large loan guarantees that were necessary because the tens of thousands of Jews from the former Soviet Union had grown to hundreds of thousands, and still they kept coming. Israel's government economists made their calculations, computing that over the next five years the nation would have to spend over $50 billion to absorb all the new immigrants. It seemed certain that $10 billion would have to be borrowed from commercial markets, so that was the sum that Israel felt it should ask to be guaranteed.

The figures, already given to Lawrence Eagleburger almost casually during the Gulf War, were sent from Jerusalem to Washington in July 1991, and U.S. government economists started examining them. Secretary of State Baker, however, was turning his mind back to the possibilities for Arab-Israeli peace. And it seemed only natural to link the two.

First, Baker was warned by his advisors, the Arabs would be extremely angry if the United States were to issue guarantees for $10 billion in loans to Israel, just when the Shamir government was accelerating its settlements program. "It would appear as though America were subsidizing Sharon," one American official recalls, referring to the Israeli minister—long loathed in Washington—who was in charge of the settlements drive.

AIPAC's Tom Dine, being well plugged in, had realized in June that the administration was leaning toward linking loan guarantees to a freeze on settlements. And while the lobby took no official stand on Jews living in the disputed territories, AIPAC was always committed to securing U.S. aid without strings attached.

Dine called for an "all-out campaign" by the pro-Israel community, "because the whole world will be watching to see if we succeed or fail." His advice to American Jews who disliked settlements was: "Swallow hard, roll up your sleeves, and get to work to fight linkage."

Widely divergent interpretations begin at this point. To Israel and many of its supporters in America, Bush and Baker were so emboldened by the Gulf War victory over Iraq that they assumed they could solve all the world's problems. With the prestige they had earned in defeating Iraq, they saw a real chance to persuade their Arab allies to sit at the peace table with their Israeli ally. They were "obsessed" by settlements, according to this interpretation, and seemed to believe that if Israel stopped building them the entire Middle East would turn into a peaceful Garden of Eden.

The highest-level Jew in the White House's Middle East team, however, told a different tale. Richard Haass, on the staff of the National Security Council and often working personally with President Bush, also stayed in touch with friends in the Jewish community. "The relationship with Israel feels frustrating," he told them. "Because after the Gulf War, instead of having any sense of mutual accomplishment, we aren't enjoying it together. Our meetings with the Israelis haven't gone well. It's not that we fought the war for Israel's sake, but it did improve Israel's security situation. That doesn't show up in many of the conversations we have. Instead, we're working on the peace process, so there's friction over that. And it's not simply that the president and the prime minister don't have the greatest chemistry."

"Precisely," one Jewish community activist responded. "It's because you guys brought up the settlements issue. Even the Arabs weren't bringing it up."

"You're kidding yourselves if you think that!" Haass replied. "Symbolically and substantively, settlements are a real problem. They're real! It's not an American invention!"

Haass conceded that Secretary of State Baker was especially adamant because of the personal affront of seeing the Israelis set up new settlements, repeatedly, on the precise days that Baker arrived to negotiate details of a Middle East peace conference. And the conference was no minor project. It was Baker's great focus from the moment that Iraq surrendered in the Gulf War.

Like Nixon and Kissinger after the Yom Kippur War of 1973, Bush and Baker felt that they now had a once-in-a-lifetime opportunity to shape a new world order in the Middle East. Setting up a peace conference was America's biggest foreign policy initiative of 1991, matched only by watching and nudging along the dissolution of the Soviet Union. The peace conference was an integral part of ending the Cold War in victory for the United States.

Yet here were the Israelis, from Baker's point of view, only haltingly interested and throwing up physical obstacles: the settlements. The Syrians, the Lebanese, the Jordanians, and nominees to the Palestinian delegation being assembled in the summer of 1991 all insisted to the United States that Israel would have to freeze its settlement program. Otherwise, they said, no Arabs would attend the peace conference.

President Bush hoped to settle the issue with the Israelis by the time-tested route of sending a Jewish envoy. Bush asked an old friend, Jacob (Jack) Stein, a former chairman of the Conference of Presidents of Major American Jewish Organizations, to fly to Jerusalem as a quiet emissary to Prime Minister Shamir in July 1991.

The oral message from Bush was: "Mr. Shamir, it would be very much in our mutual interest if you would put a halt to settlements. Or I believe we will have major problems."

According to Stein, Shamir replied: "The territory belongs to Israel. It doesn't belong to the Turks. It doesn't belong to the British Mandate. It belongs to Israel."

"Do you want me to convey that to the president?" Stein asked. Shamir said yes, and Stein did.

At that point, Bush and Baker saw no way of persuading Shamir to defy his Likud ideology and key members of his cabinet. The United States told the Arabs that their demand was a "nonstarter," so they had just better show up at the peace conference Baker was organizing. Score one round for Shamir: The Arabs would show up, on his terms.

Bush and Baker did ask Israel for one favor: not to submit the request for loan guarantees until after Labor Day. They only hinted at the reason why: that they did not trust Israel, in the wake of the Levy letter and the first $400 million guarantee, and thus were probably headed for a sharp clash over settlements that could derail the path to the peace conference. Reluctantly Shamir agreed to wait until September.

As the end of summer approached, however, the Israeli economy truly needed the loans. The $2 billion, although not yet borrowed, was already in Israel's state budget. And yet, with the peace conference not firmly set, Baker telephoned Shamir to ask again that the request for loan guarantees be postponed.

This time a crackly phone line played a role in a key diplomatic decision. Shamir could hear Baker, but not very well. The Israeli leader did not fully absorb the American's reasoning for a further delay, and anyway probably never would have agreed with Baker's view that loan guarantees to help immigrants would hurt the peace process. And Shamir began to suspect that the Bush administration was playing games with him by asking time and again for postponement.

As a further check, Shamir sought the opinion of his Likud emissary in the Washington embassy, Yoram Ettinger. And Ettinger was hearing Steve Rosen and other feisty AIPAC members loud and clear. But he was deaf to some influential lawmakers who advised the Israeli embassy to cool it.

Senator Patrick Leahy, chairman of the Foreign Operations Appropriations subcommittee, warned the Israelis that their settlements policy was a problem that would not go away. He had said so in Jerusalem, shortly after taking over the panel in January 1989. And one of his top aides, Eric Newsom, had said so to Ettinger in a friendly but firm conversation in the subcommittee's offices in the summer of 1991.

The Israeli diplomat sat on a black leather sofa in the office of senior subcommittee staffer Newsom, who puffed on a cigar while sitting at his large walnut desk. Newsom tried to keep the conversation relaxed, but he also tried to explain the new political facts of life to an Israeli who did not want to hear them.

Part of the advice was that it was a mistake, at a time of fiscal austerity in the United States, to ask for anything that has "Ten Billion Dollars" in the title. Yes, said Newsom, it isn't a grant. It doesn't cost $10 billion. But to American taxpayers, it would look bad.

Ettinger suggested that while the Jewish state might not be able to depend on the Bush administration, it had always depended on the Senate and still would. Newsom warned that now that the word "settlements" had been attached to the issue, Israel could not depend on its usual level of support.

The Israelis—and AIPAC lobbyists sent by Dine and Rosen—argued that the issues were quite separate: The need to borrow money was a humanitarian imperative for the sake of refugees whose freedom had always been sought by the United

States; the settlements were a political issue that could be discussed later in peace negotiations with the Arabs. "Don't do the Arabs' job for them," the lobbyists told American legislators and policy makers. "They'll eventually demand a settlements freeze, but at least they'll have to offer some concessions to Israel in return."

As far as Newsom's boss, Leahy, was concerned, however, it was natural to link the issues because the loan guarantees were needed to *settle* people in Israel and that connects to the *settlements* issue. The time had come, the Vermont Democrat believed, to stress a principle only hinted at by previous presidents but strongly believed in by Bush: Settlements represent "creeping annexation," and the United States should not help pay for it.

Leahy told the embassy and AIPAC that he would propose deducting one dollar from the loan guarantees for every dollar spent by the government of Israel on settlements in the West Bank, Gaza Strip, and Golan Heights. He cautioned that "the old days" of unquestioned aid were gone, because the U.S. economy had fallen on hard times. He warned, "It's no longer business as usual." But Ettinger was not listening.

At AIPAC, Rosen derided the "defeatism" of lobbyists who despaired at the thought of battling a president enjoying post–Gulf War popularity. "This will be our greatest fight since AWACS," he told leaders of several Jewish organizations, who found the prospect of uniting the entire community for a good cause very appealing. Based on fact sheets from AIPAC, the various magazines of B'nai B'rith, Hadassah, and other mass-membership Jewish groups ran full pages on Israel's need for the loan guarantees.

Prime Minister Shamir heard that American Jews were united, which was a refreshing thought. And his man in Washington, Ettinger, was citing AIPAC as his source for the assertion that the case could be won on Capitol Hill. Ettinger sent

Shamir a diplomatic cable on September 4, 1991, that spoke of President Bush's "very limited ability to dictate the agenda" and said settlements were not the most important element in U.S. decision making.

"It is inconceivable that our great friend the United States will change its ways and not help Israel in the massive enterprise of absorbing immigration," Shamir declared publicly. "Settlement in every part of our country continues and will continue."

On September 6 the Shamir government formally applied for the loan guarantees by submitting a letter through the Israeli embassy. Within an hour Secretary of State Baker summoned leaders of AIPAC and implored them not to lobby for the guarantees at that time.

President Bush then urged Congress to ignore the Israeli plea for 120 days—so that Middle East negotiations could get under way starting in late October. "Let's not blow it," he said. He signaled that talking about loans would mean arguing about settlements, and "we don't need an acrimonious debate just as we're about to get this peace conference convened."

For six days Washington and Jerusalem quibbled and quarreled. The subject came up at all of Bush's White House photo opportunities, and hoping for a compromise he offered to compensate Israel for any additional borrowing costs incurred because of the delay he was seeking.

Still, Israel and AIPAC stubbornly pressed on. Senators Bob Kasten and Daniel Inouye, the reliably pro-Israel Republican-Democrat pairing, drew up the amendment that would grant the loan guarantees. AIPAC lobbyists worked tenaciously to gather a "veto-proof majority" of over sixty-six senators to cosponsor the amendment.

The stubbornness was extraordinary, even blinding. AIPAC assumed wrongly that just because senators signed on to some humanitarian assistance to Israel, they would stand firm when the president of the United States weighed in. In fact, Bush was clever enough not to urge rejection but simply a delay. And Senator Leahy, the committee chairman controlling foreign aid bills, said that that sounded fair enough.

But the pro-Israel lobby was not retreating. President Bush even invited the president of AIPAC, Mayer Mitchell, to the White House on the morning of September 12. Knowing him well enough to address him by his nickname, Bubba, Bush asked him directly to call off the massive citizen's action effort set for that day. Bush said foreign affairs were his turf, and he did not like people going over his head to Congress.

Mitchell replied that Israel deserved the humanitarian assistance and needed it now. He also said the day of action for loan guarantees had been planned long before and could not now be stopped. What he did not say is that AIPAC felt it could beat Bush on this issue.

"It was one of those historic moments," recalls David Saperstein, a leader of the National Jewish Community Relations Advisory Council that helped organize the day of lobbying. For Jews, he says, "It was like the '67 war and the Yom Kippur War, when there was overwhelming unanimity and enthusiasm in the Jewish community on behalf of a cause that would link the United States and Israel.

"The community was split—and conflicted—about many of the policy issues in Israel. It was split on the Lebanon war, on the intifada, on the settlements policy, and the Palestinian issue generally. But on this issue, thanks to the exciting rescue of the Ethiopian and Soviet Jews, everyone across the board—all the doves and all the hawks—all were in favor of the loan guarantees."

Saperstein says the pro-Israel foot soldiers were "convinced that the president would not fight the Congress on this; that we would win this battle, because Congress would stand with us. We thought the president would compromise."

Instead he counterattacked. Just after one o'clock, almost without warning, George Bush strode into the White House press room and said the harshest things that any American president has ever said about Israel—and the pro-Israel community in the United States—in public.

Glaring at the television cameras, once even pounding his fist on the lectern, President Bush said: "We're up against very strong and effective groups that go up to the Hill. I heard today there were something like a thousand lobbyists on the Hill working the other side of the question. We've got one lonely little guy down here," referring to himself. "I think the American people will support me."

To hear themselves described as if they were un-American simply shocked the pro-Israel activists who were busily meeting with legislators at that hour. It caused further hurt to hear the president portray them—and the Jewish state—as ungrateful.

"Just months ago, American men and women in uniform risked their lives to defend Israelis in the face of Iraqi Scud missiles," said Bush, as if the Gulf War had been fought for Israel's benefit. He offered no thanks for Israel's angst-ridden agreement to refrain from retaliating during the war. Ironically, Bush had drafted his statement with his Middle East expert who happened to be Jewish, Richard Haass, and with Lawrence Eagleburger, the longtime friend of Israel.

"During the current fiscal year alone," the president continued, "and despite our own economic problems, the United States provided Israel with more than $4 billion in economic and military aid, nearly $1,000 for every Israeli man, woman, and child."

In the experience of Israel and its supporters, only opponents of aid to the Jewish state bothered with the misleading mathematical exercise that suggested every Israeli was getting a U.S. welfare check.

The "one lonely little guy" said he would veto any foreign aid bill that contained the loan guarantees, pleading again for a 120-day delay "because we must avoid a contentious debate" in the first stages of a Middle East peace process.

On a positive note he did say: "For more than forty years, the United States has been Israel's closest friend in the world. And this remains the case and will as long as I am president of the United States." And as long, he hinted, as Israel does not send lobbyists to try to embarrass him on a foreign policy question.

Most of the 1,200 roaming the halls of Congress that day were ordinary citizens with few skills in political analysis. Yet, as David Saperstein recalls, Bush's statement immediately "started to ripple like a huge rock being dropped in a calm pond. It began to turn from a mood of exuberance and momentum to a feeling of crisis. We could tell it was a historical moment. We'd remember, almost like, 'I was at Woodstock,' that we were there."

Shamir happened to be visiting Paris that day. He received a full briefing on Bush's shocking remarks and then responded with typical calm: "The history of relations with the United States is a history of ups and downs. From time to time, there are changes in the character of the relations."

From the Israeli embassy, Ettinger sent Shamir another cable, warning that the new character was decidedly negative: "The power of the president's campaign gives reason to suppose that this is not an isolated chapter, but rather, perhaps, the first chapter in the administration's treatment of Israel."

"Most friends of Israel recognize this is a fight we'll lose even if we win," Congressman Larry Smith said with a sigh, warning that if a Bush veto were to be overridden, the president would be unmollifiably angry at Israel and the Jewish community.

Already his suggestions of us-and-them, of a swarm of

menacing lobbyists overwhelming the system in Washington, and of Israel receiving plenty of money so surely it can wait before borrowing cash were extremely disturbing to American supporters of Israel. The tone was hostile, and the rhetoric included code words that struck some as anti-Semitic.

"An American president was speaking out against 'powerful political forces' and 'a thousand lobbyists' working against the best interests of the United States," comments Morris Amitay, former head of AIPAC. "This came as close to the line of inciting anti-Semitism as a public figure can go."

The seven weeks that followed were among the strangest for the U.S.-Israel alliance. The White House was at first happy to receive thousands of telephone calls and letters congratulating Bush for taking a stand—but officials then realized that many of the messages were anti-Semitic. The president had let a racist genie out of America's bottle.

"I got hold of Bush on the phone," his friend and informal Jewish advisor Jack Stein recalls, "and told him this was not going to play." Together they decided on a low-key apology. Stein suggested that Shoshana Cardin, chairwoman of the Conference of Presidents, write a letter to Bush to express the worry felt by many Jews. Bush then wrote back, saying he had not meant to question the motives of U.S. citizens who are perfectly entitled to speak out for Israel.

The strongest way to impress Bush and Republican party strategists, however, was to warn him that some of the moneymen needed for his reelection campaign were upset. Max Fisher wrote a joint letter with two real estate developers who were also leading Jewish contributors to the party, George Klein and Richard Fox, urging the president to grant Israel the loan guarantees because of "the overriding moral responsibility" to help Jewish refugees.

Bush wrote back that the true test of friendship between the United States and Israel should be their ability to disagree, while respecting each other and still remaining friends.

Fisher, Klein, AIPAC's president Mitchell, Tom Dine, and a former Republican operative who had joined AIPAC to bolster its executive-branch lobbying, Howard Kohr, all found that the softest spot in the administration was the vice president. Dan Quayle might not have had the entire nation's highest respect, but Jewish activists in Washington knew that he was their best friend in the White House.

Quayle was thrust into the position of defending George Bush to Jewish leaders. "No, of course he's not an anti-Semite," he said on several occasions, "and it's not helpful even to ask that question." Quayle, who openly and proudly labeled himself a "Zionist," told the Jews who phoned him: "Let's back off for now, we're going to get the loan guarantees eventually."

The vice president was no longer masking his role as the leading pro-Israel voice in the policy debates in the Oval Office and the National Security Council. In the Gulf War, for instance, Quayle had a "back-channel" relationship with Israel's ambassador Zalman Shoval, settling misunderstandings before they could further embitter U.S.-Israel relations.

Quayle did not consider West Bank settlements to be a major impediment to peace. He endorsed the Likud party notion that Israel need only trade "peace for peace" with the Arabs, and not necessarily the "land for peace" exchange demanded by most of the outside world. And, as a big booster of the Arrow antimissile missile project and other joint endeavors, Quayle often reminded other U.S. officials that Israel is "special"—a democracy where strategic cooperation can be mutually beneficial.

In looking for a way to repair some of the damage to the alliance, Quayle pressed President Bush to give Israel a major psychological and political gift: repeal of the United Nations General Assembly resolution that had labeled Zionism as "a form of racism and racial discrimination" and "most severely condemned" it as "a threat to world peace and security."

That resolution, in 1975, had shattered Israel's already dwindling confidence in the UN. Quayle had long called for its repeal. And on September 23, addressing the General Assembly, President Bush declared: "To equate Zionism with the intolerable sin of racism is to twist history. Zionism is not a policy; it was an idea that led to the home of the Jewish people in the State of Israel."

It took another three months for the repeal vote, 111 to 25, but Bush's immediate purpose was to reestablish a measure of trust between himself and Israel—and between himself and Jewish voters. Shamir called it a "beautiful speech."

Two days later the Israeli government agreed to give up on the loan guarantees for at least 120 days. Foreign Minister Levy met with Secretary of State Baker, and the Israeli must have been biting his lip as he said: "All those shadows that were between Israel and the United States have been removed, and a better climate has been achieved."

AIPAC, meanwhile, had the satisfaction of assembling seventy cosponsors for the Kasten-Inouye legislation granting the $10 billion in guarantees—permitting lobbyists to trumpet that if it had come to a veto fight, the pro-Israel forces could have had three more than the two-thirds needed for an override. Push never came to shove, however, because the senators went along with Israel and AIPAC in agreeing to postpone action for four months.

The rationale behind the postponement had been to leave uncontentious time for an unprecedented peace conference to get under way. And on October 18, while visiting Jerusalem for the eighth time since March, Secretary of State Baker was finally able to make the momentous announcement: that twelve days later Israel, a Palestinian delegation, and three Arab states would begin negotiating an end to their war.

In declaring that a peace conference would open in Madrid,

Spain, Baker was standing alongside the foreign minister of the Soviet Union—who that very day had restored diplomatic relations with Israel after a twenty-four-year rupture. "We have no illusions," said Baker. "We will take it one step at a time." The Israelis immediately complained that the United States was not offering the Jewish state any special assurances in writing—such as a stronger commitment to Israel's technological edge in weapons systems, a promise not to renew American contacts with the PLO, or a statement that Israel would not have to withdraw from all the territory captured in 1967. Baker was offering only a letter outlining the format for the Madrid conference and the bilateral talks to follow—the same kind of letter offered to the Palestinian delegates.

Shamir, when pressed on whether Israel was going to Madrid without a pledge of U.S. support, said: "Jim Baker's word is good enough for me." And, indeed, when the Israeli leader dug in his heels on rejecting any Palestinian negotiator with PLO connections, the Americans had taken Israel's side. By then Shamir had no real choice. If he refused, as his gut feeling suggested, to go to the conference, Israel would be labeled an anti-peace nation. There was also Shamir's hope—later proved illusory—that his presence at Madrid would prompt Bush to grant the obsessively desired loan guarantees.

At just the same time, however, the United States was astounding Israel with a public scolding for flying reconnaissance missions over western Iraq. Why weren't the flights ignored, as similar ones had been for months? Why were they leaked to the press by Washington? Why did the United States publicly issue a "strong protest"? Why did Bush and Baker flip-flop between friendly rhetoric and warlike bile? Whom were they trying to impress? The major objection, it seemed, was that Israeli jets had flown over Lebanon, Syria, and Jordan on their high-altitude photographic route. But the major message, Israeli diplomats concluded, was Bush's insistence that times had changed. The golden era of Reagan was long gone.

The seven weeks leading up to the opening of the historic peace conference had been filled with mixed messages for Israel. But on October 30, 1991, the Jewish state finally achieved one of its oft-stated goals: direct negotiations with its Arab neighbors. To underline the importance of that day in the Spanish capital, both President Bush and Soviet president Mikhail Gorbachev attended the opening.

Prime Minister Shamir himself represented Israel, as if to symbolize to Bush something that the American president refused to believe: that Shamir was committed to the peace process. It was also a matter of domestic politics. Shamir did not want Foreign Minister Levy there, because of his belief that Levy's letter making all sorts of promises on the settlements was too soft.

Shamir learned quickly that the crisis in relations with the United States had not passed. He attended the peace conference, but as far as he was concerned the Bush administration did not keep its promise and refused—right into 1992—to provide the loan guarantees. "They cheated us," says his aide, Achimeir.

Three weeks after the Madrid peace conference, Shamir fully expected to be hailed as a hero when he visited Baltimore for the largest annual gathering of American Jewish leaders. Yet he found that a sizable faction was trying to get rid of him.

"It was literally an ambush," says Mark Kramer, son of a wealthy Cleveland family and now a theater impresario in Boston who helped finance the attack on Shamir. The weapon was an opinion poll.

"The liberals knew that Shamir was coming to talk at the GA," recalls one of the organizers of the General Assembly of the Council of Jewish Federations. "And they knew that the only authoritative survey of American Jews showed a shift toward Shamir's positions. So they ran around in a frenzy to get their own numbers to shove in his face."

Indeed, a broad survey by the American Jewish Committee indicated that more U.S. Jews approved of settlements in the territories than opposed them, though by a tiny margin; while the plurality favoring the return of some territories to the Arabs had shrunk. On most issues, around three out of ten said they were "not sure," reflecting the widespread desire to let Israel decide its own fate.

But the "ambush" poll, headlined in major U.S. newspapers, indicated that, by huge margins, American Jewish leaders felt that Shamir was wrong and that Labor and other liberal parties in Israel were right. When asked whether Israel should offer "territorial compromise," 88 percent said yes, only 7 percent said no.

"The poll was rather carefully constructed," says Kramer, who also contributes to New Israel Fund and Americans for Peace Now. "It described our positions in terms that were broad enough to include many people. The wording was artful. If the results had been different, they wouldn't have released it. But they wouldn't have undertaken it, unless they felt that there was a likelihood there would be a substantial showing in our favor on this set of questions."

The polling sample was an unusually narrow choice: 205 Jewish activists with average family incomes over $200,000 per year, most of them donating $20,000 or more to Jewish Federation campaigns.

When they saw their opinions waved as an anti-Shamir banner in front of the Israeli prime minister, many said they wished they had never answered the questions. After all, they were split down the middle when asked how they felt about American Jewish leaders who publicly warned Israel that it would have to choose between settlements and loan guarantees: 43 percent expressed approval, but 45 percent said they disapproved.

The ambush worked, however. The front pages of major

American and Israeli newspapers cited the survey to report that when two thousand Jewish leaders gave Yitzhak Shamir a standing ovation in Baltimore on November 21, they may have been glad he went to the peace conference, but most in fact opposed his policies and wanted him to lose the next election.

Between the U.S. government and U.S. Jewry, no wonder Shamir had the feeling that America was out to get rid of him.

CHAPTER TWENTY-TWO

ETERNAL, FOR NOW

You could hear the champagne corks popping in the White House and in the State Department on the afternoon of June 23, 1992. The news had just come in from Israel: the Labor party had trounced the Likud.

The joyful buzz in the phone conversations among Washington's leading Middle East experts, in and out of government, was similar to Menachem Begin's pleasure when Jimmy Carter lost in 1980. The word spread quickly: "Shamir's out."

And the Americans felt, rightfully, that they had contributed to his downfall.

The message had been going out from the Bush administration for over a year, roughly since the U.S.-led coalition's victory over Iraq: We've just demonstrated that we'll defend Israel in a crisis, American officials said. We are keeping the strategic alliance strong. We would love to have good relations with Shamir. But he doesn't tell us the truth about settlements, which we know are an obstacle to peace. And don't tell us we should give Israel the benefit of the doubt because it's a unique and vital ally. Because it's not, and we proved that in the Gulf War too.

Bush never did give Shamir the loan guarantees—not even after the 120-day delay. In public, Secretary of State Baker revealed in February 1992 what everyone had assumed: that there would be no guarantees unless Israel swore not to break ground on new settlements; and even then, the amount of guarantees would have to be reduced by the precise sum Israel was spending on services and expansion projects for existing settlements.

No deal, said Shamir. At the start of an election campaign in Israel, he was faced with either capitulating to the Americans or running on a platform called "I defied Bush!" Shamir chose the latter. He chose wrong. There were no low-interest loans to help 400,000 former Soviet Jews. There was an unprecedentedly sour taste in relations with the United States. And for the Likud, there was disgrace in the election.

In March, when negotiations over the guarantees broke down, American officials were not absolutely certain that Shamir would lose. But they seemed to be looking beyond Likud rule, expecting—at worst, to their view—that Labor would come back as part of another national unity coalition in Israel.

"Regardless of the differences that exist between the United States and Israel now," Dennis Ross, the State Department's policy planner and coordinator for the Middle East peace talks, told American Jewish leaders that month, "I can tell you one thing categorically: There is not going to be a wedge driven between the United States and Israel.

"Anyone who believes that they can do that is going to be mistaken. I still hope that we will be able to provide loan guarantees. I don't know when exactly it's going to happen, but I hope that it will happen."

Ross was a Jewish academic from California, then forty-three years old, who had become Baker's indispensable advisor on the Soviet Union and on the Middle East. An analyst in Democrat Carter's defense department and then a Middle East specialist in Republican Reagan's White House, Ross was far more interested in creative diplomacy abroad than party politics at home.

"We're entering a different world," he said. "We're in the midst of a major transition. The security relationship with Israel, after all, was not just a function of our commitment to Israel. It was also a function of a certain kind of strategic reality. But there isn't a Cold War anymore. We have to rethink that part of the world, including the former Soviet states in central Asia. And those decisions can't be isolated from Israel."

The atmosphere between the United States and Israel, and between American Jews and the Bush administration, was further poisoned when a columnist claimed that Baker had said: "Fuck the Jews, they don't vote for us anyway."

"I would not stay on this job if I believed that Secretary Baker had made those remarks," Ross commented with a worried look, "and he has told me personally that he did not say such things."

He once assured Steve Rosen of AIPAC that he was well aware of the anguish felt by American Jews when they saw Bush feuding with Shamir. "My mother lives in San Francisco," said Ross. "I get calls from her. Some false column is written about me, and she calls and says, 'You did *what?*' "

"Get your mother to call Baker," Rosen suggested with a smile.

But Rosen and other AIPAC chiefs had little to smile about in those months of crisis. The pro-Israel lobby had staked its reputation on getting the loan guarantees, just as it always defined its level of success in dollars and cents.

AIPAC did its best to apply the brakes and reverse the wheels of history. The annual policy conference, the largest gathering of AIPAC members, was unusually charged in April 1992: with excitement at a challenge, and with hostility toward the Bush administration. As every year, the corridors, conference rooms, and ballrooms of a Washington hotel were teeming with pro-Israel activists. Over 2,100 attended, and there was the usual turnout of VIP guests: 46 senators, 78 members of the House, 18 ambassadors, and a few administration officials who had come to repair political relations.

But whenever a Republican tried to defend the Bush-Baker record on Israel, he was booed. It was a stunning change, in an AIPAC that had appeared increasingly Republican in the 1980s. The only exception was Vice President Quayle, warmly welcomed as he addressed the delegates as "fellow Zionists."

The most striking speech, however, was executive director Tom Dine's, because it included a declaration of war. "September 12, 1991, will be a day that lives in infamy for the American pro-Israel community," said Dine, portraying President Bush's fiery remarks about Israel and lobbyists as a Pearl Harbor–like sneak attack. "Like the Indian elephant, we shall not forget!"

The AIPAC chief, himself a lifelong Democrat but proud to have broadened the lobbying organization to include plenty of members from both major parties, sounded partisan when he reminded all who might forget: "In a close presidential election, Jews could provide a 'swing vote' in states with more than half the Electoral College votes needed to win, possibly making a decisive difference to the overall outcome."

Would fifty thousand AIPAC members vote for Bush later that year, let alone contribute to his campaign and work for his reelection? It certainly did not seem so, that April in Washington.

But first came the Israeli election, and in that race most American Jews yearned simply for less pressure: less of a dilemma for people who love both the United States and Israel.

Most felt that the perfect answer would be a change in leadership from one Yitzhak to another: from Likud's Shamir to Labor's Rabin.

The Bush administration thought so too. Senior officials denied that they were trying to intervene in Israeli politics, but clearly the refusal to compromise over loan guarantees had become—at the least—a refusal to help Shamir's reelection drive in any way.

"Trying to influence elections in a democracy is a risky proposition," AIPAC's newsletter warned the administration. "Israelis may interpret things differently. They may resent the intrusion of U.S. policymakers in their domestic affairs. A majority may rally around the prime minister who stood up to the Americans."

But they did not. In a decisive turnaround from Likud's shock victory of 1977, and after a period of almost down-the-middle division of the Israeli electorate in the 1980s, voters chose the Labor party by a wide margin: 44 K'nesset seats for Labor, to 32 for Likud. Most Israelis were unhappy that Shamir had practically lost the nation's greatest ally.

Now Yitzhak Rabin, the ambassador in Washington in the Nixon period and Israel's leader in the Ford presidency, would again be prime minister. The Bush administration, indeed all of official Washington, was delighted and did not hide the fact.

Everything would be different, said a senior administration policy maker, now that Israel had a government with credibility. "Our approach to Rabin is so different because he came out immediately and said his goals and priorities were different. Bush and Baker knew him when he was defense minister in the National Unity Government. And the experience with him was always: Whatever he says, he'll do. We don't agree with anybody all the time, but the issue is whether they tell you the truth."

As if to underline that he was on the White House wavelength, Rabin independently stated: "We have to forge a better relationship between the leaders of the two countries. It doesn't mean we have to agree with every one of America's policies; it means sometimes there can be ups and downs in the relationship." No panic; no bitterness; no basic distrust. Although they voted on the basis of many issues, the Israeli people had chosen the path of improving relations with the United States—an important issue to Israelis, because they feel such a special connection with America that they cannot long tolerate a transatlantic falling out.

Bush and Shamir had been at loggerheads for only three years—a relatively short period in a long and deep alliance—but both governments saw the need for significant repair and renovation.

Bush and Rabin got right to work, and for Israel's new leader his get-acquainted visit in August 1992 was truly a $10 billion question. The triumphant Rabin was intent on getting the guarantees, if only to prove that compared with Shamir, he was a master of U.S.-Israel relations; but also because he thought that the Israeli budget was crying out for the low-interest loans.

Bush, for his part, by now desperately wanted to grant the guarantees. Just as AIPAC's Dine had warned, Jewish voters were looking like a significant swing constituency in several states. And the presidential race in November was far different from a year before: Bush, so popular just after the Gulf War, now appeared likely to lose to Arkansas governor Bill Clinton.

Clearly wishing to patch up differences, Bush arranged a far more social occasion that he had ever offered to Shamir. Rabin spent August 10 and 11 at the Bush family vacation home in Kennebunkport, Maine—a New England version of the L.B.J. Ranch—and at the end of relaxed and friendly talks the president made what was, for Israel, a momentous announcement:

that he was "extremely pleased" to grant the $10 billion in guarantees.

Rabin read Bush's concerns very wisely. The Israeli publicly stressed that he was building "a relationship of trust and confidence" with the president. And he made it clear that Israel's "change in national priorities" would mean little or no spending on settlements.

On the Israeli side, some Likud-era officials at the embassy in Washington complained that the deal was not so great. They said that Rabin had simply capitulated to all the conditions that Shamir had rejected: notably, the president's right to reduce the amount of guarantees, dollar for dollar, to match almost any Israeli spending on infrastructure in the West Bank, Gaza, and Golan Heights.

American officials, on the other hand, said privately that they were going easy on Israel—now that Shamir was gone. "We believe that Rabin will tell us exactly what he's going to do," a U.S. official said just after the Kennebunkport summit. "No misleading, no surprises. So look: We're not demanding that all settlement activity is halted." Such is the importance of personal chemistry and trust between the leaders of the two nations.

The next day Rabin was in Washington to meet the Democrat nominee, Clinton. It was just a half-hour courtesy call, largely so that Rabin could not be accused of repeating his diplomatic flub of 1972, when he was openly favoring President Nixon's reelection.

However, despite the Israeli leader's efforts to avoid any impression of interfering in U.S. politics, the warmth and pliancy with which he reached the loan-guarantee agreement with Bush spoke volumes. And Rabin's aides undiplomatically leaked his assessment that compared with the president, Clinton was "shallow" when it came to international affairs.

It emerged that Rabin would have preferred to see Bush remain in the White House. First, a change in administration could take U.S. attention away from the Middle East peace talks, and they needed shepherding by the Americans. Also, Clinton was promising to shift America's focus onto the economy. Rabin feared that that could eventually mean less U.S. aid to Israel. So ironically, while Rabin had campaigned on a pledge of changing Israel's priorities, he did not want the Americans to change theirs if the Middle East would be affected.

American Jews, however, either couldn't take Rabin's hint or didn't care. Still angry over Bush's hostile words and tone on that September 12 that would "live in infamy," Jewish voters spurned the president. During the campaign many wealthy Jews with impeccable Republican credentials—tightened during the Reagan years—told friends that they would vote for Clinton because they could not forgive Bush for his hard line on Israel. Several admit that they "pretended" to be loyal Republicans, but secretly gave the Clinton campaign both money and information: all the inside planning documents and "talking points" distributed by the Bush-Quayle reelection committee to their usually reliable big givers.

"You have the clearest choice that I can recall in any presidential contest, as far as Israel is concerned," said Morris Amitay, the former AIPAC chief who remains a political guru to many American Jews. Bush's campaign argued valiantly that he had been good for Israel: strong military ties, his help in setting Russian Jews free, and the defeat of Iraq, among other reasons. But, said Amitay: "Any Jew voting for Bush must be doing it for the sake of his pocketbook. It certainly isn't for Israel's sake."

Overwhelmingly, Jews voted on the Israel issue—and the belief, widely held among Jews, that Bush and his administration were unsympathetic toward their concerns. Whereas Bush had received 27 percent of the Jewish vote in 1988, in 1992 he received only around 10 percent.

More than eight out of ten Jews voted for Bill Clinton, and as soon as he was elected the traditional examination period began. Jewish voters, like other Americans, were wondering if they had chosen well and how much Clinton's promised "change" would cost them in new taxes.

Amitay was so exuberant that visions of a Reagan-style golden era seemed to arise. "First, we're looking to get out of the Dark Ages!" he said. "I think Bush-Baker was the Dark Ages, in terms of hostility toward Israel, so this *has* to be a better administration."

Israelis, who are remarkably well plugged in to worldwide events, did their best to sort through the new cast of characters. There was widespread relief, in Israel, that George Bush was gone. But, watching state-run television and a host of cable channels, Israeli viewers stared agape at the youthful glory of America's festivities—leading to the mini-Woodstock of the inaugural balls in Washington on January 20, 1993.

Israelis were accustomed to political gatherings filled with shouting rather than dancing and to prime ministers in their seventies who rarely smiled. But the style of Israeli politics was changing, showing signs of imitating that of the United States. The notion of holding "primaries"—and calling them that, even in Hebrew—was embraced by Israel's major parties. Likud voters, impressed by Bibi Netanyahu's American-style political marketing, chose him as their new party leader; a man in his midforties to replace the aged Shamir.

However, most Israelis were still obsessed with the old way of measuring relations with the United States. They still asked the same old questions: Is the change good for Israel? Will the Clinton administration be friendly? Will the clean sweep in

Washington put a new shine on U.S.-Israel relations or cover them with dust?

The questions were legitimate and natural considering the roller-coaster nature of the relations and Israel's great dependence on America. But they also showed Israel's great egocentrism. The searching curiosity to find hidden meanings was often coupled with a sense, encouraged by the hyperactive Israeli media, that the Jewish state was the center of the world. In newspapers and on radio and television, the narrowmindedness was often expressed, although by now half jokingly, in a simple and oft-repeated question: "Is it good for the Jews?"

The media and political circles, whose nonstop gossip goes later into the night in Tel Aviv and Jerusalem than it does in early-to-bed Washington, turned their attention to the new American ruling class. The analysis was not initiated by the prime minister or the intelligence community, but was rather the spontaneous reaction of a worried and inquisitive public.

They tried to count the number of Jews in Congress, apparently 33 out of 435. They were amazed to find 10 Jewish senators out of 100. Were there many Jews in the cabinet? And when the name-dissection and speculation ran dry, Israelis started wondering how many White House and congressional aides were Jewish. And what about their spouses?

Whatever their religious persuasion, American officials then came under the magnifying glass as to their attitudes toward Israel. The same process occurred with the beginning of every new U.S. administration, but Clinton's truly gave cause for conversation.

Israelis heard stories about Bill and Hillary Clinton's warm relationships with Jews in their home state of Arkansas and with pro-Israel activists who had worked hard for the Democratic election victory. Israel and American Jews were delighted with Vice President Al Gore. He had been a reliable friend of the Jewish state, as his father had been, both of them senators from Tennessee.

And what about Warren Christopher, the new secretary of state? Would his years in the Carter administration affect his treatment of Israel? His replies, in Senate confirmation hearings, could not have been better: "We believe that America's unswerving commitment to Israel and Israel's right to exist behind secure borders are essential to a just and lasting peace." But Israelis had heard nice words before.

At least Les Aspin, the new defense secretary, was a familiar and friendly face. But might he repudiate the strong support he had shown, as chairman of the Senate Armed Services Committee, for strategic cooperation and for the Israeli defense industries?

And what about Mickey Kantor, Clinton's friend who would now be U.S. trade representative, and Robert Reich, the new labor secretary? Were they good Jews? To the Israeli press and some politicians, that meant supporting whatever Israel's cabinet might demand of America. Were these children of the liberal sixties at all interested in Israel?

At least by religious measures, Israelis had little doubt that Dan Kurtzer was a good Jew. His son was studying at a Jewish *yeshiva* in Israel. How would that affect his remaining on the State Department's Middle East team? What about Dennis Ross, also a Jewish holdover from the Bush-Baker team for the Middle East peace talks?

And was Samuel Lewis—back in State as policy planning chief—only a former ambassador? Or was he a friend, as measured by Israel's exaggerated standards?

Whether out of naïveté or cynicism, Israeli officials were convinced that international relations were heavily affected by personal backgrounds and contacts. When the Shamir administration noticed that Bush and Baker's advisors on Israel included several Jews, Israel hoped for lenient treatment. And then when the Jewish U.S. officials showed that they could lean on Israel as much as any other American might, Shamir's officials were angry and privately labeled those U.S. policy makers as "self-hating Jews" or "Baker's Jew-boys."

Having had only half an hour with Clinton the previous August, Rabin made a point of visiting the White House on March 15, 1993—a relatively early get-acquainted call, less than eight weeks after the start of the administration. This was an encounter between a brilliant, image-conscious politician from Little Rock and the most successful product of 1930s-style Israeli macho militarism. They had little in common. Their historical experiences and cultural outlooks were worlds apart.

Over the years, in both America and Israel, voices could be heard whining that the leaders of the other country "don't understand our mentality." Malcolm Hoenlein, of the Conference of Presidents of Major American Jewish Organizations, says: "Most Israeli politicians lack a real understanding of American events, and the Israeli media is only interested in gossip." On the Israeli side, Eitan Ben-Zur, a diplomat in charge of the American desk at the foreign ministry, complains: "Some American officials may know Israelis, but they don't know Israeli society and don't understand our politics."

However, more than any previous administration, Clinton had assembled a group of advisors who were true experts on Israel: Samuel Berger, number two in the National Security Council, and Martin Indyk, the NSC's Middle East expert. Berger was known as an American Jew who supported left-of-center causes in Israel, and Indyk was a former AIPAC researcher who had set up a Middle East think tank financed by AIPAC backers. Together with Samuel Lewis, here was a team intimately familiar with Israeli society. They had friends in most walks of Israeli life—politicians, journalists, businesspeople, and intelligence officers.

It was no wonder that Rabin was uncomfortable with Clinton's new braintrust, the aides who seemed to feel that they knew better than the Israelis what was good for Israel. At the least, they would not be fooled by gimmicks that Israelis had used in the past to enhance their position in Washington. Not that it was Rabin's style to lie or play games, but no one enjoys being transparent in the eyes of others.

There was a new, softer edge to the American approach toward Israel—but still, it was an edge and not a feather duster. Unlike Bush, whose obsession with Jewish settlements created an ugly undertone to the point that relations were defined by an Israeli newspaper as "a war," Clinton spoke affectionately of Israel and warmed the once-chilly atmosphere.

Yet even when he proposed, at the March summit, to "deepen" strategic cooperation, he seemed perfectly comfortable making demands of Israel. A tiny example might demonstrate that interests and perceptions do not disappear overnight, even when there is a change in government in both countries. Bush and Shamir were defeated in their 1992 elections, and yet the United States kept probing Israel on the settlements issue. In the middle of the following year, the American government delivered a questionnaire to Israel, demanding that every penny spent in the West Bank and Gaza Strip be accounted for. Rabin's Israel felt humiliated, no less than Shamir's Israel had felt, as if its wallet were being rifled through by U.S. patrons.

But Rabin felt he had a reputation for honesty to uphold, in order to avoid the accusations of duplicity hurled at Shamir by Washington. So the new prime minister supplied precise data, which the United States then used to cut 1994's installment of the loan guarantees by $437 million, the amount spent by Israel on settlement-related development in 1992–93.

Rabin also felt compelled to promise Clinton that there would be no Begin-style surprises. Israel gave in to American pressure by joining the Missile Technology Control Regime aimed at preventing the spread of ballistic know-how.

The new administration would not go beyond Bush's offer to link Israel to a satellite early-warning system against missiles next time there was a crisis like the 1991 Gulf War. Israel did not want to wait for war to break out before receiving a satellite downlink, but Washington continued to guard jealously its intelligence. And in the background, as always, Israeli nuclear weapons were a potential source of disagreement. Clinton persisted with Bush's policy of actively tightening the market for weapons of mass destruction, and the Israelis were concerned that this could apply to them as well as to the Iraqis, Iranians, and Syrians.

Clinton had good reason to feel that he could be as firm as he was friendly toward Israel. He knew that he had political assets: Rabin's Israel being more flexible than Shamir's, the Democrats having gotten Jewish votes, and his own pro-Israel image. Now, sounding like an echo of George Bush, Clinton was calling on America's Israeli partner "to take risks for peace."

But the new administration would not be obsessively involved in the negotiations. Israel itself would have to work harder, because without peace there was no commitment to future foreign aid. Clinton's only promise was to keep the assistance level for one year at $3 billion, plus various special projects in science, technology, and military cooperation. The president said he would make his "best efforts to maintain those levels" in future years. But there was no further promise.

After his summit with Clinton, Rabin seemed to embrace the thought behind a Hebrew proverb, *"Im ein ani li mi li?"*— loosely translated as "If I do not help myself, who else will?" He could see that this U.S. administration had little passion for the Middle East and would busy itself instead with health care and other domestic reforms.

There would be no repeat of Carter's intense Camp David, nor of Kissinger's flashy shuttle diplomacy. Determined to pull

Israel's own chestnuts out of the fire, Rabin ordered his intelligence community and foreign ministry to launch secret negotiations with the state's archenemy, the PLO. The alternatives—letting the U.S.-sponsored peace talks drift and eventually facing Palestinians turned to Islamic radicals—seemed unwise to him.

The results of the clandestine meetings shocked the world. In September 1993 Israel and the PLO announced that they reached an agreement for the gradual transformation of power in the West Bank and Gaza Strip from Israeli military authority to a locally led Arab administration: basically, the autonomy rejected by the Palestinians after Camp David fifteen years earlier.

While the United States in fact played a very marginal role in bringing the two sides together, President Clinton quickly recovered from his initial surprise and unblushingly jumped on the peace wagon to reap some of its dividends in public and strategic relations. Orchestrating the historic White House handshake between Yitzhak Rabin and Yasser Arafat with great efficiency and PR flair, Clinton presided over the ceremony as if he deserved most of the credit for it. Yet he also had the grace to invite all five living former presidents, as a symbolic reminder that ever since Franklin D. Roosevelt all American presidents and administrations, in one way or another, cared and worked to see this day of reconciliation. Carter and Bush were able to attend, delighted to witness the almost unimaginable sight.

American Jews were also surprised, and it took many of them even longer than it took the Israeli public to recover from the trauma. Their perceptions of the world and its basic hostility to Israel and the Jewish people were collapsing before their eyes. During fifteen years of Likud governments in Israel, Jewish community leaders in the United States had recited the Israeli party line that had dismissed Arafat and his group as a "gang of terrorists." The demonizing and dehumanizing were so strong that, in a sense, American Jews not only swallowed them but became greater believers in these harsh prescriptions than were the Israelis who prescribed them.

Nevertheless, within days, U.S. Jewry regained its sense of direction and rallied around the Israeli government, as had been its habit since 1948. It helped that they were pointed toward a new aim: to help the fledgling peace stand on its feet by financial support—to Israel, and now wherever possible to new institutions encouraging Israeli-Palestinian coexistence.

To maintain the momentum, Secretary of State Christopher organized a conference of forty-three nations that pledged a total of $2.4 billion to help the Palestinians of the West Bank and Gaza. The U.S. share, over a five-year period, would be $500 million. Yet administration officials told a gathering of American Jews and Arab-Americans—after joyously convening them together, shattering the tradition of separate briefings—that most of the money to build a new Middle East would have to come from private investors.

Whatever the positive spin Israeli leaders put on the financial side of the rush toward peace, they were privately disappointed. While Israel would be allowed to use some of the money allocated through loan guarantees to pay for the redeployment of forces, this was nothing like the pattern set since 1973. This time, U.S. government funds would not finance Israeli withdrawals. Nixon, Ford, and Carter had doled out billions of dollars to soften troop pullbacks in Sinai and on the Golan Heights, but Clinton declined to pick up the check when Israel served up Gaza and parts of the West Bank.

It was difficult for self-centered Israelis, even for Rabin who prided himself on being an expert on the United States, to comprehend that America's national agenda was being rewritten. In what now seemed to be the good old days, Israel would have worked wonders on Capitol Hill to win financial aid and other valuable signs of support.

But there were the new political realities of domestic priorities and the turnover in Congress—with one-quarter of the seats held by newcomers. Israel and the pro-Israel lobby would have to work with them, learn about them, and work on them when needed. To teach them the facts of Israeli-American life would take time, and in the meantime the facts might change.

Some well-established lines of communication, through congressmen and senior staffers on important committees, were cut when they lost their jobs. In the Senate, Bob Kasten of Wisconsin, who had sponsored the loan guarantees for Israel, was defeated. In the House Foreign Affairs Committee, one of Israel's most vociferous Christian champions, Dante Fascell, retired; while his fellow Floridian, Larry Smith, was bounced by the House check-writing scandal. Smith was among the most solid defenders of Israel's cause, frequently visiting the Israeli embassy to be briefed, and was remembered for his ferocious attacks on Secretary of State Baker during the loan guarantees fight.

Another great loss, from Israel's point of view, was that of Steven Solarz. A senior member of House Foreign Affairs and chairman of his own subcommittee, he had become a solid pillar of support for the Jewish state. His staffers had Israeli memorabilia on their shelves, including photos of David Ben-Gurion. Solarz was a frequent visitor to Israel, enthusiastically thought up legislation to help the country, and had a solid voting record from AIPAC's point of view.

But his defeat in 1992 was not merely part of an anti-incumbent turnover. It was part of a deeper trend. On the surface, Solarz was a victim of a redistricting that eliminated his New York City district—one of only two in the nation with a Jewish majority. The purpose was to produce a Hispanic member of Congress, and while Solarz did stage a desperate run in the newly carved district, the winner was Nydia Velasquez. She was not anti-Israel and, like most New York politicians, was aware of Jewish influence and concerns. But it was telling that her first official trip abroad was not to Israel—as was almost standard for New York legislators—but to Haiti. And, totally unlike Solarz, she opposed foreign aid, saying: "Why should my constituents accept sending their tax dollars overseas when they desperately need vital housing, health services, education, drug counseling, and infrastructure investment?"

Solarz's replacement by Velasquez reflected more significant changes in America's social fabric. Since the 1960s, when non-European immigrants began to outnumber the Europeans moving to America, the country has undergone a significant political, cultural, and social transformation.

What Israelis—and some of their supporters—seem not to understand is that the United States is again becoming a nation of immigrants in the original sense, with 11 percent of its inhabitants born in foreign lands. One out of four Americans is of African, Asian, or Hispanic origin, and the proportion continues to rise.

Members of the growing minority groups, even if they are not hostile to Israel, have their own pressing priorities. A cry for attention came from the Congressional Black Caucus, which in 1992 attempted to link the loan guarantees for Israel to housing and small business aid to America's inner cities. Congresswoman Maxine Waters recognized that "Israel has to absorb hundreds of thousands of new immigrants, but our cities deserve the same priority." She warned it would be impossible to explain foreign aid to "our people."

U.S. aid to Israel is under pressure, not only because of the ethnic and demographic remaking of America, but because all politicians feel the crisis of decaying cities, deficient education, and insufficient health care. To most Americans, the $13 billion appropriated for foreign aid in fiscal 1994 was difficult to defend, even though that was 7 percent less than the previous year.

But Israel's annual $3 billion was not touched. For years pessimists had been predicting that levels of aid would be slashed—if not immediately, then soon. A "cry-wolf" syndrome developed, with the harbingers of doom ignored. Yet even as the 1994 bill passed, by a resounding 88 to 10 in the Senate, congressmen and ambassadors warned Israel that it must adjust itself to a new reality to come. It was not clear when the wolf would materialize, but it seemed it would one day appear, dressed in the cloak of urban policy, national health care, or a sudden interest in another part of the world.

Indeed there are a few voices, both Israeli and American, advocating that there would be some good in making a small cut in U.S. aid to Israel's economy. It would reduce Israeli dependence on America; it would force Israelis to work harder; and it would enhance Israel's image as a fully fledged partner.

The U.S. ambassador to Israel, William Harrop, caused a stir in early 1993 by bluntly expressing those themes. "It may prove difficult to maintain our economic aid at its current high level," said Harrop. "Perhaps it is not prudent, in any case, for a nation to rely in the long term, even on its most dependable ally, for 7 to 8 percent of its national budget."

His counterpart in Washington, Israel's ambassador Zalman Shoval, went even further. He said that unless Israel takes the first step toward reducing the economic assistance it receives from America, a hefty $1.2 billion a year, the more essential $1.8 billion military aid could be endangered. "We could be faced with a unilateral decision on the part of the United States to cut foreign aid along lines that would be less convenient for us and also politically more difficult for our friends in Congress to resist."

In a changing world, there are also new doubts about the

military side of the alliance: about the money the U.S. gives, and about the wider issue of Israel's strategic value. The early Reagan era motivation was based almost entirely on challenging a Soviet "evil empire" that no longer exists. Now that the Cold War is over, why does America need Israel? Military complexes are giving way to new concerns about poverty at home and starvation abroad. These new trends might challenge U.S.-Israeli cooperation.

In addition, the experience of the Gulf War might suggest that Israel was unneeded when America projected its power into the region—to the point that it was an obstacle to U.S. plans.

On the other hand, even without a Cold War the Middle East remains as important to the West as ever. It is close to Europe, where a cost-conscious United States is reducing its military presence. And Western economies still depend on Mideast oil.

Saddam Hussein's Iraq was a clear, unequivocal threat to the oil fields and its neighbors, and America was able to rally most Arabs into an alliance against him. But what if a different type of crisis erupts in the future, endangering the flow of oil to the West? Instead of Cold War, the United States might face a holy war by Muslim fundamentalists. The spread of Islamic influence and occasional terror, in the Middle East and in America, is and will continue to be a source of concern to Washington. While the United States might have difficulty finding local partners offering to cooperate, in almost all scenarios Israel would be willing and able to help.

America is already cooperating with Israel in trying to block Islamic fundamentalism on the edges of the Middle East. Recognizing the geopolitical importance of former Soviet republics in central Asia, with their Muslim populations, the United States appropriated several million dollars to pay Israeli agricultural and technical advisors in Kazakhstan.

But in times of genuine crisis, Israel's usefulness goes

beyond mere political will to be supportive. Being helpful also includes the tactical ability to act effectively: the similarity of weapons systems with the United States, the experience of joint maneuvers, visits by thousands of military personnel to each other's countries every year, the materiel stored by the United States in Israel, the exchange of intelligence, and the regular consultations on vital interests—all the fruits of a full decade of formal strategic cooperation.

However, the U.S.-Israel alliance cannot afford to put all its chips in a strategic basket. Tangible and practical programs—whether military or economic—do not provide sufficient fuel to keep the engine running forever.

"The ethos of America is democracy," said Senator Richard Lugar, a member of the Foreign Relations committee and long-time friend of Israel. "As long as you maintain democracy with all its symbols and expressions, your relations with the U.S. are good. If you base your relations on military necessity, as important as that might be, they stand on shaky foundations and have chances of collapsing a lot faster."

Lugar's recommendation echoed the old argument that for many years underlay U.S.-Israel relations: Should the *realpolitik* interests of strategy and defense be stressed, as AIPAC chose to do in the golden era of the 1980s? Or should Israel emphasize the emotional side of the alliance, as Teddy Kollek and Abba Eban did in the early days, stressing Holocaust memories and common values such as religion and democracy?

But the passage of time presents the challenge of narrowed choices. The demographic shifts in the direction of ethnic minorities reduce the chance of touching them by raising subjects with which they have nothing in common. The Holy Land is a much more distant concept to people not descended from Europe, where the prevailing Western culture felt a strong link with the cradle of Judeo-Christian civilization.

From a political point of view, Israel may also find its special links with Christians weakened, should Palestinians—reaping curiosity as the oppressed underdogs who deserve sympathy for their unexpected turn onto the path of peace—start emphasizing their affiliation with the Holy Land.

And then comes the Holocaust factor. To many of the newly empowered minority groups in America, this is also a distant, unfamiliar concept. It was not their families who were wiped out in the Holocaust, and they were not part of the political ruling class that failed to save the Jews and thus might feel guilty.

"The Holocaust is fading away," says Charles Schumer, a New York congressman with the only remaining majority-Jewish district in the country. As survivors and witnesses grow older and die, the atrocities that formed the background to the birth of Israel have less impact—even on American Jews. The Jewish community demonstrated political and financial clout by helping to erect the U.S. Holocaust Memorial Museum in 1993. But the moving tribute to the victims of Nazism also suggested that, as the decades pass, the Holocaust factor—so useful in building support for Israel—may become a museum piece.

The United States is, as time goes on, not the same country lobbied in Israel's early days by Teddy Kollek and Abba Eban. The audience is not the same that was thrilled by *Exodus*.

"The *Exodus* syndrome is in trouble," says David Saperstein, a veteran of Jewish activism in Washington. "When most Americans over the age of thirty were asked, 'What do you think of when I say Israeli?' they used to think of Paul Newman in the movie *Exodus*. That was the filter through which they saw Israel. President Bush changed that. People now weigh the liabilities and pluses of Israel differently."

AIPAC was slow to realize that its world was changing. President Bush, in the loan-guarantees fight, called the bluff of the pro-Israel community and won. He lost his election, but he managed to strip the lobby of its cloak of invincibility. The Clinton-Rabin era found AIPAC disoriented, not knowing whether to stress the "shared values" argument for Israel or play the "strategic" card.

AIPAC was certainly taken aback when attacked harshly by—of all people—the prime minister of Israel. In August 1992, two months after his election victory, Yitzhak Rabin went to Washington and lectured Tom Dine and other officers of the lobby. Angry at how badly the loan-guarantee fight had gone, Rabin accused AIPAC of having worked too closely with the Likud party—echoing Labor complaints in the mid-1980s that the lobby was serving Likud's interests rather than Israel's.

Rabin, plainly exaggerating, said AIPAC had done more harm than good and had not gotten Israel "a penny." Dine and his colleagues were, to put it mildly, shocked. Members who had devoted their lives to helping Israel now felt like worthless has-beens.

The prime minister also underlined his annoyance with Jews in the United States—self-styled right-wingers—who criticized his government for its stated willingness to give up some disputed territory in exchange for peace.

Heads began to roll at AIPAC, some by coincidence and some less so. A vice president of the lobby who openly told members of the Rabin cabinet that they had "chutzpah" for offering to give up the occupied Golan Heights was forced to resign at the Israeli government's insistence.

The president of AIPAC, David Steiner, had to resign in disgrace after being caught—on tape—making inflated claims to a potential contributor. Steiner claimed AIPAC was negotiating with President Clinton for White House posts. "He's got something in his heart for the Jews," said Steiner. "He's got Jewish friends. Bush has no Jewish friends. We have a dozen people in the campaign. They're all going to get big jobs."

The biggest blow to the solid AIPAC wall built in the 1980s came when Tom Dine, the executive director and chief energizer of the lobby, was forced to resign in June 1993 for a similarly stupid error. Dine was quoted, in a book about Orthodox Jews, as saying their image was "smelly." Orthodox groups were in an uproar and demanded Dine's head. Some of them had never worked with him on pro-Israel projects, and some disapproved of Dine because he was married to a non-Jew.

Had it not been for the loan-guarantees failure, followed by Rabin's strong rebuke, Dine might have toughed out the onslaught from the Orthodox. The lobby's board would have been on his side. But by now it was widely felt to be time for a change.

AIPAC will survive, however, trimming and adjusting its role in Washington to the new realities. However unpalatable it might have once seemed, AIPAC declared that it would lobby for U.S. aid to help Palestinians have a brighter future, which would in turn help Israel be more stable and strong. Many Jewish organizations started adjusting to the notion that Palestinians would raise a new, positive profile with political action groups and fund-raising mechanisms. And now, instead of opposing them, Jews could find common cause with them.

In this adjusted mission, AIPAC is still capable because it still has plenty of members, money, and lobbyists, a formula that will always have some impact so long as the nature of politics does not change dramatically.

But there is a fundamental problem for the lobby at its grassroots. The Jewish community, the traditional bridge between American society and Israel, may cease to be a rock-solid base of support. Very few bother to visit Israel, and each successive generation shows signs of being less connected to the Jewish state. Leaders of the community are desperate to stem the tide of intermarriage, which threatens to slash the number of Jews identifying themselves with Judaism and Israel. And should successive generations include half Jews, quarter Jews, and other fractional Jews who feel no allegiance to Israel, the alliance is bound to suffer.

In addition, the myth of Jewish political power has begun to be unmasked as just that: a myth. Jews are no longer exclusively tied to the Democratic party. And the Democrats are not tied exclusively to Jewish and Israeli concerns. They have taken note of the emergence of Arab-Americans as a growing ethnic lobby, ironically modeling itself on the experience and successful tactics of politically active Jews.

In any event, in the key electoral states where Jews happen to live, such as New York and California, they would have to vote almost unanimously for a single candidate to tip the balance in most races. The political power that the organized Jewish community managed to acquire, during Israel's first four decades, seems set to decline.

Especially alarming could be the shrinkage, and perhaps the abolition, of PACs. The political action committees worked almost perfectly for the Jewish community, with the rise of nearly a hundred pro-Israel PACs in the 1980s. But President Clinton and congressional leaders drew up plans to do away with "special interest" fund-raising mechanisms. And the impact of pro-Israel political contributors could be sharply reduced.

The vision of a post-PAC political scene is motivating Jewish organizations to meet the new challenge: by reshaping their fund-raising and political muscles so as to maintain influence and not be pushed aside.

It would be wrong, indeed, to assume that despite the undeniable changes and tremendous challenges, the U.S.-Israel alliance is in mortal danger. It has already outlived predictions that its pillars were crumbling. Those prophecies of doom had no eternal standing.

Some basic policies survive, and many patterns repeat themselves—as has been seen going back to 1948. Samuel Lewis urges that the basic "intangibles" be put back at the fore of the alliance. The former ambassador says "mutual values, history,

Holocaust guilt, and Israel being the only democracy in the region" were always what counted the most.

"There was added to that the icing on the cake—what the Reagan administration called 'the strategic relationship.' And now when the Cold War has been swept away, the icing doesn't look so colorful and impressive any more. You take it away, and you see the cake is a bit moldy. It needs renewing," Lewis concludes.

The interests, emotions, and perceptions that underlie the alliance have not disappeared, however. General Colin Powell, chairman of the Joint Chiefs of Staff during the Gulf War, comments: "For me, the friendship between the United States and Israel is a personal bond. It is a bond that will continue to weather any storm—a bond that will never, never be broken."

Or as Richard Nixon sums up the unique friendship of the United States and Israel: "We are not formal allies, but we are bound together by an even stronger moral commitment. Our indispensable partnership has endured some difficult times, but no American President will ever let Israel go down the tube."

Notes

CHAPTER ONE

In a letter to the authors dated October 4, 1993, former President George Bush also wrote: "As I stood on the White House lawn and watched the famous handshake, I had this wonderful feeling of elation. Just a very few years ago, who would have thought such a meeting possible? . . . And without the historic Madrid meeting, the handshake would have been impossible. I took pride in what our team had done. I thought particularly of Jim Baker, our able Secretary of State, and of all the trips he had made. And I thought of my trusted N.S.C. adviser Brent Scowcroft, who helped me through so many mine fields."

Responding to a question on the discord between himself and Israel's Prime Minister Yitzhak Shamir, Bush added: "I thought of past difficulties in dealing with some personalities in the Middle East, but I mainly rejoiced in the fact that dramatic progress had been made."

The description of the meeting between Paul Wolfowitz and Lieutenant Colonel Krimkowitz appeared in the Israeli newspaper *Ma'a-riv* the next day, January 22, 1991. Wolfowitz was interviewed in

November 1993 and Krimkowitz in December 1993, both in Washington.

Lawrence Eagleburger, former secretary of state, was interviewed from his home in Washington in March 1993.

CHAPTER TWO

One of the most informative books describing links between America and pre-Israel Palestine is David Finnie, *Pioneers East: The Early American Experience in the Middle East* (Cambridge, MA: Harvard University Press, 1967).

Other books we found useful are: Frank E. Manuel, *The Realities of American-Palestine Relations* (Washington, DC: Public Affairs Press, 1949) and Edward Robinson, *Biblical Researches in Palestine*, vol. 1 (London: Sussex Press, 1841).

U.S. Navy Lieutenant W. F. Lynch recorded his impressions of Palestine—and in particular hoisting the Stars and Stripes flag on the Dead Sea shore at Ein Gedi on April 22, 1848—in *Narrative of the United States Expedition to the River Jordan and the Dead Sea*, published in 1853; cited by Jacob Stein in *Long Island Jewish World* (Great Neck, New York), July 23–29, 1993.

Mark Twain described his impressions in *The Innocents Abroad, or the New Pilgrims' Progress* (New York: Harper and Brothers, 1911), which he wrote in 1867 and was a best-seller when first published in July 1869; quotations are from volume 2, pp. 198, 201, 224, 248.

The best source for the history of the American colony in Jerusalem is Bertha Spafford-Vester, *Our Jerusalem: An American Family in the Holy City, 1881–1949* (New York: Random House, 1950).

On Henry Morgenthau, Sr., arranging aid for the Jews of Palestine, his "cablegram" sent from Turkey to Jacob Schiff, an American Jewish philanthropist of German origin, can be found in the archives of the American Jewish Joint Distribution Committee in New York. Historian Barbara Tuchman spoke of how Morgenthau's son-in-law Maurice Wertheim—her father—carried $50,000 worth of gold coins to Jerusalem. She also spoke of support for Eliezar Ben-Yehuda, in remarks published as "The Assimilationist Dilemma: Ambassador Morgenthau's Story," in Clark M. Clifford, Eugene V. Rostow, and Barbara W. Tuchman, *The Palestine Question in American History* (New York: Arno Press, 1978), pp. 8, 9, 13.

On the Holocaust, when the information reached the West, and the inaction that followed, see: Martin Gilbert, *Auschwitz and the Allies: How the Allies Responded to the News of Hitler's "Final Solution"* (London: Michael Joseph, 1981); Walter Laqueur, *The Terrible Secret: Suppression of the Truth about Hitler's 'Final Solution'* (Middlesex, England: Penguin, 1982); Walter Laqueur and Richard Breitman, *Breaking the Silence* (New York: Simon and Schuster, 1986); and Dina Porat, *The Blue and Yellow Stars of David: The Zionist Leadership in Palestine and the Holocaust* (Cambridge, MA: Harvard University Press, 1990).

Gan-Or (Gaynor) Jacobson was interviewed, from his home in Scottsdale, Arizona, in February 1993.

CHAPTER THREE

The Truman-Jacobson partnership is related in, among other books, David McCullough, *Truman* (New York: Simon and Schuster, 1992), pp. 107–108, 145–150.

The basic attitudes of the Departments of State and Defense are laid out by Truman's aide, Clark M. Clifford, in his article "Recognizing Israel: The Behind-the-Scenes Struggle in 1948 Between the President and the State Department," *American Heritage* (April 1977): 4–14.

Truman's recitation of Deuteronomy is noted by Clifford in his book *Counsel to the President* (New York: Random House, 1991), p. 8.

Eddie Jacobson saying "I'm no Zionist" and "Mission accomplished" is in Michael J. Cohen, *Truman and Israel* (Berkeley: University of California Press, 1990), pp. 167–168.

Dean Rusk's actions at the UN are recalled by Robert Manning in *The Swamp Root Chronicle* (New York: W.W. Norton, 1993), excerpted in *Nieman Reports* (Nieman Foundation, Harvard University) (Spring 1993): 59.

The president's remark that Jesus could not please the Jews is in McCullough, *Truman*, p. 599.

Truman wrote of "extreme Zionist" pressure in his *Memoirs: Years of Trial and Hope, 1946–1952* (New York: Doubleday, 1956), pp. 188–191.

Eddie Jacobson wrote that Truman was "close to being an anti-Semite" in a letter to a friend, quoted in Cohen, *Truman and Israel,* pp. 186–187, where details of the "Andrew Jackson" comparison with Weizmann are also given.

Weizmann's lecture to Truman about the Negev is recounted in McCullough, *Truman,* p. 604; I. L. Kenen, *Israel's Defense Line: Her Friends and Foes in Washington* (Buffalo, NY: Prometheus, 1981), p. 57; and a Clifford lecture published as "Factors Influencing President Truman's Decision to Support Partition," in Clifford, Eugene Rostow, and Barbara Tuchman, *The Palestine Question in American History* (New York: Arno Press, 1978), p. 32.

Abba Eban was interviewed in New York in September 1992. On Truman's meetings with Jacobson and then with Weizmann, see also Eban, *Personal Witness: Israel Through My Eyes* (New York: Putnam, 1992), pp. 133–134; and McCullough, *Truman,* pp. 606–607, 610–612.

The Clifford-Marshall debate is recounted by Clifford in "Factors Influencing . . . ," pp. 36–40, and *Counsel to the President,* pp. 12–14. Clifford's version, as recorded by oral histories in 1949 and 1971, is used in Cohen, *Truman and Israel,* pp. 212–214.

David Niles's observation that a Roosevelt presidency might not have produced a Jewish state is in McCullough, *Truman,* p. 596.

The American Council for Judaism statement was in the *New York Times,* May 15, 1948.

Shertok's quote on "suicide" was in the *New York Times,* May 14, 1948, as was Chavez's thundering speech.

The timing of the U.S. recognition of Israel is according to Cohen, *Truman and Israel,* pp. 218–219, and corroborating sources.

James G. McDonald described his arrival in *My Mission in Israel* (New York: Simon and Schuster, 1951), pp. 9, 20, 36–37. When Truman granted *de jure* recognition in 1949, McDonald became the first full-fledged ambassador in Israel. The Soviet envoy Pavel Yershov was merely a minister in a legation rather than an embassy.

Ben-Gurion, on "independence and security," in McDonald, *My Mission in Israel,* p. 49. McDonald, on "death sentence," ibid., p. 51. McDonald, on Israel's rejecting withdrawal, ibid., p. 88.

McDonald quotes his "personal and confidential" note of February 3, 1949, in ibid., p. 137.

McDonald's five-point summary of U.S. policy toward Israel was made at a conference of U.S. Near East envoys in Istanbul in November 1949; ibid., p. 202.

Teddy Kollek's background and New York assignment are vividly described in memoirs co-authored with his son Amos Kollek, *For Jerusalem: A Life* (New York: Random House, 1978), pp. 1–17, 37–62, 67–89.

Kollek discussed his clandestine work in an interview, as mayor of Jerusalem, in March 1991.

The number of foreign volunteers in the 1948–49 war has never been established with precision, but Howard M. Sachar, in *A History of the Jews in America* (New York: Alfred A. Knopf, 1992), pp. 616–617, says there were 3,400, making up 7 percent of Israel's army.

Harry Eckerman, a retired U.S. diplomat, told of his surprising job offer on Tinian Island, while interviewed in Tucson, Arizona, in April 1992.

The Pentagon report on former army officers' files is quoted in Stephen Green, *Taking Sides: America's Secret Relations with a Militant Israel* (New York: Morrow, 1984), pp. 53–54.

Details of Hank Greenspun's colorful life are in his autobiography, written with Alex Pelle, *Where I Stand: The Record of a Reckless Man* (New York: David McKay, 1967); and from his widow, Barbara, interviewed from her *Las Vegas Sun* office in November 1993; also in *Ha'aretz*, May 7, 1993.

Greenspun was called the "Robin Hood of the gambling community" in a story by Dick Donovan and Douglass Cater in *The Reporter*, July 1953, cited in Greenspun with Pelle, *Where I Stand*, p. 193.

His knowing "every wrinkle" on a Herzl painting is in Greenspun with Pelle, *Where I Stand*, p. 4. He said Jews will always be "hounded, driven, and burned" on p. 83. Working for Bugsy Siegel is on pp. 70–71; and helping Jimmy Hoffa help Israel, pp. 273–275. When Hoffa visited Israel he was a vice president of the Teamsters, but in 1957 he became president of the powerful union. After his links with organized crime were exposed Hoffa spent time in prison and then disappeared, apparently murdered, in 1975.

The best source on organized crime connections with Israel is Robert Rockway of Tel Aviv University, who has specialized in Jewish gangsters. Interviewed in January 1993, he reconstructed Bugsy Siegel's conversation with the Zionist envoy from Palestine. That envoy, Reuven Dafni, wrote from Jerusalem to the authors in December 1993 that since he is writing his own memoirs he declines "to elaborate on the story."

Edward G. Robinson's film on behalf of the United Jewish Appeal, made in 1947 and kept in the Jewish Agency archives in Jerusalem, was shown on Israel Television on May 25, 1993.

The FBI's surveillance of the Israeli arms network is based on a March 1993 interview with Rachel Mizrachi Gronich, who was Kollek's secretary in New York; and in Teddy Kollek and Amos Kollek, *For Jerusalem: A Life* (New York: Random House, 1978), pp. 81 and 87.

On Al Schwimmer's trial, see Kollek, *For Jerusalem*, pp. 87–88; and Stephen Green, *Living by the Sword: America and Israel in the Middle East, 1968–1987* (London: Faber and Faber, 1988), pp. 217–218. Kollek revealed Sinatra's involvement in Israel's underground activities in summer 1993 during a fund-raiser at a Los Angeles restaurant. Among the sixty guests who came to support Kollek's campaign for reelection as mayor of Jerusalem (which he lost three months later) were Sinatra himself, Barbra Streisand, and Brian Greenspun. Brian, the son of Hank Greenspun, confirmed the story in a telephone interview from his *Las Vegas Sun* office in January 1994.

CHAPTER FOUR
On the origins of the American intelligence community, see Walter Laqueur, *A World of Secrets: The Uses and Limits of Intelligence* (New York: Basic Books, 1985); and Anthony Cave Brown, *Wild Bill Donovan: The Last Hero* (New York: Times Books, 1982).

The story of Fred Gronich was first published in Hebrew by Tom Segev, *1949: The First Israelis* (Jerusalem: Domino Press, 1984), pp. 252–254; and greatly expanded upon in interviews with Gronich in California and Israel in March and May 1993.

Abba Eban discussed the struggle for U.S. aid in the New York interview of September 1992.

Henry Morgenthau, Jr.'s help to Israel is recounted by his niece Barbara Tuchman in Clark Clifford, Eugene Rostow, and Tuchman, *The Palestine Question in American History* (New York: Arno Press, 1978), p. 13.

Memi de Shalit was interviewed in Tel Aviv in November 1992, on the initial contacts between Israel and the CIA and on lobbying for financial aid.

Angleton as Israel's "guardian angel" was discussed by a senior Israeli intelligence officer who asked not to be named. Angleton's appreciation of Israel as a "best friend" was conveyed to the authors by his son, James C. Angleton, in November 1993.

Further information on Mossad-U.S. relations can be found in Dan Raviv and Yossi Melman, *Every Spy a Prince: The Complete History of Israel's Intelligence Community* (Boston: Houghton Mifflin, 1990), pp. 76–94.

On the founding of AIPAC and Hollywood connections, see Teddy Kollek, *For Jerusalem: A Life* (New York: Random House, 1978), pp. 100 and 111; and I. L. Kenen, *Israel's Defense Line: Her Friends and Foes in Washington* (New York: Prometheus, 1981).

Kenen had himself previously been registered with the Justice Department as an agent of a foreign government, when he was employed by Israel's UN delegation; but his decision to register AIPAC as a domestic lobby was based on the conviction that a strong Israel was good for America. This early instinct would allow AIPAC to sidestep the stigma of being a foreign lobbyist.

Teddy Kollek, in his memoirs, gives brief and vague mention to his friendship with James Angleton; *For Jerusalem*, p. 98. He expanded in the Jerusalem interview of March 1991.

Elyashiv Ben-Horin's espionage and Chaim Herzog's activities in Washington were confirmed in interviews with de Shalit and with Kollek, and in March 1991 with Amos Manor, the former head of Shin Bet, Israel's domestic security service. The FBI refused to provide information on the Ben-Horin case without presentation of his notarized death certificate.

On American espionage activities in the 1950s and '60s in Israel, see the *Boston Globe* magazine of December 14, 1986. An article by Jeff McConnell and Richard Higgins cites Stephen Millet, a former OSS colleague brought in by Angleton for Israel-related projects. Millet acknowledged the existence of some U.S. intelligence operations against Israel but said that they were fewer in number than those that Israel mounted against the United States.

Victor Grayevski's role in supplying the secret Khrushchev speech was revealed by him, for the first time, in an interview in Jerusalem in January 1992.

CHAPTER FIVE

The description of Hubert Humphrey's Zionism is from his former aide, Max M. Kampelman, interviewed in Washington in October 1991; and Kampelman, *Entering New Worlds* (New York: Harper-Collins, 1991), pp. 70, 188.

Lobbying Richard M. Nixon at the 1952 Republican convention is recounted by Si Kenen, *Israel's Defense Line: Her Friends and Foes in Washington* (New York: Prometheus, 1981), p. 88; and Nixon's letter to Louis Lipsky on pp. 88–89.

Abba Eban, in a September 1992 conversation with the authors, gave credit for the joke about "looking for mercy" to the late Supreme Court justice Felix Frankfurter; and in *Personal Witness: Israel Through My Eyes* (New York: Putnam, 1992), p. 222, Eban writes that he said it himself to an American Treasury secretary.

Max M. Fisher recalled Eisenhower's remarks on the Dachau death camp at a seminar at Brandeis University, September 22, 1992.

Candidate Eisenhower's support for Arab rights can be found in the *Saturday Evening Post*, April 19, 1952.

Eisenhower's opinion that Israel could not absorb more weapons was recounted by Mordecai Gazit, former deputy chief of mission at Israel's embassy in Washington, at a Jerusalem seminar in honor of Max Fisher in June 1992.

Philip Klutznick, then president of the B'nai B'rith, recalled Eisenhower saying he might not have recognized Israel, in Steven L. Spiegel, *The Other Arab-Israeli Conflict* (Chicago: University of Chicago Press, 1985), p. 54.

On Dulles's visit to the Middle East, see Eban, *Personal Witness*, p. 234.

Roger Tyler's telegram from his Jerusalem consulate to the State Department, dated April 17, 1954; obtained and cited by Stephen Green, *Taking Sides: America's Secret Relations with a Militant Israel* (New York: Morrow, 1984), pp. 319–321.

Ariel Sharon's explanation of the Qibiya raid in Jordan is in his memoirs, coauthored with David Chanoff, *Warrior: An Autobiography* (New York: Simon and Schuster, 1989), pp. 89–90.

On Eric Johnston's mission, see Teddy Kollek, *For Jerusalem: A Life* (New York: Random House, 1978), pp. 110–111; and Spiegel, *Other Arab-Israeli Conflict*, p. 65.

Eisenhower, on stopping "the Soviet," in his memoirs, *The White House Years: Mandate for Change, 1953–1956* (Garden City, NY: Doubleday, 1963), p. 25. On the "New Look," in Eban, *Personal Witness*, p. 233; and "friendly impartiality," in an article by Isaac Alteras, "Eisenhower, American Jewry and Israel," *American Jewish Archives* 37, no. 2 (November 1985): 259, with thanks to Professor Alteras for oral elaboration.

Egypt's anger at Israel's Gaza Strip raid of February 1955 was reported by the U.S. Embassy in Cairo, and the Israeli political background was in a report from the U.S. Embassy in Tel Aviv; found in *Foreign Relations of the United States, 1955–1957*, vol. 14 (Washington, DC: Department of State, 1989), pp. 73, 87.

Project Alpha was outlined in State Department memos found in *Foreign Relations of the United States, 1955–1957*, vol. 14, pp. 38–41.

Prime Minister Sharett's November 1955 visit to Washington is recorded in ibid., vol. 14, pp. 795–796.

On Jews lobbying for U.S. arms to Israel, see Alteras, "Eisenhower, American Jewry and Israel," pp. 263–264.

On the United States encouraging France and Canada to sell arms to Israel, see Eban, *Personal Witness*, p. 244; and Alteras, "Eisenhower, American Jewry and Israel," p. 264.

On Project Gamma in early 1956, see Eban, *Personal Witness*, p. 244, and Spiegel, *Other Arab-Israeli Conflict*, p. 67. There is no record of a Project Beta.

Also on Robert Anderson's shuttle diplomacy, see *Foreign Relations of the United States, 1955–1957*, vol. 15, p. 26; Kollek, *For Jerusalem*, pp. 114–115; and Eban, *Personal Witness*, pp. 245–246.

Eisenhower's diary entry of March 13, 1956, is quoted in Spiegel, *Other Arab-Israeli Conflict*, p. 68.

CIA director Allen Dulles's letter to his brother, the secretary of state, is in *Foreign Relations of the United States, 1955–1957*, vol. 17: "Arab-Israeli Dispute, 1957" (Washington, DC: Department of State, 1990), pp. 590–593.

On Eisenhower's anger with Ben-Gurion over the timing of the Suez invasion, see his memoirs, *Waging Peace: The White House*

Years, 1956–1961 (Garden City, NY: Doubleday, 1965), p. 56.

Nixon expressed his concern over "Israeli votes" in a phone call to Dulles, found in *Foreign Relations of the United States, 1955–1957*, vol. 16, p. 885.

Eisenhower's phrase, "we didn't have a Jew in America," is in his November 2, 1956, letter to boyhood friend Swede Hazlett, found in his diaries at the Eisenhower Library in Abilene, Kansas; see Alteras, "Eisenhower, American Jewry and Israel," p. 259.

On America "slapped in the face" by the Suez/Sinai campaign, see Kollek, *For Jerusalem*, p. 116.

On Ben-Gurion's claim of a "Jewish kingdom" in Sinai, see Eban, *Personal Witness*, p. 275.

Ben-Gurion's "nightmarish day" is in his diary entry of November 8, 1956, quoted in Michael Bar-Zohar, *Ben-Gurion* (New York: Adama, 1986), p. 251.

On Rabbi Abba Hillel Silver seeing "an error of judgment," see Eban, *Personal Witness*, p. 259.

On "playing the string" of union support, Ephraim Evron, a special Israeli envoy to the American labor movement in the 1950s and later an ambassador to the United States, was interviewed in Tel Aviv, November 1992.

The successful lobbying of and by Senators Knowland and Johnson is recounted in *Foreign Relations of the United States, 1955–1957*, vol. 17, pp. 140, 141, 188. Dulles's complaint to the White House press secretary is on p. 196; and Eisenhower's remark on "congressional opposition" on February 20, 1957, is on pp. 214–215; the CIA's report on sanctions, dated February 19, is on p. 210.

On the threat to cancel tax deductibility, see George W. Ball and Douglas B. Ball, *The Passionate Attachment: America's Involvement with Israel, 1947 to the Present* (New York: W.W. Norton, 1992), p. 48. A similar threat arose in 1958 but was quashed when Eisenhower's most senior Jewish official, Lewis Strauss, chairman of the Atomic Energy Commission, made a rare intervention on the topic of Israel. He said the Jewish state was the only asylum for the refugees who survived the Holocaust or were expelled from Arab lands, and discouraging help by Americans would be "resented by people of both political parties, of all religions and all nationalities." See Alteras, "Eisenhower, American Jewry and Israel," p. 271.

On Dulles complaining about "the Jews," Alteras, "Eisenhower,

American Jewry and Israel," p. 269, quotes the Dulles-Herter diaries found at the Eisenhower Library, Box 6, entries dated February 12 and 20, 1957.

The 1957 U.S. guarantees have been detailed by Israeli officials, but also by Eugene V. Rostow, who had occasion to review the documents as a senior aide to President Johnson before the outbreak of the 1967 war. See Rostow, "Israel in the Evolution of American Foreign Policy," in Clark M. Clifford, Eugene V. Rostow, and Barbara W. Tuchman, *The Palestine Question in American History* (New York: Arno Press, 1978), pp. 82–83.

The "no cause to regret" cable from Eisenhower to Ben-Gurion, March 2, 1957, in *Foreign Relations of the United States, 1955–1957*, vol. 17, pp. 348, 359.

On the U.S. tanker discharging oil at Eilat (then Elath), see *Foreign Relations of the United States, 1955–1957*, vol. 17, p. 557.

On the Eisenhower Doctrine, see Spiegel, *Other Arab-Israeli Conflict*, pp. 83–84.

A memorandum on a conversation between Eban and Secretary of State Dulles, on "Israel's need for security guarantees," October 31, 1957, is in *Foreign Relations of the United States, 1955–1957*, vol. 17, pp. 779–781.

Washington's 1958 replies to Israel's request for formal defense guarantees and weapons are found in *Foreign Relations of the United States, 1958–1960*, vol. 13, Arab-Israeli Dispute, United Arab Republic, North Africa (Washington, DC: Department of State, 1992), pp. 57–58.

The "logical corollary" of supporting Israel was suggested in a paper "Issues Arising Out of the Situation in the Near East," prepared by the National Security Council's planning board on July 29, 1958; published in *Foreign Relations of the United States, 1958–1960*, vol. 12, Near East (Washington: Department of State, 1993), p. 119.

On Dulles suggesting the Jewish lobby could help, see Eban, *Personal Witness*, p. 288; and on Israel losing a friend when Dulles died, see ibid., pp. 295–296.

On the "even keel" of the intelligence relationship, Isser Harel was interviewed in December 1992 and confirmed what he had written in *Security and Democracy* (Jerusalem: Edanim, 1988), pp. 405–406.

On Israelis in Africa, with AFL-CIO support, Evron interview, November 1992.

The process of imposing a Ben-Gurion meeting on Eisenhower is compiled from "Memorandum of Conversation Between Israeli Ambassador Avraham Harman and Secretary of State Christian Herter," February 1, 1960, in *Foreign Relations of the United States, 1958–1960*, vol. 13, pp. 260–261. The White House meeting of March 10, 1960, is summarized in ibid., vol. 17, pp. 280–288. The "surprise" to "U.S. intelligence" is on p. 289.

The newly revealed U.S. arms sales to Israel are in ibid., p. 356; and entries of January 3 and May 20, 1960, in Ben-Gurion's diaries, newly declassified, at Ben-Gurion Institute, Sde Boker, Israel.

CHAPTER SIX

Kennedy, on the "national commitment," in Ernest Barbarash, *John F. Kennedy on Israel, Zionism and Jewish Issues* (New York: Herzl Press, 1965), p. 80; cited in Steven L. Spiegel, *The Other Arab-Israeli Conflict* (Chicago: University of Chicago Press, 1985), p. 96.

Secretary of State Dean Rusk's desire for a "significant gesture" by Israel is in his memo to the president, May 25, 1961, found in the John F. Kennedy Library in Boston.

The U.S. government's alarm over the nuclear reactor at Dimona can be seen in *Foreign Relations of the United States, 1958–1960*, vol. 13, Arab-Israeli Dispute, United Arab Republic, North Africa (Washington, DC: Department of State, 1992), pp. 391–392. A December 9, 1960, telegram from the State Department to the U.S. Embassy in Tel Aviv is in ibid., p. 393. Ambassador Harman's inability to give complete answers on December 20, 1960, is in pp. 396–399, with a State Department report to the Tel Aviv embassy dated December 31 in pp. 399–400.

In Dan Raviv and Yossi Melman's *Every Spy a Prince: The Complete History of Israel's Intelligence Community* (Boston: Houghton Mifflin, 1990), see p. 67 for the link between Suez/Sinai and Israel's Dimona reactor. Shimon Peres, who negotiated the reactor deal with France, confirmed for the first time, in an interview in October 1991, that in the secret talks in Sèvres, France, that led to the Suez/Sinai war in 1956, both sides connected the war with nuclear cooperation.

Details of Ben-Gurion's May 1961 meeting with Kennedy are in an oral history interview with Ben-Gurion, conducted July 16, 1965, in Tel Aviv and found in the John F. Kennedy Library. The National Security Council's advice to the president are in office files dated May 25, 1961, on "Israel's Security" and "Ben-Gurion Visit," also found in the J.F.K. Library.

The unanswered questions on Israel's nuclear plans are in a December 31, 1960, telegram from the State Department to the U.S. Embassy in Tel Aviv, *Foreign Relations of the United States, 1958–1960,* vol. 13, p. 400.

Kennedy's seventy minutes with Golda Meir were summarized in a "secret" State Department "Memorandum of Conversation," dated December 27, 1962; quoted in Green, *Living by the Sword,* pp. 180–182; and in Spiegel, *Other Arab-Israeli Conflict,* p. 106.

Ben-Gurion's "Hawk is appreciated" letter to Kennedy, dated April 26, 1963, quoted by former official in Israeli prime minister's office, Mordechai Gazit, in *President Kennedy's Policy toward the Arab States and Israel* (Tel Aviv: Edanim, 1983); cited in David Schoenbaum, *The United States and the State of Israel* (New York: Oxford University Press, 1993), p. 138.

On inspections of the Nahal Soreq reactor: The Arms Control Association said, in Washington in June 1993, that the "Atoms for Peace" program had U.S. inspectors checking the reactor for the first few years, until the IAEA was founded and took over the inspections.

Myer Feldman's recollection that Israel agreed to inspection of Dimona is in his oral memoirs, on tape at the John F. Kennedy Library in Boston; cited by Spiegel, *Other Arab-Israeli Conflict,* p. 113.

Abba Eban confirmed that Israel deceived America's nuclear experts, in the interview of September 1992.

The CIA memorandum, "Consequences of Israeli Acquisition of Nuclear Capability," dated March 6, 1963, is cited in Gazit, *President Kennedy's Policy,* pp. 70, 89, 116.

Johnson as "pro-Israel," in Kenen, *Israel's Defense Line,* p. 136. On his Christian dogma, Professor Louis Gomolak of the Southwest Texas State University in San Marcos was interviewed by Tom Tugend for the *Jerusalem Post,* international edition for week ending September 28, 1991, under a headline: "LBJ as a Philo-Semite." The article also quotes Lady Bird Johnson's memoirs, *White House Diary.*

Although Johnson's official papers, as filed in his presidential library, make no mention of Prime Minister Eshkol's personality or friendship, their relationship was described to the authors by participants in their meetings and conversations.

Ephraim Evron, later the Israeli ambassador to the United States, told in a May 1993 interview of falling into the gully with President Johnson. The adventure occurred during a May 1968 visit, when Johnson invited the entire Evron family to the ranch to say farewell at the end of one of Evron's embassy assignments.

Marilyn Monroe's "assets," as admired by John F. Kennedy, were recalled by Abba Eban in the interview. Also in *Los Angeles Times*, July 28, 1988.

Teddy Kollek, on his "jovial" party with the movie stars, and Paul Newman's "disappointment," in Kollek, *For Jerusalem: A Life* (New York: Random House, 1978), pp. 132–133.

Leon Uris, author of *Exodus*, was interviewed in New York in November 1993.

On the composition of U.S. aid to Israel in the 1960s, see Green, *Taking Sides*, pp. 185–187.

The State Department's request to Israel to turn off the anti-Jordan lobby is found in a report by Undersecretary of State for Political Affairs W. Averell Harriman, on his talks in Jerusalem, dated February 25, 1965; quoted by Spiegel, *Other Arab-Israeli Conflict*, p. 133.

State Department memo on Skyhawk deal, dated August 1, 1966, prepared for a visit by Israel's President Zalman Shazar; quoted by Schoenbaum, *United States and State of Israel*, p. 146.

On James Angleton's attitude toward Israel's nuclear program, see Raviv and Melman, *Every Spy a Prince*, p. 198.

On conventional sales slowing Israeli nuclear progress, the August 1, 1966, State Department memo is quoted by Spiegel, *Other Arab-Israeli Conflict*, p. 135.

Johnson offered "to use nuclear energy" for desalination, in a speech to the American Friends of the Weizmann Institute in New York, February 1964; quoted in Schoenbaum, *United States and State of Israel*, p. 139.

New information on the joint project for dual-purpose nuclear technology, in interviews: in May 1992 with Dan Pattir, a senior diplomat at the Israeli embassy in Washington from 1964 to 1968; and in March 1993 with Natan Arad, one of the Israeli engineers sent to the United States.

NOTES

The description of the 1967 Middle East crisis is based on interviews with Eban, Evron, the Mossad chief Meir Amit, and former CIA directors Richard Helms and William Colby; Lyndon B. Johnson, *The Vantage Point: Perspectives of the Presidency 1963–1969* (New York: Holt, Rinehart & Winston, 1971); Yitzhak Rabin, *The Rabin Memoirs* (Boston: Little, Brown, 1979); Donald Neff, *Warriors for Jerusalem* (Brattleboro, VT: Amana, 1988); and William B. Quandt, "Lyndon Johnson and the June 1967 War: What Color Was the Light?" *Middle East Journal* 46, no. 2 (Spring 1992).

The search for the Dulles *aide memoire* was recounted in the interview with Evron. See also Schoenbaum, *United States and State of Israel,* p. 151. The original *aide memoire* was found by Johnson's officials in Eisenhower's presidential library.

On Yitzhak Rabin's proposal for a formal defense treaty with the United States, Evron says Rabin knew the Americans would say no but wanted to prove to a hesitant Eshkol that Israel could not depend on America and must use its own army. Eban says Rabin was desperate and did not understand U.S.-Israeli relations.

Johnson, saying "Israel will not be alone," in Spiegel, *Other Arab-Israeli Conflict,* p. 142.

The description of the president and his Jewish friends at the L.B.J. Ranch is based on Quandt, "Johnson and the June 1967 War," p. 216, citing Neff, *Warriors for Jerusalem,* pp. 156–158.

The Abe Fortas channel is in Quandt, "Johnson and the June 1967 War," pp. 215–216, citing Laura Kalman's *Abe Fortas: A Biography* (New Haven, CT: Yale University Press, 1990).

Meir Amit said, when interviewed, that he was told by Richard Helms that the CIA's archives contain a secret document bearing a sentence in the president's handwriting that says: "We discussed the matter with General Amit." The secret document does not specify what is "the matter." But from various sources, it appears almost certain that the subject was Israel's launching a military attack and the forum was the Amit-McNamara meeting with Johnson on the telephone.

Johnson's "regret" is expressed in his memoirs, *Vantage Point,* p. 296.

NOTES

CHAPTER SEVEN

The views and reminiscences in this chapter are based on an interview with John L. Hadden at his retirement home in Maine in June 1991.

On the attack on the USS *Liberty*, a former Israeli officer also now living in Maine, Seth Mintz, wrote to the *Washington Post* that he was in an Israeli operations room on that day. He wrote that the Israelis sent aerial photos of the *Liberty* to the U.S. Embassy to ask if it was an American ship. Twice, he wrote, the embassy said no. "The consensus in the room was that the Americans would know better than the Israelis if the ship was theirs, and since they said it wasn't, it could only be an enemy vessel masquerading as American and was therefore a legitimate target." Mintz's letter was published on November 9, 1991.

CHAPTER EIGHT

AIPAC's sudden wealth was described by I. L. Kenen in *Israel's Defense Line: Her Friends and Foes in Washington* (Buffalo, NY: Prometheus, 1981), p. 198.

On the Israel Emergency Fund raising $100 million, see Peter Golden, *Quiet Diplomat: A Biography of Max M. Fisher* (New York: Herzl Press, 1992), p. 129.

Seymour Reich, president of the American Zionist Movement, former president of B'nai B'rith International, and former chairman of the Conference of Presidents of Major American Jewish Organizations, was interviewed in his New York office in May 1991.

Edward Said, professor at Columbia University and member of the Palestine National Council, was interviewed in his New York office in January 1988.

The novelist Henry Roth was interviewed from Albuquerque, New Mexico, in January 1994; and by Leonard Michaels, a professor at the University of California at Berkeley, for his article, "The Long Comeback of Henry Roth: Call It Miraculous," *New York Times Book Review*, August 15, 1993. Other quotations are from Henry Roth, *Shifting Landscapes: A Composite, 1925–1987* (Philadelphia: Jewish Publication Society, 1987), pp. 174–175.

On the "redemption and salvation" that Israel's army gave to the Jewish people, Steven Rosenfeld of the *Washington Post* wrote in

"Politica," a left-wing Israeli monthly, no. 14–15, June 1987, marking the twentieth anniversary of the war.

Steven Hartov, who wrote a thriller set in the Middle East, was interviewed in New York in November 1992.

On the Johnson Administration's "new path," Bernard Reich and Arnon Gutfeld wrote in Hebrew in *USA and the Israeli-Arab Conflict* (Tel Aviv: Ma'archot, 1977), pp. 45–48.

On legislators not returning AIPAC's calls, see Kenen, *Israel's Defense Line*, pp. 203–204.

President Johnson's five principles of June 19, 1967, are in Steven L. Spiegel, *The Other Arab-Israeli Conflict* (Chicago: University of Chicago Press, 1985), p. 154.

For Arthur J. Goldberg's pro-Israeli interpretation of UN Resolution 242, see his article, "Withdrawal Needn't Be Total," *Washington Star*, December 9, 1973.

Johnson's "go ahead and try" on secret diplomacy with Jordan was recalled by Eban in a September 1992 interview in New York. For more details on twenty-five years of secret talks with King Hussein, including his visit to Golda Meir near Tel Aviv in 1971, see Yossi Melman and Dan Raviv, *Behind the Uprising: Israelis, Jordanians and Palestinians* (Westport, CT: Greenwood, 1989).

Prime Minister Eshkol's 1968 visit to the L.B.J. Ranch was discussed in the interview with Evron.

Eshkol in Johnson's chair and biting an orange was remembered by General Mordecai Hod, former commander of the Israeli air force, who accompanied the prime minister, in *Yediot Aharonot*, April 30, 1993.

The end-of-summit declaration of January 8, 1968, is quoted by Spiegel, *Other Arab-Israeli Conflict*, p. 160.

On his "many differences" with Yitzhak Rabin, see Kenen, *Israel's Defense Line*, p. 219.

On the link between the Phantoms and the Non-Proliferation Treaty, see Seymour M. Hersh, *The Samson Option: Israel's Nuclear Arsenal and American Foreign Policy* (New York: Random House, 1991), p. 184; also Spiegel, *Other Arab-Israeli Conflict*, p. 161.

On concern that the Phantoms could deliver nuclear bombs, see

George W. Ball and Douglas B. Ball, *Passionate Attachment: America's Involvement with Israel, 1947 to the Present* (New York: W.W. Norton, 1992), p. 66.

"Lyndon B. Johnson has kept his word" is recalled by Abba Eban, *Personal Witness: Israel Through My Eyes* (New York: Putnam, 1992), p. 474. On Johnson's October 1968 announcement of the Phantoms sale, see Kenen, *Israel's Defense Line*, p. 219.

CHAPTER NINE

Max Fisher described his February 1969 meeting with President Nixon at the Brandeis University seminar of September 1992.

Candidate Nixon's call for Israeli arms superiority, at a B'nai B'rith convention, is in I. L. Kenen, *Israel's Defense Line: Her Friends and Foes in Washington* (New York: Prometheus, 1981), pp. 224–225, and Peter Golden, *Quiet Diplomat: A Biography of Max M. Fisher* (New York: Herzl Press, 1992), pp. 164–165.

Abba Eban's "assumption" about Nixon, in *Personal Witness: Israel Through My Eyes* (New York: Putnam, 1992), p. 478.

Nixon's "prejudices" about Jews, in Henry Kissinger, *Years of Upheaval* (Boston: Little, Brown, 1982), p. 202.

The AIPAC-linked newsletter, *Near East Report*, April 6, 1992, published one of many estimates indicating that 17 percent of Jews voted for Nixon and 81 percent for Humphrey in 1968.

Henry Kissinger, saying he was "emotional" about the Holocaust, *Years of Upheaval*, p. 203.

Kissinger told Max Fisher about the family Seder, according to Rabbi Israel Miller, former chairman of the Conference of Presidents of Major American Jewish Organizations. Miller was interviewed in New York in September 1992.

Eban, on no "sentimental word" from Nixon, in *Personal Witness*, p. 478.

Nixon, on Golda Meir's "extreme toughness and extreme warmth," in his *RN: The Memoirs of Richard Nixon*, vol. 1 (New York: Warner Books, 1978), p. 592.

Kissinger, on Golda as "shrewd, earthy," in *Years of Upheaval*, p. 220.

On Nixon and Kissinger's contempt for the NPT, Seymour M. Hersh, *The Sampson Option: Israel's Nuclear Arsenal and American*

Foreign Policy (New York: Random House, 1991), p. 210, quotes classified National Security Decision Memorandum number 6, no date given.

Eban recalled his 1963 conversation with Kissinger, about nuclear weapons, in the New York interview.

Golda Meir's conversation with Nixon about nuclear "toys" was reported by an Israeli who was close to the issue.

Golda Meir, on not doing "so badly with conventional weapons," is in her memoirs, *My Life* (London: Futura, 1976), p. 329.

Meir mentioned her "shopping list" in ibid., p. 324.

Nixon and Kissinger deciding to stop the inspections of Israel's Dimona plant in 1969 is in Hersh, *Sampson Option*, p. 210.

Meir's letter, "our pilots are very good," to Nixon, in his memoirs, *RN*, vol. 1, p. 595.

Fisher noting that Kissinger, as a Jew, was at first excluded from Middle East affairs, in Golden, *Quiet Diplomat*, p. 205; and Nixon, *RN*, vol. 1, p. 591.

On Kissinger and Rogers not handling the Phantom sale, John Mitchell was interviewed by Golden, *Quiet Diplomat*, p. 207.

On Nixon passing secret reassurance through Garment and Fisher, former Israeli diplomat Mordecai Gazit said it was "tremendously powerful" to receive such a promise from friends of the president. Gazit spoke at a Jerusalem seminar honoring Fisher in June 1992.

Meir's "we are passing through difficult days" letter to Fisher in Golden, *Quiet Diplomat*, pp. 199–200.

An Israeli army general involved in defense purchases in the United States was interviewed but asked that he not be named.

The same general outlined the importance of cooperation between Israeli military intelligence and the NSA.

For details of the September 1970 crisis in Jordan, see Nixon, *RN*, vol. 1, pp. 598–601; Henry Kissinger, *White House Years* (Boston: Little, Brown, 1979), pp. 618–625; Walter Isaacson, *Kissinger* (New York: Simon and Schuster, 1992), pp. 299–303; and Steven L. Spiegel, *The Other Arab-Israeli Conflict* (Chicago: University of Chicago Press, 1985), pp. 199–202.

"Israel is the only sure access point we have between Western Europe and our partners in the Far East," Eugene V. Rostow, assistant secretary of state in the Johnson administration, wrote years after leaving office, in Clark M. Clifford, Eugene V. Rostow, and Barbara W. Tuchman, *The Palestine Question in American History* (New York: Arno Press, 1978), p. 68.

U.S. military credits are based on William B. Quandt, *Decade of Decisions* (Berkeley: University of California Press, 1977), p. 163.

Ambassador Rabin's private endorsement of Nixon is based on pro-Israel activists, preferring anonymity, who introduced Rabin to candidates in 1972 and said "he got the willies from McGovern."

For an account of Senator Henry Jackson's battle with the Nixon administration to withhold trade with the Soviet Union until its Jews were allowed to leave, see Golden, *Quiet Diplomat*, pp. 276–286.

Senator Henry Jackson, on "the *American people* support Israel," quoted in "Jackson: Foreign Affairs Generalist," by James G. Roche, in Dorothy Fosdick, ed., *Staying the Course: Henry M. Jackson and National Security* (Seattle: University of Washington Press, 1987), p. 73.

Jackson's unprecedented amendment to the Defense Procurement Act, giving the president a blank check to send arms to Israel, came in 1970; see Kenen, *Israel's Defense Line*, pp. 242, 264.

On U.S. officials perceiving an Israeli nuclear warning, see Isaacson, *Kissinger*, p. 518; confirmed by several retired officials.

On Moshe Dayan's inclination to use nuclear weapons, see Dan Raviv and Yossi Melman, *Every Spy a Prince: The Complete History of Israel's Intelligence Community* (Boston: Houghton Mifflin, 1990), p. 211. The nearest that Israeli officials have come in description is saying that he advised using weapons that would be "different and painful," a euphemism used by his close aide Naftali (Lavie) Low in *Am Ke Lavi (Nation Like a Lion)* (Tel Aviv: Ma'ariv Books, 1993), p. 277.

On Fisher's October 9, 1973, visit to the Oval Office, see Golden, *Quiet Diplomat*, p. 289.

On the October 1973 airlift to Israel, see Nixon, *RN*, vol. 1, pp. 484–485; Isaacson, *Kissinger*, p. 522; Spiegel, *Other Arab-Israeli Conflict*, pp. 254–255; Quandt, *Decade of Decisions*, pp. 183–185; Meir, *My Life*, pp. 362–363; and Golden, *Quiet Diplomat*, pp. 290–292.

"We didn't get the information" is the recollection of General Mordecai "Motta" Gur, who was Israel's military attaché in Washington during the 1973 war, interviewed in *Ha'aretz*, September 3, 1992.

On Nixon wanting "a battlefield stalemate," see Nixon, *RN*, vol. 1, p. 476.

Nixon, saying Israel "will be even more impossible," quoted in Isaacson, *Kissinger*, p. 517.

Nixon, thundering "now!" to Defense Secretary James Schlesinger, in Nixon, *RN*, vol. 1, p. 483; thundering to Kissinger, in Kissinger, *White House Years*, pp. 514–515.

Nixon described the nuclear alert and airlift as "presidential decisions" in a 1992 conversation recalled by Abba Eban in an interview. For details of alert, see David Schoenbaum, *The United States and the State of Israel* (New York: Oxford University Press, 1993), p. 208.

Nixon discussed the airlift as "a measure of U.S. reliability," interviewed by Golden, *Quiet Diplomat*, p. 294.

Kissinger's joke and Nixon and Kissinger being "our heroes," according to interview with Abba Eban.

Kissinger's eleven Middle East trips, in Spiegel, *Other Arab-Israeli Conflict*, p. 269.

On Nixon's Middle East tour of 1974, see Nixon, *RN*, vol. 1, pp. 587–598; including diary entry on p. 598.

Documents about the forest episode concerning President Ford are in the Gerald R. Ford Presidential Library, University of Michigan, Ann Arbor, in the Presidential Handwriting File, Box 6/Israel.

The memorandum prepared for Treasury Secretary Simon, "Summary of Recent Developments Concerning Sales of Nuclear Power Plants to Israel and Egypt," is in the William E. Simon papers, folder 24, Lafayette College and the Ford Library.

Defense Secretary Schlesinger explained his position on Pershing missiles on the CBS News broadcast *Face the Nation* on September 21, 1975. A transcript is in the files of White House press secretary Ron Nessen, Box 64, at the Ford Library.

On the third accord, known as Sinai II, and the "reassessment" of March to August 1975, see Isaacson, *Kissinger*, pp. 631–635; Quandt, *Decade of Decisions*, pp. 267–271; and Spiegel, *Other Arab-Israeli Conflict*, pp. 294–298.

On Max Fisher's attempts to mediate between Rabin and Kissinger, see Golden, *Quiet Diplomat*, pp. 322–326 and 331–342. Fisher's entrée stemmed not only from his Republican fund-raising but from his philanthropic roles with the United Jewish Appeal (he was president), American Jewish Committee (he chaired the executive committee), Council of Jewish Federations (he was vice president), and other groups. See ibid., p. 173.

Kissinger shouting at Dinitz about "anti-Semitism" and the $2.6 billion estimate of military aid after the Sinai II accord; see Isaacson, *Kissinger*, pp. 634–635. Quandt, *Decade of Decisions*, p. 279, estimates "several hundreds of million dollars, not several billion."

Military aid to Israel after the Yom Kippur War amounting to $2.2 billion, in Karen L. Puschel, *U.S.-Israeli Strategic Cooperation in the Post–Cold War Era* (Boulder, CO: Jaffee Center for Strategic Studies/Westview, 1992), p. 22.

The story of the U.S. military inspector who looked the other way when Israel bent the rules in the Sinai was told by the Israeli officer involved, who preferred anonymity.

For Israel's Entebbe raid in 1976, see the three movies.

CHAPTER TEN

Samuel W. Lewis was interviewed in July 1991 and March 1992, when he was president of the United States Institute of Peace in Washington. In 1993 he joined the Clinton administration as director of policy planning in the State Department. See also Samuel W. Lewis, "The United States and Israel: Constancy and Change," in William B. Quandt, ed., *The Middle East: Ten Years after Camp David* (Washington: Brookings Institution, 1988), pp. 217–257.

On the United States joining Israel's espionage agency, the Mossad, in smuggling Ethiopian Jews to Israel through Sudan, Jerry Weaver, former refugee coordinator in the U.S. Embassy in Khartoum, was interviewed from his farm in Ohio in November 1993.

Quotes from President Carter are found in Steven L. Spiegel, *The Other Arab-Israeli Conflict* (Chicago: University of Chicago Press, 1985), pp. 330–335. Also, on the "reluctance to face the trouble question" of the Palestinians, see Jimmy Carter, *The Blood of Abraham* (Boston: Houghton Mifflin, 1986), p. 46.

On Begin liking Cyrus Vance, former Begin advisor Dan Pattir was interviewed in Tel Aviv.

Sam Lewis's 1,536 cocktail parties and 2,304 official functions over his eight-year period in Israel were counted by the gossip columnist of *Yediot Aharonot*, January 20, 1993.

Carter, on the "widespread support" for Israel, in *Blood of Abraham*, p. 55.

On the threat to discuss "who had what kind of weapons" and on the invitation to Camp David filled with history and destiny, see Zbigniew Brzezinski, *Power and Principle: Memoirs of the National Security Adviser 1977–81* (London: Weidenfeld and Nicolson, 1983), p. 251.

Carter finding "Begin and Sadat were personally incompatible" is in *Blood of Abraham*, p. 43.

Begin saying he would lose his "right eye" is in Brzezinski, *Power and Principle*, p. 263.

On the airbase redeployment and the structure of the $3 billion in U.S. aid to cover the cost, former Israeli government finance advisor Dan Halperin—later an attaché at the embassy in Washington—was interviewed in Tel Aviv in May 1993.

For levels of U.S. aid to Israel from 1948 to 1985, see A. F. K. Organski, *The $36 Billion Bargain: Strategy and Politics in U.S. Assistance to Israel* (New York: Columbia University Press, 1990), pp. 16, 153–179.

The Israeli diplomat who said aid talks were "on automatic pilot" asked not to be named.

Carter on Israeli leaders "tweaking the superpower's nose" is in *Blood of Abraham*, p. 55.

Several profiles of American diplomats specializing in the Middle East appear in Robert D. Kaplan, *The Arabists: The Romance of an American Elite* (New York: Free Press, 1993), including a discussion of Samuel Lewis on pp. 177–179.

The U.S. diplomat who served in Tel Aviv in the mid-1980s and later was ambassador to Jordan from 1990 to 1992 was Roger Harrison. He wrote to the authors in October 1993.

CHAPTER ELEVEN

Menachem Begin's reaction to Ronald Reagan's election victory was recalled by Yehiel Kadishai, Begin's longtime confidant, in a February 1993 interview.

The AIPAC-linked *Near East Report*, April 6, 1992, estimated Reagan's 1980 percentage of the Jewish vote at 39, compared with 45 percent for Carter. (Others voted for independents.) In 1976, the estimate said, Carter had 71 percent of Jewish votes, compared with 27 percent for President Ford.

On President Reagan's background and attitude to Israel, see Ronald Reagan, *An American Life* (New York: Simon and Schuster, 1990), pp. 30, 100, 410–412; and Lou Cannon, *President Reagan: The Role of a Lifetime* (New York: Simon and Schuster, 1991), p. 319.

Ronald Reagan, "Recognizing the Israeli Asset," *Washington Post*, August 15, 1979.

Reagan's sentiments, including "There is no nation like us. Except Israel," said to Peter Golden, *Quiet Diplomat: A Biography of Max M. Fisher* (New York: Herzl Press, 1992), p. 424.

The AWACS deal worth $8.5 billion, see Steven L. Spiegel, *The Other Arab-Israeli Conflict* (Chicago: University of Chicago Press, 1985), p. 398.

On Israel's internal debate on AWACS, General Menachem Meron was interviewed in Tel Aviv in September 1992.

The story of the Israeli navy vessel rescued from a Saudi sandbar was recounted in the Israeli newspaper *Ma'ariv*.

On AIPAC's role in the AWACS fight, former officials and activists including AIPAC lobbyist Douglas Bloomfield were interviewed. See also Reagan, *An American Life*, pp. 410–416; and Spiegel, *Other Arab-Israeli Conflict*, pp. 408–410.

In Reagan, *An American Life:* on AWACS, diary entry, p. 412; Holocaust reference, p. 410; "I didn't like," p. 415.

Saudi plans to spend $50 billion on U.S. military supplies were first reported by Scott Armstrong in the *Washington Post*, November 1, 1981; and he later wrote that the expenditures totaled over $150 billion. See *Mother Jones* (November-December 1991).

On Jacob Stein's visit to Begin on behalf of Reagan and the slogan "Reagan or Begin," Stein was interviewed in Great Neck, New York, in June 1992.

On Vice President Bush working with Saudi embassy, interviews with former AIPAC lobbyists.

Extra loans of $600 million; and "substantive, not 'cosmetic' " cooperation, from Golden, *Quiet Diplomat*, pp. 431, 433.

Caspar Weinberger's attitude toward Israel's destruction of the Iraqi reactor, plus the U.S. protest, in the interview with General Meron. Text of U.S. condemnation is in *Department of State Bulle-*

tin (August 1981): 79, including: "Available evidence suggests U.S.-provided equipment was employed in possible violation of the applicable agreement under which it was sold to Israel."

Also interviewed was Howard Teicher, on the Middle East staff of Reagan's National Security Council. See Howard Teicher and Gayle Radley Teicher, *Twin Pillars to Desert Storm: America's Flawed Vision in the Middle East from Nixon to Bush* (New York: William Morrow, 1993), p. 145.

George Bush and Weinberger wishing to cut off aid to Israel, in testimony to House Foreign Affairs Committee by Alexander Haig, Associated Press, March 17, 1993.

Alexander Haig's private pleasure with Israel's raid on Iraq in Golden, *Quiet Diplomat*, p. 432; confirmed by interviews with officials.

On Sam Lewis's diplomatic cable about the Iraqi reactor, see Teicher and Teicher, *Twin Pillars to Desert Storm*, p. 144.

A State Department veteran who prefers anonymity recalled his advice to pro-Israeli friends.

Ambassador Lewis, in an interview, described President Reagan's view of the Iraq raid.

Reagan finding it hard "to envision Israel as being a threat" is in Cannon, *President Reagan*, p. 157.

Quotes of President Reagan and Prime Minister Begin at the White House in September 1981 were recalled by Ambassador Samuel Lewis. Also see Meron Medzini, ed., *Israel's Foreign Relations: Selected Documents, 1974–77* (Jerusalem: Ministry of Foreign Affairs, 1982), p. 143.

On the beginnings of strategic cooperation, the authors interviewed several Israeli cabinet ministers and American officials who wished to remain anonymous. Also very useful was the interview with General Meron and the excellent work by Karen L. Puschel, *U.S.-Israel Strategic Cooperation in the Post–Cold War Era* (Boulder, CO: Jaffee Center for Strategic Studies/Westview, 1992).

The Begin-Weinberger meeting was recounted in interviews with Meron and Ambassador Lewis, who had been present.

The "psychological, personal" background of Weinberger's attitude toward Israel was suggested by Thomas G. Moore, a member of his staff in the Department of Defense in the early 1980s, interviewed in Washington in November 1991.

Another Pentagon official in the Weinberger era, Dov Zakheim, was interviewed in Washington in October 1991.

James G. Roche, now a vice president of Northrop Corporation, gave details of how the strategic-cooperation concept originated, interviewed at his office in Los Angeles in December 1991. Paul D. Wolfowitz was interviewed in Washington in November 1993.

The roles of Roche, Wolfowitz, and Teicher in the early stages of strategic cooperation with Israel are recounted in Teicher and Teicher, *Twin Pillars to Desert Storm*, pp. 141–153, who point out that Haig put his counselor Robert "Bud" McFarlane in charge of the issue in secret talks with top Israeli foreign ministry official David Kimche, a former Mossad operative. McFarlane and Kimche would later work on the exchange of arms for hostages with Iran.

Haig, on the "true partnership," on ABC-TV's *Good Morning America*, September 11, 1981.

The MOU negotiations, from September to November 1991, are based in part on an interview with an Israeli participant who asked to remain anonymous.

Sharon's wish for strategic cooperation "on the global stage" is in Ariel Sharon with David Chanoff, *Warrior: An Autobiography* (New York: Simon and Schuster, 1989), p. 408.

The MOU signing ceremony was described by Israeli participants and by Teicher and Teicher, *Twin Pillars to Desert Storm*, p. 162, and Puschel, *U.S.-Israel Strategic Cooperation*, p. 49. The MOU was dated November 30, 1981.

CHAPTER TWELVE

Moshe Arens was interviewed at length at his home in Savyon and at his office in Tel Aviv in 1992 and 1993.

Menachem Begin's tart response to U.S. suspension of the MOU was recounted by Samuel W. Lewis, the former ambassador to Tel Aviv at the receiving end, in an interview; and in his article, "The United States and Israel: Constancy and Change."

Arens, the seventh ambassador: His predecessors were Eliahu Eilath, Abba Eban, Avraham Harman, Yitzhak Rabin, Simcha Dinitz, and Ephraim Evron.

On the fear of U.S. officials in 1982 that Israel might not return the last part of Sinai to Egypt, see Howard Teicher and Gayle Radley Teicher, *Twin Pillars to Desert Storm: America's Flawed Vision in the Middle East from Nixon to Bush* (New York: William Morrow, 1993), p. 170.

On Arens's successful presentation to members of the Senate Foreign Relations Committee in 1977, former committee staffer Stephen Bryen was interviewed in Washington in September 1992.

The revelation of a U.S. desire to "neutralize" the PLO came from Raymond Tanter, an official with the National Security Council in 1981 and 1982. Now a professor of political science at the University of Michigan, Tanter was interviewed in September 1993 in Ann Arbor. In *Who's at the Helm?: Lessons of Lebanon* (Boulder, CO: Westview, 1990), p. 35, he writes that the "high-ranking State Department official" had "undisputed authority to speak for the Secretary."

On Ariel Sharon's "Big Pines" briefing, the State Department official who heard it along with Ambassador Lewis was identified as Phillip Habib. See Tanter, *Who's at the Helm?* pp. 65–66; and the *Washington Post,* December 5, 1981.

On the secret U.S.-Israeli meeting in London in January 1982, see Teicher and Teicher, *Twin Pillars to Desert Storm,* pp. 167–168.

The "big dripper" label for Sharon is in Tanter, *Who's at the Helm?* p. 65.

Sharon's account of his warnings to Secretaries Haig and Weinberger are in Ariel Sharon with David Chanoff, *Warrior: An Autobiography* (New York: Simon and Schuster, 1989), pp. 450–451.

On Sharon leaving "no doubt that he was itching for war," see Teicher and Teicher, *Twin Pillars to Desert Storm,* p. 195. Howard Teicher and Ambassador Lewis, who were interviewed, were both at the May 1982 meeting.

On the question of a "green light" for the Lebanon invasion, most Israeli and American officials—including Ambassadors Lewis and Arens, General Meron, and others—agree that the United States did not sanction the war but could have lived with a small-scale Israeli operation. Weinberger has written that he cannot settle the "green light" controversy, but "I do know that Sharon's line of argument had a certain amount of appeal to Al and to others who tended to view the Palestinian-Israeli problem as a subset of the Cold War." See Caspar Weinberger, *Fighting for Peace: Seven Critical Years in the Pentagon* (New York: Warner, 1991), p. 141.

The assumptions "through which Israeli tanks might rumble" are outlined in Tanter, *Who's at the Helm?* p. 37.

The Reagan administration's delay on the $2.5 billion sale of F-16s to Israel was in the *Washington Post,* June 15, 1993. Haig's warning to Ambassador Arens that "goodwill" was being lost was reported that day by Israel Radio.

On Haig's resignation and his being "a 100 percent supporter of Israel," see Weinberger, *Fighting for Peace,* p. 143n.

The story of George Shultz having been moved by the death of an Israeli student in 1967 was related by Max Fisher and other Republican Jews, and confirmed by Shultz in a letter to the authors dated February 8, 1993.

On Arens's July 17 visit to Shultz, Reagan "lost patience," and the attitudes of Reagan, Shultz, Bush, and Weinberger, see George P. Shultz, *Turmoil and Triumph: My Years as Secretary of State* (New York: Charles Scribner's Sons, 1993), pp. 39, 53, 60.

Details of Arens's August 4 visit to Shultz are in ibid., pp. 60–61; Arens on September 16 raised his voice to Shultz, ibid., p. 104; Carter's advice, ibid., p. 106.

Reagan privately told the Israelis that the Beirut siege was becoming another "Holocaust," according to Yossi Ben-Aharon, former director-general of Prime Minister Shamir's office, interviewed in Jerusalem in October 1992.

The Israeli labor attaché who contacted the Teamsters union official was Danny Bloch, who served in the Israeli Embassy in Washington from 1982 to 1988, interviewed in Tel Aviv in October 1992.

CHAPTER THIRTEEN

Reagan's announcement of the free-trade agreement and strategic cooperation, in the *New York Times,* November 30, 1983.

Shamir, as former prime minister, was interviewed in Tel Aviv in May 1993.

Nicholas Veliotes, Deputy Chief of Mission at the U.S. Embassy in Tel Aviv in the early 1970s, later ambassador to Jordan and to Egypt, and assistant secretary of state for the Near East in 1981 to 1983, was interviewed in Washington in November 1992.

On American Jews favoring military ties with Israel but opposing the military on Vietnam, see Max M. Kampelman, *Entering New Worlds* (New York: HarperCollins, 1991), pp. 197–198, amplified by Kampelman when interviewed in October 1991.

Also interviewed was Shoshana Bryen, director of special projects for the Jewish Institute for National Security Affairs (JINSA), at her Washington office in March 1992.

James Roche was interviewed in December 1991.

On the roles played by Roche and Ross in the strategic dialogue with Israel, see also Howard Teicher and Gayle Radley Teicher, *Twin Pillars to Desert Storm: America's Flawed Vision in the Middle East, from Nixon to Bush* (New York: William Morrow, 1993), p. 91.

Howard Teicher, an official in charge of Middle East policy in the Reagan White House's National Security Council, was interviewed in Washington, as was former Ambassador Samuel Lewis.

On aircraft carrier visits designed to "reward" Israel, see Dore Gold's analysis, "Strategic Cooperation or Outright Dependence," *Jerusalem Post*, March 27, 1993.

Parts of the CIA profile of Yitzhak Shamir were obtained by the authors from a confidential source.

Teicher described in an interview and in *Twin Pillars*, coauthored with his wife, pp. 222–223, how the administration saw Moshe Arens as a friend of the United States and tried to help him enhance his prestige in the Israeli cabinet.

President Reagan signing National Security Decision Directive 111 reported by Bernard Gwertzman in "Reagan Turns to Israel," *New York Times Magazine*, November 27, 1983, p. 63. In addition, senior AIPAC officials remember the late Don Fortier, of the NSC staff, as a hero of the deliberative process.

Some of the reasons for the U.S. change of mind about the importance of Israel are mentioned in Karen L. Puschel, *U.S.-Israeli Strategic Cooperation in the Post–Cold War Era* (Boulder, CO: Jaffee Center for Strategic Studies/Westview, 1992), pp. 65–68.

On Eagleburger's November 1983 talks in Israel, see Gwertzman, "Reagan Turns to Israel," p. 63.

General Menachem Meron, on Israel "taken by surprise" by strategic cooperation, was interviewed in Tel Aviv in September 1992.

On the concept of the rapid deployment force (RDF) and the early consideration of Israel as America's strategic ally, see Teichner and Teicher, *Twin Pillars to Desert Storm*, pp. 90–91.

The role of Defense Secretary Caspar Weinberger in the JPMG was discussed in the interviews with Meron, Teicher, Shamir, Arens, Roche, and Thomas Moore. Also, Dov S. Zakheim, deputy undersecretary of defense for planning and resources under Weinberger, was interviewed in Arlington, Virginia, in June 1992.

New York congressman Steven Scheuer complained publicly, in October 1983, that Weinberger did not permit the evacuation of wounded U.S. soldiers from Beirut to nearby Israel. Weinberger has written: "I was infuriated by various specious charges made later that I had refused Israeli offers of medical help. . . . The offers were made to other United States headquarters, all of whom on their own and, of course, without directions from me, decided that our own medical contingency plans, resources and facilities did not require Israeli augmentation. We did request medical body bags from Israel and were grateful to receive them." See Caspar Weinberger, *Fighting for Peace: Seven Critical Years in the Pentagon* (New York: Warner, 1991), p. 161.

On the U.S. financing a "national trauma system" in Israel, see *Jerusalem Post*, September 21, 1991.

On U.S.-Israeli cooperation against terrorism, see Ronald Reagan, *An American Life* (New York: Simon and Schuster, 1990), pp. 493–499; George P. Shultz, *Turmoil and Triumph: My Years as Secretary of State* (New York: Charles Scribner's Sons, 1993), p. 653; and Dan Raviv and Yossi Melman, *Every Spy a Prince: The Complete History of Israel's Intelligence Community* (Boston: Houghton Mifflin, 1990), pp. 338–342.

Colonel Oliver L. North's remarks are in his memoirs, *Under Fire: An American Story* (New York: HarperCollins, 1991), p. 203. Also, Amiram Nir was interviewed in Tel Aviv several times including September 1988, two months before his mysterious death in a plane crash in Mexico.

Benjamin Netanyahu was interviewed in the K'nesset parliament building in Jerusalem in October 1992.

Shultz, *Turmoil and Triumph*, p. 656, writes of the president's warning and on pp. 655–656 on the Israeli position.

Reagan's decision "to strike back" at the seajackers of the *Achille Lauro* is recounted in his memoirs, *An American Life*, p. 508.

On the intelligence information about the *Achille Lauro*'s terrorists, see Teicher and Teicher, *Twin Pillars to Desert Storm*, p. 338; and North, *Under Fire*, pp. 203, 212.

Details of the North-Nir covert operations were published by the *Washington Post*, December 4, 1988.

On August 20, 1992, *Ma'ariv* published an investigative report revealing Contra-related clues in General Hagai Regev's diaries.

Nir, when interviewed in September 1988, revealed that Israel's advice was based on the hope of killing Colonel Qadafi.

On not letting Qadafi "get away with it," see Reagan, *An American Life*, pp. 518–519.

The $70 million appropriation for prepositioning military materiel in Israel is in Puschel, *U.S.-Israeli Strategic Cooperation*, p. 90.

The U.S. Navy report that Israel's air force "could destroy the entire Soviet fleet" is cited by Wolf Blitzer, *Between Washington and Jerusalem: A Reporter's Notebook* (New York: Oxford University Press, 1985), p. 76, based on an ABC News broadcast.

On the potential value of U.S.-Israeli naval cooperation, see "America's Security Stake in Israel," a report published by the Heritage Foundation on July 7, 1986.

Ehud Olmert, health minister in the Shamir government, and later mayor of Jerusalem, was interviewed in Tel Aviv in October 1992.

Roche is quoted from the December 1991 interview.

On Israel finding it hard to cede the right to put U.S. military service personnel on trial, the Israeli ambassador to Washington from 1987 to 1990, Moshe Arad, was interviewed in Jerusalem in September 1992.

On proposals to deepen and modernize the port of Haifa, the Reuter news agency had a report on February 17, 1993. It pointed out that while the Sixth Fleet is based in Italy, there is no official home port for aircraft carriers in the Mediterranean; at least one is on "deployment" duty from the United States.

On U.S. pilots making bombing runs at practice ranges in the Negev Desert, see Puschel, *U.S.-Israeli Strategic Cooperation*, pp. 88–89.

On the "Arrow" antiballistic missile system: The Scud attacks during the 1991 Gulf War gave the project more urgency, and despite technical problems and questions raised by the General Accounting Office on behalf of Congress, the Bush and Clinton administrations continued to support the project. Even when the director of the program was jailed in Israel for taking a $75,000 bribe from a Canadian parts supplier, the United States did not lose faith; see *Long Island Jewish World*, May 7–13, 1993. Also, AIPAC's *Near East Report*, May 17, 1993, quotes the director of the SDI Organization, Major

General Malcolm O'Neill, praising Israel's Arrow in testimony to the Senate Appropriations Subcommittee on Defense. The Arrow is to go into production in 1995.

The "electro-thermal anti-missile gun" was described in *Ha'aretz*, March 18, 1993. Details of the gun and the Arizona accident were provided by Alon Pinkas, an aide to the military attaché at the Israeli embassy in Washington from 1987 to 1990, when interviewed in Tel Aviv.

Weinberger told of seeing the RPV's videotape of himself in Beirut in 1982, when he spoke to the Jewish Press Association in Washington on May 23, 1984. In *Fighting for Peace*, p. 149, he adds, however: "That Israeli drone had actually been developed by us, but the Congress had refused to fund its deployment. It was then sold to the Israelis."

The U.S. Navy's purchase of the RPV known as Mazlat from Israel opened the door to future deals. U.S. forces used Israeli drones in the 1991 Gulf War against Iraq. In 1992 Israel Aircraft Industries was involved in a joint $500 million project with the American firm TRW's avionics and surveillance group to produce the Pentagon's drone of the future: the Hunter short-range unmanned aerial vehicle, or UAV.

Israel felt further pressed to continue building its own satellites after the Gulf War, which demonstrated how heavily the Israelis depended on U.S. reconnaissance from space. The U.S. ambassador to Tel Aviv, William Harrop, criticized Israel for concealing its space program from the Americans, expressing his fear that overambitious Israeli plans would eventually dent financial resources, so that the U.S. government would, as usual, be asked to foot the bill. See *Ha'aretz*, May 21, 1992.

Another broad issue that soured the solid-gold era was the nuclear question. The Reagan and, later, Bush administration kept delaying a decision on permitting Israel to buy Cray supercomputers. The export licenses were applied for on behalf of three universities for scientific experiments, but Pentagon officials feared Israel would use them for military-oriented nuclear research. Senators Arlen Specter, Joseph Lieberman, and Frank Lautenberg, who happen to be Jewish, wrote to President Bush in November 1990, asking that he grant the export licenses because "Israel is a vital and democratic ally." The

White House still refused, and Israel eventually made do with alternative hardware.

On the MNNA status as a Major Non-Nato Ally, an Israeli diplomat who knew of the idea's genesis asked not to be identified.

The figure of 321 joint U.S.-Israeli defense projects was given to the annual AIPAC Policy Conference in Washington in April 1992 by Steve Rosen, the lobby's research director.

On the Defense Technology Security Administration, aimed at preventing technology transfers, former Pentagon official Stephen Bryen was interviewed in Washington in September 1992. He said that even if Israel had been on his list, it would not have altered Israel's pattern of arms sales.

Senator Robert Byrd, Democrat of West Virginia, looked back on the entire history of aid to Israel when he spoke in the Senate on March 26, 1992, to oppose loan guarantees to Israel. See *Congressional Record*, vol. 138, no. 48, April 1, 1992, pp. S4599–S4607.

The text of the broad MOU between the Reagan administration and Israel, dated April 21, 1988, appears in Puschel, *U.S.-Israeli Strategic Cooperation*, pp. 181–183; with further information in Elyakim Rubinstein, *Paths of Peace* (Tel Aviv: Ministry of Defense Publishing: 1992), pp. 176–190 (in Hebrew). The MOU reaffirms the close relationship "based upon common goals, interests and values" and welcomes "the achievements made in strategic, economic, industrial and technological cooperation." It spells out other areas of cooperation, including "stimulating economic growth and self-reliance," political consultations on "a wide range of international issues," and joint aid to developing countries.

April 21, 1988, was Israel's independence day based on the Jewish, lunar calendar, which Israel uses to mark all national holidays.

CHAPTER FOURTEEN

Judith Gottfried of Gottex was interviewed in Tel Aviv in May 1993.

On the claims of Israel's Labor party regarding the genesis of the free trade agreement, see *Ha'aretz*, December 13, 1983.

The primary sources on the origins of the free trade agreement, including Gideon Patt's conversation with U.S. trade representative William Block, were Patt—interviewed in Jerusalem in October 1992—and Dan Halperin, interviewed in May 1993.

Ronald Reagan wrote of free trade in *An American Life* (New York: Simon and Schuster, 1990), p. 356; as did George P. Shultz in *Turmoil and Triumph: My Years as Secretary of State* (New York: Charles Scribner's Sons, 1993), p. 442.

Reagan's announcement of the free trade area agreement was in a White House press release on April 22, 1985.

Bill Brock said "It is not any gift" in a speech to the American Israel Public Affairs Committee in Washington on April 22, 1985, just one hour before he signed the agreement. The full text is in Toby Dershowitz, ed., *The Reagan Administration and Israel: Key Statements*, vol. 13 (Washington, DC: AIPAC Papers on US-Israel Relations, 1987).

On the question of the territories and the free trade agreement, see *Ha'aretz*, June 7, 1993, reporting on U.S. officials who said that they would open an official investigation to check whether Israel was violating the agreement by exporting goods produced in its Jewish settlements in the occupied territories.

For AIPAC's interpretation of the free trade agreement, see the lobbying organization's publication: Mitchell Bard and Joel Himmelfarb, eds., *Myths and Facts* (Washington, DC: Near East Report: 1984), pp. 249–250.

The phrase "ultimate expression" was used by former Israeli prime minister Yitzhak Shamir, interviewed in Tel Aviv in May 1993.

Figures on Israeli exports to the United States are based on official data provided in June 1993 by Israel's Ministry for Trade and Industry. For further details on U.S.-Israeli wheat deals, see *Forward*, April 9, 1992.

The estimate of Israeli losses from the Arab boycott are based on the interview with Dan Halperin.

Joan M. McEntee, acting undersecretary for export administration in the U.S. Department of Commerce, explained, in a letter to the *Jerusalem Post* published April 4, 1992, that the Office of Anti-Boycott Compliance has been very active since 1982 in its effort to impose American law on U.S. companies that comply with the Arab boycott by refusing to do business with Israel.

The authors obtained the directive issued in October 1985 by Israel's Ministry of Foreign Affairs to its diplomats in the United States to mobilize Jewish organizations against South Korean companies that violated U.S. laws by complying with the Arab boycott.

Max Fisher told the Brandeis University seminar on September 22, 1992, how he made Henry Ford II a friend of Israel; see also Peter Golden, *Quiet Diplomat: A Biography of Max M. Fisher* (New York: Herzl Press, 1992), pp. 244–248.

Opponents of foreign aid point out that in addition to the $3 billion annual aid, special favors to Israel added significant value to the raw dollar figures. Annual payments include $2.7 million under the American Schools and Hospitals Grant Program, $3.5 million to fund cooperatives, $1 million from the Overseas Private Investment Corporation to insure business ventures in Israel, and special permission to Israel to convert $475 million of the yearly military aid to Israeli shekels to be spent locally rather than purchasing U.S. defense products. See Senator Robert Byrd's speech in the *Congressional Record,* vol. 138, no. 48, April 1, 1992, pp. S4599–S4607.

Oded Eran, an Israeli diplomat who served in Washington as liaison to Congress, said that Secretary of State Shultz approached Israeli diplomats and asked their help to get foreign aid legislation passed by Congress. Eran was interviewed in his Jerusalem office in February 1992.

The Israeli diplomat in Washington who spoke of Israel as a "locomotive," and who asked not to be named, was interviewed in April 1992.

The AIPAC activist who commented on the role of his lobby and of Israel in shaping America's foreign aid policy also asked not to be named and was interviewed in Washington in April 1991.

In his interview, Dan Halperin revealed how he was approached by his Romanian counterpart in Washington.

Information on the Israeli intercession on behalf of Zaire and Turkey comes from the interview with Oded Eran.

Stephen Bryen, on the staff of the U.S. Senate Committee on Foreign Affairs during the 1970s, spoke of the Merkava project when interviewed in Washington in September 1992.

On the Americans' desire to see Moshe Arens emerge as Prime Minister Begin's successor, see Howard Teicher and Gayle Radley Teicher, *Twin Pillars to Desert Storm: America's Flawed Vision in the Middle East from Nixon to Bush* (New York: William Morrow, 1993), pp. 222–224.

According to figures provided by Israel's Ministry of Defense, the

United States allocated more than $1 billion to the Lavi project during its three years of existence.

On Shultz's position on the Lavi, see his *Turmoil and Triumph*, p. 443.

Dov Zakheim—now a defense industry consultant—was interviewed in Arlington, Virginia, in June 1992.

Veteran Israeli journalist Moshe Zak, in the *Jerusalem Post*, of April 18, 1992, described Zakheim as a *"kippa*-wearing Jew." Arens's reference to Zakheim came when the former defense minister was interviewed in April 1993.

The White House memo noting "Israel's Bar Mitzvah," prepared for the president before he met with Ben-Gurion, was dated May 24, 1961, and is found in the John F. Kennedy Library in Boston.

On Shultz's views concerning Israel's economy, see *Turmoil and Triumph*, pp. 442–443.

Uriel (Uri) Savir, an aide to Prime Minister Shimon Peres during the Reagan-Shultz era, was interviewed in New York in March 1992.

Esther Alexander, an independent Israeli economist, was a major advocate of the notion that Israel must for its own benefit cut its dependence on American money. See her article in *Yediot Aharonot*, May 10, 1991.

Among Israeli economists who tried to persuade Fisher and Stein that the opportunity to put political pressure on Israel should be exploited was Professor Yoram Ben-Porat of the Hebrew University in Jerusalem, known as a peace activist. He revealed his involvement in an interview in October 1990 in Jerusalem, and in *Yediot Aharonot*, October 23, 1992.

New York Times editor Max Frankel wrote on November 16, 1982, that members of the Labor opposition in Jerusalem suggested that the U.S. reduce economic aid for Israel.

The citation from *New York Times* columnist William Safire is in Edward Tivnan's *The Lobby: Jewish Political Power and American Foreign Policy* (New York: Simon and Schuster, 1987), p. 232.

The negative description of Sharon is from the March 1992 interview with former Ambassador Samuel Lewis.

Zelig Chinitz of the World Zionist Organization was interviewed in New York in September 1992 on Project Independence, which was meant to "set in motion a trend to facilitate exports from Israel."

Also see Shultz, *Turmoil and Triumph*, pp. 442–443. Max Fisher was also interviewed on this issue.

The story of Melvin Ross was published by *Yediot Aharonot* on February 5, 1993.

Alan Greenberg was interviewed in *Ha'aretz* on May 24, 1993.

The authors calculated in mid-1993 that U.S. aid to Israel, since the country's independence in 1948, totaled $100 billion, including all the various aspects—military and economic, public and private. The *New York Times* of September 23, 1991, concluded that since 1967 alone, Israel received $77 billion from the United States.

On the other hand an opponent of aid to Israel, former Congressman Paul Findley, offers a lower estimate of $53 billion provided by the U.S. government "in aid and special benefits" from 1949 through 1991; in his *Deliberate Deceptions: Facing the Facts about the U.S.-Israel Relationship* (Brooklyn, NY: Lawrence Hill, 1993), p. 111.

Former president Jimmy Carter was interviewed by the *Los Angeles Times*, July 20, 1987, in an article headlined "Unique Situation Describing U.S.-Israeli Relations."

Senator Robert Byrd's complaint that "we have poured foreign aid into Israel," adding "and both the United States and Israel have very little progress to show for it," is in the *Congressional Record*, vol. 138, no. 48, April 1, 1992, p. S4602.

A senior Senate staffer who has worked closely with Republican leader Bob Dole, but who requested anonymity, was interviewed in Washington in January 1992.

CHAPTER FIFTEEN

Figures about staffing levels at the Israeli and American embassies were provided in April 1993 by the press office at Israel's Foreign Ministry and by the press attaché at the U.S. Embassy in Tel Aviv.

The information on the mysterious offer of Saudi airbase blueprints by an American, whose name is known to the authors, is based on reliable Israeli officials who asked not to be named. General Ben-Porat refused to comment on this matter.

For more details on the Pollard affair, see Dan Raviv and Yossi Melman, *Every Spy a Prince* (Boston: Houghton Mifflin, 1990), pp. 301–323.

Howard Teicher told of being investigated by *Time* magazine; see

Teicher and Gayle Radley Teicher, *Twin Pillars to Desert Storm* (New York: William Morrow, 1993), p. 379.

On the investigation into Stephen Bryen, former Senate committee staffer, Bryen was interviewed in September 1992. Andrew Cockburn and Leslie Cockburn, in *Dangerous Liaison: The Inside Story of the U.S.-Israeli Covert Relationship* (New York: HarperCollins, 1991), p. 199, says that the FBI "had concluded that it had enough evidence of espionage activities by Bryen to take to a grand jury," but the case was quashed by "higher authority."

Robert D. Kaplan, in *The Arabists: The Romance of an American Elite* (New York: Free Press, 1993), pp. 207–229, provides a lively portrait of Jerry Weaver. More was learned on his post-Sudan ordeal in interviews with Weaver, now a farmer in Ohio, in November 1993.

President Reagan's response to Pollard's arrest was in *The Los Angeles Times*, November 27, 1985.

Secretary of Defense Weinberger's 46-page memo to federal judge Aubrey Robinson said: "The defendant has substantially harmed the United States, and, in my view, his crimes demand severe punishment," as quoted in Wolf Blitzer, *Territory of Lies* (New York: Harper & Row, 1989), pp. 221–230.

On Israeli officials claiming that the United States spies on Israel, see Raviv and Melman, *Every Spy a Prince*, pp. 307–308. Defense Minister Yitzhak Rabin first revealed the information about American espionage activities in Israel in an interview with one of the authors in November 1986.

On Yosef Amit, the Israeli army major arrested for "spying for Syria," the New York Hebrew-language *Israel Shelanu* reported a few clues in 1986, as cited by *Ha'aretz*, April 7, 1986. Israel's prisons authority announced on October 12, 1993, that the army major was released after serving nearly two-thirds of his twelve-year sentence.

On the Amit case, *Monitin*, a small Israeli monthly, published in November 1992 an allegorical story, presumably taking place three thousand years ago, about a spy who was working for an ancient superpower. While the allegorical usage was to circumvent Israeli censorship, the story was so masked that the public did not understand it.

In large part because Amit continued sending letters from prison,

Israeli authorities in June 1993 permitted limited reporting of the espionage case—although they still found it too sensitive to confirm publicly that the army major had been employed by the United States. His full story is based on interviews with intelligence officers involved in the case and Amit's lawyers, Shmuel Tsang and Amnon Zichroni.

For Senator Dave Durenberger's revelation that the United States had a spy in Israel's army and Secretary of Defense Weinberger's denial, see *Los Angeles Times*, June 5, 1993.

That Pollard "fouled up the atmosphere," Alon Pinkas, assistant to Israel's military attaché in Washington from 1987 to 1990, was interviewed in Tel Aviv in May 1992.

"Collection of information on secret U.S. policy" said to be a target for Israeli intelligence in a March 1976 report by the Central Intelligence Agency, *Israel: Foreign Intelligence and Security Services*, classified "secret" but published by Iranian Islamic militants who seized the U.S. Embassy in Tehran in late 1979, p. 9. The CIA report, cited in Raviv and Melman, *Every Spy a Prince*, pp. 169, 201, is not generally available in the West but is sold in Tehran bookstores.

On Richard Smyth, charged with smuggling krytron switches to Israel, see Ravi and Melman, *Every Spy a Prince*, pp. 304–305; and Arnon Milchan's link to Milco was in an NBC News broadcast on March 23, 1993, reported two days later by *Yediot Aharonot*.

The Nafco smuggling case was reported in *Ha'aretz*, February 7, 1992, and elsewhere in the Israeli press.

The long dispute between Israel and Recon over industrial espionage was settled during the Gulf War. See *Wall Street Journal*, January 27, 1991, and Cockburn and Cockburn, *Dangerous Liaison*, pp. 197–200.

State Department allegations of military technology transfers by Israel are in a report by the Office of the Inspector General, *Report of Audit: Defense Trade Controls* (Washington, DC: Department of State, March 1992). The inspector, Sherman Funk, identified the "major recipient" as Israel when speaking with reporters; see *New York Times*, April 2, 1992, and *Wall Street Journal*, April 3, 1992.

More accusations regarding Israeli re-exports were leaked to the *Washington Times*, NBC News, and *Wall Street Journal*, European edition, March 13–14, 1992. The leak from a U.S. intelligence report appeared on the eve of a visit to Washington by Defense Minister Arens.

Commenting on the Funk report, Stephen Bryen said that the Reagan administration had "painstakingly established" controls over arms technology transfers, and he charged that the only country the Bush administration bothered to worry about was Israel. See "The Anti-Israel Double Standard," by Bryen and Michael Ledeen, in the *Jerusalem Post* international edition for week ending March 28, 1992.

General Bin-Nun's response to the charge that Israel transferred Patriot missile technology to China was quoted by Associated Press, March 21, 1992.

Defense Minister Arens on Israeli modifications making their way into U.S. weapons systems for Arab countries, in interview of April 1993.

On bribery charges involving General Zvi Schiller and Uri Simhoni, see *Ha'aretz*, June 30 and July 11, 1991. In May 1993 federal prosecutors asked Israel to extradite them to the United States.

The arrest and imprisonment of corrupt General Rami Dotan was covered, at length, through most of 1992 by the Israeli press. In addition to paying $70 million in fines and compensation, General Electric quietly dismissed around a dozen employees. The firm's representative in Israel, Chester Walsh, was given immunity from prosecution and—for helping the investigation—was paid a "whistleblower's" reward of $11 million.

The chairman of United Technologies, the parent corporation of Pratt & Whitney, Robert Daniell, said the diversion of cash to General Dotan's consulting affiliates was "an embarrassment to me personally and to the corporation." See *Associated Press*, October 26 and 27, 1993.

Congressman John Dingell's suggestion that military aid to Israel be stopped to protest the Dotan affair was in a statement to the oversight subcommittee of the House Committee on Energy and Commerce on July 29, 1992.

On the Israeli failure to read the 1989 U.S. military aid contract before signing it: Israel's state comptroller, Miriam Ben-Porat, in her forty-third annual report on the Treasury and the Defense Ministry, in *Ha'aretz*, May 11, 1993.

The new Pentagon restrictions on Israel's use of FMS aid money were reported in *Ha'aretz* on June 14, 1993.

CHAPTER SIXTEEN

The quotations from President Reagan's conversation with Thomas A. Dine of AIPAC were obtained from the White House by Wolf Blitzer of the *Jerusalem Post*, October 28, 1983.

Dine's background as a Reform Jew and details of AIPAC's membership and budget were in the *New York Times*, July 6, 1987; with further information from an AIPAC spokeswoman in June 1993.

Morris J. Amitay, former executive director of AIPAC and the founder of Washington PAC, was interviewed in October 1991 and in September and November 1992.

On Dine's sense of Jewish ethics, see *New York Times*, July 6, 1987, where he was interviewed. As for personal reward, Dine's annual salary at AIPAC was reported at $177,000 before his resignation in June 1993, about average for the executive directors of large American Jewish organizations.

On expecting Reagan to be a friendly president, Douglas Bloomfield, former legislative director of AIPAC, was interviewed in Washington in March 1992.

The Israeli who took part in lobbying on Capitol Hill, while interviewed about "good cooperation" with AIPAC, asked not to be identified.

Douglas Bloomfield described the Reagan administration's attempt to cut aid to Israel in December 1982, through Senator Mark Hatfield's amendment, in "Shultz's Turning Point," *Jerusalem Post* international edition, week ending May 29, 1993.

Senator Daniel Inouye, Democrat of Hawaii, was interviewed on his support for Israel by CBS News' *60 Minutes*, broadcast October 23, 1988.

George P. Shultz recalled being "astonished" by "Israel's leverage in our Congress" in his memoirs, *Turmoil and Triumph: My Years as Secretary of State* (New York: Charles Scribner's Sons, 1993), p. 112.

Jonathan S. Kessler, co-author of *The AIPAC College Guide: Exposing the Anti-Israel Campaign on Campus* (Washington, DC: America-Israel Public Affairs Committee, 1984), was interviewed in Washington in October 1991 and September 1992.

Senator Bob Packwood's campaign fund-raising letter, aimed at Jewish voters, was reported by the Associated Press on June 28, 1993.

Rabbi Israel Miller was interviewed in New York in September 1992 and by CBS News' *60 Minutes* in October 1988.

Contributions by pro-Israel PACs were said to total $43,475 in 1978, growing phenomenally to $5,432,055 in 1988, according to Richard H. Curtiss, *Stealth PACs: How Israel's American Lobby Took Control of U.S. Middle East Policy* (Washington, DC: American Educational Trust, 1990), pp. 16, 103. Curtiss suggests that the 1988 figure represents 10 percent of all contributions by all PACs.

George W. Ball, a former State Department official highly critical of Israel, estimates "perhaps 90 percent" of the money given to Democrats and "nearly 60 percent" to Republicans comes from Jews, in George W. Ball and Douglas B. Ball, *The Passionate Attachment: America's Involvement with Israel, 1947 to the Present* (New York: W.W. Norton, 1992), p. 218.

Then-president of AIPAC Robert H. Asher, on the other hand, estimated in 1987 that contributions by pro-Israel PACs were no greater than 2.6 percent of all PAC campaign giving, the proportion of Jews in the U.S. population. It is impossible to determine how much more is contributed to campaigns, privately, by individual supporters of Israel. See *New York Times,* July 7, 1987.

Brent Erickson, legislative assistant to Senator Allan Simpson of Wyoming, was interviewed in Washington in September 1991.

For further information on the ADL scandal, see Jeremy Kalmanofsky's article in *Moment* (August-September 1993): 38–43. ADL officials contend that they did nothing illegal and that the League upheld its eighty-year-old principles: defending civil rights for Jews and other minorities, and defending Israel against unfair criticism. San Francisco authorities decided in November 1993 not to press charges.

Charles D. Brooks, legislative assistant and later consultant to Senator Arlen Specter of Pennsylvania, was interviewed in Washington in October 1991 and July 1992.

M. J. Rosenberg, former editor of AIPAC's *Near East Report* and a congressional staffer, was interviewed in Washington in September 1992 and paraphrased his own *Village Voice* article of 1969, "To Uncle Tom and Other Such Jews."

"Leaders of 3 U.S. Jewish Groups Take Issue With Pro-Israel Lobby," said a *New York Times* headline on October 18, 1988. The new "First Tuesday Club" meetings were described by activists in the Jewish organizations.

Jonathan E. Mitchell was interviewed in Los Angeles in November 1991, before he became a national officer of AIPAC.

The newsletter *Activities*, sent to senior AIPAC members, monitors vocal opposition to Israel and to AIPAC. Similar information, collected by AIPAC in a book, *The Campaign to Discredit Israel* (Washington: America-Israel Public Affairs Committee, 1983), was criticized as an inaccurate "enemies list" by Anthony Lewis of the *New York Times* in his columns of December 22, 1983, and January 16, 1984.

In *The Village Voice* of August 4 and 25, 1992, Robert I. Friedman attacked the Policy Analysis "opposition-research unit" at AIPAC and charged that research director Steven J. Rosen "has many dossiers on people whom he perceives to be anti-Israel." Dine and Rosen both denied the charges.

Andrew S. Carroll, interviewed in Washington in September 1992, claimed he lost his job as editor of the *Washington Jewish Week* that year in part because Rosen—based on a dossier—showed a negative report on Carroll to his publisher. Carroll said AIPAC seemed annoyed that the pro-Arab complaint to the Federal Election Commission in 1988 was based largely on articles in *Washington Jewish Week* and added: "What bothers me is how narrowly they've defined who is pro-Israel and who isn't. But I appreciate about 95 percent of what AIPAC has done. It's painful for me to be in a dispute with them, because I'm glad they're there."

Rosen told the Jewish Telegraphic Agency in August 1992 that the memo was a one-time affair and he had no secret file system on individuals. The Jewish Telegraphic Agency added: "People with a firsthand knowledge, however, insist that Rosen does have such files."

Dine and AIPAC board chairman Mayer Mitchell wrote, in the *Washington Post* of November 14, 1992: "No one at AIPAC conducts 'investigations' of anyone, beyond collecting speeches, clipping published articles and attending public conferences." Dine and Rosen declined repeated invitations to be interviewed. Rosen's 1982 "night flowers" memo was quoted in the *Washington Post,* January 7, 1986.

Yossi Sarid, member of the Israeli parliament, was interviewed in Tel Aviv in July 1993.

Dine's denial of a rightward drift was in his letter to the *Washington Post,* November 14, 1992, with Mayer Mitchell.

CHAPTER SEVENTEEN

Robert Rosenberg was interviewed in Tel Aviv's Café Tamar in October 1992.

The estimate of 60,000 Americans living in Israel was in an Associated Press report on June 24, 1993. This figure is confirmed by the authoritative annual survey by Steven M. Cohen for the Institute on American-Jewish Relations cited in Stuart Eizenstat, "Loving Israel: Warts and All," *Foreign Policy* (Winter 1990–91): 87–105. According to Israel's Bureau of Statistics, the Israeli population at the end of 1992 was 5.3 million, comprising 4.4 million Jews and 0.9 million Israeli Arabs of Christian and Muslim origins.

Among the ex-Americans: Shimon Agranat, born in the United States and educated in the progressive environment of America's judicial system, was president of Israel's Supreme Court in the 1960s and '70s. The members of parliament were Shlomo Rosenberg and his son Yehuda Ben-Meir, who in the early 1980s was a K'nesset member and the deputy foreign minister.

Joshua Schoffman was interviewed in July 1993 following a *New York Times* article on January 15, 1993.

Miriam Levinger was interviewed in July 1993; see also *Yediot Aharonot,* July 7, 1992.

There are no precise figures on the number of Israelis who left for America. In Yossi Melman's *The New Israelis: An Intimate View of a Changing People* (New York: Birch Lane, 1992), p. 215, Israeli officials estimated the number of Israelis who have left the country for America since 1948 at between 250,000 and 500,000. *Ma'ariv,* on July 2, 1993, said 250,000 Israelis moved to the United States. Jewish organizations in America believe the figure is a bit lower.

The reference to Abba Eban as a *yored,* or emigrant, was made by his fellow Israeli diplomat and former ambassador to Washington, Ephraim Evron.

The *Jewish Journal* reported on April 19, 1993, that "the Jewish

Federation Council of Los Angeles now has an Israeli Division" established in October 1992.

The estimate of 1.4 million American Jews having visited Israel is based on a survey that found 31 percent of the 4.2 million Americans who were born as Jews and still identify as Jews had visited Israel; plus 11 percent of the 1.1 million who were born Jewish but no longer identify as Jews and 11 percent of the 210,000 who were born and raised Jewish but converted to other religions. See *Highlights of the CJF 1990 National Jewish Population Survey* (New York: Council of Jewish Federations, 1991), pp. 4, 35.

Some reflections on the "Americanization" of Israeli society are adapted from Melman, *New Israelis*, chapter entitled "The Subaru Syndrome," pp. 207–214.

Mike Mitchell was interviewed in Tel Aviv in February 1992 by *Ma'ariv*.

Benjamin Netanyahu was interviewed in Jerusalem in October 1992. His brief change of name to Nitay was reported by *Ma'ariv*, March 26, 1993.

Malcolm Hoenlein, of the Conference of Presidents of Major American Jewish Organizations, was interviewed in February 1992 in Jerusalem.

On 60,000 U.S. Jews having moved to Israel and other statistics, see Steven M. Cohen's survey for the Institute on American Jewish-Israeli Relations, cited in Eizenstat, "Loving Israel: Warts and All," p. 95.

Colette Avital, the Israeli consul-general in New York, was interviewed there in November 1992.

Among the Israelis who called for the dismantling of the UJA was the novelist and essayist A. B. Yehoshua.

On the origins of Israel's relations with the Jewish diaspora, see Yigal Eilam, *The Jewish Agency: First Years* (Jerusalem: The Zionist Library, World Zionist Federation, 1990).

Eleanor (Elly) Friedman and her husband Jonathan Cohen, cofounders of the New Israel Fund, were interviewed at their home in Lincoln, Massachusetts, in September 1992.

Dr. Sanford Kuvin was interviewed, from his home in Palm Beach, Florida, in October 1993.

Professor Franklin Fisher was interviewed in his office at MIT in

Cambridge, Massachusetts, in September 1992.

New Israel Fund does have bitter opponents, including Herbert Zweibon, chairman of Americans for a Safe Israel, a New York–based group strongly opposing any territorial concessions by Israel in the Middle East peace talks. One of AFSI's publications is entitled *The New Israel Fund: A New Fund for Israel's Enemies*. Zweibon proposed dismantling the Conference of Presidents of Major American Jewish Organizations after it admitted Americans for Peace Now as a member in 1993.

CHAPTER EIGHTEEN

The story of oil prospector Harris Darcy was in the *Wall Street Journal*, August 22, 1985. In the Bible, Zebulun and Issachar are promised "the hidden treasures of the sand" in their tribal lands (Deuteronomy 33:19), and of Asher it is said, "Let him dip his foot in oil" (Deuteronomy 33:24). The authors interviewed some Americans involved in the project in October 1985.

On the history of the connections between American Christians and Israel, Yaakov Ariel wrote an excellent article in Hebrew, "American Fundamentalists in Israel," published by the Leonard Davis Institute for International Relations at the Hebrew University in Jerusalem, July 1989.

Sister Rose Thering of the National Christian Leadership Conference for Israel was interviewed in New York in April and June 1993.

Richard Hellman, who heard the voice of God and went on to form the Christians' Israel Public Action Campaign, was interviewed in Washington in March 1992.

AIPAC's deputy legislative director, Arne Christenson, called himself a "Christian Zionist" when speaking to members of Adas Israel Congregation in Washington in December 1993.

Jacques Torczyner, veteran member of the executive of the World Zionist Organization, was interviewed in New York in May 1992.

The White House briefing on President Clinton and his biblical reflections on Middle East peace was conducted by the State Department's Dennis Ross and Martin Indyk of the National Security Council on September 12, 1993. See also the *New York Times*, September 14, 1993.

On Pat Robertson and his support for "Jews for Jesus" revealed by the newspaper *Forward* on May 14, 1993, the director of the Israel

Government Tourist Office in North America, Raphael Farber, expressed his backing for Robertson in *Ha'aretz*, May 31, 1993, adding: "Pat Robertson is a big friend of Israel. The problem isn't Robertson or the activities of 'Jews for Jesus.' The problem is that American Jews will disappear in twenty years because of mixed marriages."

Rabbi Yehiel Eckstein, founder and director of the International Fellowship of Christians and Jews, was interviewed in Chicago in June 1992 and in December 1993.

Robert Zimmerman of the American Jewish Congress was interviewed in New York in April 1993.

CHAPTER NINETEEN

Dan Rather and Peter Jennings were on videotape, but stars of Broadway and Hollywood and Mayor David Dinkins were on hand to honor Israel's consul, Uriel (Uri) Savir, at a farewell party thrown by the American Friends of Tel Aviv University on August 28, 1992, at the Essex House Hotel in New York.

Savir was interviewed at his New York consulate in March 1992, before becoming director-general of Israel's foreign ministry in Jerusalem.

General Eisenhower's role in ensuring that Americans saw the shocking newsreels of liberated concentration camps, and the audience reactions, are quoted from Thomas Doherty, *Projections of War: Hollywood, American Culture and World War II* (New York: Columbia University Press, 1993), as reviewed in *The New York Times*, December 28, 1993.

Edward R. Murrow's frequent visits to Israel are recounted by Teddy Kollek in his memoirs, *For Jerusalem: A Life* (New York: Random House, 1978), p. 133.

The Arab diplomats' complaint to Secretary of State Christian Herter on March 7, 1960, is in *Foreign Relations of the United States, 1958–1960*, vol. 13, Arab-Israeli Dispute, United Arab Republic, North Africa (Washington, DC: Department of State, 1992), pp. 279–290.

The numbers of foreign correspondents accredited in Israel were provided by the Government Press Office in Jerusalem in May 1993.

The Israeli diplomat, who spoke of the Lebanon invasion as "a lost battle" for Israel's image makers, worked in Washington in 1982 but asked not to be named.

NOTES

Benjamin Netanyahu wrote of his investigation into the photograph of the armless Palestinian girl in *A Place Among the Nations: Israel and the World* (New York: Bantam, 1993), pp. 385–386. Reagan used the word "holocaust" in complaining to Begin about the bombing of Beirut, according to several officials and Bernard Gwertzman, "Reagan Turns to Israel," *New York Times Magazine*, November 27, 1983, p. 69.

Gallup polls on support for Israel versus support for Arab nations from 1980 to 1991 were summarized in AIPAC's *Near East Report*, March 11, 1991. The smallest margin was 32 to 28 percent in Israel's favor after the Sabra and Shatila refugee camps massacre of September 1982. When Iraq's Scud missiles were hitting Israel in February 1991, the margin was 64 to 8 percent.

The Israeli diplomat in Washington who spoke of "blue-eyed boys" asked not to be identified.

Examples of front-page photographs of Israeli-Palestinian confrontations, almost devoid of news, abounded at the height of the intifada in early 1988. Thomas L. Friedman discusses one, in *From Beirut to Jerusalem* (New York: Farrar Strauss Giroux, 1989), pp. 431–432.

Richard Schifter, assistant secretary of state for human rights and humanitarian affairs from 1985 to 1992, was interviewed by Miami's Jewish Family Television on November 15, 1992.

Andrea Levin, executive director of the Committee for Accuracy in Middle East Reporting in America, was interviewed in CAMERA's Boston office in June 1992.

Quotes from Alan Dershowitz are found in his fund-raising letter on behalf of CAMERA, sent in late 1992.

On frequent targets of criticism: AIPAC protested in the *Washington Post*, March 11, 1991, about "another 'slam piece' " by Evans and Novak. CAMERA aimed a minute-by-minute monitoring effort at National Public Radio in 1992, charging that Arab and Israeli voices that were critical of Israel's government far outweighed any government supporters who were aired; NPR denied any bias. NBC's Gumbel was criticized in the AIPAC newsletter, *Near East Report*, on July 8 and August 5, 1991. On ABC, CAMERA's Levin said: "Jennings stands out, and I don't know his personal dynamics or anything." Jennings firmly stood by his reporting, at length, in the *Baltimore Jewish Times*, May 24, 1991.

Abraham Foxman, national director of the Anti-Defamation League of B'nai B'rith, was interviewed in his New York office in February 1992.

Jonathan Mitchell was interviewed in Los Angeles in 1991, before becoming a national officer of AIPAC.

Vice President George Bush told the Washington Press Club on September 23, 1982, that the truth about the Beirut massacre that month would come out because of Israel's "investigative reporters"; quoted in Wolf Blitzer, *Between Washington and Jerusalem: A Reporter's Notebook* (New York: Oxford University Press, 1985), p. 166.

Abba Eban's assessment of the Lebanon war as "a dark age in the moral history" was in *Ma'ariv* in mid-July 1982, quoted by him in *Personal Witness: Israel Through My Eyes* (New York: Putnam, 1992), p. 611.

Yossi Sarid, member of the K'nesset and Yitzhak Rabin's cabinet, was interviewed in Tel Aviv in July 1993.

CHAPTER TWENTY

Defense Minister Moshe Arens was interviewed at home in Savyon in September 1992; also interviewed in *Yediot Aharonot*, January 10, 1992.

America's strategic shift from Iran to Iraq is chronicled by Howard Teicher, former National Security Council official, interviewed in Washington in November 1991, and in the book he wrote with Gayle Radley Teicher, *Twin Pillars to Desert Storm: America's Flawed Vision in the Middle East from Nixon to Bush* (New York: William Morrow, 1993).

The Israeli prediction that Iraq would rapidly win the war against Iran was recounted to the authors by several Israeli intelligence officers.

On the secret U.S. support for Iraq, see Bob Woodward, *Veil: the Secret Wars of the CIA, 1981–1987* (London: Headline, 1988), p. 439.

General Amos Gilboa, a senior veteran of Israeli intelligence, published an investigative report in *Ma'ariv*, March 29, 1991, in which he argued that Israeli intelligence passed on warnings of Saddam Hussein's aggressive intentions to its American counterparts, but they either rejected or ignored them.

On being treated as "paranoid" and "virtually shouting," a senior

Israeli intelligence officer was interviewed but asked to remain anonymous.

Although the name of the Mossad director is not generally published in Israel, he was identified as Shabtai Shavit by the British newsletter *Foreign Report,* August 12, 1993.

Some Israelis had the impression that the United States was stuck in a "concept" that Iraq would not do anything grossly unacceptable; rather like Israel's self-described and self-deluding "concept" before the Yom Kippur War of 1973 that the Arabs would never dare start a war. Almost three years after the invasion of Kuwait, there was a measure of confirmation by Richard Haass, the Middle East expert on the White House's National Security Council: "Our policy of 'constructive dialogue' toward Iraq failed. . . . I admit guilt. At that time, we were prisoners in a conceptual trap." Haass was interviewed by *Yediot Aharonot,* May 25, 1993.

The senior diplomat in Israel's embassy in Washington who recalled the elation after Iraq invaded Kuwait asked to remain anonymous.

General Michael Dugan was quoted in the *Washington Post* on September 16, 1990, and was forced to resign that week. But he told the authors, in October 1991, that he had only been speaking hypothetically.

Lawrence Eagleburger was interviewed in March 1993, after retiring as secretary of state. Wolfowitz was interviewed in November 1993. Other U.S. officials who were involved in the planning and implementation of the Eagleburger-Wolfowitz visits to Israel were interviewed, asking to remain anonymous.

The description of early warning by satellites is based on explanations to the authors by physicist Dror Sadeh, a former director-general of Israel's space agency.

The telephone calls from Washington were recounted in a special war summary by *Ma'ariv,* March 29, 1991.

Descriptions of the atmosphere in the Israeli government are based on interviews with most of the ministers and with close aides of Prime Minister Shamir.

Mayor David Dinkins recalled the Scud-induced singing of "We Shall Overcome" when he spoke to the American Friends of Tel Aviv University in New York on August 28, 1992.

On NSA eavesdropping, ABC News reported on October 7, 1993,

that British protesters who penetrated an NSA installation seized Hebrew documents confirming that Israel is a target for U.S. intelligence gathering.

In recent years several books and articles have claimed that Israel put its nuclear forces on special alert and intended to use them during the Gulf War. Our research, however, found that this was not the case.

On the Jericho's inability to strike Iraqi cities: When the Gulf War was over, some Likud party ministers accused Labor's Yitzhak Rabin—who had been defense minister from 1984 until nine months before the war—of responsibility for the inadequacy of the missiles. They charged that he had not invested sufficient funds in improving the Jericho. Rabin contended that there were more important priorities.

Yossi Achimeir, an aide to Shamir, was interviewed in Jerusalem in October 1992.

Details of the Patriots' deployment and the participation of American Jews in the mission are based on a January 1993 interview with Rabbi Jacob Goldstein, the chief chaplain to the U.S. forces in Israel during the Gulf War, and a December 1993 interview with Lieutenant Colonel Harry Krimkowitz.

Among the analyses of the Patriots' effectiveness, noteworthy are Reuven Pedatzur's studies for the newspaper *Ha'aretz*, April 17 and 30, 1991. Rabin was quoted by *Yediot Aharonot*, January 10, 1992.

General Avihu Bin-Nun's demand to clear an air corridor for Israeli planes is based on the recollections of Israeli participants, and *Ma'ariv*, March 29, 1991.

Achimeir, on the need for U.S. aid, is cited in the *New York Times*, January 23, 1991.

The *Ha'aretz* editorial appeared on January 23, 1991.

President Bush on the Scud hunt is cited in the *Washington Post*, January 19, 1991.

Dan Meridor, member of Shamir's cabinet, was interviewed in Jerusalem in September 1992.

General Bin-Nun's bitter assessment of the U.S. Scud-hunting effort came during an interview on Israeli television on March 4, 1992, and at a public forum in Tel Aviv in June; see *Yediot Aharonot*, June 19, 1992.

In a reply to the authors from the United States Central Command at MacDill Air Force Base in Florida, Captain R. S. Prucha wrote in November 1993: "Approximately 110,000 coalition sorties were flown, of which 65,000 were U.S. Of these, 2,500 counter-Scud missions were flown, approximately 4 percent of total U.S. sorties. When logistics, reconnaissance, and the multitude of combat and other support missions are considered, 4 percent is a significant figure."

A study conducted for the U.S. Air Force by Eliot Cohen of the School for Advanced International Studies in Washington said, in May 1993, that 5 percent of the bombing missions were directed at Scud installations in western Iraq. Cohen, in an interview that month, added that there was "no hard evidence" that any mobile launchers were hit; and he confirmed that American pilots had not trained for this type of bombing. The study was published as *Gulf War Air Power Survey* (Washington, DC: Government Printing Office, 1993).

The Israeli government received an unpublished report on Scud hunting by Oded Eran, deputy director-general of the ministry of foreign affairs, compiled while he was on leave at the Washington Institute for Near East Policy. Eran provided one of the authors with his main findings during an interview in Jerusalem in July 1992.

Israel's government decided not to raise publicly its suspicions about Bush's motives, so as not to cause further harm to relations with Washington. Thus Eran's and other studies were kept secret.

While General Colin L. Powell did not comment, his wartime aide Colonel Bill Smullen responded briefly by telephone in October 1993 to the Israeli allegations that U.S. officials did not do all they could to stop the Scud attacks. The allegations, said Smullen, were "inaccurate and untrue."

As the former president, George Bush spoke of "crushing Saddam's vaunted army," thus making Israel safer, in a speech to the Joint Israel Appeal in London, England, on December 2, 1993.

General H. Norman Schwarzkopf, interviewed in Tampa, Florida, in November 1993, told the authors that he had been informed by Lieutenant General Charles A. Horner, commander of the U.S. Ninth Air Force, "that fully 25 percent of the attack missions by F-15's, F-16's, and low-flying A-10's at one time were dedicated to the mobile missile chase," apparently during the first weekend after Scuds struck Israel.

Schwarzkopf added: "I say that we didn't fail in our mission. When you have multiple Scud launches of eight or nine missiles in a given day at the start of the war, but later the average is less than one a day, you have accomplished your mission. You may not have destroyed every one, but what's important is that you prevent missiles being launched."

Edward Luttwack, an analyst and lecturer at the Center for Strategic and International Studies in Washington and an occasional consultant to the U.S. military, was interviewed by telephone from Washington in November 1993.

CHAPTER TWENTY-ONE

Descriptions of the day of lobbying by 1,200 supporters of Israel are based on the recollections of several of them.

The roles of Yoram Ettinger and Steve Rosen, advising Israel to challenge President Bush over loan guarantees, were recounted in confidential interviews by participants in the lobbying effort. Ettinger, in charge of the Senate side of the Israeli embassy's Capitol Hill lobbying, was considered a Likud protégé of Moshe Arens and Benjamin Netanyahu.

President Reagan was described as not losing any sleep over Middle East peace by an Israeli diplomat who asked not to be identified.

George P. Shultz discussed the 1988 recognition of the PLO in his memoirs, *Turmoil and Triumph: My Years as Secretary of State* (New York: Charles Scribner's Sons, 1993), pp. 1035, 1040.

Congressman Larry Smith was interviewed at his Capitol Hill office in July 1991. He was one of many who identified White House chief of staff Sununu, the president's national security advisor Scowcroft, and budget director Darman as unsympathetic to Israel.

Yossi Ahimeir, a senior aide to Shamir, was "astonished" when Bush raised settlements. Yossi Ben-Aharon, director-general of Shamir's office as foreign minister, from 1984 to 1986, and then as prime minister from 1986 to 1992, recalled the "slap in the face." Both were interviewed.

Prime Minister Shamir, asking his aides, "Have you ever seen . . . ?" was recalled by Yossi Achimeir when interviewed in October 1992.

Ehud Olmert called Bush "aggressive and cruel," frequently punishing Israel, when interviewed in 1992.

On Secretary of State James Baker reciting the White House telephone number to the Shamir government, see the *New York Times* and other newspapers, June 14, 1990.

Foreign Minister David Levy's letter to Secretary of State Baker, dated October 2, 1990, is summarized in an internal State Department report, "Israeli Settlement in the Occupied Territories," dated March 4, 1991; released to the authors under the Freedom of Information Act. It notes that around three thousand Soviet Jews who arrived in 1990 chose to reside in the West Bank or Golan Heights, which was "only 1.2 percent of the 1990 immigration flow from the Soviet Union, [but] they represent approximately 20 percent of the 1990 growth in settlement population." The report also includes East Jerusalem, to the displeasure of Israel's government.

Baker said "it is a matter of great importance" in testimony to the House Foreign Affairs Committee, quoted in AIPAC's *Near East Report*, February 18, 1991.

Bush, saying "I accept the fact" that Shamir would build settlements, and the Israeli expenditure of "3x," is according to confidential interviews with members of the White House staff. The president told leaders of the Union of Orthodox Jewish Congregations of America that he could not support future Israeli requests for loan guarantees unless Israel froze the settlement program; see Reuter, "Shamir Says Settlements to Go On Despite Bush Warning," June 12, 1991.

The House vote on June 19, 1991, rejecting Congressman Bryant's proposed cut in aid to Israel, followed by the approval of foreign aid for Fiscal Years 1992 and 1993, is in AIPAC's *Near East Report*, July 1, 1991. The Senate vote is in *Near East Report*, August 5, 1991.

Richard Haass's statement on the White House view of a "frustrating" relationship with Israel is according to the recollection of Jewish community officials with whom he spoke in 1991 and 1992.

AIPAC's Tom Dine, calling for an "all-out campaign" in a closed meeting with major donors to AIPAC, quoted by Reuter, "Could U.S. Squeeze Israel on $10 Billion Loan Request?" June 20, 1991.

Jacob (Jack) Stein, a White House official in the Reagan years, a friend of George Bush, and previously chairman of the Conference of Presidents of Major American Jewish Organizations, was interviewed at his home in Great Neck, New York, in June 1992.

An Israeli diplomat who was based in Washington in 1991 and

asked not to be named said: "The line wasn't very good and Shamir didn't hear Baker properly."

Details of the advice from Senator Patrick Leahy and his aides to the Israelis were obtained from officials fully aware of the conversations.

Among the magazine features was "Loan Guarantees Now" in B'nai B'rith's *Jewish Monthly* (August-September 1991): 5, which said: "Since the 1970s, the United States and Israel have joined together in the struggle to secure the internationally guaranteed right to free emigration for Soviet Jews. Now that the gates finally have been opened, it is appropriate that the United States assist in the absorption of these immigrants in Israel."

Ettinger's two cables to Shamir are quoted in *Yediot Aharonot*, October 11, 1991.

Shamir, on settlements "will continue," was quoted by Reuter, June 12, 1991.

The president's first request for a 120-day delay is in Associated Press, "Despite Bush Appeal for Delay Israel Asks for Help in Settling Soviet Jews," September 7, 1991.

Mayer (Bubba) Mitchell's September 12 visit to President Bush at the White House was recounted by Jacob Stein in an interview.

President Bush's precedent-shattering appearance in the White House press room was broadcast by CBS News, on radio, on September 12.

Morris Amitay gave his opinion when interviewed on September 16.

The letter to Bush from three Jewish Republican activists, Max Fisher, George Klein, and Richard Fox, was obtained by Associated Press, September 16, 1991.

Vice President Dan Quayle's conversations with Jews and in the administration were recounted by participants.

Bush's speech at the UN and the repeal of the Zionism-equals-racism resolution are in *Near East Report*, December 23, 1991; *New York Times*, September 22 and 24, 1991; and Associated Press, "Shamir Pleased by Bush Call to Nix Zionism is Racism Resolution," September 23, 1991.

Foreign minister Levy, giving up on the loan guarantees, was in the *New York Times*, September 26, 1991.

The U.S. protest to Israel on reconnaissance flights over Iraq was reported by Reuter on October 9 and 10, 1991, including the defense secretary, Dick Cheney, saying: "We have been involved in extensive sharing of information with our Israeli friends. Problems that might arise from these overflights we can do without." *Yediot Aharonot* headlined its account, on October 11: "The Washington-Jerusalem War."

Mark Kramer, financial backer of New Israel Fund and other groups, was interviewed in Boston in September 1992.

The official of the Council of Jewish Federations who spoke on the background to the anti-Shamir opinion survey asked not to be identified.

The 1991 National Survey of American Jews, conducted by Professor Steven M. Cohen for the Institute on American Jewish-Israeli Relations and the American Jewish Committee, was based on questionnaires returned by 1,159 Jews chosen nationwide by a marketing firm. Published October 3, 1991, it states: "In the aftermath of the Gulf War, American Jewish attitudes shifted in a hard-line direction." It also found, incidentally, that 40 percent of American Jews feel emotionally "extremely attached" or "very attached" to Israel, and 37 percent have visited the country.

The anti-Shamir poll, now revealed to have been "an ambush," was conducted by Steven M. Cohen and Seymour Martin Lipset and entitled "Attitudes Toward the Arab-Israeli Conflict and the Peace Process Among American Jewish Philanthropic Leaders, 1991." It was published in November 1991, on the eve of the General Assembly of the Council of Jewish Federations, by the Wilstein Institute of Jewish Policy Studies at the University of Judaism in Los Angeles. Out of 339 board members and presidents of Jewish Federations, the pollsters were able to question 205. In this group, 97 percent felt "extremely" or "very" emotionally attached to Israel; and 96 percent had visited the country.

The "ambush" poll was featured in the *New York Times*, November 21, 1991, under the headline: "Shamir's Visit Will Find U.S. Jews More Dovish."

CHAPTER TWENTY-TWO

Martin Indyk, when interviewed in September 1992 at the Washington Institute for Near East Policy, which he headed, said:

"Metaphorically, you could hear the champagne corks popping in Washington when the Israeli election returns came in. There was no lack of private glee. People were very pleased." In 1993 Indyk became Middle East specialist—Richard Haass's old job—on the National Security Council.

While there were no low-interest loans under a U.S. guarantee program, Israel's need for funds to house and educate Soviet and Ethiopian refugees did yield a successful Operation Exodus campaign by the United Jewish Appeal and a record sale of $1.1 billion in State of Israel Bonds in 1992, for a total of $12.7 billion in bond sales in thirty-one years. See *Long Island Jewish World*, May 7–13, 1993.

Quotes from Dennis Ross, the State Department's coordinator for the Middle East peace talks, are from participants in several meetings he had with American Jewish leaders in early 1992.

James Baker's alleged profanity about Jewish voters was reported by former New York mayor Edward Koch in a *New York Post* column, March 6, 1992. See also Reuter dispatch, "Bush May Face Jewish Backlash Over Israeli Loans," March 18, 1992.

AIPAC's warning against "intrusion of U.S. policymakers" in Israeli politics appeared in the lobby's *Near East Report*, March 23, 1992.

The senior Bush administration policy maker, who was interviewed in 1992 about Rabin's high credibility, asked not to be identified.

Morris Amitay, former executive director of AIPAC and now head of Washington PAC, was interviewed about the Bush-Clinton race in September 1992.

Warren Christopher's testimony in his confirmation hearings for secretary of state were excerpted in *Near East Report*, January 25, 1993.

The fact that Israeli officials referred to some U.S. counterparts as "self-hating Jews" and "Baker's Jew-boys" is according to Yossi Ben-Aharon and Yossi Achimeir, two senior aides to Yitzhak Shamir.

On President Clinton and Prime Minister Rabin being "worlds apart," Nahum Barnea wrote in *Yediot Aharonot*, March 12, 1993.

Malcolm Hoenlein was interviewed in Jerusalem in February 1992 and at his New York office in August 1992.

Eitan Ben-Zur, who held three diplomatic posts in the United

States since 1967, was interviewed in Jerusalem in May 1991.

Samuel Berger was profiled in a pro-Israel newsletter, *The Caucus Current* (Great Neck, New York), April 1993.

U.S.-Israel relations under Bush and Shamir were described as "The Washington-Jerusalem War" in a headline in *Yediot Aharonot* on October 11, 1991.

President Clinton "deepening" the relationship with Israel as a "strategic partner" was cited in *Yediot Aharonot*, March 19, 1993. See also Associated Press, March 15, 1993.

The reduction in U.S. loan guarantees, from $2 billion to under $1.6 billion for fiscal 1994, was reported by Reuter, October 5, 1993, and the *New York Times*, October 6, 1993.

When Israel and the PLO announced their peace accord, among the hostile reactions was that of Ruth R. Wisse, professor of Yiddish at Harvard University: "It's the first time that an Israeli government is doing something for which I, as an American Jew, would not like to bear moral responsibility," she told the *New York Times*, September 3, 1993.

Representative Nydia Velasquez's remark opposing foreign aid was cited in *Near East Report*, June 28, 1993.

The Congressional Black Caucus demand to link foreign aid to urban aid was in *Ha'aretz*, August 2, 1992.

A survey of 1,662 randomly selected Americans in 1990 said 45 percent favored decreasing or stopping aid to Israel, 38 percent favored keeping it the same, and only 8 percent favored an increase. Among 377 "leaders" of public opinion, 54 percent favored decreasing or cutting aid. See *American Public Opinion and U.S. Foreign Policy 1991* (Chicago: Chicago Council on Foreign Relations, 1991), pp. 23–24.

Among many voices warning, in 1993, that foreign aid to Israel would eventually be cut were Rabbi Arthur J. Hertzberg, former president of the American Jewish Congress, in *Ha'aretz*, January 8, 1991; and Congressman David Obey, chairman of the House Appropriations subcommittee dealing with foreign aid, who warned: "We cannot forever assume that we are going to provide this high percentage of aid to the region." See *Near East Report*, March 15, 1993.

U.S. ambassador William Harrop suggested a cut in aid to Israel in a speech to the Rotary Club of Tel Aviv on March 4, 1993. The State

Department disavowed his speech, and two months later he was replaced after barely one year in Israel.

Israeli ambassador to Washington Zalman Shoval warned of future aid cuts in *Forward*, February 12, 1993.

Among articles doubting Israel's strategic value after the end of the Cold War was an editorial in the *New York Times*, March 22, 1992.

On U.S.-Israeli cooperation in Kazakhstan and other former Soviet republics, Ehud Gol, in charge of the project in the Israeli foreign ministry, was interviewed in Jerusalem in February 1993.

Senator Richard Lugar, Republican of Indiana, was quoted by *Ha'aretz*, February 2, 1990.

Congressman Charles Schumer, Democrat of New York, was interviewed in his Capitol Hill office in April 1991.

David Saperstein, Washington representative of the National Jewish Community Relations Advisory Council, was interviewed in September 1991.

On Rabin's clash with AIPAC, several members of the organization were interviewed anonymously. See also *Forward*, August 21, 1992, and the *New York Times*, August 22, 1992.

On the resignation of AIPAC vice president Harvey Friedman, see the *New York Times*, July 2, 1993, and *Forward*, July 9, 1993. The breaking point was Friedman calling Israel's deputy foreign minister Yossi Beilin "a little slime ball."

On the resignation of AIPAC president David Steiner, see Associated Press and the *Washington Times*, November 4, 1992.

In his resignation letter, dated June 28, 1993, and obtained from AIPAC, executive director Thomas A. Dine gave a three-page review of the huge growth in AIPAC under his leadership. "Our relationships with Executive branch officials and our record of achievement on Capitol Hill are widely acknowledged," he wrote. "Our collective lobbying efforts are bipartisan because Israel is a bipartisan issue, and must always so remain. The respect accorded to our information—accurate, timely, relevant, and thus credible—extends across the political and policy spectrums."

An example of AIPAC's adjustment came immediately after the signing of the Israel-PLO accord in Washington in September 1993, when the lobby's new president, Steve Grossman, happily met with the PLO's Faisal Husseini, leader of the Palestinian delegation to the peace talks. "If the Israeli and Palestinian economies are linked," said Grossman, "the leaders of the two communities in this country should be, too." The AIPAC chief proposed a Jewish-Arab "think tank, created for joint ventures between American-Jewish business-people and Arab-American businesspeople." See *Long Island Jewish World*, September 24–30, 1993.

The notion that the political power of American Jews is set to decline and that they rarely can decide elections is in Earl Raab and Seymour Martin Lipset, *The Political Future of American Jews* (New York: American Jewish Congress, 1992), pp. 2–3.

The vision of a post-PAC political scene helped motivate a restructuring of the American Zionist Federation in early 1993, renamed the American Zionist Movement. As an umbrella for twenty-two organizations with combined membership rolls of over 1 million American Jews, it has a formidable mailing list. And if 100,000 would contribute just $100 each to a political campaign, they would form a $10 million bloc. "As Congress makes efforts to tighten up on campaign giving and the noose tightens around PACs," says AZM president Seymour D. Reich, it will become impossible to wield political power based on fifty or one hundred wealthy Jews giving $25,000 apiece to PACs and candidates. "The small givers will fill that void."

In the meantime, AZM officers began visiting legislators and plan annual political and youth conferences in Washington—just like AIPAC. "We don't intend to replace AIPAC," says Reich. "We have a broader base. And AIPAC was not available to many of them, because they have not been the big givers. They now have an outlet for political activity on a grassroots level, where they won't be ashamed of not being among the big givers." Reich was interviewed in New York in July 1993.

Ambassador Samuel Lewis's analysis of the "icing" and the "cake" was in an interview in April 1992. In 1993 Lewis became director of policy planning—Dennis Ross's old job—in the State Department.

General Colin L. Powell spoke of his "personal bond" with Israel at Yeshiva University in New York on December 20, 1992.

America will not let Israel go "down the tube," Richard Nixon wrote in a letter to the authors on October 7, 1992.

INDEX

INDEX

101–2, 106; *see also* Warplanes; Weapons
Arms deals, 90, 93
Arms deliveries to Israel, 167–68
Arms embargo, 39, 72, 111
Arms for hostages deal, 239–40
Arms race, 78, 144
Arms sales to Arab countries, 112
Arms sales to Israel, 101, 111–12, 144, 152, 157
Arms smuggling, 39–40, 43, 44, 51
Arms suppliers, Communist, 77
Arrow antimissile missile, 246, 390, 429
Ashdod, 114
Aspin, Les, 445
Assembly of God, 361
Association for Civil Rights (Israel), 332
Atom bomb, 38, 211; *see also* Nuclear capability
Atomic Energy Commission (Israel), 114
Atomic Energy Commission (U.S.), 96, 166
Atomic plant (Dimona), 96–100, 102–4, 113, 149–50
Atoms for Peace program, 102
Auschwitz, 17, 19, 72, 134
Avital, Colette, 344
AWACS (Airborne Warning and Control Systems) controversy, 189–96, 199, 204, 213, 231, 309, 312, 408, 423

Baghdad, 196, 198, 386–87
Baghdad Pact, 77
Baker, James, 356–57, 388–89, 410, 439, 445–46; and Gulf War, 397–98, 403; hostility to Israel, 408, 437, 438, 443; and loan guarantees issue, 415–16, 417, 419, 421–22, 424, 430, 436, 451; and Middle East peace initiatives, 409, 412, 418, 431; and U.S./Israeli relations, 413, 438
Baker, Mrs. James, 356–57
Balaban, Barney, 54
Balfour Declaration of 1917, 16, 26
Bechtel Corp., 188, 201, 221, 231, 281
Begin, Aliza, 224
Begin, Menachem, 172, 178, 179, 180, 198–99, 230, 268, 310, 340, 367, 370, 410, 435, 447; and Arens, 213; and American Christians, 353–55, 360–61; and AWACS controversy, 191, 193, 194–95; cabinet, 181; and Camp David accords, 181–84; and Carter, 176–78, 187–88; demonology surrounding, 173–75, 185; depression, passivity, 265; economic policy, 270; and invasion of Lebanon, 217, 219, 221–22, 223, 224;

"Jerusalem Law," 358; and proposed strategic cooperation agreement, 202, 203, 204–5, 206, 208–10, 213; and Reagan, 189, 199–200, 214; reelection, 196–97; resignation, 225; and U.S./Israeli relations, 269; Zionism, 211–12
Beirut, 219, 220, 222, 231, 366–67
Belzec, 17
Ben-Gurion, David, 16, 17, 18, 25, 26, 33, 36, 46, 55, 68, 80, 101, 103–4, 128, 201, 212, 226–27, 340, 364, 451; and American Christians, 352; and Arab-Israeli conflict, 73, 74; and atomic plant (Dimona), 96, 99, 102; Begin's competition with, 175; and cooperation of intelligence communities, 62; death of, 148; as defense minister, 76; and Eisenhower Doctrine, 87, 88–89; Gronich advisor to, 48–49, 50; Hadden's contacts with, 124–25; and international support, 86–87; and invasion of Egypt, 81–82, 83; Israel's declaration of independence, 30, 31–32; Marcus advisor to, 38; meetings with U.S. presidents, 90, 92, 99–100, 105–6, 270; negotiations with Egypt, 79, 80; relationship with Eisenhower, 411; responding to pressure from U.S., 85; retirement, 104; as statesman, 108–9; visit to U.S., 57, 59, 60
Ben-Gurion, Paula, 125
Ben-Horin, Elyashiv, 63–64, 65
Ben-Porat, Yoel, 278, 280–82
Ben-Yehuda, Eliezer, 15
Ben-Zur, Eitan, 446
Berger, Samuel, 446
Bible, 10, 185, 347, 363; and search for oil in Israel, 349–50, 355
Big Pines, 217
Bin-Nun, Avihu, 301, 396, 398–99
Blackstone, William, 351
Bloomfield, Douglas M., 308, 309, 310–11, 320–21, 323
B'nai B'rith, 27, 28, 39, 133, 235, 317–18, 423
Boston Consulting Group, 341
Brandeis, Louis, 351
Bridges for Peace, 358
Brock, William, 253–55, 256, 257
Brooks, Charles D., 318
Brown, Harold, 229, 248
Bryant, John, 417, 418
Bryen, Stephen, 249–50, 264, 265, 286–87, 301
Brzezinski, Zbigniew, 178, 180, 182

INDEX

Bush, George, 4, 197, 229, 341, 377, 445,
448, 449, 456, 457; attack on Israeli
lobby, 425–27, 429; and Gulf War, 5–7,
383–84, 386, 392, 397–98, 399–400; and
Jewish settlements loan guarantees
issue, 407–8, 410–11, 412–13, 415–16,
419, 420–21, 423, 424–29, 431; and
Madrid peace conference, 432; and
Middle East peace initiatives, 409;
relationship with Israel, 256, 408, 414,
438, 443, 447; on UN resolution,
429–30; vice-presidency, 195, 221, 240,
375
Bush administration, 4, 235, 382; and aid
to Israel, 417; and loan guarantees issue,
415; relationship with Israel, 300–1,
412–14, 418–21, 426–27, 432, 435–36,
437, 439–43
Byrd, Robert, 250, 276

Call It Sleep (Roth), 135
CAMERA (Committee for Accuracy in
Middle East Reporting in America),
372–74
Camp David accords, 182–84, 214, 221,
244, 410
Canada, 78–79, 255, 257, 261
Cardin, Shoshana, 428
Carlucci, Frank, 244
Carmon, David, 123
Carter, Jimmy, 4, 189, 223, 228, 253, 435,
437, 448, 449, 450; on aid to Israel, 277;
Christianity of, 354, 357; loss of
reelection bid, 187–88; and Middle East
peace initiatives, 178–80, 182–84,
185–86; relationship with Iraq, 379;
relationship with Israel, 175, 176–86,
206
Carter administration, 198, 202, 227, 250,
445; and strategic cooperation, 229–30
Casey, Bill, 213–14
Cast a Giant Shadow (film), 109
CBS News, 365
Ceausescu, Nicolae, 262
Central Intelligence Agency (CIA), 46, 47,
51, 59, 76, 79, 84, 99, 158, 177, 230–31,
297, 381; agency chief in Tel Aviv, 120,
121–31; intelligence about Israel,
134–35, 140; and Israeli atomic plant, 96,
97; and Israeli invasion of Egypt, 80–81;
liaison with Mossad, 61, 62–68, 89–90,
119, 120, 153, 226, 279, 284, 288, 383;
Near East department, 61; Office of
National Estimates, 103; and theft of
technology, 299
Chavez, Dennis, 32

Checkmate project, 402–3
Chelmno, 17
Cheney, Dick, 381–82, 386, 388, 389,
397–98, 399, 403
China, 155, 250, 300, 301
Christian dogma, 105
Christians: and Holy Land, 9, 10, 13;
interest in/relationship with Israel, 13,
347, 350–61, 456
Christopher, Warren, 445, 450
Churchill, Winston, 18–19
CIPAC (Christians' Israel Public Action
Campaign), 356
Clemens, Samuel, 12
Cleveland, Grover, 14
Clifford, Clark, 30–31, 34
Clinton, Bill, 3–4, 357, 440, 441, 446–50,
456, 457, 459; Jews voted for, 442–43
Clinton, Hillary, 444
Clinton administration, 233, 235, 423–25,
444–47
Coca-Cola Corp., 259
Cohen, Jonathan, 346
Cohen, Mickey, 41
Cold War, 34, 52, 58, 59, 101, 110, 420,
437; aid as weapon in, 102; end of, 454,
455, 460; realpolitik of, 148
College representatives (AIPAC), 312
Communist bloc. *See* Soviet bloc; Soviet
Union
Conference of Presidents of Major
American Jewish Organizations, 55, 78,
408
Congress, 180, 213; aid appropriations for
Israel, 58, 243, 270–71; antiboycott
legislation, 257–59; Begin and, 219–20;
change in membership of, 451–52;
Israel's influence in 255, 256; Jews in,
444; and loan guarantees issue, 406–8;
415, 417–18, 424–28; lobbied by AIPAC,
193–94, 195, 307, 308, 309, 310–11,
313–22; lobbied by Israelis/friends of
Israel, 53–54, 144, 145, 156–57, 266,
406–8; and Pollard affair, 285; pro-Israel
sentiment/support for Israel, 70–71, 84,
228, 247, 248, 261, 319–20, 408;
sponsored trips to Israel for members of,
316–17
Congressional Black Caucus, 452
Conservative Jews, 312–13, 332
Constituents (U.S.): mobilized to support
Jewish causes, 307, 308, 316
Corruption, 302–5
Council of Jewish Federations, General
Assembly, 432
Counterterrorism, 236, 237, 239, 241

INDEX

International Atomic Energy Agency
(IAEA), 103, 166
International Christian Embassy
(Jerusalem), 358, 359
International Ladies' Garment Workers
Union (ILGWU), 57
Intifada, 313, 412, 425; media coverage of,
363, 368, 370, 373, 374
Iran, 77, 78, 152, 223, 231, 302; American
hostages in, 189; and arms for hostages
deal, 239–40; Islamic revolution in, 379
Iran-Iraq war, 190, 231, 379–80, 381
Irangate affair, 46
Iraq, 5, 77, 169, 191, 245; government
overthrown, 88; Israeli reconnaissance
missions over, 431; nuclear program,
285; nuclear reactor bombed by Israel,
196–99, 203, 213, 231, 354, 382; seizure
of Kuwait, 378–405; as threat, 205, 454;
U.S. policy toward, 379–84; victory over,
419, 420, 422, 435
Islamic fundamentalism, 190, 454
Isolationism (U.S.), 15
Israel, xv, 13, 26; bending to U.S. pressure,
74–75, 84, 85; borders, 77, 165, 176;
dependence on U.S., 227, 254, 269,
271–72, 277, 399–400, 444, 453;
egocentricity, 444; elections, 34; exports
to U.S., 252, 253, 254, 257; image of,
changed by coverage of Lebanon war,
363, 366, 368, 372; independence, 22,
32–33; and leverage system, 24; myth of,
109–10; new, 172–86; new society in,
36–37; perception of freedom to bend
rules in psychology of, 283;
pro-Western orientation of, 59; U.S.
recognition of, 24–32, 126; recognition
of right to exist, 142; society of
immigrants, 331–32; usefulness to U.S.,
95 (see also Strategic value of Israel);
War of Independence, 37–38, 95, 212,
363
Israel Aircraft Industries, 46, 212, 247, 268,
302
Israel Bonds, 56–57, 154, 275, 296, 414
Israel Defense Forces, 7, 48–49, 242
Israel Military Industries, 300
Israeli air force, 39, 192–93, 242, 285, 388;
destruction of Iraq's nuclear reactor,
197–99; and Gulf War, 383, 394, 398–99
Israeli army: foreign volunteers in, 37–39,
82
Israeli navy, 242, 247
Israelis: emigrants to U.S., 335–37, 343;
relations with American Jews, 343–48
Ivri, David, 382, 392

Jabotinsky, Ze'ev, 177
Jabotinsky Medal, 355
Jackson, Andrew, 10, 29
Jackson, Henry "Scoop," 156–57, 264
Jacobson, Eddie, 24–29, 30, 37, 126
Jacobson, Israel Gaynor, 19–22, 24, 36
Jacobson, Morris, 20
Jaffa, 12, 15
Jennings, Peter, 362, 374
Jericho missiles, 389
Jerusalem, 10, 11, 105, 132, 365; as capital
of Israel, 358–59; Christians' interest in,
346–47; protection of, in Gulf War, 395
"Jerusalem Law," 358–59
Jerusalem Post, 329
Jew, definition of, 312–13
Jewish Agency for Palestine, 18, 25, 28, 32,
49, 60, 344–45
Jewish Federations, 344
Jewish Institute for National Security
Affairs (JINSA), 228, 241
Jewish National Fund, 276
Jewish refugees, 24, 36, 71, 105; denied
entry in West, 16, 18, 20–21
Jewish settlements (occupied territories),
142–43, 176–77, 188, 215, 333, 335, 360,
447; American Jews' attitudes toward,
433; dispute with U.S. over, 407–12;
legality of, 256; proposed freeze on, 221,
224; tied to loan guarantees issue,
414–15, 418–25, 429, 436, 440; see also
Gaza Strip; Golan Heights; West Bank
Jews, 21–22; instant citizenship in Israel
331; political power of, 458–59; return to
homeland, 10, 11, 14–15; see also
American Jews
"Jews for Jesus," 358
Jihad, 359–60
Johnson, Lady Bird, 105
Johnson, Lyndon B., 31, 84, 110, 174, 199;
relationship with Israel, 105–6, 110–11,
117, 118–20, 130, 155
Johnson administration: and Egypt's threat
to Israel, 116; peace efforts in Middle
East, 141; strategic alliance with Israel,
143–45
Johnston, Eric, 75, 79
Joint military exercises, 226, 234–35, 241,
242, 244, 245
Joint Political-Military Group (JPMG),
226, 233–34, 238, 241, 243, 245
Jonathan Institute for the Study of
Terrorism, 341
Jordan, 80, 81, 158, 185, 121, 197, 431;
Arab nationalists in, 88; arms sales to,
112, 285; and Gulf War, 388; Israel

INDEX

Miller, Israel, 315
Minority groups (U.S.), 452, 455
Missile Technology Control Regime, 447–48
Mitchell, Edward, 323–24
Mitchell, John, 150–51
Mitchell, Jonathan E., 323–27, 374–75
Mitchell, Mayer, 425, 429
Mitchell, Mike, 339
Mobotu Sese Seko, 252
Moda'i, Yitzhak, 404
Monetary reform (Israel), 271
Monroe, Marilyn, 108
Moral Majority, 354, 355
Morgan, J. P., 351
Morgenthau, Henry, Jr., 56
Morgenthau, Henry, Sr., 14, 15, 20
Mossad, 51, 114–15, 126, 129, 177, 197, 198, 209, 222; cooperation with Saudi Arabia, 191–92; cooperation with U.S. intelligence, 226; and Ethiopian Jews rescue, 288–89, 290; and Gulf War, 383; liaison with CIA, 61–68, 89–90, 122, 153, 284, 383; operatives at embassy in Washington, 279; "peripheral concept," 78; and terrorism, 236
Mount Sinai, 82, 85
Murrow, Casey, 364
Murrow, Edward R., 364
Muslim states, 78

Nafco (co.), 300
Nahal Soreq, 102–3, 114, 246, 292
Nasser, Gamal Abdel, 75–76, 77, 78, 79–80, 82, 88, 89, 91, 158; death of, 156; threat to Israel, 115, 117, 118
Nation of Islam, 318
National agenda (U.S.): changes in, 450–60
National Basketball Association, 338–39
National Christian Leadership Conference for Israel (NCLCI), 355
National Institutes of Health, 346
National Jewish Community Relations Advisory Council, 425
National PAC, The, 315–16
National Public Radio, 374
National Religious Broadcasters, 357
National Security Agency (NSA), 65, 120, 226, 391; Aman links with, 153
National Security Council (NSC), 88, 99, 151, 165, 194–95, 429, 446; counterterrorism, 236; and Israeli atomic plant, 96; of Reagan, 265, 266; and strategic cooperation, 233
National Security Decision Directive 111, 232

National Security Decision Memorandum, 149
National Unity Government (Israel), 413, 439
Naval cooperation, 242–43
"Nazi Atrocities," 364
Nazi Germany, 16–19, 352
Negev Desert, 28, 76, 79, 124, 183, 244, 399; atomic plant in, 96–100; irrigation of, 73; Voice of America transmission facility in, 232–33
Netanyahu, Benjamin, 237, 340–42, 343, 366–67, 443
Netanyahu, Yehonathan (Jonathan), 171, 341
New Israel Fund, 332, 346–47, 348, 433
"New Look" policy, 75
New York State, 26
New York Times, 352, 363, 370, 371, 374
Newcomers (the), 13
Newman, Paul, 109, 110, 456
Newsom, Eric, 422, 423
Nicaragua, 240
Niebuhr, Reinhold, 351
Niles, David, 30, 31, 39, 53, 165
Niles, Elliot, 39
Nir, Amiram, 236, 239
Nixon, Richard M., 97, 144, 167, 177, 183, 199, 420, 441, 450; offered nuclear plants to Egypt and Israel, 164, 166, 175; reelection campaign, 266; relations with Israel, 146, 147–52, 154, 155, 158; resignation, 164, 330; on U.S.-Israel special relationship, 460; support for Israel, 71, 156, 160–63; vice-presidency, 81
Nixon administration, 202, 245
Nixon Doctrine, 148
Nonalignment ideology (Israel), 58
Non-Proliferation Treaty, 112, 145, 149, 299
North, Oliver, 236, 238, 239, 240
North American Free Trade Agreement, 257
North Atlantic Treaty Organization (NATO), 201, 263
NSA. *See* National Security Agency (NSA)
Nuclear capability: Iraq, 196–97, 198, 380
Nuclear capability (Israel), 95–100, 102–4, 113–14, 124, 145, 181, 284; Nixon and, 149–50, 164, 166, 175; U.S. opposition to, 99, 100; U.S. spying on, 292–93
Nuclear weapons (Israel), 448; proposed use of, 159, 393

INDEX

INDEX

INDEX